Historic Christianity and the Federal Vision

Historic Christianity and the Federal Vision

A Theological Analysis and Practical Evaluation

Dewey Roberts

Historic Christianity and the Federal Vision
A Theological Analysis and Practical Evaluation

© 2016 Dewey Roberts
www.solafidepublications.org

ISBN: 978-0-99726666-3-4

Original (clothbound) ISBN: 978-0-9972666-0-3

Prepared for publication by www.greatwriting.org. This 2021 edition is re-typeset and has minor revisions and improvements.

All rights reserved. No part of this publication may be reproduced, stored in a retrieval system or transmitted in any form by any means, electronic, mechanical, photocopy, recording or otherwise without prior permission of the publisher, except as provided by USA copyright law.

Cover design: www.greatwriting.org
Book layout and design: www.greatwriting.org

Unless noted otherwise, Scripture quotations are taken from the New American Standard Bible® (NASB), Copyright © 1960, 1962, 1963, 1968, 1971, 1972, 1973, 1975, 1977, 1995 by The Lockman Foundation Used by permission. www.Lockman.org

SOLA FIDE PULICATIONS
Destin, Florida

About the Author

Dr. Dewey Roberts was born in Cleveland, Mississippi, and raised in the southeastern states of the USA. He studied Bible and English at Belhaven College and earned his Master of Divinity from Reformed Theological Seminary (both institutions in Jackson, Mississippi). He is the founding pastor of Cornerstone Presbyterian Church in Destin, Florida, where he has served since 1995. He was an Army Reserve chaplain for twenty-four years and served three tours on active duty. He retired in the rank of Colonel in 2011 and spent the last eight years of his chaplain career as a writer / instructor at the US Army Chaplain School and Center in Fort Jackson, SC. In addition to his pastoral duties, he also serves as Executive Director of Church Planting International (CPI) which promotes reformed indigenous missions in Russia, Uganda, Myanmar, India, and Portugal. CPI was founded by Rev. Donald Dunkerley in 1993.

Dewey received a PhD in Historical Theology from Whitfield Theological Seminary in 2017 for his work on Historic Christianity and the Federal Vision.

Dewey and his wife, Jane, have two children and four grandchildren.

To Jane:

*My loving wife and best friend
whose encouragement means more to me than she realizes.*

Chapter Contents

Appreciations 9
Acknowledgements 13
Foreword 15
Preface... 19
What is the Federal Vision?...31
The Federal Vision and Regeneration.................................... 41
The Federal Vision and Grace... 61
The Federal Vision and Covenant Theology 79
The Federal Vision's Paradigm for Baptism 103
The Federal Vision's Wrong View of Efficacy 115
The Federal Vision and Baptismal Efficacy 125
The Federal Vision and Baptismal Regeneration................ 143
The Federal Vision and the Order of Salvation 167
The Federal Vision and Theonomy 183
The Federal Vision and the Reformed Symbols.................. 201
The Federal Vision and Unconditional Election 213
The Federal Vision and Union with Christ 231
The Federal Vision and Justification by Faith Alone 245
The Federal Vision and Imputation..................................... 267
The Federal Vision and Covenant Faithfulness 289
The Federal Vision and Apostasy 303
The Federal Vision and Assurance of Salvation 319
The Federal Vision and Perseverance.................................. 335
The Federal Vision and Final Justification 345
The Federal Vision and Gnosticism..................................... 359
The Federal Vision: Another Gospel 373
Appendix A 387
Appendix B.. 391
Select Bibliography... 392
Index of Names 402

Appreciations

Roberts' book is a marvelous critique of the Federal Vision heresy and an outstanding piece of writing.

R C SPROUL, FOUNDER OF LIGONIER MINISTRIES

This book breathes passionate concern. It comes from the heart of the author, but thankfully the affections of Dewey Roberts have been illuminated and purified by a knowledge of the Bible. So this is a safe book to read, but also it is an exciting journey through the pilgrimage of the church and the attacks that have been launched on the gospel over hundreds of years. But if you thought such matters as how a sinner could get right with God, how are we justified freely, and what is our only hope in life and death had all been settled and sealed in the great past controversies and confessions of faith, then this book sounds an alarm.

The armies are at the gates of the City of God today. But there are watchmen awake and alert who have not been bought by the smiles of the enemies. So this book is essential and gripping reading. It reminds us of our courageous fathers who stood, sometimes very alone, and declared the sovereign grace of God. It exhorts us to be alert and to understand and contend as they also did. God grant that in all humility, and all boldness, and in reliance on God, we may also fight the good fight of faith. We may not be onlookers or neutrals in this battle. We may only be good soldiers of Jesus Christ.

GEOFFREY THOMAS, PASTOR, ALFRED PLACE BAPTIST CHURCH, ABERYSTWYTH, WALES

Dewey Roberts has done us a great service in writing this book. With cogent logic, based on Reformed biblical theology, he exposes the errors present in "Federal Vision" thinking, running rampant in some circles in the church today. He is fair to those who differ, but leaves no doubt as to where he stands: any doctrine that chips away at the doctrines of grace set forth in Reformed theology is heresy, and must be called out. He does a masterful job in doing just that.

MARK BELZ J.D. / MBLS LLC, RETIRED ATTORNEY AND FORMER MODERATOR OF THE PRESBYTERIAN CHURCH IN AMERICA

With assiduous clarity, Rev. Roberts has provided a steady, orthodox examination of the soteriological/sacramental scheme known as the *Federal Vision*, and its related theological iterations. A highly readable work, this steady, orthodox appraisal blends pastoral concern with scholarly methodology, yielding a truly valuable contribution for the benefit of earnest inquirers.

JOHN T. SOWELL, PRESIDENT, REFORMED THEOLOGICAL SEMINARY, ATLANTA, GEORGIA

"The ear tests words as the palate tastes food," says Job 34:3. Today we hear tantalizing words that sound sweet, but are often laced with the strychnine of primordial deception; lies made more sinister for they have been refuted by godly men in times past. The controversy that Reverend Dewey Roberts addresses in this remarkable volume may well qualify as one of those infamous deceptions. The *Federal Vision* matter comes at a critical time when so many in the modern Protestant Church and, especially, Presbyterian and Reformed branches of the Church, in North America (and, increasingly, in Canada and in Great Britain), are, understandably, longing for a more consistent sacramental theology, as well as a more historically sustainable ecclesiology. But our quest for a more satisfying worship experience or even a more sensible church order must never be advanced at the price of even the minutest theological point of truth. When we are (unwittingly) willing (because our liturgical zeal surpasses our doctrinal fidelity) to trade our birthright of John 3:16 truths for a pot of incense-stewed propositions, we are likely to introduce theological error into the divinely composed and revealed plan of faith and life. Introducing error into a human syllogism can result in losing an argument. Introducing error into the plan of salvation might result in losing a soul. This is, therefore, no small issue, to say the least.

To investigate the matter carefully will require knowing, teaching, and, in a word, teaching the truth of the divine plan of God. Then, one would need to expose the error, name it, distinguish it from the truth and from other errors, dismantle it piece by piece, demonstrating how and when it made its way into the companionship of holy verities and by what manner it can be removed. This is the work of a researcher, a scholar, a fair-minded churchman, an evangelist, and, above all, a faithful Christian minister. This is not work to be taken up by a novice. Neither is this a task to be done by a hot-headed party-man who is eager to advance his case so to score another point for his side. There are too many good ministers who have inquired into the tenets of the case at hand or been swayed by other arguments. There are too many sensitive spirits who long for beauty in theology. They have found it missing in the austerity of certain Western confessions and have seen it present in other places. Someone must be there to not just write them off as heretics, but comfort them with the poetry of our own traditions; to help them to see the beauty, again, in the porcelain layers of grace that didactic realism has stripped away.

The power of the Federal Vision has been that it has drawn extraordinarily gifted ministers, many of them being young ministers, filled with commendable enthusiasm for the things of God, as well as hard-working older shepherds who have grown understandably discontent with the vacuous pop-worship and dry-creek-bed-evangelicalism of the day. Yet the man to stand to speak truth to each and all of these as well as the more treacherous in the crowd—and there are those as well—will need to be capable of discriminating between erring lamb and a wolf in sheep's clothing. In other words, we need an experienced pastor to take on this challenge.

I am thankful to commend this book and this author, The Reverend Dewey Roberts. Dewey, as a fellow army chaplain and fellow minister of the gospel in the Presbyterian Church in America, is the right man at the right time to shed gospel light on the shadows encircling the question and subsidiary questions of the Federal Vision.

May God bless and increase the Light of His Word through this book and cause many to see clearly unto eternal life through Jesus Christ our Lord. My prayer for this book is the text from Job 34:

> Hear my words, you wise men,
> and listen to me, you who know.
> For the ear tests words
> as the palate tastes food.
> Let us choose for ourselves what is right;
> Let us know among ourselves what is good. (Job 34:2-4)

MICHAEL A. MILTON, PH.D., NINTH SUNDAY AFTER PENTECOST

The Federal Vision is a significant movement that has sprung up within conservative Calvinist churches in North America, Europe, and Russia. Dewey Roberts has made an exhaustive study of their teaching, and here explains fully why and how it departs from Reformed theology as this has been traditionally understood. Those who wish to understand the Federal Vision cannot afford to ignore this book.

DR. ANTHONY N. S. LANE,
PROFESSOR OF HISTORICAL THEOLOGY AT LONDON SCHOOL OF THEOLOGY

Acknowledgements

It is impossible to finish a work of over 100,000 words without the help of numerous other people. There are many people who greatly assisted me with the writing of this book. First, I want to thank my wife for patiently bearing with me numerous evenings as I read through material germane to this work. Second, I want to thank my congregation, particularly my elders, for encouraging me to write this book.

There were many people who provided valuable suggestions to me concerning this book. My editors, Jim and Sue Holmes of Taylors, SC, offered very valuable comments and edited the whole. Their help has been immeasurable. Dr. Morton H. Smith of Brevard, NC, read the entire manuscript and made very important observations that contributed to the improvement of this book. He also kindly wrote the Foreword.

The following distinguished church leaders read the manuscript and gave their endorsements of it for which I am very thankful: Dr. John Sowell, President of Reformed Theological Seminary in Atlanta, GA; Dr. Anthony N. S. Lane, professor of historical theology at London School of Theology; H. Geoffrey Thomas, pastor of Alfred Place Baptist Church in Aberystwyth, Wales; Dr. Michael A. Milton, a minister in the Presbyterian Church in America, a former Chancellor of Reformed Theological Seminary, and an Army Reserve chaplain who serves as an instructor / writer at the US Army Chaplain Center and School at Fort Jackson, SC; and, Mark Belz, a retired attorney who lives in St. Louis, MO, and is a former Moderator of the Presbyterian Church in America.

Finally, but not least, there are several members or friends of my congregation in Destin, FL, who proofread the formatted manuscript and found grammatical errors that had been overlooked or missed: Chuck Stoyer, Linda Wohleber, Kathy Orr, Rich and Gail Rogers, Bob Good, and Ed Maney. This book is greatly improved because of their help.

Foreword

MORTON H. SMITH

My former student, Dewey Roberts, has written a great book for us and the whole church in sounding a needed warning of the insidious dangers of the Federal Vision. The Federal Vision is wrongly viewed by many people within the PCA as an acceptable interpretation of the gospel that represents little cause for concern despite the fact that it is a legalistic system that is contradictory to the Scriptures and the Reformed Standards. Too many ministers and Christians within the PCA or other Reformed denominations are unaware of the deep inroads that have been made by this erroneous system within the body of Christ. Error thrives under the cloak of darkness unless it is vigorously opposed by courageous voices that raise the flag of warning for God's people. Truth is for the purpose of godliness and error / heresy is always destructive of true piety. The author of this book, therefore, is to be commended for plumbing the depths of the theological errors of the Federal Vision and exposing those errors by the light of truth for all to see. This is a book that is both timely and a necessary warning against those errors. It should be read by all who are concerned with the purity of the gospel. And the sooner the better.

In the first half of the twentieth century, J. Gresham Machen raised his voice of protest against the liberalism / modernism of the Presbyterian Church in the United States of America (the old Northern Presbyterian Church) with the result that he himself was excommunicated from that body despite his unquestioned orthodoxy. A different approach was taken by ministers and elders in the Presbyterian Church in the United States (the old Southern Presbyterian Church). The PCUS decided to tolerate liberalism / modernism within their body through a gentleman's agreement that they hoped would preserve the peace. They sacrificed truth for the sake of a false peace. While heresy grew much more rapidly in the PCUSA than the PCUS, it nonetheless eroded the evangelical foundations of the latter body and her gold became dim. Thus, the Federal Vision cannot be tolerated within any Reformed or evangelical denomination without causing irreparable damage to that body. Thankfully, this book provides us with the information to properly assess the Federal Vision and the ammunition to defend the gospel against the errors of that system. The author has dug down deep into the system of the Federal Vision in order to let the gospel shine more clearly in contrast with it. His work represents careful research into original source material both by the Federal Vision proponents and the greatest minds in the history of the Church.

Dr. Morton Howison Smith

Academic Career:
Bachelor of Divinity from Columbia Theological Seminary in Decatur, Georgia (1952)
Doctor of Theology from the Free University of Amsterdam (1962).

Ministerial Career:
Pastor of the Springfield and Roller churches in Sykesville, Maryland (1954);
Professor at Belhaven College in Jackson, Mississippi (1954-1963);
Guest Lecturer at Westminster Theological Seminary in Philadelphia, Pennsylvania (1963-1964);
First professor and one of the founders of Reformed Theological Seminary in Jackson, Mississippi (1964-1979);
A member of the committee that paved the way for the founding of the Presbyterian Church in America;
The first Stated Clerk of the Presbyterian Church in America (1973-1988);
A Founder, Professor, and Dean of Greenville Presbyterian Theological Seminary in Greenville, South Carolina (1987-2014)

He is the author of the following works:
Studies in Southern Presbyterian Theology
How is the Gold Become Dim
Harmony of the Westminster Confession of Faith and Catechisms
Commentary on the PCA Book of Church Order

Systematic Theology
Reformed Evangelism
Testimony
The Subscription Debate: Studies in Southern Presbyterian Polity
The Case for Full Subscription to the Westminster Standards in the Presbyterian Church in America

And a contributor to:
Encyclopedia of Christianity
Baker's Dictionary of Theology
Interpreting God's Word Today
Reformed Theology in America

Preface

The writing of this book is the result of several providential circumstances in my service to the church, particularly as a member of the Presbyterian Church in America's Standing Judicial Commission (SJC). *First*, I was a juror on the SJC in 2007 when a complaint against Louisiana Presbytery for providing safe harbor to the theological errors of Teaching Elder Steve Wilkins was upheld by the higher court. *Second*, I was appointed as the prosecutor for the trial of Louisiana Presbytery in March of 2008 when the SJC brought charges against the lower court for failure to comply with the decision of the higher court in the case. That trial was the first time in American Presbyterian Church history that a General Assembly or its commission has censured a presbytery. *Third*, I was the chairman of the SJC panel in 2009 that upheld the first complaint against Pacific Northwest Presbytery for its refusal to censure Teaching Elder Peter Leithart. *Fourth*, I was the representative of the complainant, Ruling Elder Gerald Hedman, in the hearing before the full SJC in March of 2013 concerning the second complaint against Pacific Northwest Presbytery in the matters of Peter Leithart.

Over a period of six years, I was a juror, a prosecutor, a panel chairman, and the representative of a complainant in some of the most important cases concerning the Federal Vision that have been decided by Reformed churches in the twenty-first century. The trial documents of those cases, particularly the cases concerning Peter Leithart, taught me many things that I would not have learned by reading the various pieces of literature of the Federal Vision proponents. Thus, I began work on this book in earnest sometime in 2012 with a series of sermons I preached to my congregation clarifying the differences between the Christian faith and the Federal Vision.

In addition to the trial documents in the various cases before the SJC, I have also read the writings of people on both sides of this issue. Guy Prentiss Waters' two books, *Justification and the New Perspectives on Paul* and *The Federal Vision and Covenant Theology*, and Cornelis P.

Venema's *The Gospel of Free Acceptance in Christ*, are, in my opinion, the best books that expose the soteriological errors of both the Federal Vision and the New Perspectives on Paul.[1] The denominational reports of the Presbyterian Church in America, the Orthodox Presbyterian Church, and the Reformed Church in the United States all make very valuable contributions in identifying the errors of these views.

The Federal Vision and Legalism

The Federal Vision represents a full-scale frontal attack against all the essential doctrines of the gospel that is disguised as an attempt to improve the Reformed faith. This book agrees substantially with the analysis of the Federal Vision in the books and articles written against it by Guy Prentiss Waters, Cornelis Venema, R. Scott Clark, John V. Fesko, John Otis, David J. Engelsma, and others.

After completing this manuscript, I came across the following quote from Dr. R. Scott Clark, professor of church history and historical theology at Westminster Theological Seminary in Escondido, California, concerning the Federal Vision and the New Perspectives on Paul:

> It is an historical fact that moralism (the confusion of justification with sanctification) never dies, it just goes dormant periodically. The Reformation defeated 1000 years of moralism only to see forms of it re-emerge in the Protestant churches even before Luther died.
>
> It resurfaced in the Remonstrant theology, in Richard Baxter (and in those orthodox Reformed whom he influenced), in the Scottish neonomians in the 18th century, in the Oxford (Tractarian) movement in the 19th century, in Charles Finney, and has more or less dominated American Protestantism (whether "evangelical" or liberal) for most of American history. Over the last few years in the NAPARC[2] world and in satellite groups, the orthodox have won several strategic victories in the courts and assemblies of the Reformed churches. The following denominations or federations have rejected the Federal Vision / NPP and related forms of moralism (justification by grace and cooperation with grace) in no particular order (from memory): The United Reformed Churches, The Orthodox Presbyterian Church, The Presbyterian Church in America, The Bible Presbyterian Church, The

---

1 There are differences between the Federal Vision and the New Perspectives on Paul, but those differences are not on the doctrines of salvation. On soteriology, they are virtually identical.

2 NAPARC stands for North American Presbyterian and Reformed Churches, an organization that promotes fraternal relations between evangelical Reformed denominations throughout North America.

Reformed Church in the United States, The Orthodox Christian Reformed Church, The Reformed Presbyterian Church in North America, The Reformed Presbyterian Church in the United States. It isn't over, however.³

Clark rightly identifies this problem of moralism, or legalism, as existing for a thousand years before the Reformation (which would be back to Pelagius). It resurfaced after the Reformation with the Remonstrants through Arminius, with Richard Baxter, with the neonomians of Scotland, with the Tractarians in the Church of England, with Charles Finney, with Albert Barnes, and with others. Interestingly, this book traces the same historical connections between the Federal Vision theology and the various moralism heresies of the past (including several more that are not mentioned in his brief quote). The Federal Vision/ New Perspectives on Paul are moralistic or legalistic systems, as Clark observes. They are not new. They are just the same old salvation-by-works scheme from the past dressed up in new theological nomenclature to confuse the undiscerning.

In a more recent article, Clark goes beyond identifying these movements as merely moralism and singles out one of them, the Remonstrants (the followers of Arminius), as Pelagianism. As he says:

> The Remonstrants always find a way to put the believer "on the hook" for his final salvation. Grace is never really free. It is never really amazing. As with Rome, grace is reduced to a helper. The Remonstrants wrote of "the assisting grace of the Holy Spirit" and that Jesus Christ "assists" us poor sinners "if only" we are "ready for the conflict and desire his help, and are not inactive. . ." Here the true nature of the Remonstrant doctrine of perseverance emerges: God helps those who help themselves by cooperating with his "assisting grace." This is quite another picture of salvation. Here God has not parted the Red Sea and led us through, by the hand, as it were (Jer 31:32; Ex 14:16). Rather, according to the Remonstrants, God has covenanted to co-act with those who do what lies within them *(facientibus quod in se est, Deus non denegat gratiam)*. The Remonstrants turned Reformed theology into the Pelagian covenant theology of the Franciscan theologian Gabriel Biel (c. 1420–95). Those who meet these antecedent conditions—the Remonstrants turned the covenant of grace into a covenant of works—cannot be plucked out of Christ's hands. If we only read the first few lines and then let our eyes slip down to quotation of John 10:28 we

---

3 R. Scott Clark, "After the Federal Vision: The Return of Moralism," August, 2008 (rev. 2012). http://rscottclark.org/2008/09/after-the-federal-vision-the-return-of-moralism/ Accessed on June 30, 2015.

might get entirely the wrong impression. Once, however, we read the words in between the picture becomes much clearer. The Remonstrants re-contextualized John 10:28 and the evangelical (in the original, sixteenth-century sense of the word), Protestant, Reformed doctrine of the perseverance of the saints.[4]

Of course, that is not Clark's opinion alone concerning the Remonstrants. The Synod of Dort called the Remonstrants Pelagians eight different times in their response to them. What Clark and the Synod of Dort say about the Remonstrants can also be said about the other forms of moralism that have surfaced since the Reformation, including the most recent forms known as the Federal Vision and the New Perspectives on Paul. These movements are not only moralism but also Pelagianism.

The Federal Vision as a Worldwide Problem
The New Perspectives on Paul, as taught by N. T. Wright, has influenced ministers and Christians throughout the English-speaking world. The Federal Vision is also a worldwide problem. A correspondent in South Africa informed me that many of the Reformed churches there have been infected with the Federal Vision heresy. A missionary friend in Ukraine emailed me with concerns that students trained in a Reformed seminary there have adopted Federal Vision views after graduation. Some of the Federal Vision advocates have made mission trips to the former Soviet Union countries, infecting ministers there with the poison of their system. My own mission trips to Russia have revealed how deep those inroads are. Legalism is and always has been the greatest enemy of the church because it is a denial of the gospel. Moralism is legalism. Pelagianism is legalism. Both are natural religion and both deny the gospel.

The Federal Vision and Pelagianism
Most modern authors agree that the errors of the Federal Vision and the New Persepectives on Paul are at least the heresy of Semi-Pelagianism,[5] which was condemned by the Council of Orange in 530.

---

4 R. Scott Clark, "The Synod of Dort on Election, Conditions of Salvation, and Fruit: Does the Doctrine of Perseverance Turn the Covenant of Grace into a Covenant of Works?", November 13, 2015. Accessed at: http://theaquilareport.com/the-synod-of-dort-on-election-conditions-of-salvation-and-fruit-2/ on November 16, 2015.

5 Guy Prentiss Waters, *Justification and the New Perspectives on Paul: A Review and Response*

The errors of the Federal Vision are certainly within the Pelagian spectrum of heresies—Pelagianism, Semi-Pelagianism, Arminianism, Neonomianism, and Roman Catholicism. Over fifty quotes from thirty of the greatest theologians of the church over a period of fifteen hundred years (from Augustine to Geerhardus Vos) as Pelagianism to one degree or another. The great theologians of the past unanimously defined Pelagianism (and its offshoots) primarily in terms of the doctrine of grace and secondarily in terms of the doctrine of man.

There are subtle differences in the various forms which moralism or legalism has adopted over the centuries, but those differences are dismissed by the great Southern Presbyterian theologian, James Henley Thornwell, in the following quote:

> Now the reigning error of Arminianism, Pelagianism, and this Neonomianism—for they are all substantially the same, they rest upon identically the same principle—is an utter disregard of the true Scripture doctrine of grace, and a fatal misapprehension of the present condition of man in the sight of God. The friends of these systems will all admit that a man is justified by grace, but when they undertake to explain their meaning, "grace is no more grace."
>
> The source of the error in many minds is the unfounded notion that grace is whatever is opposed to merit.[6]

Anyone who has read much of the writings of the Federal Vision authors will be aware how often they oppose grace to merit. Thornwell's remarks are, therefore, both historically accurate and prescient. In one sense, it is not worth our time to debate whether the views of the Federal Vision are actually closer to Arminianism, Pelagianism, Semi-Pelagianism, Romanism or Neonomianism because all those systems are substantially the same in their 'utter disregard of the true Scripture doctrine of grace, and a fatal misapprehension of the present condition of man in the sight of God,' as Thornwell said. Yet, the Federal Vision generally denies or mutes the subjective grace of the Holy Spirit in their emphasis on baptismal efficacy which makes them, on that point, more Pelagian than Semi-Pelagian. In other instances,

---

(Phillipsburg, New Jersey: P&R Publishing, 2004), 174, 186-187. See also: Cornelis P. Venema, *The Gospel of Free Acceptance in Christ* (Edinburgh, Scotland and Carlisle, Pennsylvania: The Banner of Truth Trust, 2006), 127-128, 156-158, 161, 257.

6   James Henley Thornwell, *The Collected Writings of James Henley Thornwell*, Volume II: Theological and Ethical (Edinburgh, Scotland and Carlisle, Pennsylvania: The Banner of Truth Trust, 1974), 390-391.

their positions will be closer to Semi-Pelagianism or Neonomianism.

A. A. Hodge correctly taught that Pelagianism is a complete, self-consistent system of theology:

> There are, in fact, as we might have anticipated, but two complete self-consistent systems of Christian theology possible. 1st. On the right hand, Augustinianism completed in Calvinism. 2nd. On the left hand, Pelagianism completed in Socinianism. And 3rd. Arminianism comes between these as the system of compromises, and is developed Semi-pelagianism.[7]

Semi-Pelagianism (or Arminianism) is an unstable theological system which is always vacillating between the only two complete self-consistent systems. Semi-Pelagianism sometimes leans more towards Pelagianism and other times more towards Augustinianism.

Reformed Churches and the Pelagian Heresy

It might seem unimaginable that any form of Pelagianism could appear within a Reformed church. Yet, it should not surprise us. Reformed churches have often been infected by Pelagian doctrines in the past and will continue to face this problem until the end of time. In words that now appear prescient, Geerhardus Vos wrote over a century ago in *Reformed Dogmatics* (recently translated and published for the first time in English) that the apparent failure of the covenant to live up to the breadth of God's promises concerning baptized covenant children would be the way in which Pelagianism could enter into Reformed doctrine:

> We here face the difficulty that the covenant relationship appears powerless to bring covenant fellowship in its wake. We get a covenant that remains unfruitful. A barren, juridical relationship, an "ought to be," appears to take the place of the glorious realities that mention of the covenant brings to our minds. This is in fact the point where, by means of the covenant idea, the Pelagian error could gain access to Reformed doctrine.[8]

In other words, Vos foresaw the day that some people, seizing on the reality that not all baptized covenant children truly live in the fel-

---

[7] Archibald Alexander Hodge, *Outlines of Theology* (Grand Rapids, Michigan: Zondervan Publishing House, 1972), 96.

[8] Richard B, Gaffin, Jr. and John R. DeWitt, trans. and eds., Geerhardus Vos, *Reformed Dogmatics*, Volume Two: *Anthropolgy* (Bellingham, Washington: Lexham Press, 2013), 107-8.

lowship of the covenant, would try to make changes to the doctrine of the covenant to account for this apparent contradiction. Those changes, Vos said, would provide the opportunity for Pelagianism to be taught under the banner of Reformed doctrine. That is exactly what has happened with the Federal Vision movement. The Federal Vision proponents have tinkered with the doctrine of the covenant in order to try to reconcile God's promises concerning children of the covenant with the reality that not all of them appear to be living in fellowship with God. In so doing, they have substituted their doctrine of baptismal efficacy for the efficacious grace of the Holy Spirit and placed the responsibility for the fulfillment of the covenant on the individual, rather than God. That is a Pelagian modification of the sacrament of baptism, the doctrine of grace, and the doctrine of the covenant.

The Orthodox Presbyterian Church Report on the Federal Vision
A committee report adopted by the 2004 General Assembly of the Orthodox Presbyterian Church (OPC) listed twenty errors of the Federal Vision, among which are the following:

1. Pitting Scripture and Confession against each other;
2. Regarding systematic theology as rationalistic;
3. A mono-covenantalism that denies the distinction between the covenant of works and the covenant of grace;
4. Election as primarily corporate and covenantal;
5. The covenant is conditional;
6. A denial that the law before the Fall was more fully published at Mt. Sinai, requiring perfect obedience;
7. A denial of the imputation of the active obedience of Christ in our justification;
8. Defining justification exclusively as the forgiveness of sins;
9. The reduction of justification to the inclusion of the Gentiles in the church;
10. Including works (by use of "faithfulness," "obedience," etc.) in the very definition of faith;
11. Failing to affirm an infallible perseverance and the indefectibility of grace;
12. Teaching baptismal regeneration;
13. Denying the distinction between the visible and invisible church;
14. An overly objectified sacramental efficacy that downplays the need for faith and that tends toward an *ex opere operato* [automatically effective] view of the sacraments;

15. Ecclesiology that eclipses and swallows up soteriology.[9]

All of these errors coalesce in the Federal Vision system as an attack on the great doctrines of salvation. Therefore, this book will deal with the errors of the Federal Vision identified by the Orthodox Presbyterian Church and with various others. My purpose is to oppose the Federal Vision system as a whole and not to analyze every statement of an advocate of that system. Thus, I will consider their errors as a whole in light of the great battles for the truth in the history of the church (as Clark rightly outlined above). Guy Prentiss Waters has already written an excellent book, *The Federal Vision and Covenant Theology: A Comparative Analysis*, which responds in detail to numerous quotes from the Federal Vision authors. There is no need for this book to be redundant of his work, but it will build on his research. There will be several quotes from the Federal Vision authors in every chapter that identify the Federal Vision view on various aspects of theology. Those views will then be put into the context of historical theology, the teaching of Scripture, and the great Reformed creeds.

My approach in this book was confirmed to me as the right one when I read an article by Archibald Alexander in *Princeton Versus the New Divinity*. Alexander, along with several other professors at Princeton Seminary in the early nineteenth century, was involved in exposing the theological errors of the "New Divinity" taught by Charles G. Finney, Albert Barnes, and others within the Presbyterian Church. The Princeton professors identified those errors as a revival of Pelagianism. Alexander's comments on the best way to combat such errors is very telling:

> There has never yet been an instance in the history of the church of the rejection of any doctrines of the gospel, where the opposers of the truth have been contented to stop at the first departure from sound doctrine. If they who first adopt and propagate an error are sometimes restrained by habit, and by a lurking respect for the opinions of the wise and good, as also by a fear of incurring the censure of heresy, from going the full length which their principles require; yet those who follow them in their error will not be kept back by such considerations.
>
> Indeed, the principles of self defence require that men who undertake to defend their opinions by argument should endeavor to be consistent with themselves; and thus it commonly happens that what

---

9 Accessed at http://www.opc.org/nh.html?article_id=478 on October 19, 2015

was originally a single error draws after it the whole system of which it is a part. On this account it is incumbent on the friends of truth to oppose error in its commencement, and to endeavour to point out the consequences likely to result from its adoption; and to us it appears that nothing is better calculated to show what will be the effect of a particular error than to trace its former progress by the lights of ecclesiastical history.[10]

I agree with Alexander that the best way to show what any heresy is, including the Federal Vision, is to "trace its former progress by the lights of ecclesiastical history." As much as the Federal Vision already represents a significant departure from historic Christianity, it will be much worse in the hands of its second and third generation followers. They will take the system to its logical conclusions. If the system stops short of full-blown Pelagianism at the present time, it will not do so in the future.

Key Figures in the Federal Vision
Some of the key figures in the Federal Vision who will be quoted in this book are:

(1) Peter Leithart (formerly a PCA minister in Pacific Northwest Presbytery serving a Confederation of Reformed Evangelical Churches (CREC) congregation out of the bounds of his presbytery in Moscow, Idaho, and a theological instructor at New St. Andrews, also in Moscow, Idaho. He has since taken a teaching position in Birmingham, Alabama, and has transferred his membership to the CREC). Leithart has written extensively and, therefore, many quotes will be taken from his writings. Additionally, the two judicial cases concerning his theology that came before the Standing Judicial Commission of the PCA comprised nearly 900 pages of material. There are several statements within the record of those cases that reveal the thinking of Federal Vision proponents.

(2) Steve Wilkins, pastor of Auburn Avenue Presbyterian Church in Monroe, Louisiana; (a former PCA minister who is now in the CREC). Steve was a classmate and close friend during our days together at Reformed Theological Seminary and afterwards. His con-

---

10 Archibald Alexander, "Original Sin," in *Princeton Versus the New Divinity* (Edinburgh, Scotland and Carlisle, Pennsylvania: The Banner of Truth Trust, 2001), 114.

gregation hosts a pastors conference each year, the Auburn Avenue Presbyterian Church Pastors Conference (AAPCPC).

(3) Douglas Wilson, pastor of Christ Church (CREC), Moscow, Idaho. He has written over two dozen books published by his printing company, Canon Press; he is the publisher of *Credenda/Agenda*; and he has been instrumental in the revival of classical Christian schools across North America.

(4) James Jordan, a graduate of Westminster Theological Seminary in Philadelphia, Pennsylvania; a former student at Reformed Theological Seminary during Greg Bahnsen's professorship; studied under Norman Shepherd during his controversial time at Westminster. Jordan was also a close friend at RTS during our days together at that seminary. He is a popular conference speaker at churches sympathetic to the Federal Vision.

(5) Steve Schlissel, pastor of Messiah's Congregation (CREC), New York City.

(6) Mark Horne, without call according to the latest information I have, but an ordained minister in the PCA. He was once pastor of First Reformed Presbyterian Church of Minco, Oklahoma, (where I served from 1986-1989).

(7) Ralph Smith, CREC missionary to Japan.

(8) John Barach, pastor of a United Reformed Church (URC) in Alberta, Canada.

(9) Rich Lusk, former assistant to Steve Wilkins in Monroe, Louisiana; graduate of Covenant Theological Seminary in St. Louis, Missouri; and, pastor of Trinity Presbyterian Church in Birmingham, Alabama.

(10) Joel Garver, a PCA officer in the Philadelphia area who serves as an assistant professor at LaSalle University.

Additionally, this book will quote from both N. T. Wright (well-known former Bishop of Durham in the Church of England) and Norman Shepherd (former professor at Westminster Theological Seminary now serving in the Christian Reformed Church).

–1–
What is the Federal Vision?

"When old truths are attacked with new weapons, they must be vindicated by new defences, adopted to meet the most recent forms of error; and this is pre-eminently the case, at the present day, with the cardinal doctrine of Justification"[1]

JAMES BUCHANAN, NINETEENTH-CENTURY SCOTTISH THEOLOGIAN

"We do not baptize because the one to be baptized is already regenerate. Rather we baptize in order that the one who is baptized be made regenerate."[2]

JOEL GARVER, FEDERAL VISION PROPONENT

"Baptism marks the objective starting point of the Christian life. There is no question that baptism has 'conferred and sealed' grace. But that grace must be received by faith, and by continuing in the Faith."[3]

MARK HORNE, FEDERAL VISION PROPONENT

---

1 James Buchanan, *The Doctrine of Justification: An Outline of its History in the Church and of its Exposition from Scripture* (London: The Banner of Truth Trust, 1961), 24.

2 Guy Prentiss Waters, *The Federal Vision and Covenant Theology: A Comparative Analysis* (Phillipsburg, New Jersey: P & R Publishing, 2006), 243.

3 Ibid., 248.

Historic Christianity and the Federal Vision

Since the 1970s, there has been a growing attack on the doctrine of justification by faith alone within the broader Reformed community. Some of it began with the teaching of Norman Shepherd at Westminster Theological Seminary in Philadelphia, Pennsylvania, who denied the covenant of works; denied the imputation of Christ's active obedience to believers; viewed election in terms of the covenant instead of God's eternal decrees; defined baptism as a marker of those within the covenant who are recipients of all the benefits of Christ (though those benefits can be lost); and, especially, taught that justification is based on faith plus non-meritorious works rather than faith alone.

Shepherd's teaching soon aroused great concern among many ministers and theologians within the Reformed community, with the result that a letter was sent to the board of Westminster Seminary containing forty-five signatories; including Roger Nicole, R. C. Sproul, D. Martyn Lloyd-Jones, O. Palmer Robertson, Robert Reymond, George Knight III, W. Stanford Reid, Morton Smith, Albert N. Martin, Robert Godfrey, William Hendriksen, and Meredith Kline.

Soteriological views similar to Shepherd's views have also been taught in more recent days by such men as N. T. Wright (New Perspectives on Paul), Peter Leithart (Federal Vision), Steve Wilkins (Auburn Avenue Theology), and numerous others. The different labels that are used by them are mostly irrelevant. The thing that *is* relevant is their doctrine of salvation. These new theologies are really not new at all. They are simply using new weapons to make the same old attack on the doctrines of grace taught in the Bible as the quote at the beginning of this chapter by James Buchanan (1804-1870), Professor of Apologetics at New College in Edinburgh, Scotland, underscores. These new weapons of our opponents must be countered by a vindication of the old truths—a vindication particularly adapted to show the errors of these new attacks. This book is written to provide that vindication and to confront the present form of this heresy head on.

Modernism and Sacramentalism

The title for this book was inspired by J. Gresham Machen's classic work, *Christianity and Liberalism*. Machen was determined to prove that Liberalism or Modernism was not a true branch of historic Christianity, but a different plant altogether. The issue at stake for

Machen was the true nature of the gospel. He knew that every generation must "contend earnestly for the faith which was once for all handed down to the saints" (Jude 3). As he wrote:

> The type of religion which rejoices in the pious sound of traditional phrases, regardless of their meanings, or shrinks from "controversial" matters, will never stand amid the shock of life. In the sphere of religion, as in other spheres, the things about which men are agreed are apt to be the things that are least worth holding; the really important things are the things about which men will fight.[4]

Our generation is facing an attack on the gospel from a somewhat different quarter than Machen battled against in his day. The gospel is now being subverted in evangelical circles by the Pelagian spectrum of heresies—Semi-Pelagianism, Nomism (of various types), the allure of Roman Catholic theology, and Pelagianism. The errors which necessitated the Protestant Reformation are now being taught in denominations which hold to an evangelical and Reformed confession. The purpose of this book, therefore, is the same as Machen expressed in *Christianity and Liberalism*:

> The purpose of this book is not to decide the religious issue of the day, but merely to present the issue as sharply and clearly as possible, in order that the reader may be aided in deciding it for himself.[5]

Definition of The Federal Vision

People often ask me to give a succinct definition of the errors of the Federal Vision or New Perspectives on Paul.[6] My answer is that those who hold to such teaching are guilty of the same errors as the Pharisees and Judaizers who said concerning the Gentile converts:

> It is necessary to circumcise them and to direct them to observe the Law of Moses. (Acts 15:5b)

The Judaizers asserted that circumcision conveyed some necessary grace which could not be obtained simply by faith in Christ, and that keeping the law was essential to complete the work of salvation initi-

---

4 J. Gresham Machen, *Christianity and Liberalism* (Grand Rapids, Michigan/Cambridge, U.K.: William B. Eerdmans Publishing Company, 2009), 1-2.

5 Ibid., 1.

6 Whatever differences there are between the Federal Vision and the New Perspectives on Paul (as held by N. T. Wright, in particular), those differences do not affect their doctrines of salvation. On the doctrine of salvation, they hold the same views.

ated by circumcision. The Federal Vision says the same thing as evidenced by the quotes at the beginning of this chapter. Its proponents say that baptism conveys all the benefits of Christ's redemption to everyone who outwardly receives the ordinance, but it must be augmented by the faithful obedience and perseverance of the baptized person to the end of his life in order to result in final justification. If the Federal Vision advocates had been at the Council at Jerusalem, their response likely would have been something like this:

> It is necessary to baptize them with water and to direct them to be faithful to their covenant baptism.

In both instances, salvation is a result of sacramental grace plus obedience, to which Peter responded:

> Now therefore why do you put God to the test by placing upon the neck of the disciples a yoke which neither our fathers nor we have been able to bear? But we believe that we are saved through the grace of the Lord Jesus, in the same way as they are also. (Acts 15:10, 11)

Like the Judaizers, the Federal Vision endorses the same yoke of slavery to the law which the Apostles, the Pharisees, the new converts to Christianity, and the fathers of the Old Testament could not keep. It teaches that final justification is by works of righteousness, though Federal Vision advocates nuance their position to make it seem more palatable with evangelical Christianity. Therefore, it denies that salvation is through the free grace of Christ alone. It is a theological system as old as the fall of mankind that has been perpetuated throughout the history of the church by the Pharisees and Judaizers; by various fathers of the church; by Pelagius; by many of the Scholastics of the Medieval church; by the Council of Trent and the Papacy; by Arminius and the Remonstrants; by Richard Baxter; by Albert Barnes and Charles G. Finney; and others. Therefore, this is my definition of the Federal Vision:

The Federal Vision is a scheme of salvation by works, both moral and ceremonial, set within the framework of a conditional covenant that depends on the covenant faithfulness and perseverance of the baptized for its efficacy and for their final justification.

This definition comprehends in a single sentence almost everything that will be covered in this book and is very similar to what a definition of legalism would be. The Federal Vision is a new scheme of legalism that conflicts with salvation by grace alone.

Rationalism and Ritualism

The Federal Vision can accurately be called a ritualistic heresy, but it is not heretical in every area of theology. The proponents of the Federal Vision agree with historic Christianity concerning many important doctrines of the Bible. They believe in the Trinity, the virgin birth, and the resurrection of Christ, among other doctrines. Semi-Pelagianism, Pelagianism, Neonomianism, and Roman Catholicism also agree with many important doctrines of Scripture, but that does not make those heresies any less dangerous. Heresies necessarily have many tentacles. One error inevitably leads to another and both lead to even further errors. This point was made well by J. C. Ryle, who had firsthand experience with theological errors almost identical to the Federal Vision:

> There is a close connection between false doctrines. It is almost impossible to take up one alone. Once let a man get wrong about the Church and the sacraments, and there is no saying how far he may go, and where he may land at last. It is a mistake at the fountain-head, and it influences the whole course of his religion. The mistake about baptism is a striking illustration of what I mean. It throws a colour over the whole of a man's divinity. It insensibly affects his views of justification, sanctification, election, and perseverance. It fills his mind with a tangled maze of confusion as to all the leading articles of the faith. He starts with a theory for which no single plain text of Scripture can be alleged, and before this theory he tramples down plain passages of the Bible by the score! They interfere forsooth, with his favourite theory, and therefore cannot mean what common sense tells us they do! We ought to be as jealous over a little false doctrine, as we would be about a little sin![7]

The gospel is continuously being attacked from opposite sides by the false doctrines of rationalism (which makes reason the chief source of knowledge) or ritualism. Rationalism, whether Liberalism or the Neo-orthodoxy of Barthianism, takes away from the Word of God. Both Liberalism and Barthianism are forms of rationalistic modernism. Ritualism is the opposite problem. It adds to the Scripture. It overlays the Scripture with so many superstitions that the truth becomes obscured. Revelation 22:18, 19 sounds an anathema against

---

7 John Charles Ryle, *Old Paths: Being Plain Statements on Some Weightier Matters of Christianity* (Cambridge & London: James Clarke & Co. LTD., 1972), 504.

both adding to the Scripture or taking away from it.

The greatest danger for the evangelical church in this generation is not rationalism, Liberalism, Barthianism, modernism, or infidelity; but it is ritualism, Romanism, and superstition. The Federal Vision has veered from the faith in the direction of adding to the Word of God and leading the misguided back into the ritualistic superstitions of the Papacy. The errors of the Federal Vision affect all the cardinal doctrines of salvation—election, effectual calling, regeneration, justification by faith alone, saving faith, adoption, union with Christ, forgiveness of sins, the Holy Spirit, apostasy, assurance, the visible and invisible church, and the perseverance of the saints.

Yet, there is this correlation between rationalism and ritualism, modernism and Romanism. Both deny the scriptural way of salvation. They approach salvation from different perspectives, but they both conclude that salvation is not by faith in Christ alone. Modernism says, "Christianity is a life, not a doctrine."[8] Ritualism says that the essence of Christianity is to receive the sacraments and to live obediently. The emphasis in both is on the life of the individual as the path to salvation. Both rationalism and ritualism downplay doctrine. In combating the rationalistic liberalism of his day, Machen referred to the same error of the Judaizers in Acts 15 which is referenced above concerning the Federal Vision. Heresy only has one message: Salvation is by the works of the flesh. The gospel has a different message: Salvation is through faith in Christ alone. In the Cunningham Lectures of 1871, James Walker commented:

> It has been oftentimes remarked that there are deep connections between Romanism and Rationalism.[9]

No Intramural Debate

There are those who tell us that this controversy with the Federal Vision is a tempest in a teapot, an intramural debate over semantic differences. The same types of arguments were made in J. C. Ryle's day concerning the ritualistic errors of the Church of England, to which he replied:

> Men sometimes say it makes no difference whether we think all bap-

---

8 Machen, *Christianity and Liberalism*, 17.

9 James Walker, *Theology and the Theologians of Scotland, 1560-1750* (Edinburgh, Scotland: Knox Press, 1982), 28.

tized persons are regenerate or not. They tell us it all comes to the same thing in the long run. I cannot say so. To my humble apprehension it seems to make an immense difference. If I tell a man that he has grace in his heart, and only needs to "stir up a gift," already within him, it is one thing. If I tell him that he is dead in sins, and must be "born again," it is quite another. The moral effect of the two messages must, on the very face of it, be widely different. The one, I contend, is calculated by God's blessing to awaken the sinner. The other, I contend, is calculated to lull him to sleep. The one, I maintain, is likely to feed sloth, check self-examination, and encourage an easy self-satisfied state of soul: he has got some grace within him whenever he likes to use it,—why should he be in a hurry, why be afraid? The other, I maintain, is likely to rouse him to self-inquiry, and frighten him out of his dangerous security: he has nothing within him to rest upon,—he must find a refuge and remedy, he is lost and perishing,—what must he do to be saved?[10]

While this book is primarily written against the theological errors of the Federal Vision, there will be references to the New Perspectives on Paul also. The differences between the Federal Vision and the New Perspectives on Paul are not as great as are often assumed or even asserted. The New Perspectives on Paul provides the scholarly rationale, albeit from a mostly liberal viewpoint, for the doctrines which are popularly taught as the Federal Vision. For instance, the New Perspectives on Paul asserts that when the Temple was rebuilt following their return from captivity in Babylon or Assyria, the Jews had been purged from their theories of works salvation. That "scholarly" position allows the advocates of the New Perspectives on Paul to assert that the Reformers misinterpreted Paul concerning justification. The Federal Vision proponents reach the same conclusion about the doctrine of justification in the Scripture as a result of their wrong view of the covenant, while buttressing their position by the scholarship of the New Perspectives on Paul authors. Both deny that justification is once-for-all through faith in Christ alone; both assert that a correct doctrine of justification must go back to the teaching of the church before the Reformation; and, both assert that there is a final justification at death for every baptized person. The New Perspectives on Paul and the Federal Vision are in basic agreement on many other deviations from the doctrines of salvation taught in the Bible.

---

10 John Charles Ryle, D. D., *Knots Untied: Being plain statements on disputed points in Religion from the standpoint of an Evangelical Churchman* (Cambridge, England: James Clarke & Co. LTD., 1977), 122-123.

The Federal Vision and the Holy Spirit

The Federal Vision ties the operation of the Holy Spirit to the objective application of the sacraments (as the quote from Mark Horne at the beginning of the chapter states) and, thereby, denies His real work of grace in the hearts of the elect. The desire to restore the objectivity of the covenant leads the Federal Vision proponents, wittingly or unwittingly, into the denial of the subjective work of God's grace. Grace is limited to the objective acquisition of it through the atonement of Christ, while the subjective application of it to the believer by the work of the Holy Spirit is denied or ignored. Then, even the objective side of grace is undermined by denying justification by faith alone, by denying the imputation of Christ's righteousness, by denying the covenant of works, and by denying other objective truths of Scripture.

Yet, for two reasons it is not readily apparent to many people that the problem with the Federal Vision is a part of the Pelagian spectrum of heresies. First, Pelagianism is wrongly reduced to the single doctrine that all humans are born sinless. Thornwell rightly defined the Pelagian spectrum of heresies as first of all a wrong view of God's grace. Flowing out of that wrong view of grace was a wrong view of man, one which emphasized his complete freedom of will. In order to support his theory on the sinless birth of all humans, Pelagius developed other unscriptural doctrines in the areas of sacramentology and soteriology, which were essential to his system.

Second, there is a failure to distinguish between the Federal Vision system and the Federal Vision proponents. One is a system; the other consists of those who hold to that system. The Federal Vision system is within the Pelagian spectrum of heresies; the Federal Vision proponents inconsistently espouse both the Federal Vision and Reformed theology. They profess the doctrines of the Reformed faith when compelled to do so by the courts of the church, but there are no books written by them on unconditional election, regeneration, the perseverance of the saints, justification by faith alone, effectual calling, the subjective grace of the Holy Spirit, or any of the other great doctrines of salvation. Rather, their books and articles contradict the great scriptural doctrines of salvation. We must conclude, therefore, that the Federal Vision proponents believe what they write and teach—not what they *say* they believe about the confession or the Scripture when backed into a corner by their presbyteries.

The errors of the Federal Vision are the same ones that were the great battleground of the Protestant Reformation, as Scott Clark rightly noted. The Reformers knew that the sacramental theories of Rome were a large part of the delusion of the masses concerning the true way of salvation. Those sacramental theories also led the Church of Rome into grievous errors concerning soteriology. The views of the Federal Vision would lead the church back into those same Pelagian/Semi-Pelagian errors that predominated before the Reformation. Therefore, this book will show that the views of the Federal Vision are contrary to the Scripture, to all the Reformed creeds, and to the views of the greatest Reformed theologians of all ages.

Of course, the great question for us is this: Is the Federal Vision a real problem, and, if so, why? Yes, the Federal Vision is a problem because it is an attack on the gospel. Antinomianism (anti-legalism) denies the Law. Legalism (which the Federal Vision is) denies the gospel. Antinomianism primarily attacks the doctrine of sanctification. Legalism primarily attacks the doctrine of justification. All things considered, the Federal Vision is a greater enemy of the truth than even antinomianism because of its attack on the gospel.

-2-

The Federal Vision and Regeneration

"My thesis is that there is no such thing as 'regeneration' in the sense in which Reformed theology since Dort has spoken of it. The Bible says nothing about a permanent change in the hearts of those elected to heaven."[1]

JAMES JORDAN, FEDERAL VISION PROPONENT

"The Bible does not teach that some people receive incorruptible new hearts, i.e., that some people are as individuals 'regenerated'."[2]

JAMES JORDAN

"My position: everyone who is baptized has been given the same thing. No one has been given a permanently changed 'regenerated heart'."[3]

JAMES JORDAN

"In baptism we are brought covenantally and publicly out of union with Adam and into union with Christ. When this occurs, one is 'born again,' not in the sense we have come to speak of regeneration as an irresistible, irreversible change of heart, but in the covenantal sense of being brought out of Adam's family into God's family."[4]

RICH LUSK, FEDERAL VISION PROPONENT

---

1 Guy Prentiss Waters, *The Federal Vision and Covenant Theology: A Comparative Analysis* (Phillipsburg, New Jersey: P&R Publishing, 2006), 295.

2 Ibid.

3 Ibid.

4 Ibid., 226.

In 2007, several ministers who hold to the Federal Vision agreed on a summary of their beliefs. This statement was titled "A Joint Federal Vision Profession" and was signed by four ministers in the Presbyterian Church in America (Mark Horne, Peter Leithart, Jeff Meyers, and Steve Wilkins), six ministers in the Confederation of Reformed Evangelical Churches (John Barach, Randy Booth, Tim Gallant, Rich Lusk, Ralph Smith, and Douglas Wilson), and one teacher at large, Jim Jordan. Two of the PCA signatories, Wilkins and Leithart, have since transferred their membership to the CREC. Concerning regeneration, their joint document says:

> Another difference is whether or not personal regeneration represents a change of nature in the person so regenerated. Some of us say yes while others question whether we actually have such an "essence" that can be changed.[5]

This quote is found in the section of the "Profession" concerning "intramural disagreements" and supposedly does not represent the views of every person in the Federal Vision. It wrongly contrasts personal regeneration with the idea that man has an "essence" which is changed in regeneration. These signatories equate nature with essence, but those terms are not the same thing. Regeneration is a change of nature, but it is not a change of the essence or the substance of the soul. The latter is the error of Manichaeism and is "inconsistent with the nature of sin and holiness."[6]

Regeneration is Necessary for Salvation

There are two great parts of the biblical doctrine of salvation—regeneration and saving faith. The good news of the gospel requires that we affirm both of them. First, we must tell sinners the same thing Christ told Nicodemus: "You must be born again" (John 3:7). This fundamental change of regeneration is a vital aspect of salvation. It is life

---

5 http://www.federal-vision.com/resources/joint_FV_Statement.pdf, accessed October 20th, 2014. This document was formulated in 2007 and was signed by John Barach, Rich Lusk, Randy Booth, Jeff Meyers, Tim Gallant, Ralph Smith, Mark Horne, Steve Wilkins, Jim Jordan, Doug Wilson, and Peter Leithart

6 Charles Hodge, *Systematic Theology*, Volume III (Grand Rapids, Michigan: Wm. B. Eerdmans Publishing Company, 1970), 32. The Manichees were a major Gnostic religion founded by the Iranian prophet, Mani. Like all Gnostics, they believed in the dualistic struggle between good and evil. Augustine was once a Manichee, but opposed it when he was converted. The Manichees said that their religion was for the whole world because Christianity, Buddhism, and Zoroastrianism were incomplete religions.

from the dead. It is taking away the heart of stone and giving a heart of flesh. It is a new creation in Christ. The Scripture is clear about this great change called the *new birth*. Yet, there is confusion and even disagreement among the Federal Vision proponents about the nature of "personal regeneration." This *confusion* by the Federal Vision was the vanguard of its position in 2006 when Guy Prentiss Waters wrote, *The Federal Vision and Covenant Theology*, in which he said:

> Few FV proponents, after all, deny the necessity of individual regeneration.[7]

Yet, Waters predicted that the Federal Vision proponents would grasp at some point that individual regeneration is extraneous to their core doctrines. Today, it is apparent that they mean something radically different about regeneration than what evangelical Christians have always believed about it. Their ideas on regeneration are further explored in Chapter 8, "The Federal Vision and Baptismal Regeneration," but James Jordan's quotes at the beginning of this chapter show both his position and the direction of the Federal Vision concerning regeneration. He states that the Reformed position since Dort is wrong when it describes regeneration as a permanent change of our hearts.

Second, we must be able to proclaim as Paul did to the Philippian jailer: "Believe in the Lord Jesus, and you will be saved" (Acts 16:31). This saving faith results in the justification of a sinner, which is the forensic side of salvation. It is a change of status. It is a legal declaration of being in a right relationship with God. By faith in Christ, the guilt of our sin is wiped away and we are put in a right relationship with God. On the other hand, regeneration breaks the power of sin through our new life in Christ. Both regeneration and saving faith are necessary to salvation. A denial of either one is a fundamental error.

The third chapter of John's Gospel gives the account of Nicodemus, a ruler of the Jews, who came to Jesus at night to inquire about His teaching. Jesus responded to Nicodemus with the startling statement, "Unless one is born again he cannot see the kingdom of God" (John 3:3). In other words, Jesus told Nicodemus that he could not even comprehend His teaching without a spiritual rebirth. The abruptness of Jesus' words—before Nicodemus could even ask Him a question—is explained by Calvin:

---

7 Waters, *Federal Vision and Covenant Theology*, 152.

> Christ saw that Nicodemus' mind was so full of thorns and choked with many noxious weeds that there was scarcely any room for spiritual teaching. This exhortation was therefore like a ploughing to clean him, that nothing should make the teaching unfruitful.[8]

Concerning the question of whether or not man has a nature which can be changed, Jesus' words to Nicodemus are determinative, "You must be born again" (John 3:7). The same power of God that Nicodemus acknowledged was present in Jesus' miracles must radically and fundamentally change the heart of man before he can even enter into the kingdom of God. This is a new birth by water and the Spirit (John 3:5), but it cannot be reduced merely to a so-called "new life" received in the ordinance of baptism. True regeneration is supernatural. Thus, Calvin comments that water in John 3:5 refers to the "inward cleansing and quickening of the Holy Spirit."[9] The nineteenth-century Presbyterian minister, C. R. Vaughan, makes the following assessment of Jesus' conversation with Nicodemus in *The Gifts of the Holy Spirit*:

> All attempts to identify this change with the mere ordinance of baptism, or with the mere modification of thought or feeling produced by the influence of written words, are useless. All attempts to construe it as a mere change in any outward or merely legal relations of a man are failures, complete in abortiveness. It is a change inward, not outward, a change of nature, not of relations. It is not a change of mere *state*, defined by relations to an outward order or law of action. Even when contemplated as an inward change, it is not merely a change of *habits*, or even some modifications of *character*; for these may be effected by human energies and associations, by human will and moral culture. It goes deeper than any such influences can reach. It is a profound movement on that inner moral energy which determines thought and feeling—which forms character, which dictates action, and thus creates habits. It goes to the bottom of the deep radical disorder of the human heart.[10]

Regeneration is not merely a change of culture or habits. It is not merely a change of opinions or thoughts about the Scripture. It goes deeper than all those things and is at the bottom of every true change

---

8   T. H. L. Parker, trans., David W. Torrance and Thomas F. Torrance, eds., *Calvin's Commentaries: The Gospel According to St. John* (Grand Rapids, Michigan: Wm. B. Eerdmans Publishing Company, 1959), 62-3.

9   Ibid., 65.

10   C. R. Vaughan, *The Gifts of the Holy Spirit: To unbelievers and believers* (Edinburgh, Scotland and Carlisle, Pennsylvania: The Banner of Truth Trust, 1975), 136.

in a man's life. As Vaughan says, it determines a man's thoughts and feelings; it dictates action and creates habits; and, it changes the radical disorder of the heart.

If man does not have a nature that can be changed (as some in the Federal Vision state), then Jesus was mistaken in telling Nicodemus that he needed to be born again. Without a spiritual rebirth, whatever change happens in a person's life must be the result of some greater enlightenment or the exercise of one's will. Jesus' words to Nicodemus rule out the possibility of mere enlightenment effecting this radical change, and John 1:13 makes it clear that being born of God is not a result of the will of man. Yet, the joint statement by the Federal Vision permits its signatories to deny the new birth without offering any other solution for how a person undergoes a change in his actions or character.

J. C. Ryle faced many of the same theological issues in the nineteenth century which the Federal Vision presents to our own generation. Concerning the wrong views of regeneration held by some people in his day, he said:

> Some hold that regeneration only means admission into a state of ecclesiastical privileges, by being a member of the Church, but does not mean a change of heart. Some tell us that a regenerate man has a certain power within him which enables him to repent and believe if he thinks fit, but that he still needs a further change in order to make him a true Christian. Some say there is a difference between Regeneration and being born again. Others say there is a difference between being born again and conversion.
>
> To all this I have one simple reply, and that is, *I can find no such Regeneration spoken of anywhere in the Bible*. A Regeneration which only means admission into a state of ecclesiastical privilege may be ancient and primitive for anything I know. But something more than this is wanted. A few plain texts of Scripture are needed; and these texts have yet to be found.
>
> Such a notion of Regeneration is utterly inconsistent with that which St. John gives us in his first Epistle. It renders it necessary to invent the awkward theory that there are two Regenerations, and is thus calculated to confuse the minds of unlearned people, and introduce false doctrine.[11]

Ryle, in his simple and inimitable way, puts his finger on the heart of the issue with all these false theories of regeneration. Despite the

---

11 John Charles Ryle, *Knots Untied* (Cambridge, England: James Clarke & Co. LTD, 1977), 91-2.

passing of time, the same basic issues are plaguing the church today that did so in Ryle's day and earlier times. In his trial before Pacific Northwest Presbytery of the Presbyterian Church in America in 2011[12], Peter Leithart distinguished between an ecclesiastical new life conveyed through baptism, and supernatural regeneration as described by the Westminster Confession of Faith. A theory of two regenerations is necessarily confusing to Christ's little ones because it is utterly unscriptural. There is no scriptural warrant for saying that the new birth or new life is merely an ecclesiastical birth. That requires the teaching of two different regenerations—one ecclesiastical and the other spiritual.

Regeneration is a supernatural change

The Scripture is perspicuous concerning the change called regeneration or the new birth. It attributes this change throughout to the supernatural power of the Holy Spirit. In Ezekiel, the Lord proclaims thus: "Moreover, I will give you a new heart and put a new spirit within you; and I will remove the heart of stone from your flesh and give you a heart of flesh. I will put My Spirit within you and cause you to walk in My statutes. . ." (Ezekiel 36:26, 27). This new heart is the result of the Holy Spirit dwelling within us. Numerous New Testament verses confirm that the Holy Spirit indeed dwells within His people, which fact proves that the change is the result of a super-

---

12 Following the adoption in June of 2007 by the General Assembly of the Presbyterian Church in America of the Ad-Interim Study Committee Report on Federal Vision, New Perspective and the Auburn Avenue Theologies, Teaching Elder Peter Leithart of Pacific Northwest Presbytery informed that court in writing his differences with the nine points affirmed by the vote of the assembly. That led to an investigation and exoneration of his views by Pacific Northwest Presbytery. A complaint against the actions of that court was then filed with the lower court and that complaint was submitted to the General Assembly's Standing Judicial Commission in 2009. It was heard by a panel chaired by Teaching Elder Dewey Roberts in November of 2009 that unanimously voted to uphold it. The full Standing Judicial Commission voted in March of 2010 to send the case back to the lower court, Pacific Northwest Presbytery, for further judicial action. When Leithart refused to transfer his membership into another denomination, such as the Confederation of Reformed Evangelical Churches, he submitted to a trial in 2011 by Pacific Northwest Presbytery concerning his views. That trial resulted in the lower court exonerating Leithart of any theological errors and another complaint was brought to the General Assembly's Standing Judicial Commission against the actions of Pacific Northwest Presbytery. The complainant, Ruling Elder Gerald Hedman, was represented before the Standing Judicial Commission by Teaching Elder Dewey Roberts. The General Assembly's Standing Judicial Commission heard the complaint on March 5, 2013 and voted 15-2 to deny the complaint without considering the theological issues involved. The reasoning of the Standing Judicial Commission was that Pacific Northwest Presbytery had followed the right procedure in conducting a trial and that their decision was, therefore, not reviewable by the higher court. It was a decision in which church polity trumped the doctrinal beliefs of the church.

natural Person. Christians are born again not of the flesh, but of the Spirit (John 3:5, 6, 8). Christ baptizes not with water, but with the Spirit (Matthew 3:11; Mark 1:8; Luke 3:16; and John 1:33). We once were dead in our trespasses and sins, but have been made alive with Christ (Ephesians 2:1, 5). Peter describes us as being made partakers of the divine nature (2 Peter 1:4). John in his first epistle says that we are born of God (1 John 2:29; 3:9; 4:7; 5:1, 4, 18). James says that it was by the exercise of God's will that we were brought forth to new life (James 1:18). Paul describes this new life as being new creatures in Christ in which all things have become new (2 Corinthians 5:17; Galatians 6:15). Thus, we have the united testimony of the apostles and prophets, along with Christ Himself, that the new birth, or regeneration, is a supernatural work of the Holy Spirit in which a new heart is given. Whoever denies that regeneration is a supernatural work of God's free grace is capable of infidelity concerning any doctrine of Scripture. Yet, some in the Federal Vision deny that regeneration is a supernatural work of God's Spirit.

One of the signatories to this joint Federal Vision Profession was Doug Wilson, who wrote an article, "Can a Nature/Grace Dualism be Born Again?" in his magazine, *Credenda-Agenda*. In this article, Wilson referred to Yale Professor Harold Bloom's book, *The American Religion*, which criticizes most religious faiths as being essentially gnostic in their psychological hold on their members. This book helped Wilson supposedly gain a greater insight into the doctrine of regeneration. He was also assisted by Peter Leithart and James Jordan in divesting regeneration of what he claims is the nature/grace dualism held by many evangelical Christians. Is Wilson correct in what he says about regeneration in this article? Here is a quote from Wilson in this article which gets to the heart of what he is trying to say:

> If you assume that in the supernatural act of regeneration God comes down and implants a grace node in your heart, then this is a form of gnosticism, and it helps perpetuate that pestilent nature/grace dualism. But if you hold that the act of regeneration is supernatural, and that the results are entirely "natural", then this is not gnostic.[13]

There are several problems with these two sentences in Wilson's article. First, how are the results of God's supernatural regeneration

---

13 Doug Wilson, "Can a Nature/Grace Dualism Be Born Again?", Credenda Agenda, Volume 19, Series 3, Special Edition, (2007): 22.

entirely "natural," as Wilson asserts? He does not tell us. Where does Wilson find that statement in Scripture? He never refers to any Scripture passage or verse which teaches that theory. What are those natural results of regeneration? Wilson does not list a single one of those supposed natural results of regeneration. Which Reformed theologian has ever said that regeneration is God coming down and supernaturally implanting a "grace node" in our hearts? This writer has never seen that phrase used by anyone except Wilson. Wilson's use of the term, "grace node," appears to be a pejorative to make his denial of the supernatural more palatable. And, finally, by distinguishing between supernatural and natural with respect to regeneration, is not Wilson guilty of the same nature/grace dualism that he is supposedly trying to combat?

Key Assessment: Some Federal Vision proponents deny a personal, supernatural regeneration, while others are willing to accept the denial of such regeneration as an intramural debate of no consequence.

When regeneration has been defined as natural, it has generally resulted in a denial of the supernatural work of the Holy Spirit in the new birth. The Spirit's agency in regeneration is then restricted to influencing the mind of the sinner through moral suasion or illumination. The Spirit certainly does influence and enlighten sinners, but regeneration includes more than that. It includes a change of the will and a spiritual rebirth which can only be accomplished by the almighty power of God. Without this latter element, regeneration is at best synergistic and dependent on the cooperation of man. Synergistic regeneration is the error of Semi-Pelagianism, the Council of Trent, and Arminianism. The scriptural position is that regeneration is a monergistic act of God. It is incumbent on Wilson and those in the Federal Vision to explain how their view that regeneration is entirely natural in its results is not a violation of Reformed theology and Scripture.

The position staked out by Wilson is almost identical to the view of Claude Pajon, a seventeenth-century French Protestant who taught for two years at the French Huguenot school, the University of Saumur, in western France. Pajon was forced to resign in 1668 for teaching that the Holy Spirit works indirectly, not directly, on an individual in salvation by influencing his judgments. After his resignation, Pajon became a pastor at Orleans, France, where his views were accused in 1677 of

The Federal Vision and Regeneration

being Pelagian and Arminian. Pajon's views were revived a century later by two German Protestant authors, Johann Ernst Schubert and Johann Z. Junckheim. Junckheim's work in 1775 was the more formidable of the two and attempted to reconcile the supernatural in the work of grace. George Smeaton describes Junckheim's position:

> He asserted that the operation of God in men's regeneration and conversion was not to be designated SUPERNATURAL, or, if that style of language was still retained, only in so far as the Scriptures were of supernatural origin. For the rest, there was nothing that was not wholly natural. The moral power of the word effected all. This was an erratic tendency, which, though it called forth less alarm than Pelagianism, or Synergism, or Arminianism, was as perilous as any of them, and proved, perhaps, more calamitous. It was a theory that recognized the Scriptures, but left the Spirit nothing further to do. The propounder of this theory did not perceive that without an inward supernatural work of grace, admitted and believed, men will not long believe in an external supernatural revelation. More than that: if the Spirit does nothing on the individual, His personality will not long be believed in, in any proper sense of the term. And both results necessarily followed, in due course, in the religious history of Germany.[14]

In Wilson's earlier quote above, he denies the immediate, inward, supernatural operation of the Holy Spirit in the work of grace. He does not altogether deny that the act of regeneration is supernatural in some sense, but he asserts that the results are entirely natural. Junckheim, according to Smeaton, referred to the work of regeneration as wholly natural. The terms "wholly" and "entirely" mean the same thing. The denial of this scriptural truth of a supernatural regeneration will have all the same devastating consequences today that rationalism has produced in German theological circles over the past 250 years. It will lead to infidelity concerning God's supernatural revelation; to a denial of the Divine personality of the Holy Spirit; and, to opposition to the supernatural work of the Spirit in the hearts of believers.

Another Federal Vision advocate who denies the supernatural work of God in regeneration is Rich Lusk, who wrote:

> Baptism will consummate the process of regeneration begun by the Word preached.[15]

---

14 George Smeaton, *The Doctrine of the Holy Spirit* (Edinburgh, Scotland and Carlisle, Pennsylvania: The Banner of Truth Trust, 1974), 373-4.

15 Waters, *Federal Vision and Covenant Theology*, 212.

Lusk's view is that regeneration is a process, not an instantaneous act of God. He also mentions only two things involved in this process—the preaching of the Word and baptism. Moreover, he says that baptism consummates what the preaching of the Word began. Such a view of regeneration relegates the work of the Holy Spirit to an influence on the mind or moral suasion at most. That is rationalism. When the Word and baptism are combined as the means of regeneration without the supernatural work of the Spirit in the hearts of men, rationalism and ritualism are then joined together. Vaughan repudiates such rationalistic and ritualistic views of regeneration as being contrary to the Scripture:

> We affirm this supernatural origin of regeneration, *first*, as against the theory of it as a mere natural change wrought by the force of mere religious ideas, just as other written or spoken thoughts modify character, on the one side, and on the other, as against the theory of it as a mere ritual change wrought by the sacraments administered by human agents in an official character.[16]

The denial of the supernatural work of the Holy Spirit in the regeneration of sinners is an area where the ritualism of the Federal Vision clearly also becomes rationalistic. Rationalism and ritualism are sometimes found on the same side of theological issues because they have a common enemy in the scriptural doctrine of salvation, including supernatural regeneration by God's free grace. Pelagius himself took a rationalistic approach to regeneration when he taught that man could purpose to obey God without the assistance of free grace. He was also the first person to develop a full-orbed theory of baptismal regeneration which became the model for the Roman Catholic heresy on the sacraments. His theology was both rationalistic and ritualistic; and that is the tendency of all forms of Pelagianism. Thus, William Cunningham is certainly correct when he states that:

> Modern Socinians[17] and Rationalists are the only consistent Pelagians. When men reject what Pelagius rejected, they are bound in consistency to reject everything that is peculiar and distinctive in the Christian system as a remedial scheme. Upon Pelagian principles, there is no oc-

---

16 Vaughan, *The Gifts of the Holy Spirit*, 168.

17 Socinianism is a system of doctrine that denies the Trinity and strips Christ of His deity. It was named for Faustus Socinus, a sixteenth-century Protestant leader in Poland who departed from evangelical and Reformed theology in the area of soteriology.

casion for, and really no meaning in, a Saviour, an atonement, a Holy Spirit.[18]

In every generation, there have been some who moved in the direction of Pelagianism or Semi-Pelagianism while professing allegiance to other theological systems. When the Pelagian controversy erupted within the Presbyterian Church in America in the 1800's, Albert Barnes was charged with teaching synergism concerning regeneration among several other charges. The specific charge stated that he taught:

> That unregenerate men are able to keep the commandments, and convert themselves to God.[19]

Barnes, like so many others who fell into error, claimed that he had not departed from the Westminster Standards in his views or teaching. Nonetheless, the General Assembly in 1836 found him guilty of heresy, and his subsequent history proved the justice of the charges against him. Barnes' theology developed in all the wrong ways Cunningham said such rationalism would.

Regeneration is a Change of Nature but Not a Change of Substance or Essence

The denial by some in the Federal Vision that man does not have an "essence" that can be changed is misguided. The only Protestant advocate of the view that man's essence is changed in regeneration was Matthaias Flacius Illyricus (1520-1575), a pupil of Luther and a second-generation Reformer.[20] Every orthodox Protestant denomination believes both in personal regeneration and that such regeneration is not a change of the essence or substance of the soul of man. Moreover, the position of Illyricus was condemned by the Lutheran *Formula of Concord*[21] as a revival of the Manichean (Gnostic) heresy. Charles Hodge's comment about Illyricus is enlightening:

---

18 William Cunningham, *Historical Theology*, Volume I (London: The Banner of Truth Trust, 1969), 329-330.

19 Samuel J. Baird, *A History of the New School* (Philadelphia: Claxton, Remsen, and Haffelfinger, 1868), 476.

20 Hodge, *Systematic Theology*, III, 6.

21 Philip Schaff, ed., and David S. Schaff, rev., *The Creeds of Christendom: With a History and Critical Notes*, Volume III, "The Evangelical Protestant Creeds" (Grand Rapids, Michigan: Baker Book House, 1983), 103.

> Always extreme in his opinions, he held that original sin was a corruption of the substance of the soul, and regeneration such a change of that substance as to restore its normal purity.[22]

Illyricus' view of regeneration is further illumined by the comment of Augustine concerning his own experience during his time as a Manichean heretic:

> I still thought that it is not we who sin but some other nature that sins within us. It flattered my pride to think that I incurred no guilt and, when I did wrong, not to confess it so that you might *bring healing to a soul that sinned against you*. I preferred to excuse myself and blame this unknown thing which was in me but was not part of me. The truth, of course, was that it was all my own self, and my own impiety had divided me against myself. My sin was all the more incurable because I did not think myself a sinner.[23]

If regeneration is a change of the essence or substance of the soul of man, then man is not blamable for his sins. The problem of sin is blamed on the sinful substance (essence) of the soul within man, but the sinner incurs no guilt. Augustine was correct in acknowledging that the real problem was his own impiety which had divided his heart. Schaff's comments about Augustine's Anti-Manichean writings are worth noting:

> His [Augustine's] doctrine of the nature of evil is particularly valuable. He has triumphantly demonstrated for all time, that evil is not a corporeal thing, nor in any way substantial, but a product of the free will of the creature, a perversion of substance in itself good, a corruption of the nature created by God.[24]

Therefore, the intramural debate about regeneration among the Federal Vision proponents wrongly contrasts nature and essence. Regeneration is a change of nature, but that nature is not the essence or substance of man. Sin is a matter of the will and is not corporeal; it does not consist in physical substance or matter. Essence is corporeal and does consist in physical substance. This statement of their "Profession" concerning regeneration is both troubling and nonsensical.

---

22 Hodge, *Systematic Theology*, III, 5-6.

23 R. S. Pine-Coffin, trans. and introduction, Saint Augustine, *Confessions*, Book V, Section 10 (London, England: Penguin Books, 1961), 103.

24 Philip Schaff, *History of the Christian Church*, Vol. III, Nicene and Post-Nicene Christianity (Grand Rapids, Michigan: Wm. B. Eerdmans Publishing Company, 1981), 1013.

Did this Federal Vision "Profession" intend to say that some of them believe in personal regeneration and others of them do not? Or, did they intend to say that some of them believe that regeneration is a change of nature and others of them do not? Or, did they intend to say that some of them believe regeneration is a change of the essence of the soul and others disagree? Or, did they intentionally contrast personal regeneration with an heretical view of it? Like so many things about the Federal Vision, they promote confusion by making theologically imprecise statements.

While regeneration is not a change of the substance or essence of the soul, the whole soul is the subject of this great work of God—the intellect, the feelings, and the will. It is a spiritual resurrection and the beginning of new life. The Holy Spirit inclines the will of man to holiness and against sin in regeneration. Before regeneration, the will is inclined to sin and wholly incapable of seeking God. As Charles Hodge states about regeneration:

> Sometimes the word expresses the act of God. God regenerates. Sometimes it designates the subjective effect of his act. The sinner is regenerated. He becomes a new creature. He is born again. And this is his regeneration. . . Its metaphysical nature is left a mystery. It is not the province of either philosophy or theology to solve that mystery.[25]

In a chapter on regeneration in *Introduction to Dogmatic Theology*, Edward A. Litton, a nineteenth-century evangelical Church of England minister and scholar, makes the following observation:

> The union with Christ, and through Christ with God, of which Scripture speaks, is of an ethical, not a metaphysical character; a union effected by faith, and moral in its nature; not of essences, whether Divine or human. Physical conceptions on the subject are an intrusion of the natural creation into the higher region of supernatural grace.[26]

In the nineteenth-century theological controversy with the "New Divinity" held by Charles G. Finney, Albert Barnes and others, the Princeton Seminary professors clearly saw that the issue was between Calvinism and Pelagianism. Charles Hodge wrote an article for the *Biblical Repertory and Theological Review* (later known as the *Princ-*

---

25 Hodge, *Systematic Theology*, 5.

26 Philip E. Hughes, ed., Edward Arthur Litton, *Introduction to Dogmatic Theology* (London, England: James Clarke & Co. Ltd, 1960), 329.

eton Review) on the subject of regeneration. Hodge's article was a review of a sermon preached by Samuel H. Cox before the Synod of New York in 1830. Cox was the pastor of Laight Street Presbyterian Church in New York City and was an advocate of the New Divinity. In that sermon, he misrepresented and falsely caricatured the doctrine of regeneration held by his opponents as stating that:

> Regeneration consists in some secret physical motion on the soul which restores its dislocated powers and cures the connatural diseases of its texture.[27]

The false caricature by Cox that the orthodox doctrine of regeneration consists in a physical change was the primary concern of Hodge in his article. He saw Cox's false caricature as an attack on the older Calvinists who were accused of also teaching "that man's depravity is a 'physical defect'—that regeneration is a 'physical change', etc."[28] In his review, Hodge shows that referring to regeneration as a physical change is the same thing as referring to it as a change of the essence or substance of the soul (similar to what the Federal Vision "Profession" states). Moreover, he proves that any description of regeneration as a physical change necessarily results in caricaturing original sin as a physical change also. The two doctrines hang together and fall together. Indeed, Cox also falsely caricatured total depravity as a physical change in the introduction to his sermon.[29] As Hodge says:

> We cannot pass this subject without a single remark on the charge of physical depravity. The futility and unfairness of the same charge as it regards the subject of regeneration we have endeavored to expose above. As this rests on precisely the same grounds, it must stand or fall with the other.[30]

In other words, if either regeneration or native depravity consists in a physical change, the other must also. The two stand or fall together on the same ground. Of course, the purpose of Hodge's review article was to prove that such a doctrine was neither the doctrine of the older Calvinists nor those Calvinists of his age. (Rather, that the

---

27 Charles Hodge, "Regeneration" in *Princeton Versus the New Divinity* (Edinburgh, Scotland and Carlisle, Pennsylvania: The Banner of Truth Trust, 2001), 4.

28 Ibid., 5.

29 Ibid., 4. "Total depravity and physical depravity are nearly synonymous."

30 Ibid. 46.

false caricature of either regeneration or native depravity is the result of a theological system moving in the direction of the Pelagian spectrum of heresies by defining regeneration as moral suasion only and not a change of heart.)[31]

B. B. Warfield refers to another quote wherein Finney denied original sin for the very same reason he denied that regeneration is a change of substance or physical nature of the soul:

> We deny that the human constitution is morally depraved. . . because it is impossible that sin should be a quality of the substance of the soul or body. It is, and must be, a quality of choice or intention, and not of substance.[32]

All of this is relevant with respect to the Federal Vision because there are some of their advocates who assert that regeneration is not a change of the essence of the soul. Hodge saw that position as cover for a denial of both regeneration and original sin. Some modern opponents of the Federal Vision have overlooked their denial of regeneration and have not realized how that denial leads to a denial of original sin also. Thus, the Federal Vision cannot and does not hold to an Augustinian view of sin and grace.

Some opponents of the Federal Vision consider them guilty of Semi-Pelagianism instead of Pelagianism because they think they have neither denied regeneration nor original sin. Hodge's review of Cox's sermon proves the falsity of that idea. Whenever someone claims that man does not have an essence or substance that can be regenerated, he has already denied both regeneration and original sin. That is a cover position for Pelagianism according to Hodge. Hodge's review article is fifty pages long and thoroughly exposes this false caricature of regeneration. Anyone doubtful of the connection between regeneration and original sin or of the problem in falsely caricaturing them as physical changes should read Hodge's article with great carefulness.

Therefore, the statement concerning regeneration by those who signed the "Profession" appears to be an instance where they have delved into mysteries which God has not fully explained in His Word. Their intramural debate about regeneration cracks open the door for the entrance of error and heresy in both directions. On the one hand,

---

31 Ibid., cf. especially pages 11-20, 26-27, 45-49.

32 Benjamin Breckinridge Warfield, *Perfectionism* (Philadelphia, Pennsylvania: The Presbyterian and Reformed Publishing Company, 1974), 188.

they have opened the door for the heresy of Manichaeism. On the other hand, they have relegated the scriptural doctrine of regeneration to being a non-essential doctrine of no great importance. They have determined that fundamental differences concerning it are irrelevant.

The Denial of Regeneration in the Pelagian Heresy

These intramural debates among the Federal Vision proponents push the subject of regeneration in the direction of the Pelagian spectrum of heresies. One of the great fault lines between Augustinianism/Calvinism and Pelagianism concerns the necessity of regeneration. Pelagius held that the ability to live according to God's commands is within the power of every individual. For instance, Pelagius and his disciple, Coelestius, were condemned by the Council of Carthage in 418 as follows:

> If any man says that this grace only helps not to sin, in so far that by it we obtain a better insight into the Divine commands, and learn what we should desire and avoid, but does not also give the power gladly to do and to fulfil what we have seen to be good, let him be anathema.[33]

The Council of Carthage contrasted the enlightenment of the mind with the power of God to do and to fulfill what is seen to be good. The Pelagians said that man has the capacity in his freedom of will to do whatever his mind is enlightened to do. The Council of Carthage, on the other hand, anathematized anyone who restricted God's grace to just the enlightening of the mind. God's grace must give us the power to do and to fulfill.

Pelagius' chief nemesis was Augustine, the great stalwart of orthodoxy. Augustine differed from Pelagius by holding that grace precedes every good thing in man, even though he failed to define this grace as regeneration. He quotes the Pelagians as saying:

> That grace also assists the good purpose of every one, but that it does not infuse the desire of virtue into a reluctant heart.[34]

The effect of Pelagius' teaching is to deny the necessity and reality

---

33 Patristics in English Project, Council of Carthage, May 1, 418.

34 Philip Schaff, ed., *A Select Library of the Nicene and Post-Nicene Fathers of the Christian Church*, Volume V, "Saint Augustine: Anti-Pelagian Writings" (Grand Rapids, Michigan: Wm. B. Eerdmans Publishing Company, 1978), 401.

of the new birth. Grace is viewed by Pelagius as assisting a "good purpose" already begun in the heart but not infusing the desire for such a purpose. That makes man, not God, the originator of any good thing in his heart. Pelagius also denies the invincibility of God's grace to overcome the reluctance of man's heart. Thus, Augustine states in reply:

> Subsequent grace indeed assists man's good purpose, but the purpose would not itself exist if grace did not precede. The desire of man, also, which is called good, yet does not begin without grace, but is inspired by Him of whom the apostle says, "But thanks be to God, who has given us the same desire for you in the heart of Titus."[35]

Augustine's position is that grace precedes both the purpose and the desire of man to do good. What he calls preceding grace is the same thing Jesus told Nicodemus he needed in order to see the kingdom of God. Augustine clearly believed that a work of grace in the heart of man was necessary before he could desire and purpose to do any good thing. Yet, Jordan's position on regeneration quoted at the beginning of this chapter is pure Pelagianism and is the direction in which the Federal Vision is necessarily moving. By denying personal regeneration through the Holy Spirit, Jordan makes any change in the human heart the result of man's efforts.

Key Assessment: Both Augustine and Bernard define the Pelagian heresy as a denial of regeneration or preceding grace. Philip Schaff says Pelagianism leaves no place for regeneration.

More than seven centuries after Pelagius, Bernard of Clairvaux wrote to Pope Innocent a book, *On the Errors of Peter Abelard*, against some of the disputed points of Abelard's theology. Bernard accused him of some of the errors of Pelagianism, particularly with respect to regeneration:

> If the life that Christ gives us is nothing but education, then certainly the death that Adam gave will likewise be nothing but education, so that they both teach people—the one by his example to sin, the other by example to live well and love him. But if, assenting to the Christian faith and not the Pelagian heresy, we confess that it is by generation, not education, that the sin of Adam has been transmitted [*traductum*] to us, let us also acknowledge that it is necessary for Christ to restore

35 Ibid.

righteousness to us (and through righteousness, life) not by education but by regeneration...

He attributes the whole of salvation to our commitment, none of it to regeneration; he locates the whole of our redemption and essence of salvation not in the power of the Cross, not in the value [*pretium*] of the blood, but in the improvement of our way of life.[36]

Both Bernard and the Council of Carthage confirm that one of the grand differences between the true gospel and Pelagianism concerns the matter of regeneration. The Pelagians deny that regeneration is anything more than commitment, improvement of our way of life, and a better insight into the Law. Such a view necessarily means that the difference consists in the knowledge which is put into practice. It denies the necessity of a new birth by the Holy Spirit which alone can give us the power to obey God's commands. Regeneration, for them, consists only in enlightenment and a commitment to live according to God's law or teaching.

Summary
There are some in the Federal Vision who still hold to personal regeneration, however contradictory it is to their main principles. Yet, others within that movement differ with them. On the other hand, all of the signatories to "A Joint Federal Vision Profession" believe that their differences about regeneration are only an intramural debate. Some of the Federal Vision proponents might actually be closer to Semi-Pelagianism in their views; i.e., they believe that a supernatural "regeneration" of the Holy Spirit is bestowed in baptism that can be lost. Others of them clearly deny regeneration or define regeneration as only an ecclesiastical new birth. There is no explanation by them how someone who receives only an ecclesiastical new birth can attain eternal life through covenant faithfulness. Those who deny the necessity of regeneration are taking a more Pelagian position on that doctrine. They are denying the great change that is essential to salvation. Guy Waters is certainly correct when he says that regeneration is extraneous to their core doctrines.

Regeneration is necessary because of the natural depravity of all humans. If regeneration is denied or explained away, it can only be because original sin is also denied or explained away. It is assumed by

---

36 Anthony N. S. Lane, *Bernard of Clairvaux: Theologian of the Cross* (Collegeville, Minnesota: Liturgical Press, 2013), 99-101.

some opponents of the Federal Vision that its advocates still hold to an Augustinian view of sin despite their other problems, but Charles Hodge shows that to be a false assumption. When people falsely caricature regeneration as a physical change of essence or substance, their doctrine of regeneration also assumes that original sin is a physical change. That false caricature is cover for the denial of both, as church history clearly reveals. Thus, the Federal Vision's position on regeneration is also a denial of original sin which is the primary identifying characteristic of Pelagianism.

Conclusion

Doug Wilson, James Jordan, Rich Lusk, and others in the Federal Vision have taken a Pelagian and/or rationalistic position by denying that regeneration is a supernatural work of the Holy Spirit. Perhaps they are not thoroughgoing Pelagians on all points of theology, but they are moving in that direction. The Pelagian scheme leaves us nothing of the redemptive system of the Scripture. It strips us of a Divine Savior. It makes the Holy Spirit a mere force to persuade us. It destroys the meaning of the atonement. For all the pretended devotion to Scripture itself, the Federal Vision will ultimately leave us with a Bible which resembles the one read by Thomas Jefferson after he had cut out with scissors every semblance of the miraculous. It will be a Bible full of holes with everything supernatural removed. It will be the Bible of higher criticism and of rationalists who have destroyed the faith of Christ's little ones. As Philip Schaff wrote:

> The Pelagian system has really no place for the ideas of redemption, atonement, regeneration, and new creation. It substitutes for them our own moral effort to perfect our natural powers, and the mere addition of the grace as a valuable aid and support.[37]

What Schaff and others wrote concerning Pelagianism may also be said about the Federal Vision. Inasmuch as some in the Federal Vision deny regeneration and the new creation, they are bound to also deny the free, efficacious grace of God in salvation. In the end, the great question is this: How can anyone who has been born again by the all-powerful grace of God deny that regeneration is supernatural? The answer is obvious. It is as impossible for a true child of God to

---

37 Philip Schaff, *History of the Christian Church*, Vol. III, 815.

deny that he has been begotten by the Father as it would be for the man born blind to deny that he once was unable to see, but now can. As Malachi wrote concerning those who were divorcing the wives of their youth, "... not one has done so who has a remnant of the Spirit" (Malachi 2:15). The same may be said concerning this Federal Vision heresy.

As Charles Hodge proclaimed in his sermon at the memorial service for James Waddell Alexander on October 9, 1859, held at the Fifth Avenue Presbyterian Church in New York City:

> A faith founded on argument may be shaken by arguments; but a conviction arising from religious experience, that is, from a state of consciousness produced by the Spirit of God, is not to be moved.[38]

Such a state of consciousness, such a religious experience, God has given to all those He has regenerated by the supernatural power of the Holy Spirit. That firm conviction in their hearts is an immovable proof to them of the reality of personal regeneration.

---

38 James M. Garretson, *Pastor-Teachers of Old Princeton*, "He Preached Christ" (Edinburgh, Scotland and Carlisle, Pennsylvania: The Banner of Truth Trust, 2012), 141.

-3-

The Federal Vision and Grace

"If grace is the favor of God manifested in the bestowal of favors, then baptism is and confers grace: the grace of standing in the house of God, the grace of membership in the community of the reconciled, the grace of immersion in the history of the bride of Christ, the grace of God's favorable regard upon us."[1]

PETER LEITHART, FEDERAL VISION PROPONENT

"The grace of God is not 'that blue Pepsi, Gatorade stuff that really juices up your system, its [sic—DR] favor—it means being in a favorable, and receiving the favor of God, and that is only found in Christ, He was the one whom God favored, he is the Beloved of the Father, and it is in him that we are granted favor as well.'"[2]

STEVE WILKINS, FEDERAL VISION PROPONENT

---

[1] Peter Leithart, *The Priesthood of the Plebs: The Baptismal Transformation of Antique Order* (Eugene, Oregon: Wipf and Stock Publishers, 2003), 183.

[2] Guy Prentiss Waters, *The Federal Vision and Covenant Theology: A Comparative Analysis* (Phillipsburg, New Jersey: P&R Publishing, 2006), 237.

The denial by James Jordan and others in the Federal Vision that regeneration represents "a permanent change in the hearts" of God's people lays an ax at the root of biblical Christianity. Such a denial also changes the meaning of the grace of God. Thus, Peter Leithart's definition of grace leaves out any reference to an inner renewal or redemptive grace. Steve Wilkins defines grace in terms of union with Christ, but also makes no reference to redemption or supernatural regeneration. In other places, union with Christ is defined by the Federal Vision advocates as an ecclesiastical relationship as a result of baptism. Any obscuring of the importance of supernatural regeneration has the same effect as a denial of it. If regeneration is neither necessary (as all the signatories of their "Profession" must believe) nor possible (as some of the those signatories assert), then it is because, as B. B. Warfield wrote in the preface to Augustine's *Anti-Pelagian Writings*, the nature of man is such that it does not need "divine grace in the sense of an inward help to man's weakness."[3] If regeneration is not a supernatural act of God, then the subjective experience of redemptive grace in the inner man is not needed. It is not enough, therefore, that the adherents of the Federal Vision speak about grace. What do they mean by the use of the word grace? Is it the internal, subjective, efficacious grace bestowed by the Holy Spirit in regeneration? Or is it external, objective, and non-efficacious "grace" bestowed by water baptism? These are questions of great moment. One Federal Vision advocate, Rich Lusk, contends that all the covenant community has an "objective standing in grace."[4] His position is similar to the views of other Federal Vision proponents. Such a position is not new, as Warfield further observed concerning the Pelagian controversy:

> It was upon this last point [i.e., that grace is an inward help to man's weakness—DR] that the greatest stress was laid in the controversy, and Augustin was most of all disturbed that thus God's grace was denied and opposed. No doubt the Pelagians spoke constantly of grace, but they meant by this the primal endowment of man with free will, and the subsequent aid given to him in order to its proper use by the reve-

---

3 B. B. Warfield, "Introductory Essay on Augustin and the Pelagian Controversy," in Philip Schaff, ed., Saint Augustin, *Anti-Pelagian Writings*, Volume V of *A Select Library of the Nicene and Post-Nicene Fathers of the Christian Church* (Grand Rapids, Michigan: Wm. B. Eerdmans Publishing Company, 1978), xv.

4 Rich Lusk, "New Life and Apostasy," in Steve Willkins and Duane Garner, eds., *The Federal Vision* (Monroe, Louisiana: Atahanasius Press, 2004), 274-275.

lation of the law and the teaching of the gospel, and, above all, by the forgiveness of past sins in Christ and by Christ's example[5]

A more comprehensive definition of the Pelagian view of grace is given by Herman Bavinck:

> Hence, in Pelagius's theory there could be no internal grace, no regenerating grace of the Holy Spirit which not only illumined the mind but also bent the will. He admittedly did speak of grace but meant by it only: (a) natural ability, the gift of being able to will, which God grants to every person—creating grace; (b) the objective grace of the proclamation of the law or the gospel and of the example of Christ, which was directed to the human intellect and instructed people in the way of salvation—illuminating grace; and (c) the forgiveness of sins and future salvation, which would be granted to the person who believed and did good works.[6]

The doctrine of regeneration can never be allowed to become an intramural debate as the Federal Vision advocates have made it. The denial of the regenerating grace of the Holy Spirit, as Bavinck states, necessarily results in a Pelagian view of salvation.

Grace in the Federal Vision System

An essential issue at stake with the rise of the Federal Vision / New Perspectives on Paul theology is the correct definition of grace. Grace is a term which is used frequently in Scripture with various shades of meaning. Reformed theology has generally categorized grace as either common grace or redemptive grace. Calvin was especially instrumental in developing an understanding of common grace as an expression of God's favor which does not necessarily result in salvation. Not all grace is saving grace. Not every operation of the Holy Spirit is a saving operation. There are common operations of the Holy Spirit which are manifestations of God's grace which do not result in salvation.

Though the proponents of the Federal Vision frequently refer to the grace or gifts of God, they generally fail to define what they mean by grace. In the trial of Peter Leithart by Pacific Northwest Presbytery of the Presbyterian Church in America, an expert witness for the defense, Dr. William Barker,[7] whose orthodoxy is not in question,

---

5   Schaff, ed., *Augustin, Anti-Pelagian Writings*, xv.

6   John Bolt, ed., John Vriend, trans., Herman Bavinck, *Reformed Dogmatics*, Volume 3, Sin and Salvation (Grand Rapids, Michigan: Baker Academic, 2006), 508-9.

7   My respect for Dr. Barker is immense and his theology is not in question. My purpose is not

struggled to define the Federal Vision's view of grace. He was twice asked about the assertions of Leithart that the differences between God's covenants with man before the fall and after the fall were not at the level of a contrast between grace and law. Barker rightly explained that grace before the fall was beneficent favor—not redeeming grace. The prosecutor in that trial, Jason Stellman (who has since defected from the PCA to become a Catholic priest), should have then asked Dr. Barker if he could point to any places where Leithart or other Federal Vision advocates distinguish grace in that way (there are no places of which I am aware). Then, Barker said that as long as salvation was understood to be by grace alone through faith alone, that was sufficient. In other words, he answered essentially the same question in two contradictory ways. First, he distinguished between the beneficent grace before the fall and the redemptive grace after the fall. Second, he asserted that as long as grace was understood to be redeeming grace, he had no concerns. That is begging the question. The grace before the fall was not redemptive grace. The grace after the fall is more than beneficent favor to God's elect. Thus, the proponents of the Federal Vision never clearly distinguish grace before the fall from grace after the fall in any place of which I am aware. Indeed, they cannot define grace after the fall as both redemptive *and* efficacious without abandoning their other views.

In all those statements about grace at the beginning of this chapter, Leithart never defines it as the redemptive grace of Christ or the regenerating grace of the Holy Spirit. Grace is being in the community of God, however that came to pass, according to Leithart. Some Federal Vision proponents do speak of the principle of works in the covenant before the fall and the redemptive grace of the second covenant, but they strongly assert that the two covenants are bound together by grace. Both are gracious covenants, according to them. Yet, they never define how that grace is the same in both covenants. Such ambiguity in defining grace is not a new phenomenon. Augustine accused Pelagius of the same thing:

> That which he seems to regard as the grace which helps us to turn aside from evil and to good, he describes in such a manner as to keep to his

---

to embarrass him, but to show the errors with the Federal Vision/New Perspectives on Paul. He chose to be an expert witness in this trial and the trial documents reveal the difficulty he had in defining the Federal Vision's view of grace. His personal view of grace is correct, but he necessarily struggled in attempting to exonerate Leithart.

old ambiguity of language, and thus have it in his power so to explain to his followers, that they may suppose the assistance which is rendered by grace, for the purpose of helping our natural capacity, consists of nothing else than the law and the teaching.[8]

This chapter is not the place to delve into the Federal Vision's teaching about the law, or covenant faithfulness, and regeneration. Regeneration was covered in Chapter 2 and covenant faithfulness will be considered in Chapter 16. It will be evident when those chapters are read in light of this one (and vice versa) that they mean nothing more by grace than what Pelagius taught. They necessarily restrict "grace" to common grace, to the law and to teaching (including the example of Christ). Many of those in the Federal Vision deny the supernatural work of God's Spirit in the hearts of believers. Therefore, they cannot unequivocally believe that grace is efficacious and redemptive unto eternal life. Thus, they use the word grace without defining its meaning.

If the "grace" conferred in baptism is defined as redemptive and efficacious grace, the whole Federal Vision theory falls apart. Its position would then be as follows:

> When a person is baptized with water, he receives all the saving benefits of Christ's redemptive grace which grace is efficacious unto eternal life.

Thus, salvation would be guaranteed for all the baptized who have all received redemptive, efficacious grace *in their baptism*—a teaching manifestly contradicted by Scripture. Yet, if the "grace" conferred in baptism is defined as common grace or beneficent favor, there are other difficulties. The position of the Federal Vision then becomes:

> When a person is baptized with water, he receives the common grace of God, and if he perseveres in this grace he will be saved.

That position would mean that a person can persevere unto salvation without receiving the special, redemptive grace of God. To obviate this difficulty, the Federal Vision proponents have modified their earlier teaching. They once taught that the baptized receive everything that Christ has to offer. They now say that baptism bestows all the benefits of Christ except perseverance. Yet, that position causes additional problems for them.

---

8 Schaff, ed., *Augustin: Anti-Pelagian Writings*, 232.

Key Assessment: Proponents of the Federal Vision are ambiguous in their definition of grace; they avoid defining it as either redemptive grace or common grace; and they illustrate it by reference to externals.

Peter Leithart evaded defining grace as either special or common at his trial. Instead, he stated that the grace conferred in baptism is something like "ordination grace." Ordination grace is a view held by Catholics wherein they include "divine orders" among the so-called seven sacraments of the church, but it is not a doctrine of the Reformed churches. There is no scriptural warrant for teaching that grace is conferred in the act of ordination. Ordination acknowledges the grace that is already present in the ordinand, but does not confer grace. The whole of the Bible testifies to this truth. The priests of the Old Testament were ordained in solemn ceremonies by having the blood of the sacrifice sprinkled on them which symbolically cleansed them. Yet, the general disregard by the priests for God's ordinances is proof that they did not receive "ordination grace" in those ceremonies. Leithart does not even define what he means by "ordination grace." It is apparently a term he uses to find a middle ground between common grace and redemptive grace.

The Pelagian View of Grace

Pelagianism is typically defined as a system that denies grace altogether. Such an analysis is a *reductio ad absurdum*. Pelagius believed in grace of a sort, but limited grace to the law, to the forgiveness of past sins, and to the illumination of the Holy Spirit. His view of grace left no place for the inward work of God in the hearts of His people. He believed in objective grace, but not subjective grace. He believed in the common grace of God as the Creator, but not the special grace of Christ as the Redeemer. Bavinck is correct in his assessment of Pelagius on grace:

> This trend culminated in the teaching of Pelagius, who did not deny grace but understood it as a universal gift to all people enabling them to choose the good and refuse evil. Grace is emptied of its real meaning since our appropriation of grace depends on our will: God helps those who help themselves. Objectively and subjectively, from beginning to end, the work of salvation is a work of God's grace and of his grace alone.[9]

---

9 John Bolt, ed., John Vriend, trans., Herman Bavinck, *Reformed Dogmatics*, Volume 3: *Sin and*

Thus, it is incorrect to define Pelagianism as a graceless system. The denial of subjective grace and the emphasis that grace is objective only are the touchstones of Pelagianism. Likewise, the Federal Vision emphasizes the objectivity of grace and either denies or neglects subjective grace. Those are the chief reasons that the Federal Vision is guilty of the Pelagian spectrum of heresies. Yet, true grace is both objective and subjective. True grace encompasses both the objective acquisition of salvation through the Mediator and the subjective application of salvation through the Holy Spirit. Even the Council of Trent at least recognized the subjective work of the Spirit in bestowing grace. Yet, Julian, a disciple of Pelagius, ignored the subjective grace of the Spirit in the following quote from Augustine's writings:

> We maintain . . . that men are the work of God, and that no one is forced unwillingly by His power either into evil or good, but that man does either good or ill of his own will; but that in a good work he is always assisted by God's grace, while in evil he is incited by the suggestions of the devil.[10]

Augustine's response to Julian was that by defining grace as assisting man he was necessarily denying that God's grace works "both to will and to do for His good pleasure."[11] The first error of the Pelagians concerning grace was to make it subservient to the will of man. Pelagius himself objected concerning those who accused him of denying grace:

> Let them acknowledge how unfair is their determination to disparage us for a denial of grace, when we throughout almost the whole work acknowledge fully and sincerely both free will and grace.[12]

Pelagius was very adept, as Augustine observed in other places, at defining grace in such a way that it was "by no means clear from the passage either what grace he means, or to what extent he supposes our nature to be assisted by it."[13] Yet, Pelagius was not always able to refrain from telegraphing his views as, for instance, when he defined what he meant by God's help:

Salvation in Christ (Grand Rapids, Michigan: Baker Academic, 2003), 486

10 Schaff, ed., *Augustin, Anti-Pelagian Writings*, 388.

11 Ibid.

12 Ibid., 232.

13 Ibid., 220.

> God helps us by His teaching and revelation, whilst he opens the eyes of our heart; whilst He points out to us the future, that we may not be absorbed in the present; whilst He discovers to us the snares of the devil; whilst He enlightens us with the manifold and ineffable gift of heavenly grace.[14]

Key Assessment: Pelagians are ambiguous in their definition of grace, as Augustine proved, and define it in terms of externals rather than the internal, subjective grace of the Spirit.

In his battle against the Pelagian heresy, Augustine clearly saw that the crucial issue was the necessity of subjective grace. Thus, he wrote:

> Therefore let them read and understand and confess that not by the law and doctrine sounding externally, but by an internal and hidden, a wonderful and ineffable power, God works in the heart not only true revelations, but also a good will.[15]

James Buchanan, a keen student of truth, commented concerning Augustine's debate with the Pelagians on the proper definition of grace:

> The Pelagians, with whom he was called to contend, admitted the doctrine of Grace in the free remission of sins, while they denied the necessity of efficacious grace for the conversion of the sinner.[16]

Buchanan makes an important distinction concerning Pelagianism and grace. Pelagians do not deny all grace; just internal and efficacious grace. As is shown in other chapters, they affirmed the grace of forgiveness and sacramental grace. What they denied was the free, sovereign, efficacious grace of God which results in salvation. Calvin makes this same point in a quote from Augustine:

> But this effectual working of the Holy Spirit is described in the thirty-second chapter of Jeremiah, where he thus speaks in the name of God, "I will put the fear of my name into their hearts, that they decline not from my commandments." In short, their error lies in making no distinction between the grace of Regeneration, which now comes to the succour of our wretchedness, and the first grace which had been

---

14 Ibid.

15 James T. Dennison, Jr., ed., George Musgrave Giger, trans., Francis Turretin, *Institutes of Elenctic Theology*, Volume 2 (Phillipsburg, New Jersey: P&R Publishing, 1994), 527.

16 James Buchanan, *The Doctrine of Justification: An Outline of its History in the Church and of its Exposition from Scripture* (London: The Banner of Truth Trust, 1961), 102.

given to Adam. This Augustine carefully expounds. "Through Christ the Mediator," he says, "God makes those who were wicked to be good for ever after. The first man had not that grace by which he could never wish to be bad; for the help given him was of that nature that he might abandon it when he would, and remain in it if he would, but it was not such as to make him willing. The grace of the second Adam is more powerful. It makes us will, will so strongly and love so ardently, that by the will of the spirit we overcome the will of the flesh lusting against it. . . Through this grace of God in receiving good and persevering therein, there is in us a power not only to be able to do what we will, but to will what we are able."[17]

Special grace has always been understood by evangelical Christians to consist in the power to will and to do God's good pleasure; redemption through Christ's atonement; the renovation of the human heart by the supernatural power of God; and, the indwelling of the Holy Spirit. Augustine correctly assessed Pelagius as limiting grace to the law and teaching and the forgiveness of past sins. The work of the Spirit, in Pelagius' system, was limited to moral suasion in enlightening us.

Why are these references to the Pelagian view of grace necessary? Because there is a chain of errors bound up in the Federal Vision system which lead back to the Pelagian spectrum of heresies. They speak incessantly of grace, but they use the term in an undefined way. In either denying or dismissing the necessity of supernatural regeneration, they necessarily also deny the grace of God in the gospel. That leads them to deny the indwelling of the Holy Spirit and the natural enslavement of the will to sin. If the present-day proponents of the Federal Vision have not yet worked out these connections in their theology, their children certainly will. The novelty of Pelagius' doctrine, as Warfield observes, is "that, in emphasizing free will, he denied the ruin of the race and the necessity of grace."[18] The Federal Vision starts at the opposite pole but will eventually include all the errors of Pelagianism. It first denies or obscures the necessity of regenerative grace and will eventually deny the ruin of the race. The Federal Vision proponents, or their children, will someday unmistakably also deny "the bondage of the will," as Luther called it. The ruin of the race,

---

17 Henry Beveridge, ed. and trans., *John Calvin: Tracts and Letters*, Volume 3: Tracts, Part 3 (Edinburgh, Scotland and Carlisle, Pennsylvania: The Banner of Truth Trust, 2009), 111-112.

18 Schaff, ed., *Augustin, Anti-Pelagian Writings*, xiii.

the necessity of grace, and a scriptural view of the will are truths that hang together or fall together. Thus, Calvin quotes Augustine on the will as follows:

> The will to believe too is not conceived by innate goodness but is made and formed by the Holy Spirit.[19]

In denying either that regeneration is possible or that it is an essential doctrine, the Federal Vision has redefined grace in a Pelagian manner. The Holy Spirit cannot enable us to will and to do after His good pleasure if regeneration and subjective grace are denied. The will to believe is then conceived by innate goodness, not by the Holy Spirit. The Federal Vision and Pelagianism approach grace from opposite directions, but they view it similarly. Thus, a syllogism for Pelagianism on grace would look like this:

> All people are born in a state of innocence and are capable of obeying God's laws by an act of their will.
>
> Therefore, people do not need the internal, supernatural grace of regeneration.

A syllogism for the Federal Vision would start with the conclusion of the syllogism for Pelagianism and would look like this:

> Regeneration is not a supernatural, internal work of God's grace.
>
> Therefore, all who are baptized have a good heart and are capable of obeying God's laws by an act of their will.

Federal Vision proponents do not overtly adhere to free will, but it is implicit in their whole position. The Federal Vision promises all the baptized that they will be saved if they persevere in covenant faithfulness. Augustinianism / Calvinism teaches that only the elect can persevere unto salvation and only by God's efficacious grace. How can anyone persevere in covenant faithfulness apart from God's efficacious grace? Once efficacious grace is either denied or muted, the only logical answer to that question is that such a person must persevere by an act of his own will. His salvation under that scenario is not owing to God's grace, but to his own free will. Otherwise, the whole Federal

---

19   A. N. S. Lane, ed., G. I. Davies, trans., John Calvin, *The Bondage and Liberation of the Will* (Grand Rapids, Michigan: Baker Books, 1996), 119.

Vision system would be merely hypothetical, serving no practical purpose. Free grace and free will are opposites in the matter of salvation. By failing to define grace as efficacious, the Federal Vision has necessarily chosen free will. Thus, Francis Turretin shows the connection between the denial of subjective, efficacious grace and free will:

> Since universal objective grace is vain and illusory without subjective grace, we must either say that sufficient strength is restored to each and all, by which they can (if they will) obey God and be received into the covenant (which is nothing else than to sacrifice to the idol of free will and wholly to abolish discriminating grace, against Paul; as if something is or can be in us which is our own [according to Pelagius] and does not proceed from the unmerited grace of God, 1 Cor. 4:7; or that God intends something under an impossible condition which neither man can have of himself, nor does God, who alone can, will to bestow upon him).[20]

In this quote, Turretin connects free will to any theory that separates objective grace from subjective grace. Such a theory necessarily requires a power that the natural person does not have and cannot have except under the Pelagian theory. Thus, the Westminster Confession devotes an entire chapter to the doctrine of free will, but defines it as follows:

> Man, by his fall into a state of sin, hath wholly lost all ability of will to any spiritual good accompanying salvation; so as, a natural man, being altogether averse from that good, and dead in sin, is not able, by his own strength, to convert himself, or to prepare himself thereunto. (WCF 9.3)

Free Grace, Free Will, and Pagan Philosophy

Free will, as it has been taught in many branches of the church since Pelagius, is opposed to free grace and is not derived from the Scripture. Rather, it is a doctrine of the pagan philosophers that was brought into the church by Pelagius and others. This connection between Pelagius' doctrine of free will and the views of the ancient philosophers is brought out in Warfield's article:

> Jerome. . . speaks of Pelagianism as the "heresy of Pythagoras and Zeno;" and modern writers of the various schools have more or less fully recognized it. Thus Dean Milman thinks that "the greater part" of Pelagius' letter to Demetrias "might have been written by an ancient

---

20 Turretin, *Institutes of Elenctic Theology*, Volume 2, 211.

academic;" Dr. DePressense identifies the Pelagian idea of liberty with that of Paganism; and Bishop Hefele openly declares that their fundamental doctrine, "that man is virtuous entirely of his own merit, not of the gift of grace," seems to him "to be a rehabilitation of the general heathen view of the world."[21]

One of those pagan philosophers who taught free will was Marcus Tullius Cicero who died in 43 B.C., just short of his sixty-fourth birthday. Voltaire, the eighteenth-century French philosopher, was of the opinion that Cicero's *On The Nature of the Gods* was the best book of all antiquity. That work was written in 45 B.C. as a textbook on theology based on the views of the different Greek and Roman philosophers—Stoics, Epicureans and Skeptics. In the third volume of this work, Cicero stated:

> Every one obtaineth virtue for himself; never any wise man thanked God for that; for our virtue we are praised; in virtue we glory, which might not be were it a gift of God.[22]

In another place, Cicero stated:

> For gold, lands, and all the blessings of life, we have to return thanks to the Gods; but no one ever returned thanks to the Gods for virtue.[23]

The idea that goodness is the natural property of every person was also held by Marcus Aurelius, a Stoic philosopher and emperor of Rome from 161 to 180. In his *Meditations*, Aurelius wrote:

> Dig inside yourself. Inside there is a spring of goodness ready to gush at any moment, if you just keep digging.[24]

The great John Owen in his work, *A Display of Arminianism*, wrote concerning Cicero's statement, "truly this, in softer terms, is the sum of the Remonstrants' arguments in this particular."[25] Owen wrote those words in his tenth chapter, "Of the cause of faith, grace, and righteousness." The Remonstrants, to whom he was referring,

---

21 Schaff, ed., *Augustin, Anti-Pelagian Writings*, xiii.

22 William H. Goold, ed., *The Works of John Owen*, Volume X (London: The Banner of Truth Trust, 1967), 106.

23 Schaff, ed., *Augustin, Anti-Pelagian Writings*, xiv.

24 Martin Hammond, trans., Marcus Aurelius, *Meditations* (New York, New York: Penguin Group (USA), 2006), 67.

25 Goold, *Works of John Owen*, Volume X, 106.

were a group of forty-six Dutch ministers who met at The Hague on January 14, 1610, to formulate their differences with the Calvinistic doctrines and their support for the teaching of Jacobus Arminius who had died the year before. In those documents, they stated:

> Faith and conversion cannot be acts of our obedience if they are wrought by God in us. That God should require that of us which himself will work in us is a ridiculous action, scarce fit for a stage.
>
> There is nothing more vain and foolish than to ascribe faith and regeneration to the merit of Christ.
>
> That saying of Augustine, that "God crowneth his own gifts in us," is not easily to be admitted.[26]

One of the Remonstrants at that meeting in 1610 was Simon Episcopius (1583-1643) who stated his understanding of grace:

> Whether any immediate action of the Spirit upon the will or mind is necessary or promised in the Scriptures, in order that anyone may be able to believe the word externally presented? We maintain the negative.
>
> Anyone can, provided only he has the use of reason, without any peculiar immediate or internal enlightenment, most easily understand and perceive all the meanings of the Scriptures, which are necessary to be known, believed, hoped for, or done, in order to salvation.[27]
>
> In all of these statements, the Remonstrants (or Arminians) approximate the same position that Cicero declared sixteen centuries earlier. They chide the idea that faith and regeneration are the product of God's supernatural grace. They exalt the free will of man at the expense of God's free grace. They ridicule the exaltation of God's grace as an action unworthy even of the stage. Owen was correct. There is no discernible difference, real or imaginary, between the position of the heathen philosopher and the Remonstrants concerning faith, grace, and righteousness (or virtue). The Remonstrants stated their opinions on grace as follows:
>
> We believe with the Word of God the Spirit of God puts forth no strength in us for conversion, except by the Word, since this is the only seed of our regeneration.[28]

Simon Episcopius was one of thirteen delegates from the Remonstrants to the Synod of Dordt in 1618. He lost his standing and was refused a hearing when he failed to submit to the order by which the

---

26 Ibid., 108.

27 Turretin, *Institutes of Elenctic Theology*, Volume 2, 528.

28 Ibid.

Synod determined to proceed. The Synod required that the Remonstrants first present scriptural arguments for their positions, which they could not do and refused to attempt. Their arguments were philosophical in nature, not scriptural. Owen is not the only person to note the identity of the positions of the Arminians and Pelagians with ancient philosophy rather than with Scripture. Arminian theology is not merely based on philosophical reasoning. It is based on heathen philosophy. It has more in common with Cicero or Aristotle than with Scripture.

Grace in the History of the Church
In his masterful work on Scottish theology for the Cunningham Lectures of 1871, *The Theology and Theologians of Scotland, 1560-1750*, James Walker said:

> With the growth of mere externalism, the theology of Anselm and Bernard passed away, till you have the Pelagianism of the Jesuits and the Council of Trent, and the deeper views of the atonement to all intents put under brand.[29]

When grace is defined concerning externals, as it is in the Federal Vision theories, then the atonement of Christ takes a back seat and eventually is removed altogether. Such theories lead to viewing Christ as an example for our own obedience rather than the only Savior of human beings. It is a very short step from that position to Socinianism in which the deity of Christ is denied altogether.

The failure to distinguish between the grace which Adam had in the time of his innocence and the grace which believers receive in the gospel is a fundamental mistake of the Federal Vision. The difference between the two is brought out clearly by Augustine:

> Did not Adam have the grace of God? Yes, truly, he had it largely, but of a different kind. He was placed in the midst of benefits which he had received from the goodness of his Creator; for he had not procured those benefits by his own deservings; in which benefits he suffered absolutely no evil. But saints in this life, to whom pertains this grace of deliverance, are in the midst of evils out of which they cry to God, "Deliver us from evil." He in those benefits needed not the death of Christ: these, the blood of the Lamb absolves from guilt, as well inherited as their

---

29 James Walker, *The Theology and Theologians of Scotland, 1560-1750* (Edinburgh, Scotland: Knox Press, 1982), 67.

own. He had no need of that assistance which they implore when they say, "I see another law in my members warring against the law of my mind, and making me captive in the law of sin which is in my members. O wretched man that I am! who shall deliver me from the body of this death? The grace of God through Jesus Christ our Lord."[30]

The Augustinian view of grace and free will based on the renewal of the inner man by the Holy Spirit is brought out in Warfield's comment:

> It was by free will that man passed into this state of death; but a dead man needs something else to revive him,—he needs nothing less than a Vivifier. But of vivifying grace, Pelagius knew nothing; and by knowing nothing of a Vivifier, he knows nothing of a Saviour; but rather by making nature of itself able to be sinless, he glorifies the Creator at the expense of the Saviour.[31]

In denying either the fact or the importance of the supernatural regeneration of sinners, proponents of the Federal Vision have necessarily limited grace to the Creator at the expense of the Savior. They define grace as objective, but not subjective; given through baptism, but not bestowed internally by the Holy Spirit. Their position is not new, as Herman Bavinck writes concerning the struggles in France:

> In France, therefore, the theological struggle especially concerned the nature of subjective grace. Cameron restricted it to the illumination of the intellect, Amyrald made objective grace universal, and Pajon taught that special subjective grace was superfluous. All this prepared the way for deism and rationalism.[32]

In its quest to restore the objectivity of the covenant and its dismissal of subjective grace, the Federal Vision has opened the door for the denial of evangelical Christianity altogether. Thus, Francis Turretin underscores the necessity of subjective grace:

> These propositions being thus established, if the question is now asked whether besides the objective and mediate grace by which the Spirit acts upon minds by the word preached with whatever opportunity and accompanied by whatever circumstances and helps, there is required another grace subjective and immediate by which he operates upon the

---

30 Schaff, ed., *Augustin, Anti-Pelagian Writings*, 483.

31 Ibid., xxxiii.

32 John Bolt, ed., John Vriend, trans., Herman Bavinck, *Reformed Dogmatics*, Volume 1: Prolegomena (Grand Rapids, Michigan: Baker Academic, 2003), 187.

faculties themselves to dispose them to a saving reception of the word and by whose efficacy conversion is necessarily and infallibly brought about. We answer affirmatively, as the church formerly determined against the Pelagians and most recently against the Remonstrants.[33]

John Chrysostom, like so many of the Greek theologians, emphasized free will to the detriment of free grace. He said: "God draws, but He draws the willing one."[34] As such, he sided with objective grace over subjective grace. About him, Smeaton commented:

> Chrysostom's opinions on the application of Christ's saving work can only be described as defective. . . His view of grace to us is only grace in the objective sense, or as coincident with the salvation-work of Christ. . . The tenor of his language sets forth that God's grace offers salvation, and that man's free will applies it; and that as no one is effectually inclined to receive the objectively offered salvation, those only are true partakers of it, who by their own free choice are inclined to receive it.[35]

Both a wrong view of the sacraments and a wrong view of free will stand in the place of the work of the Holy Spirit. The necessity of the Spirit's work within is diminished by an unscriptural view of free will. Thus, the Word of God becomes sufficient without the internal work of the Holy Spirit in such a system. In these ways, subjective grace is denied or diminished.

At the time of the Reformation, there were Augustinians, Pelagians, and Semi-Pelagians in the Catholic Church. As a result, there were very different definitions of grace within Catholicism, even though Augustinianism still predominated. For instance, a Dutch priest, Albert Pighius (1490-1542), zealously defended the Pelagian position against Calvin by denying the subjective work of the Holy Spirit. Thus, Turretin commented on Calvin's insistence on subjective grace in this dispute with Pighius:

> This opinion Calvin frequently endorses against Pighius. For as the latter acknowledged with Pelagius no other means of our conversion than the external and objective, the former (on the contrary) maintains that

---

33 Turretin, *Institutes of Elenctic Theology*, Volume 2, 529.

34 George Smeaton, *The Doctrine of the Holy Spirit* (Edinburgh, Scotland and Carlisle, Pennsylvania: The Banner of Truth Trust, 1974), 329.

35 Ibid.

God works in the elect in two ways: "externally by the word, internally by his Spirit."[36]

The internal work of the Spirit is what make grace efficacious for the elect and bestows on them a new nature in regeneration.

The Rediscovery of Grace in the Reformation

The Protestant Reformation was the period when the great Augustinian doctrines of God's saving grace were further developed and articulated. Just as the church wrestled with numerous errors before formulating confessional statements concerning God and Christ, so the Reformers gave the church a better understanding of the doctrines of grace. The great confessions defining salvation all were drawn up during or after the Reformation. This new understanding of salvation by the Reformers was really only a rediscovery of the doctrines of Scripture which had never been extinguished from the church. As Louis Berkhof wrote:

> No dogma was ever added to the sacred deposit, and no dogma contained in it was ever changed. The Church only has power to declare a truth to be revealed by God and to give it an infallible interpretation.[37]

Summary

The Federal Vision proponents define grace as beneficent favor that can be lost. They emphasize objective grace to the neglect or denial of subjective grace. Pelagius also emphasized objective grace and denied the necessity of internal grace. Perhaps, it is not proper to classify every Federal Vision proponent as Pelagian, but those who deny supernatural regeneration and subjective grace are certainly taking the Pelagian position on grace. Likewise, those Federal Vision advocates (if there are any) who assert that supernatural regeneration and subjective grace can be lost are more Semi-Pelagian in their positions.

Conclusion

Thus, the testimony on both sides clarifies this issue for us. Pelagians take the position that grace is external, mediate, and objective. In their view, God does not work within the heart of a person, but

---

36 Turretin, *Institutes of Elenctic Theology*, Volume 2, 529.

37 Louis Berkhof, *The History of Christian Doctrines* (Edinburgh, Scotland and Carlisle, Pennsylvania: The Banner of Truth Trust, 1975), 21.

gives him the Word and the law. The Spirit of God persuades and illumines through the Word, but does not change the heart inwardly, according to this false theory. On the other hand, the Reformed view is that the Spirit of God renews the will and changes the heart. Grace is thus internal and subjective, as well as external and objective. The insistence by many Federal Vision proponents on objective grace only places such views within the camp of the Pelagians. We would be happy to learn that the Federal Vision proponents affirm both the necessity and possibility of subjective grace and supernatural regeneration. We would be happy to learn that Federal Vision proponents affirm that grace is redemptive and efficacious. Such affirmations by them, though, would undermine their whole system. For that reason, the most that the Federal Vision proponents do is remain silent about subjective grace and supernatural regeneration while emphasizing the restoration of the objectivity of the covenant.

–4–
The Federal Vision and Covenant Theology

"This law/Gospel dichotomy is a false one. It is unbiblical. It is a result of asking and demanding that Scripture answer the *wrong* questions."[1]

STEVE SCHLISSEL, FEDERAL VISION PROPONENT

"The bi-covenantal[2] construction badly skews the covenant by turning it into a rather impersonal contract. The legal swallows up the filial, subordinating theology to anthropology. . . "[T]his is the picture the covenant of works construction seems to paint since it reduces everything to a matter of merit and strict justice."[3]

RICH LUSK, FEDERAL VISION PROPONENT

---

1 Guy Prentiss Waters, *The Federal Vision and Covenant Theology: A Comparative Analysis* (Phillipsburg, New Jersey: P&R Publishing, 2006), 50.

2 The bi-covenantal view of Scripture emphasizes the distinction between the covenant of works before the fall and the covenant of grace after the fall. Most Federal Vision proponents take a mono-covenantal view of Scripture and emphasize that both covenants were gracious covenants. Some of them formerly repudiated the covenant of works, but most of them now try to nuance their position. Yet, I am aware of none of them that takes a truly scriptural and confessional view of the covenants according to the Reformed tradition.

3 Waters, *Federal Vision and Covenant Theology,* 48.

Historic Christianity and the Federal Vision

The name for the Federal Vision is derived from a Latin noun, *foedus*, which means "treaty, agreement, or contract." In theological circles, *foedus*, or federal, is used as a synonym for covenant theology which is sometimes called federal theology or federalism. Federal or covenant theology is not the same thing as the Federal Vision, though. To prevent confusion in this book, therefore, we will distinguish them as the Federal Vision and covenant theology. The Federal Vision purports to be a vision of covenant theology which is consistent with Reformed theology, but it is not. The purpose of this book is to prove that the Federal Vision is neither scriptural, nor Reformed, nor true to federal theology. Rather, the Federal Vision is simply old heresy dressed up in new garments.

As the quotes above illustrate, the proponents of the Federal Vision deny the bi-covenantal structure of Scripture and assert that the law/gospel distinction is unbiblical. They flatten the distinction between the covenant of works and the covenant of grace. They contend there is only one covenant—a view known as monocovenantalism. They disagree with the essential distinctive of covenant or federal theology. Such wrong views of the covenant affect their soteriology, making their views of salvation hostile to the Scriptures and contrary to the Reformed faith. Thus, the Federal Vision is a misnomer. It is not a vision for covenant theology. It is a vision for sacramental theology. It is a view of the sacraments which is nearly identical to the false views of the Roman Catholic Church. It would be more accurate to call this new theology the Sacramental Vision (or the Sacerdotal Vision) and ascribe to it an attempt to restore the objectivity of the sacraments. That is what it is and that is what it attempts to do. There would be far less confusion about this new heresy if it were called the Sacramental Vision.

One Federal Vision proponent, Douglas Wilson, tells us what the fundamental issue of covenant theology is for their side:

> One of the fundamental concerns is this: we want to insist upon believing God's promises concerning our children.[4]

In other words, the Federal Vision maintains that God has made a promise to save every person, particularly every child of believing parents, who receives the sign of the covenant. It is interesting that a system that says it wants to restore the *objectivity* of the covenant ar-

---

4 Ibid., 26.

gues for its primary premise on the basis of *subjectivism*—"we insist on believing God's promises concerning our children." Yet, not all who receive the sign of the covenant are saved which even the Federal Vision proponents acknowledge. The Federal Vision says that such covenant members failed to persevere in covenant faithfulness. In that way, they make the covenant promises conditional (and uncertain) which conflicts with their stated concern to make God's promises certain concerning their children.

Key Assessment: The Federal Vision holds to mono-covenantalism, denies the bi-covenantal structure of the Scripture, and teaches that the one covenant is a covenant of grace which requires covenant faithfulness for its fulfillment.

In this chapter, we will show that the bi-covenantal structure of historic reformed theology is scriptural and confessional. The law/gospel distinction of covenant theology is an organic principle of the Scripture and is not artificially imposed on it, as Schlissel and Lusk assert above. We will first trace the development of covenant theology in historic reformed theology and then deal consecutively with the covenant of works and the covenant of grace.

The Historical Development of Covenant Theology

Covenant theology did not arise out of a vacuum at the time of the Reformation. The primary elements of Covenant Theology existed before the Reformation and some of them can be found in the writings of the early church fathers. Though covenant theology was not fully developed until after the Reformation, that should not be understood to mean that the church before the Reformation, and even the Reformers themselves, were agnostic about the basic principles of it. As Louis Berkhof astutely observes concerning the development of Christian doctrine:

> The development of the dogma of the Church moved along organic lines and was therefore in the main a continuous growth, in spite of the fact that leaders of the Church in their endeavors to apprehend the truth often wandered into blind alleys, chasing will-o'-the-wisps and toying with foreign elements; and that even the Church itself, as a whole or part, sometimes erred in its formulation of the truth.[5]

---

5 Louis Berkhof, *The History of Christian Doctrines* (Edinburgh, Scotland and Carlisle, Pennsylvania: The Banner of Truth Trust, 1975), 22.

There is sometimes the mistaken idea that the Protestant Reformation was a movement disconnected from the rest of the historical development of Christian doctrine. That wrong idea lies behind much of the criticism of the Reformers by the Federal Vision proponents and N. T. Wright. Concerning one doctrine or another, they will assert that the Reformers misunderstood Paul or moved the church in a wrong direction which now needs to be corrected. That idea is patently false. The Reformers continually appealed not only to the Scripture but also to other church leaders throughout the history of the church. Calvin copiously quoted Augustine and the early church fathers as well as various theologians of the medieval church. The other Reformers did likewise.

Interestingly, the Federal Vision advocates try to erect a fence between the first and second generation Reformers on the doctrine of the covenant, particularly the Reformers in Holland. They claim that the covenant theology developed by second generation Reformers espoused views contrary to what Calvin taught. That is their way of trying to rid covenant theology of the doctrines which are most essential to it. Yet, it is actually the Federal Vision which is out of lockstep with the Reformed tradition. David J. Engelsma is certainly correct when he asserts that the Federal Vision is the heretical view of a conditional covenant taught by Jacobus Arminius in the sixteenth century and condemned by the Synod of Dordt.[6]

Specifically, the Federal Vision proponents charge that the distinction between the covenant of works and the covenant of grace was a departure from the views of the Reformers by second generation Reformed theologians which first found creedal expression in the Westminster Confession of Faith. For instance, Federal Vision proponent Ralph Smith asserts without proof that the Westminster divines, in developing their doctrine of the covenant of works, embraced "a notion borrowed from the nominalist school of thought and the covenantal thinking of medieval Franciscans."[7] Yet, the doctrine of the covenant was seen as a unifying principle of the Scripture in *The Epistle of Barnabas*[8], in Justin Martyr's

---

6 David J. Engelsma, *Federal Vision: Heresy at the Root* (Jenison, Michigan: Reformed Free Publishing Association, 2012), 33.

7 Ralph Smith, *Eternal Covenant: How the Trinity Reshapes Covenant Theology* (Moscow, Idaho: Canon Press, 2003), 63.

8 J. R. Harmer, ed., J. B. Lightfoot, "The Epistle of Barnabas" in *The Apostolic Fathers* (Grand Rapids, Michigan: Baker Book House, 1973), 139-140.

Dialogue with Trypho[9], and, in Irenaeus' *Adversus Haereses*[10], among others. It is certainly correct that the Apostolic Fathers did not have a fully developed doctrine of the covenant, but the doctrine was developing organically. While Augustine, Bishop of Hippo, did not use the distinctions of covenant of works and covenant of grace, he held to the theology inherent in those terms. In *The City of God*, he wrote:

> There are many covenants or testaments of God besides these two great ones, the Old and New Testaments, which everyone can get to know by reading them. There is the first covenant made with the first man: "On the day you eat thereof you shall die the death.". . . Circumcision was a type of regeneration or new birth. Not undeservedly does a child lose his birthright, by reason of that original sin by which God's first covenant was broken, unless he regain it by being born again. It is thus said: "He who is not regenerate, that soul shall perish from among his people", because he has broken the covenant of God when together with all others he sinned in Adam.[11]

Augustine acknowledges that there are two great covenants of Scripture, the old and new covenants, but he asserts that there are many others as well. He was, without doubt, thinking of the covenants made with Adam, Abraham, Noah and David. It is important to note that he calls that probationary period under which Adam was governed before the fall a "covenant." The breach of that covenant was the basis of original sin whereby all descendants of Adam sinned in him.

The development of covenant theology by the Reformers took place very early during the Reformation and was not hijacked later by second generation Reformers or by Lutherans. Geerhardus Vos wrote a definitive paper on this subject, "The Doctrine of the Covenant in Reformed Theology," in which he proved that the doctrine of the covenant was in development from the very beginning of the Reformation. As early as 1525, Ulrich Zwingli was using the covenant to prove infant baptism against the Anabaptists. This development was continued and carried forth into the latter part of the sixteenth century by Bullinger, Olevianus, and Ursinus when it became permanently

---

9   Anne Fremantle, ed., "Dialogue with Trypho the Jew" in *A Treasury of Early Christianity* (New York: Viking Press, 1953), 275.

10 John Keble, trans., Irenaeus, *Against the Heresies* (Oxford, London and Cambridge: James Parker and Co., 1872), 339-361.

11 J. W. C. Wand, trans., *St. Augustine's City of God* (London: Oxford University Press, 1963), 271-2.

entrenched in Reformed theology. In response to the false idea that covenant theology was a wrong development by Dutch Reformers, Alexander F. Mitchell wrote in his Baird lectures for 1882:

> With respect to the doctrine of the Covenants, which some assert to have been derived from Holland, I think myself now, after careful investigation, entitled to maintain that there is nothing taught in the Confession which had not been long before taught in substance by Rollock and Howie in Scotland, and by Cartwright, Preston, Perkins, Ames, and Ball in his two catechisms in England, while there is perceptible advance beyond what is exhibited in the general teaching of the Dutch Divines in the *Synopsis Purioris Theologiae* as late as 1642. The work of Cocceius, even in its earliest form, was not given to the world till after the Confession had been completed and published.[12]

The idea that the covenant theology of the Westminster Standards was a minor development in Reformed theology which was borrowed from the Dutch Reformers is patently incorrect. The leading ideas of covenant theology predated the Reformation and were in mature development from that period onwards. The Westminster Standards give in creedal form the bi-covenantal structure of Scripture that had been believed by all branches of the Reformed church long before 1643.

The basic ideas of covenant theology were present also in the sermons of John Calvin. In 1557-58, he preached through Paul's Epistle to the Galatians to the congregation of St. Peter's Church in Geneva, Switzerland. In his sermon on Galatians 3:11, 12, he contrasted the righteousness of the law with the imputed righteousness of Christ received through free grace:

> Now what man is so proud that he would dare boast he has fully discharged his duty towards God? None but a hypocrite who has been overtaken by devilish pride, or a profane person who despises God and who has never truly repented, whose conscience is either asleep or bewitched. Only such a person can deceive himself into thinking he deserves anything. Thus, since the righteousness of the law is unattainable, and is something from which we are utterly barred, we need to find another righteousness. Put another way, we need God to accept us through his free grace. Instead of God receiving anything from us, we need the obedience of the Lord Jesus Christ to be imputed to us, though we do not deserve it. . .
>
> In the same way, with reference to salvation, we must come to the

---

12 Alexander F. Mitchell, *The Westminster Assembly: Its History and Standards* (Philadelphia: Presbyterian Board of Publication, 1897), 387-8.

original and chief contract God made with us. Now, that contract is the law. Therefore, if men are seeking to be paid according to their service, they will find that this will banish them from everlasting life rather than enable them to obtain it. For God has declared that they have to perform all that he has commanded them, before they can inherit the salvation he has in store.[13]

What Calvin refers to as the "original and chief contract" is known to us as the covenant of works. Calvin clearly states that salvation under that original contract was based on performing all God's commands. Yet, according to him, righteousness cannot be found in that way. We need the obedience of Christ imputed to us in order to be counted righteous before God. Thus, Calvin enunciated the basic outline of covenant theology in his sermons almost nine decades before the Westminster Assembly deliberated on the matter.

The true position is that covenant theology has been in progressive, organic development from the very beginning of the New Testament church. Therefore, the covenant theology of the Westminster Confession of Faith is not a departure from the views of the first generation Reformers, but an enrichment of those views.

The Covenant of Works
The question of first importance in this chapter is this: Does the Scripture teach two covenants; one a covenant of works which leads to works righteousness, and the other a covenant of grace which leads to salvation through faith in Christ? The particular phrases, covenant of works and covenant of grace, are nowhere to be found in the Scripture, but the ideas concerning them are everywhere throughout the Bible. The covenant of works refers to the covenant made by God with Adam before the fall. After Adam's sin, there was only the possibility of being saved by God's free grace. Thus, that second covenant is called the covenant of grace.

Guy Waters is certainly correct when he states that many of the Federal Vision advocates have tried in recent years to walk their position back from an overtly mono-covenantal (a single covenant) view. For instance, Peter Leithart refused to state at his trial whether he believed in a mono-covenantal view or a bi-covenantal view of Scripture. The Federal Vision proponents will acknowledge that the cove-

---

13 Kathy Childress, trans., John Calvin, *Sermons on Galatians* (Edinburgh, Scotland and Carlisle, Pennsylvania: The Banner of Truth Trust, 1997), 272, 273.

nant before the fall was not a covenant of redemption, but they still insist that there is a continuity between the gracious character of the covenant before the fall and the covenant after the fall. For instance, Andrew Sandlin, a Federal Vision proponent, writes:

> There are not two ways of gaining eternal life, one in the prelapsarian era and one in the postlapsarian era, or one in the Mosaic era and one in the resurrection era. There is only one way of obtaining eternal life, *and there has always been only one way.*[14]

In asserting that "there has always been only one way" of obtaining eternal life, Sandlin dismisses the problem of sin with a few key strokes. If the way of salvation is the same both before and after the fall, then sin must have caused no problem for God. Of course, then, the question becomes: Why do we need redemption after the fall—and why did Adam *not* need redemption before his fall—if the way of salvation is the same despite the entrance of sin?

Central to true covenant theology is the bi-covenantal view of Scripture which recognizes two distinct covenants; the covenant of works before the fall and the covenant of grace after it. Even the Merriam-Webster online dictionary gives the following definition of federal or covenant theology:

> The theological system which rests upon the beliefs (1) that before the Fall man was under a covenant of works by which God through Adam promised man eternal blessedness if he kept his commandments and (2) that since the Fall man has been under a covenant of grace by which God by his grace promises the same blessings to all who believe in Christ—called also *covenant theology.*[15]

That definition of covenant or federal theology is in line with what Wilhelmus a' Brakel wrote about the covenant of works in the seventeenth century:

> Acquaintance with this covenant is of the greatest importance, for whoever errs or denies the existence of the covenant of works, will not understand the covenant of grace, and will readily err concerning the mediatorship of the Lord Jesus. Such a person will very readily

---

14 P. Andrew Sandlin, "Covenant in Redemptive History," in P. Andrew Sandlin, ed., *A Faith That Is Never Alone: A Response to Westminster Seminary California* (LaGrange: Kerygma Press, 2007), 68.

15 http://www.merriam-webster.com/dictionary/federal%20theology, accessed September 9th, 2014

deny that Christ by His active obedience has merited a right to eternal life for the elect. This is to be observed with several parties who, because they err concerning the covenant of grace, also deny the covenant of works. Conversely, whoever denies the covenant of works, must rightly be suspected to be in error concerning the covenant of grace as well.[16]

The Federal Vision proponents deny the covenant of works / covenant of grace structure of Scripture, as the quotes by Schlissel and Lusk at the beginning of this chapter show; they deny the imputation of the active obedience of Christ (as a' Brakel said such people will always do); and, they are erroneous in their view of the covenant of grace. They affirm mono-covenantalism and assert even God's covenant in the Garden of Eden was a covenant of grace. There certainly was grace in the first covenant, but it was not the same grace as in the second covenant. Therefore, they deny the distinction which Paul lays out in Galatians 4 between the promise and the law. Thus, the Federal Vision is a new vision of covenant theology which is contrary to classical Reformed theology and the Scripture.

In contradiction to the Federal Vision position, the Westminster Confession of Faith 19.1, 2 teaches that there was a covenant of works which Adam was under, and connects it with the law given through Moses at Sinai:

> God gave to Adam a law, as a covenant of works, by which he bound him and all his posterity to personal, entire, exact, and perpetual obedience, promised life upon the fulfilling, and threatened death upon the breach of it, and endued him with power and ability to keep it.
>
> This law, after his fall, continued to be a perfect rule of righteousness; and, as such, was delivered by God upon Mount Sinai, in ten commandments, and written in two tablets.

Concerning the moral law as the standard for Adam's obedience, Tertullian, in *An Answer to the Jews*, wrote nearly the same thing:

> That primordial law given to Adam in paradise was, as it were, the matrix of all God's precepts.[17]

---

16 Bartel Elshout, trans., Wilhelmus a' Brakel, *The Christian's Reasonable Service, Vol 1* (Ligonier, Pennsylvania: Soli Deo Gloria Publications, 1992), 355.

17 James T. Dennison, Jr., ed., George Musgrave Giger, trans., Francis Turretin, *Institutes of Elenctic Theology*, I (Phillipsburg, New Jersey: P&R Publishing, 1992), 579.

James Henley Thornwell makes a similar comment on Adam's test of obedience:

> The tree was a test of man's obedience; it concentrated his probation upon a single point, and implicitly contained the whole moral law.[18]

Likewise, Romans 2:14, 15 says: "For when the Gentiles who do not have the Law do instinctively the things of the Law, these, not having the Law, are a law to themselves, in that they show the work of the Law written on their hearts, their conscience bearing witness and their thoughts alternately accusing or else defending them." The law written on the hearts of all mankind was necessarily written at their creation. Thus, the same law which was the basis of the covenant of works made with Adam is the law written on the hearts of all men and was reinstated at Mount Sinai through Moses. As Robert Haldane wrote concerning Romans 2:15:

> This is an allusion to the law written by the finger of God upon tablets of stone, and afterwards recorded in the Scripture. The great principles of this law were communicated to man in his creation, and much of it remains with him in his fallen state. This natural light of the understanding is called the law written in the heart, because it is imprinted on the mind by the Author of creation, and is God's work as much as the writing on the tables of stone.[19]

There is a false hope in the heart of every person of finding peace with God through some form of works righteousness. As George Whitefield said,

> We cry out against popery, and that very justly, but we are all Papists; at least, I am sure, we are all Arminians by nature; and, therefore, no wonder so many natural men embrace that scheme.[20]

That hope of works righteousness is a deceptive lie, but it is the result of every person having the law written on their hearts. Ever since the fall of Adam, only deceivers or hypocrites have thought they could be reconciled to God by their works. It is not our obedience to the law that earns salvation, but the imputation of Christ's obedience

---

18 James Henley Thornwell, *The Collected Writings of James Henley Thornwell*, Volume I: Theological (Edinburgh, Scotland and Carlisle, Pennsylvania, 1974), 284.

19 Robert Haldane, *An Exposition of the Epistle to the Romans* (MacDill AFB, Florida: MacDonald Publishing Company, n.d.), 91.

20 *Select Sermons of George Whitefield* (London: The Banner of Truth Trust, 1964), 116.

to us by the free grace of God. It is, therefore, integral to the Scripture that the only way for mere creatures to have a relationship with God is through a covenant. As Westminster Confession of Faith 7.1 says:

> The distance between God and the creature is so great, that although reasonable creatures do owe obedience unto him as their Creator, yet they could never have any fruition of him as their blessedness and reward, but by some voluntary condescension on God's part, which he hath been pleased to express by way of covenant.

In Galatians 4:24, Paul contrasts two covenants. The one is from Mount Sinai and is a covenant of law which leads to slavery and bondage. The other is from Jerusalem above and is based on the promise which results in salvation for those who believe. In Galatians 3:10-14, Paul had shown that the promise of salvation in Christ (the promised seed of Abraham) was not invalidated by the law which was given 430 years later. The promise and the law are antithetical in that Scripture. Salvation cannot be earned by the keeping of the law without invalidating the promise made to Abraham. The law commands us: "So you shall keep My statutes and My judgments, by which a man may live if he does them; I am the LORD" (Leviticus 18:5). Life is indeed promised to those who are obedient to God's commandments, but it must be perfect, personal and exact obedience. One slip and all is ruined. As James says, "For whoever keeps the whole law, and yet stumbles in one point, he has become guilty of all" (James 2:10). Any sin, large or small, is enough to ruin forever our hopes of attaining salvation through keeping the law. God does not grade on the curve. He does not accept sincere obedience in the place of perfect obedience.

The Mosaic law is a gracious covenant to believers, but a covenant of works to all who are without faith in Christ. In his penetrating work on the law in Puritan theology, *The Grace of Law*, Ernest F. Kevan quoted from William Strong's work on *The Two Covenants*:

> The Lord's intention in giving the Law was double, unto the carnal Jews to set forth to them the old Covenant which they had broken; and yet unto believing Jews it did darkly shadow and set forth unto them the Covenant of Grace made with Christ... and therefore it was delivered after a sort in the form of a Covenant of Works.... It was to the carnal Jews plainly a Covenant of Works, not in God's intention, but by their own corruption.[21]

---

21 Ernest F. Kevan, *The Grace of Law: A Study of Puritan Theology* (Grand Rapids, Michigan: Baker

Concerning Paul's words in Galatians 4:24, 25, Kevan further observes:

> Paul's reference to the covenants in Galatians iv creates a problem at first sight, for he seems to suggest that Sinai was merely a Covenant of Works, but Henry Burton offers the solution that Paul is speaking of the Law only in the killing sense given to it by the carnal Jews, for Sinai and Sion are opposite only as the unbelieving makes them opposite.[22]

Despite their denial that the Mosaic law is a covenant of works, the Federal Vision adherents ironically make it such by holding forth the hope of final justification through the keeping of it. Their approach to the law then becomes the carnal view of it that is condemned by Paul in Galatians 4.

The law and the promise, as contrasted in Galatians 4, are two different covenants. The law, in that sense, is a covenant of works. The promise is a covenant of grace. Yet, Federal Vision proponent, Ralph Smith, asserts that "the covenant of works is unbiblical" and that "to truly have a covenant of works, Eden and all its blessings would have to be off limits until Adam and Eve had obtained the merit by which they would be justified and therefore qualified to enjoy the rewards of the covenant."[23] It is certainly true that God did not use the word covenant when he commanded Adam not to eat from the tree of the knowledge of good and evil and threatened him with death if he disobeyed. We cannot expect the opening chapters of the Bible to have a fully developed doctrine of the covenant. The progressive nature of God's special revelation requires us to read Genesis 1-3 through the lens of later passages of Scripture, particularly the New Testament. One of the key New Testament passages, in that respect, is Romans 5:12-19, where the federal headships of both Adam and Christ are contrasted and compared.

Many of the Federal Vision proponents claim John Murray in support of their denial of the covenant of works. Murray gave a lecture to his students at Westminster Theological Seminary in Philadelphia, subsequently published by the Banner of Truth Trust in the *Collected Writings of John Murray, Volume 2: Systematic Theology* titled, "The Adamic Administration." In that paper, he denied that Adam was un-

---

Book House, 1976), 129.

22 Ibid., 131.

23 Waters, *Federal Vision and Covenant Theology*, 35.

der a covenant of works which, after the fall, was delivered at Mount Sinai in the form of the Ten Commandments. Murray's position is regrettable and, at that point, is contrary to Westminster Confession of Faith 19.1, 2 (quoted earlier in this chapter).

Murray's denial of the covenant of works unintentionally cracked open the door just enough to allow certain heresies of the Federal Vision to enter in through it—positions with which Murray himself did not agree. Indeed, Murray's conclusions are contrary to the positions of the Federal Vision. Moreover, that heretical system would have developed without his contributions to biblical theology.

It is certainly a matter of debate among Reformed scholars and commentators whether the Scripture ever uses the word covenant to describe the period of Adam's probation. Hosea 6:7 says, "But like Adam they have transgressed the covenant." The words "like Adam" are alternately translated as "like men" by some translations and as "at Admah" by at least one version. The name Adam also means man in the Hebrew. B. B. Warfield has an in-depth analysis of this verse, and the various translations of it, in which he concludes that "like Adam" is the correct translation. As Warfield says:

> The translation, "They have like men transgressed the covenant" remains vapid and meaningless until a sense beyond the suggestion of the words themselves is forced upon it. The simple "men" must be made in some way to bear a pregnant sense—either as mere men, as opposed to God, or as common men opposed to the nobility or the priestly, or as heathen as opposed to the Israelites—to none of which does it seem naturally to lend itself here. . .
>
> No such exegetical objections lie against the rendering, "Like Adam". . . The transgressing of Adam, as the great normative act of covenant-breaking, offered itself naturally as the fit standard over against which the heinousness of the covenant-breaking of Israel could be thrown out.[24]

Those who agree with Warfield's position include Cyril of Alexandria, Jerome, Francis Turretin, Martin Luther, Wilhelmus a' Brakel, Hermann Witsius, Jonathan Edwards, Herman Bavinck, A. A. Hodge, Gerrhardus Vos, James Orr, C. F. Keil, Francis Delitzsch, Gustav Oehler, James Henley Thornwell, and John Colquhoun. If Warfield is correct, then Hosea clearly points to Adam being under a covenant

---

24 John E. Meeter, ed., *Selected Shorter Writings of Benjamin B. Warfield*, I (Nutley, New Jersey: Presbyterian and Reformed Publishing Company, 1970), 127-8.

which he transgressed. In the context of Hosea, it seems more likely that "like Adam" is a reference to our first parent because it is a book that has several references to historical characters or historical events—David (3:5); Jacob (12:2-5; 12); and the prophet who led Israel out of Egypt—that is Moses (see 12:13).

Additionally, the phrase "like Adam" is used only one other time in Scripture, in Job 31:33, where Job asks, "Have I covered my transgressions like Adam, by hiding my iniquity in my bosom?" That verse is an obvious reference to the action of Adam hiding from God after he ate from the tree of the knowledge of good and evil. While it is not necessary to interpret phrases the same way in every instance, the reference in Job is a strong argument that Hosea was also referring to Adam—and not man in general. If so, then Hosea 6:7 would be a clear reference to a pre-fall covenant with Adam, the covenant of works.

One of the most impressive articles on the covenant of works was written by the nineteenth-century Southern Presbyterian theologian, James Henley Thornwell. In my opinion, few impartial persons could read the papers of both Thornwell and Murray without being convinced that the arguments of the former are more cogent, persuasive, and compelling. (For a longer work, John Colquhoun's *A Treatise on the Covenant of Works* is unparalleled). Thornwell compares the effects of Christ's federal headship to the failure of the law as follows:

> The work of redemption has only achieved for us the same blessings—the same in kind, however they may differ in degree—which the law previously prepared as the reward of obedience. Christ has done for us what the law was ordained to do, but failed to do only through the fault of man.[25]

Notwithstanding, Federal Vision proponent Peter Leithart, flattens the distinction between the covenant of works and the covenant of grace by asserting that 'covenant faithfulness' is required in both:

> That the differences between Adamic and post-lapsarian covenants are not at a "soteriological" level, but at the level of covenant administration.[26] And, yes, covenant faithfulness is the way of salvation, for the

---

25 Thornwell, *The Collected Writings*, 288.

26 Record of the Case, Standing Judicial Commission of the Presbyterian Church in America, Case 2012-5, RE Gerald Hedman vs. Pacific Northwest Presbytery, 78.

"doers of the law will be justified" at the final judgment.[27]

Yet, the Westminster Confession of Faith 7.3 says "man, by his fall, . . . made himself incapable of life by that covenant" (that is the covenant of works). Thus, the Westminster Standards teach that the difference between those covenants is at the soteriological level. The basic problem in the mono-covenantalism of the Federal Vision is that justification is then based on covenant faithfulness, which the Scripture and the Westminster Standards say is impossible. When Federal Vision proponents conflate covenant faithfulness with saving faith, they take a position which is similar to the Pelagians, as the following quote of the Pelagian position shows:

> But we do praise God as the Author of our righteousness, in that He gave us the law, by the teaching of which we have learned how we ought to live.[28] We confess that even the old law, according to the apostle, is holy and just and good, and that this could confer eternal life on those that kept its commandments, and lived righteously by faith, like the prophets and patriarchs, and all the saints.[29]

The Pelagians taught that covenant faithfulness ("lived righteously by faith") is the way of salvation. In point of fact, Pelagius taught that the law and the gospel have essentially the same effect in leading us to heaven. In Pelagius' mind, there was no antithesis between law and gospel, such as the covenant of works / covenant of grace distinction. For Pelagius, grace is law; the New Testament is law.[30] Christ is not the Savior for Pelagius, but an example to be followed. The law is an example of God's will for our lives and the law requires obedience, as Pelagius says:

> First, then, get to know God's will, as contained in his law, so that you may be able to do it, since you can be certain you are a Christian only when you have taken the trouble to keep all God's commandments.[31]

---

27 Ibid.

28 Philip Schaff, editor, *Nicene and Post-Nicene Fathers*, Volume V, (Grand Rapids: Wm. B. Eerdmans, 1971), 88.

29 Ibid., 420.

30 Robert F. Evans, *Pelagius: Inquiries and Reappraisals* (London: Adam & Charles Black, 1968), 106.

31 B. R. Rees, *The Letters of Pelagius and His Followers* (Rochester, New York: Boydell Press, 1991), 160.

Key Assessment: Pelagius taught that living righteously in obedience to the law was the path to salvation. He saw no antithesis between the law and the gospel; the covenant of works and the covenant of grace.

The teaching of the Federal Vision is eerily similar to the above quotes from Pelagius. They fail to take serious account of the strict and perpetual requirement of the law which condemns us all (for example, Galatians 3:10).

In the trial of Peter Leithart before Pacific Northwest Presbytery (PCA), the Defense quoted Richard Baxter in support of the proposition that Leithart's views are within the Reformed tradition. We will have more to say about the Reformed tradition in Chapter 10, "The Federal Vision and the Reformed Symbols," but it should be obvious to everyone that the errors or heresies of one man can never be used to prove the orthodoxy of another man. Baxter and his followers were known as Neonomians. And their views were not orthodox in the area where quoted in support of the Federal Vision. Their covenantal nomism undermined the doctrine of justification by faith alone. Dr. John MacLeod, former principal of the Free Church College in Edinburgh, Scotland, wrote concerning Baxter's views:

> This name they got from their type of teaching which at this point was of a generally Arminian character. They spoke of a new law of works, compliance with whose demand was held graciously to be a righteousness that won life for the Christian. The Gospel that calls for faith was to them such a new law as called for faith and sincere obedience.[32]

J. I. Packer's assessment of Baxter's theology was:

> As a theologian he was, though brilliant, something of a disaster.[33]

Packer further assessed the damage done by Baxter's theology:

> Thus, Baxter, by the initial rationalism of his "political method," which forced Scripture into an *a priori* mould, actually sowed the seeds of *moralism* with regard to sin, *Arianism* with regard to Christ, *legalism* with regard to faith and salvation, and *liberalism* with regard to God.[34]

---

32 John MacLeod, *Scottish Theology: In Relation to Church History Since the Reformation* (Edinburgh, Scotland and Carlisle, Pennsylvania: The Banner of Truth Trust, 1974), 139.

33 J. I. Packer, *A Quest for Godliness: The Puritan Vision of the Christian Life,* (Wheaton, Illinois: Crossway Books, 1990), 159.

34 Ibid., 160.

It is hardly a ringing endorsement to be compared with someone whose errors led to moralism, Arianism, legalism, and liberalism. Baxter's denial of the distinction between the law and the gospel was a major contributor to his errors in theology, even as it is with the Federal Vision proponents. Concerning this fundamental error, Bavinck writes:

> In the Christian church this antithesis between law and gospel was even exacerbated and made irreconcilable, on the one hand, by antinomianism in its various forms: Gnosticism, Manichaeism, Paulicianism, Anabaptism, Hattemism, and so forth. . . On the other hand, the antithesis between law and gospel was weakened and canceled out by nomism in its various forms: Pelagianism, semi-Pelagianism, Romanism, Socinianism, rationalism, and so forth.[35]

As different as antinomianism and legalism appear superficially, they are actually aligned in their opposition to the antithesis between law and gospel. Both blur the distinction between law and grace, the covenant of works and the covenant of grace. Antinomianism collapses the law into grace and nomism or legalism collapses grace into the law. Thus, antinomian proponents of cheap grace often fall into the trap of legalism. On the other hand, proponents of nomism constantly refer to the law as grace. Yet, both groups deny that law and grace are distinct and that denial is their common bond.

The Covenant of Grace

The advocates of the Federal Vision say even God's covenant with Adam in the Garden of Eden was a covenant of grace. Whatever grace was in the covenant of works with Adam in the Garden of Eden, we know that it was not redeeming grace. Certainly, some Federal Vision proponents acknowledge that there was no redeeming grace in the first covenant, but that only exacerbates their position. They do not define the grace that they assert unifies both covenants. Yet, there are certain things we can say about such grace in the first covenant. It was not grace that provided a renovation of the hearts of Adam and Eve. Our first parents were created upright and holy and did not need any inward renovation. The grace of God to our first parents before the fall was not the same grace as Christ experienced in His temptations,

---

35   John Bolt, ed., John Vriend, trans., Herman Bavinck, *Reformed Dogmatics*, Volume 4: Holy Spirit, Church and New Creation (Grand Rapids, Michigan: Baker Academic, 2008), 451.

or even that believers daily experience. As Westminster Shorter Catechism #14 says:

> Our first parents being left to the freedom of their own will, fell from the estate wherein they were created, by sinning against God.

The redeeming grace of God never leaves believers to the complete freedom of their own will or they would all be lost. God's grace in the gospel is efficacious, but whatever grace was in the covenant of works was not efficacious grace. God's grace to the saints includes the gift of perseverance which Adam did not have or else he could not have fallen. As Augustine in his *Treatise on Rebuke and Grace* says:

> What then? Did not Adam have the grace of God? Yes, truly, he had it largely, but of a different kind. He was placed in the midst of benefits which he had received from the goodness of his Creator; for he had not procured those benefits by his own deservings; in which benefits he suffered absolutely no evil.[36]

There are many differences between the grace that God gave to Adam before the fall and the grace that believers have in the gospel. Adam had everything in perfect order. Believers today live in a world of sin. Adam had no sin raging in his heart. Believers are engaged in the battle of the flesh against the Spirit (Galatians 5). Adam had no need of forgiveness or redemption. Believers need both. Adam did not have need of a Mediator to reconcile him to God, but believers do. Adam did not have efficacious, persevering grace or he would not have (and could not have) fallen. Believers have both or they could not resist in the evil day. So, the grace given to Adam in the garden cannot be equated with the grace given to believers in the covenant of grace. This is a fundamental error of the Federal Vision, and it is a denial of the gospel.

Jean-Marc Berthoud, as interpreted by Douglas F. Kelly, writes about the grace that Adam and Eve had in their first estate:

> Everything came to them from the grace of God, a grace which enabled them to do all the works which had been ordained for them by God.[37]

---

36 Philip Schaff, ed., *Augustin: Anti-Pelagian Writings*, Nicene and Post-Nicene Fathers, First Series, Volume 5 (Peabody, Massachusetts: Hendrickson Publishers, 1999), 483.

37 Jean-Marc Berthoud, *L'Alliance de Dieu a Travers L'Ecriture Sainte; Une Theologie Biblique* (Lausanne: Messages, L'Age d'Homme, 2012), 71-89. Quoted in Douglas F. Kelly, *Systematic Theology: Grounded in Scripture and Understood in Light of the Church*, Volume Two, "The Beauty of Christ: A

Such a quote is troubling. Our first parents had the power and ability to fulfill the conditions of the Covenant of Works (WCF 19.1) because they were created upright and holy, but they did not have the persevering grace to prevent their fall. They were left to the freedom of their own wills and they could either obey God or disobey Him. The decrees of God permitted the fall but did not make God responsible for the sin of our first parents. There was a limit to the grace God gave Adam and Eve. Otherwise they could not have fallen if *everything* came to them from the grace of God. Berthoud's quote gives no explanation for the fall.

Neither was the grace given to Adam equal to the grace given to Christ. The one point of similarity between Christ and Adam is that they both were devoid of sin in their hearts which means their temptations were solely from outside of them. In every other respect, the temptations of Christ were much more severe. Adam was tempted in one point. Christ was tempted in all points. Adam was tempted to be like God. Christ was tempted to be a mere man. Adam was tempted among tame animals in a garden. Christ was tempted in a wilderness among wild animals. Adam's temptations were concentrated for a probationary period only. Christ was tempted from cradle to grave. Adam was tempted with food readily available. Christ was tempted for forty days and nights without food. Adam had a helpmeet. Christ was alone. Christ resisted every temptation by clinging to the Word of God. Adam rejected God's words and succumbed to the beguiling lies of the devil. As James Henley Thornwell wrote concerning Christ's temptations:

> Here was a human being who actually did pass through the world from cradle to grave without sin. If He had been placed in only ordinary circumstances, this is a truly astonishing phenomenon. The most humble and retired man is seduced on all hands in a world like this, where sin has reigned for thousands of years. But the case of Jesus is remarkable in that He was exposed to special and extraordinary trials. He was providentially dealt with as if He had been a sinner. The world and the Devil were let loose on Him. The severity of the conflict was condensed into two periods—one at the commencement and the other at the close of His career—and yet he held fast His integrity. This is godlike virtue.[38]

Trinitarian Vision," (Fearn, Ross-Shire, Scotland: Christian Focus Publications, 2014), 331.

38 *The Collected Writings of James Henley Thornwell*, Volume II—Theological and Ethical (Edin-

One result of the Federal Vision proponents denying this antithesis between the law and the gospel is that they deny that the law requires personal, perpetual, and perfect obedience. For instance, Rich Lusk writes:

> Those [elements of the Mosaic covenant] are all gracious elements. The sacrifices in the law are also a gracious element in the law. The law was never meant for a sinless people. It's not as if the law required you to keep the commandments perfectly and was very disappointed when you didn't and had no provisions for lawbreaking. The law was meant for a sinful people. The Lord knew His people would sin, and every sacrifice is a promise in the law.[39]

Yet, Hebrews 9:16 says, "Where a covenant is, there must of necessity be the death of the one who made it." The author's argument in that section is that a covenant is a testament that requires the death of the testator before it goes into effect. Yet, that simple truth points out that there is definitely a difference at the soteriological level between the covenant before the fall and the covenant after the fall. The two cannot be conflated into the same thing because the first did not require the death of anyone for its fulfillment. Yet, the second required the death of the Testator, Jesus Christ, for its fulfillment. The death that resulted from the first covenant was the death and condemnation of all the seed of Adam. The death required by the second covenant resulted in what John Owen called the death of death in the death of Christ. The covenant made with Adam promised life, but resulted in death for all men through the disobedience of our first parent. The covenant of grace required the death of the Testator, but resulted in life for all the elect. The soteriological difference between the covenant of works and the covenant of grace is the difference between life and death. Eternal life is possible only through faith in the Testator of the covenant of grace as a result of His death for the elect. As John Brown wrote in his commentary on Hebrews 9:16:

> Where there is a divine covenant, the object of which is the communication of benefits to fallen men, there must be of necessity the death of that which ratifies it, or the sacrificial victim. . . . It is not the life, but the death of the victim, which confirms the covenant. . . . The death of

---

burgh, Scotland and Carlisle, Pennsylvania: The Banner of Truth Trust, 1974), 297. The ideas in the previous paragraph were also borrowed from this part of Thornwell's writings.

39 Waters, *Federal Vision and Covenant Theology*, 50.

Christ was necessary to His being the successful Mediator of the New Covenant.[40]

The covenant made with Adam did not require death for its fulfillment but resulted in death for all his posterity through his disobedience. Thus, the covenant made with Adam is absent of the most important distinction of the covenant of grace—the death of the Testator. This necessarily means that the grace in the covenant made with Adam (the covenant of works) cannot be equated with the grace in the covenant of grace. The covenant of grace stipulates a Mediator and requires the death of that Mediator for the communication of all its benefits. The covenant before the fall (the covenant of works) did not have a Mediator and did not require death to make it valid (Hebrews 9:17). Therefore, the covenant before the fall can never be considered as a part of the covenant of grace. They are two different covenants.

This is an essential point. The whole Federal Vision system depends on being able to conflate the covenant of works before the fall with the covenant of grace after the fall. Proponents of the Federal Vision attempt to flatten the distinctions between the covenant of works and the covenant of grace. Unless they can do so, there is nothing of substance left to their system. Yet, Hebrews 9 clearly shows that the covenant of grace is built on the foundation of the death of Christ, the Testator. His death was shadowed in the sacrifices and types of the Old Testament and was prophesied from Genesis 3:15 (immediately after the fall) to Malachi. The covenant of grace was ratified by the blood of Christ, but the covenant of works knew nothing about His sacrifice. Therefore, the covenant before the fall cannot be equated with God's covenant of grace after the fall.

Summary

The main emphasis of the Federal Vision concerning covenant theology is a position that was held also by Pelagius. They teach salvation is by covenant faithfulness. He taught that 'believers' must live righteously by faith. They deny the distinction between the law and grace. He taught that both the law and the gospel inform us how to live. They deny the distinction between the covenant of works and the

---

40 John Brown, *Hebrews* (London, England and Carlisle, Pennsylvania: The Banner of Truth Trust, 1972), 415.

covenant of grace. He saw no distinction between the relationship of Adam with God before the fall and that which we have with Him after the fall. Both the Federal Vision and Pelagius hold to a mono-covenantal view of Scripture. On the other hand, the Reformed churches have always held to the bi-covenantal view of Scripture as essential to sound theology.

Conclusion

Any theory of nomism, such as the Federal Vision, necessarily must have a relaxation of the law which accommodates human sinfulness. This also reveals how far from the Scripture the Federal Vision really is. The gospel proclaims a perfect Savior who has fulfilled all the demands of God's law in our behalf. The Federal Vision constructs a scheme of salvation which denies that Christ's perfect righteousness is imputed to believers and asserts that final justification will be based on the totality of one's life. Instead of the perfect life of Christ imputed to believers, the Federal Vision teaches that one's own sincere obedience will be the basis for God's declaration of righteousness in the day of judgment.

John Calvin, in his antidote to the canons of the Council of Trent, defined the distinction between the law and the gospel as follows:

> The difference between the Law and the Gospel lies in this, that the latter does not like the former promise life under the condition of works, but from faith.[41]

A fuller distinction is beautifully given by the pen of Herman Bavinck:

> The law was temporary and designed for one people; the gospel is eternal and has to be carried to all peoples. The law was imperfect, a shadow and an example; the gospel is perfect and the substance of the good things themselves. The law fostered fear and servitude; the gospel generates love and freedom. The gospel embodied in the sacrament, however, confers the power of grace that enables its recipients to keep God's commandments and to gain eternal life. In a word, the law is the incomplete gospel; the gospel is the complete law. The gospel was contained in the law as a tree in a seed, a grain in an ear of corn.[42]

---

41 Henry Beveridge, ed. and trans., John Calvin, *Tracts and Letters*, Volume 3: Tracts, Part 3 (Edinburgh, Scotland and Carlisle, Pennsylvania: The Banner of Truth Trust, 2009), 156.

42 Bavinck, *Reformed Dogmatics*, Vol. 4, 452.

Then, Bavinck gathers several Scripture passages to show the differences between the law and the gospel which he summarizes as follows:

> In these texts law and gospel are contrasted as demand and gift, as command and promise, as sin and grace, as sickness and healing, as death and life. . . The law proceeds from God's holiness, the gospel from God's grace; the law is known by nature, the gospel only from special revelation; the law demands perfect righteousness, but the gospel grants it; the law leads people to eternal life by works, and the gospel produces good works from the riches of eternal life granted in faith; the law condemns people, and the gospel acquits them.[43]

These distinctions are very important. The Federal Vision proclaims a message that you can be saved if you persevere in faithfulness and if your works meet the approval of God at the final judgment. That is the message of the law. That is not the message of the gospel.

---

43 Ibid., 453.

–5–

The Federal Vision's Paradigm for Baptism

> "In my work on baptism, I have exactly taken the paradigm of infant baptism as the model of baptism."[1]
>
> PETER LEITHART, FEDERAL VISION PROPONENT

> "The child's pre-baptismal faith means that he is able to receive what God offers to him in baptism, namely, Christ and the promise of forgiveness through participation in His death and resurrection. Paedofaith prevents us from viewing paedobaptism as an empty, outward sign. It ensures that the child's baptism is efficacious, not empty. Baptism, then does not create faith in the heart of the child (as the Lutherans sometimes claim). Rather, through faith the child receives what God offers in baptism, namely, Christ and the benefits of the new covenant."[2]
>
> RICH LUSK, FEDERAL VISION PROPONENT

---

[1] Record of the Case, Standing Judicial Commission of the Presbyterian Church in America, Case 2012-5, RE Gerald Hedman vs. Pacific Northwest Presbytery, p. 524.

[2] Rich Lusk, *Paedofaith: A Primer on the Mystery of Infant Salvation and a Handbook for Covenant Parents* (Monroe, Louisiana: Athanasius Press, 2005), 50.

There are two erroneous presuppositions, or fatal flaws, of the Federal Vision which fundamentally affect all their other positions on the doctrines of salvation. These flaws were discovered during my work representing Ruling Elder Gerald Hedman in his complaint against Pacific Northwest Presbytery (PCA) concerning the trial of Peter Leithart—a prominent apologist for the Federal Vision theology. For the most part, the Federal Vision proponents have been guarded about revealing their basic presuppositions, but Leithart expressed two fundamental presuppositions in his trial. The first presupposition makes infant baptism a new paradigm for all baptism. The second presupposition is a redefinition of "efficacy" which will be the subject of the next chapter. These two presuppositions are essential to the whole system of the Federal Vision. Every person who holds to the Federal Vision must also hold to them. Their system cannot be erected without them.

Key Assessment: The Federal Vision makes infant baptism the paradigm for all baptism, contrary to Scripture. The Scripture makes adult baptism the paradigm of baptism.

The confusing statements Federal Vision proponents make concerning baptism cannot be understood without realizing that they have a different paradigm concerning it. Their paradigm of baptism is not new, though. It represents a sacramental view that is at least as old as the Judaizers. It combines the theory of the magical efficacy of sacraments with the doctrine of infant baptism. The Federal Vision's theories of efficacy and baptism will be explored more in Chapters 6 and 7. At this point, it is important to note that the Federal Vision is not the first system to develop around the theory of what baptism means to an infant. Pelagius, in order to defend his theory of the native innocence of all mankind, was compelled to devise a new view of infant baptism. As G. F. Wiggers wrote in his book, *Augustinism and Pelagianism*, concerning the first principle of Pelagianism:

> It is difficult to say whether the contest began with infant baptism or with original sin. . . So much, however, is certain; from the close connection between the doctrine of infant baptism with that of original sin, the controversy on both doctrines must have been nearly simultaneous.

The doctrine of infant baptism was, therefore, as we have seen, either the first on which the controversy began, or at least one of the first.[3]

This new paradigm of baptism places the Federal Vision in the unenviable position of doing the same thing Pelagius did over 1,600 years ago. Pelagius was pressed hard by Augustine concerning the purpose of baptizing infants. Augustine challenged him that the church had always believed that baptism is for the remission of sins, which could not be the case if the theory of the innocence of infants was true. Pelagius' response was to redefine the meaning of baptism on the basis of what that rite meant for infants. Wiggers, therefore, is vindicated in his assertion that it was at least one of the first doctrines on which the controversy centered. The Federal Vision, in making the same mistake, is at best Semi-Pelagianism; at worst, it is Pelagianism.

The Scriptural Paradigm of Baptism

A paradigm of infant baptism as the model for all baptism cannot be constructed from the New Testament and is nowhere found in the Westminster Confession of Faith. There is not one single infant baptism mentioned in the New Testament, and infant baptism is not taught as the paradigm of all baptism in the Scripture.

My systematic theology professor at Reformed Theological Seminary, Dr. Morton Smith, taught us that the role of a theologian is "to think God's thoughts after Him." This first presupposition of Federal Vision proponents undermines that role and allows them to think of theology *apart* from God's thoughts. They can pour whatever meaning into baptism that suits their fancy. They have framed the debate in such a way that most people do not know how to respond to their assertions about baptism. Instead of proving their position from Scripture, the Federal Vision proponents make their opponents disprove those assertions. They frame the question this way: Are there any biblical passages which deny that baptism gives new life, justification, adoption, sanctification, the fullness of the Spirit, union with Christ, and forgiveness of sins to baptized infants? No, of course there are not. In fact, there are no New Testament passages which even mention infant baptism. Yet, that is the wrong question altogether. The

---

3 G. F. Wiggers, *An Historical Presentation of Augustinism amd Pelagianism from the Original Sources* (Andover, Connecticut: Gould, Newman & Saxton, 1840), 58, 61.

proper question should be this: What is the New Testament paradigm for all baptism? Does the New Testament use infant baptism or adult baptism as that paradigm? The church has always understood Scripture to teach that adult baptism is the paradigm for all baptism. Even Leithart admits that fact.[4] In support of adult baptism being the proper paradigm, Charles Hodge wrote:

> The difficulty on this subject is that baptism from its very nature involves a profession of faith; it is the way in which by the ordinance of Christ, He is to be confessed before men; but infants are incapable of making such confession; therefore they are not the proper subjects of baptism.[5]

Hodge is not arguing against infant baptism. He is simply saying that infants cannot fulfill the prerequisite of a profession of faith which is required by baptism. Herman Bavinck wrote to the same effect:

> Nowadays, most churches know baptism virtually exclusively as infant baptism. Aside from mission fields abroad and in Baptist churches, the baptism of adults is an exception. Yet, in Scripture the reverse is true. Nowhere does it speak explicitly of infant baptism. It always assumes the baptism of adults. Also the Christian creeds and Christian theologians have always followed the example of Scripture in this respect insofar as they took their point of departure in the baptism of adults and only then went on to infant baptism. . . Scripture tells us beyond any doubt baptism has been exclusively instituted for believers.[6]

James Bannerman in his two-volume work, *The Church of Christ*, wrote about the scriptural model of baptism:

> The proper and true type of baptism, as a sacrament in the church of Christ, is the baptism of adults, and not the baptism of infants. In consequence of the altered circumstances of the Christian Church at present, as compared with the era when baptism was first appointed, we are apt to overlook this truth. . . It is abundantly obvious that adult baptism is the rule, and infant baptism the exceptional case; and we must take our idea of the ordinance in its nature and effects not from the exception, but from the rule. . . It is very plain, and very important

---

4 Record of the Case, Standing Judicial Commission, 524.

5 Charles Hodge, *Systematic Theology*, Volume III (Grand Rapids: Wm. B. Eerdmans Publishing Company, 1970), 546.

6 Herman Bavinck, *Reformed Dogmatics*, Volume IV (Grand Rapids: Baker Publishing Group, 2008), 514.

to remember, that the only true and complete type of baptism is found in the instance of those subjects of it who are capable of faith and repentance, not in the instance of those subjects of it who are not capable of either. The Bible model of baptism is adult baptism, and not infant.[7]

J. C. Ryle, the Anglican Bishop of Liverpool from 1880 to 1900, summed up the situation well:

> The right of Christian infants to baptism is only through their parents. The precise effect of baptism on infants is never once stated in the New Testament. There is no description of a child's baptism: and to say that children, born in sin, as all are, are in themselves worthy to receive grace, appears to me a near approach to the old heresy of Pelagianism.[8]

It is interesting that Ryle, who was very familiar with the "baptismal regeneration" heresies propagated by many within the Church of England, says that they make "a near approach to the old heresy of Pelagianism." Many people are reluctant to go that far, but those who knew the issues the best, such as Ryle, did not hesitate to do so.

Another quote from Herman Bavinck reaches a similar conclusion about infant baptism as these other great theologians:

> Adult baptism is therefore the original baptism; infant baptism is derivative; the former must not be conformed to the latter, but the latter must be conformed to the former.[9]

In other words, Bavinck says that infant baptism cannot be the paradigm for adult baptism, but adult baptism must be the paradigm for infant baptism. Of course, Rich Lusk thinks he has found the answer to this apparent dilemma. In the quote at the beginning of this chapter, he asserts that infants are baptized not on the basis of their parents' faith, but on the basis of their own faith. What Lusk does not seem to realize is that his theory, wholly unsupported by the clear teaching of Scripture, would completely undermine the doctrine of covenant baptism and federal theology. If infants are baptized on the basis of their own faith, then all baptisms are

---

[7] James Bannerman, *The Church of Christ: A treatise on the nature, powers, ordinances, discipline and government of the Christian Church*, Volume 2 (Edinburgh: The Banner of Truth Trust, 1974), 108-109.

[8] G. E. Duffield, ed., J. C. Ryle, *Knots Untied: Being Plain Statements on Disputed Points in Religion from the Standpoint of an Evangelical Churchman* (Cambridge, England: James Clarke & Co., Ltd, 1977), 105.

[9] Bavinck, *Reformed Dogmatics*, Volume IV, 526.

baptisms of believers. In such a system, covenant or federal theology would no longer be necessary.

The Necessity of Repentance and Faith for Baptism
The views of Hodge, Bavinck, Ryle, and Bannerman are in perfect agreement with what the New Testament teaches about baptism. Both John the Baptist and Jesus began their ministries by preaching, "Repent, for the kingdom of heaven is at hand." (Matthew 3:2; 4:17). Once repentance took place, both John and Jesus baptized the people (Matthew 3:6, John 4:1). Repentance, therefore, was a requirement for baptism. Peter told the crowds on the day of Pentecost, "Repent, and each of you be baptized in the name of Jesus Christ for the forgiveness of your sins. . . " (Acts 2:39).

Repentance and faith are different sides of the same coin. Where one is present, the other will be found also. Luke records concerning Peter's sermon at the Feast of Pentecost that "those who had *received* his word were baptized" (Acts 2:41). Philip preached the good news to the Samaritans and they were baptized after believing. As Acts 8:12 says, "But when they *believed* Philip preaching the good news about the kingdom of God and the name of Jesus Christ, they were being baptized, men and women alike." The Ethiopian eunuch was also evangelized by Philip, and he asked the evangelist upon seeing some water in the desert, "What prevents me from being baptized?" (Acts 8:36). Philip responded, "If you *believe* with all your heart, you may" (Acts 8:37). The Philippian jailer tremblingly asked Paul and Silas, "Sirs, what must I do to be saved?" (Acts 16:30). Paul responded, "Believe in the Lord Jesus, and you will be saved, you and your household" (Acts 16:31). Paul then spoke the word of God to the jailer and his household and they believed it. Immediately after believing in God, the jailer and his household were baptized (Acts 16:33, 34).

In the Bible, faith and repentance are never the response to baptism, as the proponents of the Federal Vision wrongly teach. Faith and repentance always precede baptism in the case of adults. They are a response to the gospel message before baptism. Only after believing in the gospel is an adult believer a proper candidate for baptism. The early church was diligent in examining converts concerning their faith prior to baptism and had special classes for catechumens. Even those baptized in infancy are to be called on to trust in the gospel when they are old enough to understand it. They are not to look to their baptism and respond to it. Baptism cannot save us, but faith in the gospel of Christ does save us. As Louis Berkhof wrote:

> [B]aptism presupposes regeneration, faith, conversion, and justification, these surely are not to be conceived as wrought by it. . . . Neither does baptism work a special sacramental grace, consisting in this that the recipient is implanted into the body of Jesus Christ. The believer's incorporation into mystical union with Christ is also presupposed.[10]

This fatal presupposition of the Federal Vision allows its proponents to teach that baptism confers graces which the Scripture clearly teaches are conferred to believers by the Holy Spirit. Regeneration, justification, adoption, sanctification, forgiveness of sins, the outpouring of the Spirit, and union with Christ are not conferred through baptism. They are conferred *before* baptism in the case of adult believers and are not tied to the moment of baptism even for infants.

The Federal Vision also says that baptism bestows the *arrabon*, or earnest, of the Holy Spirit to every recipient of water baptism. The New Testament teaches otherwise. First, the reception of the Holy Spirit preceded baptism on the Day of Pentecost. The Holy Spirit was poured out on the crowds at Pentecost before any of them were baptized (Acts 2:1-4). On another occasion, Peter preached the good news to the Gentiles at Caesarea and the Holy Spirit fell on them, to which the Apostle responded, "Surely no one can refuse the water for these to be baptized who have received the Holy Spirit just as we did, can he?" (Acts 10:47). Baptism did not effect the reception of the Holy Spirit for them, but evidenced that they had already received the Spirit.

This same view of the outpouring of the Spirit is given by Paul in the first chapter of Ephesians:

> In Him, you also, after listening to the message of the truth, the gospel of your salvation—having also believed, you were sealed in Him with the Holy Spirit of promise, who is given as a pledge of our inheritance (Ephesians 1:13, 14).

The Spirit of promise is given to those who believe, which means He is not conferred through baptism *before* saving faith. The giving of

---

10 Louis Berkhof, *Systematic Theology* (Grand Rapids: Wm. B. Eerdmans Publishing Company, 1972), 632.

the Spirit was the great promise of Christ to His people both during His last days before the crucifixion and to the gathered crowds at His ascension. As Jesus said, "You will receive power when the Holy Spirit has come upon you" (Acts 1:8). If this promise is understood to take place at baptism, then it is denuded of the spiritual reality and power which Jesus promised. This promise of the Spirit was for the purpose of equipping believers with the power to live the Christian life and to be witnesses for Christ. This happens only when a person experiences the reality of baptism in a true conversion to Christ. It does not happen to every person who is baptized with water, but the Spirit *is* given immediately to every person who believes.

Faith and repentance also assume that the new birth takes place before baptism. In John 3, Jesus mentions both the new birth and saving faith. Concerning the new birth, Jesus said, "Truly, truly, I say to you, unless one is born again he cannot see the kingdom of God" (John 3:3). Seeing the kingdom of God is the same as believing the gospel. The new birth is assumed to be prior to saving faith, and that is the order in which they are mentioned by Christ—first the new birth, then saving faith. Other Scriptures support the necessity of the new birth prior to any spiritual activity. They include: John 1:12, 13; 6:37, 44, 65; Romans 8:8; Ezekiel 36:26, 27; 1 Peter 2:9; Ephesians 2:1-10; 1 Corinthians 2:12; Acts 16:14; Acts 26:18, etc.

William Cunningham notes the problem with making infant baptism the fundamental paradigm for all baptism:

> It becomes practically, as well as theoretically, important to remember, that we ought to form our primary and fundamental conceptions of baptism from the baptism of adults, in which it must be, *in every instance*, according to the general doctrine of Protestants, *either* the sign and seal of a faith and regeneration *previously existing*—already effected by God's grace—or else a hypocritical profession of a state of mind and feeling which has no existence.[11]

In adult baptism, the benefits of redemption are bestowed on believers *prior* to baptism and not *by* baptism. As Bavinck notes:

> All these benefits have already been bestowed on the baptized in the word of the gospel. They were received on the part of the baptized by faith; but now these benefits were further signified and sealed to them

---

11 William Cunningham, *Historical Theology*, Volume II (London: The Banner of Truth Trust, 1969), 126.

in baptism. Hence the situation must not be pictured as one in which before baptism only a few and in any case not all the benefits were granted in faith and that the one(s) still lacking are now bestowed in baptism. The Word contains all the promises, and faith accepts them all. There is not a single grace that is not conveyed by the Word and only by the sacrament.[12]

The Westminster Standards on Baptism

The great change resulting in salvation is described by the Westminster Standards in the chapter on effectual calling:

> All those whom God hath predestinated unto life, and those only, he is pleased, in his appointed and accepted time, effectually to call, by his Word and Spirit, out of that state of sin and death, in which they are by nature, to grace and salvation, by Jesus Christ; enlightening their minds spiritually and savingly to understand the things of God, taking away their heart of stone, and giving them a heart of flesh; renewing their wills, and, by his almighty power, determining them to Jesus Christ; yet so, as they come most freely, being made willing by his grace (Westminster Confession of Faith 10.1).

In the Westminster Standards, and frequently in the New Testament also, the new birth is subsumed under effectual calling. Before Nicodemus could see the kingdom of God, he had to be born again. Before Lydia could respond to the things spoken by Paul, her heart had to be opened by the Lord. Before the Philippian jailer could earnestly and sincerely inquire about salvation, God had to perform a work of grace in his heart. That work of grace was missing in the heart of the rich young ruler and he parted from Jesus with sadness, despite asking Him what good thing he must do to be saved. Jesus told the inquiring Jews, "This is the work of God, that you believe in Him whom He has sent" (John 6:29). The work of God to which Jesus refers is the work of giving His elect a new heart. Regeneration precedes saving faith and, therefore, also precedes baptism in the case of adults.

Justification is an act of God's free grace, according to the Shorter Catechism, and is conferred immediately, once for all, whenever a person believes in Christ. Since the Scripture teaches that faith and repentance precede baptism, justification also precedes baptism. Adoption is an also act of God's free grace which is coincident with justifica-

---

12 Bavinck, *Reformed Dogmatics*, Volume IV, 521.

tion, so that also is assumed to precede our baptism. The forgiveness of our sins is a result of saving faith and that is assumed to precede baptism. Justification, adoption, the new birth, the outpouring of the Spirit, and the forgiveness of sins are all given to believers before they are baptized. All the benefits of Christ which Leithart says are bestowed in baptism are actually given to adult believers before they are baptized. Moreover, these benefits of Christ's redemption are not given to every infant who is baptized according to the Westminster Confession of Faith 28.6:

> The efficacy of baptism is not tied to that moment of time wherein it is administered; yet, notwithstanding, by the right use of this ordinance, the grace promised is not only offered, but really exhibited, and conferred, by the Holy Ghost, to such (whether of age or infants) as that grace belongeth unto, according to the counsel of God's own will, in His appointed time.

The benefits of Christ, therefore, do not belong to every person who is baptized. They belong only to the elect, whether of age or infants, who are effectually called by God's grace. Believing adults receive these benefits before they are baptized. Some adults who are baptized without true faith may receive these benefits at a later time, but only if they come to repentance and faith in God's appointed time. Otherwise, such adults are baptized on a hypocritical profession of faith. Infants, who are baptized, do not have the benefits of Christ's redemption "conferred" on them unless such graces belong to them, according to the counsel of God's will and in His own time. The view held by Federal Vision proponents, that every baptized person receives the benefits of Christ, is completely without support in the Scripture or the Westminster Confession of Faith. It assumes a wrong paradigm by making infant baptism the model for all baptism. This error results in other errors which are hostile to the fundamental doctrines of the Bible. The proponents of this view make a fundamental and fatal mistake in interpreting the plain passages of Scripture by their own imaginations concerning what is the "paradigm of baptism." The Westminster Confession of Faith Chapter 1.9 says:

> The infallible rule of interpretation of Scripture is Scripture itself; and therefore, when there is a question about the true and full sense of any Scripture (which is not manifold but one), it must be searched and known by other places that speak more clearly.

Summary

By making infant baptism the paradigm of all baptism, the Federal Vision proponents have made the same mistake as Pelagius. He also devised a new way of thinking about baptism in that he rejected the doctrine of the native depravity of all of Adam's descendants. Leithart and others in the Federal Vision perhaps disagree with Pelagius about the native sinfulness of all humanity, but they are following his example by making infant baptism the paradigm of all baptism. In so doing, they are not only making a change to baptism, but they are undermining the soteriology of the Scripture after the example of Pelagius.

Conclusion

It is not enough for the Federal Vision proponents to appeal to antiquity in support of their flawed positions. It is ill-advised for Federal Vision proponents, like Leithart, to even consider new ways of thinking about baptism. The thoughts of ancient theologians are not sufficient. The thoughts of the greatest theologians of today are not sufficient. What is required is some clear passage of Scripture to show God's thoughts about baptism. There are no passages of Scripture that teach infant baptism is the paradigm of all baptism. Scripture is silent on this matter and so must we be. Thus, the Federal Vision makes a fundamental mistake when it asserts that infant baptism is the paradigm for all baptism. Their mistake places them in conflict with the Scriptures, the Reformed standards, and the overwhelming consensus of the greatest theologians in the Reformed churches.

-6-
The Federal Vision's Wrong View of Efficacy

"Baptism, I argued, is efficacious in the way that the ordination rite is efficacious. That is still my position. This analogy opens up a new way of thinking about baptismal efficacy that avoids two extremes. It avoids the view that baptism has little or no effect, and it avoids the view that baptism invariably and permanently confers grace."[1]

PETER LEITHART, FEDERAL VISION PROPONENT

"Baptism is covenantally efficacious. It brings every baptized person into an objective and living relationship with Christ, whether the baptized person is elect or reprobate."[2]

DOUGLAS WILSON, FEDERAL VISION PROPONENT

---

1 Record of the Case, Standing Judicial Commission of the Presbyterian Church in America, Case 2012-5, RE Gerald Hedman vs. Pacific Northwest Presbytery, 188.

2 Douglas Wilson, "Credos: On Baptism," #6, *Credenda/Agenda* 15/5:24.

The second fundamental flaw of the Federal Vision is a wrong view of baptismal efficacy. Efficacy is the power to produce an effect. What is the effect of baptism? That is the question. All sides believe in baptismal efficacy of some sort or another, but there are disagreements concerning the parties to whom that efficacy applies and when it applies. The Reformed position has always been that the efficacy of baptism applies only to the elect as a *sealing* ordinance and is not tied to the moment of baptism. In this way, both the objective grace and the subjective grace of the sacraments are upheld. The Federal Vision's view is that the same objective grace of the covenant is given to everyone who receives the sacrament of baptism. In their emphasis on the objectivity of the covenant, its proponents have essentially denied the subjective work of the Holy Spirit in conversion and the sealing aspect of the sacrament. Thus, their view of efficacy ultimately depends on the response of the individual to his baptism rather than God's grace through the Holy Spirit.

In his trial, Peter Leithart explained his view of baptismal efficacy:

> Like ordination, baptism confers benefits—"graces" in the original sense—and these are truly conferred by baptism. Baptism marks the baptized with God's favor and grants favor, but baptism does not guarantee that the baptized will remain in God's favor forever.[3]

There is a reason why it is necessary for many, if not most, proponents of the Federal Vision to define efficacy in the way Leithart does. That reason is that they deny that personal regeneration by the Holy Spirit is an essential doctrine of the Scriptures, as Chapter 2 of this book demonstrates. Rather, they believe personal regeneration is an intramural debate that can be affirmed or denied without harm to one's theological position. Yet, efficacious grace is particularly the work of the Spirit in the souls of God's people and is, therefore, vitally connected with a supernatural and personal regeneration. As A. A. Hodge said in his commentary on the Westminster Confession of Faith,

> Effectual calling, according to the usage of our Standards, is the act of the Holy Spirit effecting regeneration. Regeneration is the effect produced by the Holy Spirit in effectual calling. The Holy Spirit, in the act of effectual calling, causes the soul to become regenerate by implanting a new governing principle or habit or spiritual affection and action.

---

3 Record of the Case, 188.

The soul itself, in conversion, immediately acts under the guidance of this new principle in turning from sin unto God through Christ.[4]

There are really only two options concerning efficacious grace and baptismal efficacy. First, we can believe rightly, as the Scripture teaches, that the Holy Spirit works powerfully and efficaciously in the hearts of the elect to bring them to salvation and secure their eternal destiny. Second, we can believe wrongly that the sacraments perform their work in the very action of receiving them. This latter view has been called by the Latin term, *ex opere operato*, which means "from the work done." It is a phrase which is generally taken to mean that the sacraments perform their work regardless of the attitude of the recipient or the minister.

Key Assessment: The Federal Vision defines the efficacy of baptism as more than nothing but less than permanently conferring the grace of eternal salvation. That is a definition of efficacy which is contrary to the meaning of the word in the Scripture and the Reformed creeds.

The Federal Vision's Definition of Efficacy

When the sacramental view of efficacy is chosen, it necessarily results in a different meaning of efficacy. Efficacy becomes something which does not always result in eternal salvation. Efficacy is hedged in by the will of man. This becomes apparent in reading what the Federal Vision proponents mean by the efficacy of baptism. There is no clearer proof that the Federal Vision is teaching a view of salvation that is radically different from the Bible than in these efforts to redefine efficacy. In fact, Wilson and other Federal Vision advocates define efficacy to mean that it results in either election *or* reprobation, as Chapter 16, "The Federal Vision and Apostasy," will show.

Such a definition of efficacy is contrary to the plain meaning of the word. Efficacy, according to this definition, would actually be non-efficacious unto salvation unless completed by man. The doctrine of efficacy has been the great watershed between the Augustinian-Calvinistic systems on the one hand and the Pelagian-Semipelagian-Arminian systems on the other hand. The latter have always defined efficacy in such a way that grace must be assisted by man's free will in order to actually result in eternal salvation. The Westminster Standards are very clear about efficacious grace. Efficacious grace always results in

---

4 A. A. Hodge, *The Confession of Faith* (London: The Banner of Truth Trust, 1961), 171.

eternal salvation. It is powerful and effective because it is based on the omnipotence of God. God overcomes all the obstinacy of man's sinful will and secures his eternal salvation. This grace is efficacious because it is God's powerful, unchanging grace.

The Federal Vision makes a fundamental mistake in describing baptismal efficacy to be like "ordination grace." Evangelical and Reformed denominations, like the Presbyterian Church in America or the Orthodox Presbyterian Church, do not have a doctrine of ordination grace. They do not believe ordination is efficacious or that it conveys grace. Rather, they require that all candidates for the ministry must give evidence of experiential grace and a call to the ministry before they can pass the trials for ordination. Ordination does not bestow the grace which is required, but assumes it is already present. In this respect, ordination is like baptism. It does not bestow or confer grace but requires it to be present already. Yet, the Federal Vision definition of sacramental efficacy is similar to the Council of Trent which says:

> A sacrament is something presented to the senses, which has the power, by divine institution, not only of signifying, but also of efficiently conveying grace.[5]

Of course, the Federal Vision differs with Rome on the matter of subjective, internal grace. They think they have avoided the errors of Romanism by emphasizing the objective grace, but they have thereby fallen into an even greater heresy—Pelagianism—than the Semi-Pelagianism of the Council of Trent.

The Catholic Church teaches that the sacraments contain grace, but the free will of man is necessary to make them completely efficacious. Yet, the Scripture never uses the word grace in the context of the sacraments, according to McClintock and Strong:

> The word grace appears 128 times in the New Test. (Cruden). Wilson presents all these passages in a tabular form, with explanations, and remarks that a comparison of them will show that "there is not one text in which the word grace occurs in any connection with either of the sacraments."[6]

---

[5] A. A. Hodge, *Outlines of Theology* (Grand Rapids, Michigan: Zondervan Publishing House, 1972), 589.

[6] John McClintock and James Strong, *Cyclopedia of Biblical, Theological, and Ecclesiastical Literature*, Volume III (Grand Rapids: Baker Book House, 1981), 968.

The Westminster Confession of Faith on Efficacy

There is no doctrine more essential to the teaching of the Westminster Standards than efficacious grace. As B. B. Warfield wrote:

> The distinguishing mark of Calvinism as over against all other systems lies in its doctrines of "efficacious grace."[7]
>
> Predestination is rather a logical consequence of, and an essential element in, than the determining principle of, Calvinism.[8]

Warfield's statement is confirmed by a perusal of the Westminster Standards which refer specifically to efficacious grace in nine different chapters of the Westminster Confession of Faith (WCF 3.6; 7.5; 8.6; 8.8; 10.1-4; 11.1; 13.1; 17.2; 27.3; 28.6) and in answer to various questions of the Larger and Shorter Catechisms (LCQ 2, 35, 58, 59, 66, 67, 68, 155, 161; SCQ 29, 30, 31, 32, 88, 89, 90, 91). The Standards also indirectly refer to efficacious grace by describing the work of the Spirit in the hearts of His people in various other sections.

The Westminster Standards teach that the elect are effectually called to faith in Christ by the Holy Spirit.

> Wherefore, they who are elected, being fallen in Adam, are redeemed by Christ, are *effectually* called unto faith by His Holy Spirit working in due season, are justified, adopted, sanctified, and kept by His power, through faith, unto salvation (WCF 3.6).

In other places, the Westminster Standards teach that:

1. The covenant of grace was "sufficient and *efficacious*, through the operation of the Holy Spirit" during the time of the law (WCF 7.5).
2. "The virtue, *efficacy*, and benefits [of Christ] were communicated unto the elect" before Christ became a man (WCF 8.6).
3. Particular redemption is *effectually* applied only to the elect (WCF 8.8).
4. Justification by faith flows from *effectual* calling (WCF 11.1).
5. Sanctification is the result of *effectual* calling and regeneration (WCF 13.1).
6. Perseverance is the result of the *efficacy* of Christ's merit and

---

7 John E. Meeter, editor, *Selected Shorter Writings of Benjamin B. Warfield*, Volume II (Nutley, New Jersey: Presbyterian and Reformed Publishing Company, 1973), 415.

8 Ibid., 414.

intercession, the abiding of the Spirit, and the covenant of grace (WCF 17.2).
7. The sacraments are *efficacious* only through the working of the Spirit (WCF 27.3).
8. Baptismal *efficacy* is not tied to the moment of baptism, but grace is offered and conferred to such as that grace belongs, according to the counsel of God's own will, in His appointed time (WCF 28.6).
9. Chapter ten of the Westminster Confession of Faith is devoted completely to the doctrine of *effectual* calling (italics added for emphasis).

Concerning baptismal efficacy, the Westminster Standards restrict it to the elect alone who are the subjects of God's efficacious grace. A wrong view of baptismal efficacy changes the meaning of all the most important doctrines of salvation. Efficacious grace means that the elect alone are: redeemed by Christ; given a new heart; justified, adopted, and sanctified; given the Holy Spirit; forgiven their sins; enabled to persevere; kept by God's power; and, made heirs of eternal salvation. The Federal Vision's view of baptismal efficacy totally redefines the efficacious grace of the Westminster Standards and replaces it with a view of efficacy that is completed by man. Grace, in the Scripture and the Westminster Standards, is efficacious solely through the work of the Spirit and the power of God.

Common and Special Grace as Bearing on Efficacy
The Federal Vision attempts to evade this problem by saying that "baptismal efficacy" is different than efficacious grace or effectual calling. In fact, one Federal Vision proponent, Mark Horne, specifically states that the efficacy of baptism must not be understood solely in terms of "special grace", but "common grace" and the promise as conditional.[9] Where does special grace end and common grace begin in such a convoluted scheme of baptismal efficacy? There simply is no basis for distinguishing between efficacious grace and baptismal efficacy. Efficacy is the same no matter where it is found in the scheme of salvation. The answer to Shorter Catechism question 88 clarifies to whom baptism is made effectual:

---

9 Guy Prentiss Waters, *The Federal Vision and Covenant Theology: A Comparative Analysis* (Phillipsburg, New Jersey: P&R Publishing, 2006), 249-250.

> The outward and ordinary means whereby Christ communicateth to us the benefits of redemption, are his ordinances, especially the word, sacraments, and prayer; all which are made effectual to the elect for salvation.

The efficacy of baptism is the same as the efficacy that comes through reading the Scripture and praying. We can pray fervently for a person, but our prayers are ineffectual for them unless the ones we are praying for are chosen of God. Paul sought urgently to convince King Agrippa of the Christian gospel, but his efforts fell on deaf ears. The preaching of the word and prayer are made effectual only to the elect. Baptism is likewise restricted to the elect, according to our standards. The Word of God is only efficacious to the salvation of those whose hearts are opened by the Holy Spirit, as in the case of Lydia. Prayer is only efficacious to the salvation of the elect who, in due time, call on the name of the Lord according to the promise of Scripture and believe in Christ. Likewise, baptism is only effectual to the salvation of the elect and is not efficacious in any sense for the non-elect, despite the assertions of the Federal Vision to the contrary. This is the clear teaching of the Westminster Standards and the Scripture. The true position on baptismal efficacy is given by James Bannerman in *The Church of Christ*:

> In the case of adults, we know that baptism is fitted and designed not to confer faith, but rather to confirm it,—not to originate grace, but to increase it—not to effect that inward change of regeneration by which we are numbered with the children of God, or that outward change of justification by which we are accepted of Him, but to seal these blessings before bestowed. With adults, baptism is not regeneration or justification, but the seal of both to the regenerated and justified man . . . infant baptism is not infant regeneration or justification, any more than in the instance of adults.[10]

Perhaps Federal Vision advocates would still contend that "baptismal efficacy" is not to be understood in the same sense as efficacious grace. Yet, that dichotomy simply will not work. The Federal Vision states that baptism confers new life, justification, adoption, sanctification, the earnest of the Spirit, and forgiveness of sins. If such efficacy of water baptism is different than the efficacious grace mentioned

---

10 James Bannerman, *The Church of Christ: A treatise on the nature, powers, ordinances, discipline and government of the Christian Church*, Volume II (Edinburgh, Scotland and Carlisle, PA: The Banner of Truth Trust, 1974), 112.

in the Westminster Standards, then what does that make these other graces? Does the new life that is supposedly conferred by baptism in the Federal Vision system become non-efficacious or temporarily efficacious new life for those who do not persevere? Does the justification that is supposedly conferred by baptism become non-efficacious justification without perseverance? Of course those graces must be non-efficacious for all the baptized who fail to persevere. Yet, the system of the Federal Vision fails to see that perseverance is included in the efficacious grace of the Scripture and the Westminster Standards for all the elect.

An even more troubling question is how some benefit of Christ's redemption that is supposedly conferred by God's common grace, as for instance in Horne's position, can become the effectual grace of God? There are only two options. It would have to be either from God or through man. If it is the latter, then that would make man the ultimate determiner of his salvation. That is a position contrary to the Scripture and Reformed theology. If it is from God, then how can such grace fail to be special and efficacious, and how could the baptized ever fail to persevere? We reject Horne's paradigm of baptism and common grace. Common grace can never morph into special grace through the faithfulness and perseverance of the baptized. Only special, efficacious grace can ever save anyone.

Summary
Proponents of the Federal Vision define efficacy in a manner similar to the Council of Trent. Their position is not consistent with the Scriptures or the Westminster Standards. Efficacy in their system depends on the response of the baptized in order for it to become truly effectual. Therein, they deny the true teaching about God's efficacious grace.

Conclusion
Any denial or redefinition of efficacious grace rips the heart out of the Westminster Standards. Warfield rightly said that efficacious grace is the distinguishing mark of Calvinism. If efficacious grace is not one of the fundamentals of the system of doctrine, indeed *the* fundamental doctrine, then there is no fundamental doctrine of the Standards. The Federal Vision is hostile to the whole system of the Westminster

Standards in its rejection of efficacious grace. This teaching cannot be tolerated without permitting doctrines which undermine the most basic and essential doctrine of the Westminster Standards—efficacious grace. Thus, the nineteenth-century Southern Presbyterian theologian, Robert L. Dabney, concluded his analysis of the doctrine of sacramental grace with these words:

> We may say of this doctrine as of all forms of sacramental grace, it is the prompting of that tendency to formalism and to a sensuous religion which exhibits itself in popery and paganism.[11]

---

11   Robert L. Dabney, *Discussions: Evangelical and Theological,* Volume I (London: The Banner of Truth Trust, 1967), 349.

–7–

The Federal Vision and Baptismal Efficacy

> "If external events and realities cannot penetrate to the inner man, then we have no grounds for sacramental theology at all, since sacraments are outward bodily acts."[1]
>
> PETER LEITHART, FEDERAL VISION PROPONENT

> "The Bible doesn't know about a distinction between being internally in the covenant, really in the covenant, and being only externally in the covenant, just being in the sphere of the covenant. The Bible speaks about the reality, the efficacy of baptism. Every baptized person is truly a member of God's covenant."[2]
>
> JOHN BARACH, FEDERAL VISION PROPONENT

---

1 Record of the Case, Standing Judicial Commission of the Presbyterian Church in America, Case 2012-5, RE Gerald Hedman vs. Pacific Northwest Presbytery, 200.

2 John Barach "Covenant and History" (2002 Auburn Avenue Presbyterian Church Pastors Conference sermon). Quoted in Guy Prentiss Waters, *The Federal Vision and Covenant Theology: A Comparative Analysis* (Phillipsburg, New Jersey: P & R Publishing, 2006), 15.

Historic Christianity and the Federal Vision

The first quote above by Federal Vision proponent, Peter Leithart, acknowledges the fundamental problem of the Federal Vision system. It is based on a flawed theory that something external can penetrate to the inner person. It is a system which substitutes the sacrament of baptism for the subjective work of the Holy Spirit in the souls of believers. The Federal Vision teaches that the water of baptism accomplishes that inner change. Guy Waters was certainly correct when he wrote about the Federal Vision:

> Distinctions within the covenant of grace based on subjective considerations are either muted or rejected.[3]

Yet, it is impossible for such proponents to be completely consistent in emphasizing the objectivity of the covenant and rejecting (or muting) the subjective aspect of the same. This inconsistency is seen throughout the Federal Vision system. Thus, Leithart tries to explain the supposed power that water baptism has to penetrate into the soul of the baptized. One of the greatest theologians of the church, Francis Turretin, addressed this matter decisively:

> Third, the word does not confer grace by any power implanted in the sound or in the letters, but by the power of the Spirit who accompanies it. There is, however, the same relation here of the word and the sacraments and they confer grace in the same way. . .
>
> Fourth, if the sacraments physically contained grace in themselves and conferred it by an inherent force, grace would be tied to the sacraments. This cannot be said without absurdity. . .
>
> Fifth, nothing corporeal can by its own power effect anything spiritual or act upon the soul.[4]

Leithart's views are not without precedent in the church, though. The Council of Trent endorsed the same idea when it stated:

> If anyone says that in the three sacraments, to wit, baptism, confirmation and order, a mark is not impressed upon the soul, that is, a certain spiritual and indelible sign, whence they cannot be repeated, let him be anathema.[5]

Leithart's comparison in Chapter 6 of the efficacy of baptism to

---

3 Ibid.

4 James T. Dennison, ed., George Musgrave Giger, trans., Francis Turretin, *Institutes of Elenctic Theology*, Volume 3 (Phillipsburg, New Jersey: P&R Publishing Company, 1997), 364-365.

5 Ibid., 375.

the efficacy of ecclesiastical orders is an inherently Catholic position. The Council of Trent, in the above quote, connects baptism, confirmation, and holy orders together as supposed spiritual marks that are impressed on the soul. It is not the Westminster Confession of Faith, or some other Reformed confession, that is the basis for the Federal Vision's views on baptismal efficacy. Rather, it is the Council of Trent and the Catholic Church that is the mother of such views.

Key Assessment: The Federal Vision says that the outward sacrament of baptism has the inherent power to penetrate to the inner heart of the recipients.

Leithart's quote in this chapter reveals a glimpse into the doubts that he and other Federal Vision proponents must have about their system. He is correct. The Federal Vision cannot be maintained unless those who hold to it can prove that water baptism has the power to efficaciously penetrate into the inner person of the recipients. Yet, that is something they cannot do. Interestingly, Leithart's quote is an instance of the inconsistency and inherent contradictions of the Federal Vision system. They can never quite decide if they believe in the "objectivity of the covenant" or if they believe that the sacraments convey internal grace as well. In his quote above Leithart argues that his sacramental theology requires that an external reality must have the power to penetrate to the inner man, or else the Federal Vision has no grounds for their views. Yet, penetrating to the inner man means that the sacraments are doing something that is internal and subjective—and that the sacraments are no longer external and objective only.

The Sign and the Thing Signified

Much of the confusion about the sacraments is due to a failure to distinguish between the sign and the thing signified. The outward sign is a symbol of the inward spiritual grace conferred by the Holy Spirit to the elect alone. Larger Catechism Question 163 defines the sacraments in this way:

> The parts of a sacrament are two, the one an outward and sensible sign used according to Christ's appointment; the other an inward and spiritual grace thereby signified.

In the context of Paul's epistle to the Romans, Romans 2:28, 29 is part of his proof that even the Jews were under the wrath of God. Matthew Henry gives us the key to Paul's meaning in these verses when he transposes them into Christian terms:

> He is not a Christian, that is one outwardly, nor is baptism, that which is outward in the flesh; but he is a Christian, that is one inwardly, and baptism is that of the heart, in the spirit, and not in the letter; whose praise is not of men, but of God.[6]

If circumcision is not outward in the flesh, neither is baptism. If Jews are not such on the basis of fleshly descent alone, then neither are Christians such on the basis of outward baptism alone. Paul's words in the second chapter of Romans are based on the Old Testament interpretation of circumcision. The law and the prophets with one united voice proclaimed that true circumcision was a matter of the heart. They distinguished between those who were circumcised in the flesh, but whose hearts were still uncircumcised. As Jeremiah 9:25, 26 says:

> "Behold, the days are coming", declares the LORD, "when *I will punish all who are circumcised and yet uncircumcised*—Egypt, and Judah, Edom and the sons of Ammon, and Moab and all those inhabiting the desert who clip the hair on their temples; for *all the nations are uncircumcised, and all the house of Israel are uncircumcised of heart.*

The nations Jeremiah mentions in the last quote—Egypt, Edom, Ammon, and Moab—all practiced the rite of circumcision.[7] Yet, Jeremiah accuses those nations of being uncircumcised in heart and Israel to be just like them. Thus, Calvin made the following valuable comment on Jeremiah 9:26:

> Hence the prophet says, that though they had the visible symbol in the flesh, they were yet uncircumcised in heart, and ought therefore to be classed with the nations. We see how sharply he reproves them; for God cares not for the external symbol, but regards the chief thing, the circumcision of the heart. . .
>
> It is a common thing with Moses and the Prophets to call an unre-

---

6 Geoffrey B. Wilson, *Romans: A Digest of Reformed Comment* (Edinburgh: Banner of Truth Trust, 1977), 49.

7 Cf. "Circumcision" in John McClintock and James Strong, *Cyclopedia of Biblical, Theological, and Ecclesiastical Literature,* Volume II, C-D (Grand Rapids: Baker Book House, 1981), 347-353. Cf. also "The Epistle of Barnabas" in J. B. Lightfoot, *The Apostolic Fathers* (Grand Rapids: Baker Book House, 1973), 145.

newed heart, uncircumcision, and to say that the people are uncircumcised in heart: for circumcision, while an evidence of free salvation in Christ, at the same time initiated the Jews into the worship, and service of God, and proved the necessity of a new life; it was in short a sign both of repentance and of faith. . . And hence Paul calls the external rite, when the sign separated from its reality and substance, the letter of circumcision; and on the other hand he calls that the true circumcision, which is in secret and in the spirit. We may say the same of baptism, — that the literal baptism avails hypocrites nothing, for they receive only the naked sign; and therefore we must come to the spirit of baptism, to the thing itself; for the interior power is renovation, when our old man is crucified in us, and when we rise again with Christ into newness of life.[8]

Water baptism, according to Calvin, is never sufficient. True Christians are not those who are merely baptized with water. Water baptism is a symbol of an even greater work of God in the hearts of His people. This work of grace is neither extended to all who are circumcised nor to all who are baptized with water. Rather, the work of grace is bestowed through the Holy Spirit to the elect alone. Otherwise, the prophet could not upbraid the Israelites for being uncircumcised of heart.

Theories of the Magical Efficacy of Sacraments
In his work, *Biblical Theology: Old and New Testaments*, Geerhardus Vos comments on Satan's suggestion to Eve in Genesis 3:5 that eating of the fruit of the tree of the knowledge of good and evil would open her eyes, and Adam's eyes too, and cause them to be like God knowing good and evil:

> This carries a twofold implication: first that the tree has in itself, magically, the power of conferring knowledge of good and evil. This lowers the plane of the whole transaction from the religious and moral to the pagan-magical sphere. And secondly, Satan explains the prohibition from the motive of envy. This also we have already found to be a piece of pagan-mythological interpretation.[9]

Vos' analysis of Genesis 3:5 is indirectly a damning indictment of the Federal Vision's theory that sacramental theology depends on ex-

---

8 John Calvin, *A Commentary on Jeremiah*, Volume One (Edinburgh, Scotland and Carlisle, Pennsylvania: The Banner of Truth Trust, 1989), 507-508.

9 Geerhardus Vos, *Biblical Theology: Old and New Testaments* (Edinburgh, Scotland and Carlisle Pennsylvania: The Banner of Truth Trust, 1975), 32-33.

ternal realities having the power to penetrate to the inner man. We agree with Vos. It is not the external reality of either the tree of the knowledge of good and evil or the New Testament sacraments that penetrate to the inner man. The Scripture nowhere teaches such a pagan-magical idea. Rather, it is the Spirit of God who penetrates the inner man of the elect, and only the elect, in making the sacraments efficacious unto salvation.

Likewise, the idea of the efficacy of water of baptism predates the New Testament church. For several centuries before Christ, many pagan religions practiced a form of baptism among their sacred rites. Such pagan religions generally believed that the water of baptism has a magical, cleansing efficacy to forgive sins and to regenerate. The doctrine of *ex opere operato* did not originate with the Catholic Church, but predated it several centuries among the pagans. In his book, *The Axioms of Religion*, E. Y. Mullins, the late nineteenth- and early twentieth-century Southern Baptist theologian, wrote:

> Paganism had certain rites and ceremonies which were analogous in some respects to baptism and the Lord's Supper. With these rites certain mysteries were connected. Weak and carnal Christians lately won from paganism would naturally bring some of their heathen conceptions with them. . .
>
> It was but a single step to transfer the idea of magical efficacy in the heathen rites over to baptism and the Lord's Supper. Accordingly, in the second and third centuries men began to connect remission of sins with water baptism.[10]

There is not a single verse in the Bible that connects magical efficacy with the Old Testament or New Testament sacraments. The theory of baptismal efficacy did not enter the church through the faithful exposition of the Scriptures. Its entrance was from another direction altogether. Henry Hart Milman wrote a three-volume work on church history called, *The History of Christianity, From the Birth of Christ to the Abolition of Paganism in the Roman Empire*. In his first volume, Milman showed that the Jews contracted the religious views of the pagans both through the Babylonian captivity and through the Diaspora during the Roman Empire. Both directly and indirectly, they were influenced by pagan ideas. Both Babylon and Alexandria changed the Jewish religion. As Milman said:

---

10   E. Y. Mullins, *The Axioms of Religion* (Macon, Georgia: Mercer UniversityPress, 2010), 93.

Hence came the mystic Cabala of the Jews, the chief parent of those gnostic opinions, out of which grew the heresies of the early Church: here the Jews, under the Prince of the Captivity, held their famous schools, where learning was embodied in the Babylonian Talmud.[11]

The view of the magical efficacy of baptism entered the church through various avenues. It entered through the Judaizers who were influenced in their views by pagan religious views both in the east (Babylon) and the west (Greeks and Romans). It entered directly through various church fathers who tried to synthesize pagan philosophy with the Scripture. It entered through the recent converts to Christianity from paganism who brought with them their views of the magical powers of rites to convey grace.

Baptismal regeneration did not begin with the fathers of the early church. Rather, the idea of sacramental regeneration was a part of pagan religions centuries before Christ was born in Bethlehem. The Hindus of India were familiar with the term long before the Christian era, and the Brahmins boasted that they were "twice-born" men. The Babylonians connected the second birth with baptism and used the phrase, "baptismal regeneration," to describe their religious experience.[12] Thus, Tertullian stated:

> Well, but the nations, who are strangers to all understanding of spiritual powers ascribe to their idols the imbuing of waters with the self-same efficacy." (So they do) . . . and they presume that the effect of their doing that is their regeneration and the remission of the penalties due to their perjuries. Among the ancients, again, whoever had defiled himself with murder, was wont to go in quest of purifying waters.[13]

Regeneration, remission of sins, and purification from the defilement of capital crimes, such as murder, were believed by the heathen to be the result of being baptized with water. All of this was a part of pagan religious belief before Christ, before the Apostles, and before the doctrine of baptismal regeneration became the official doctrine of the Catholic Church. Where did the pagans get this doctrine of baptismal regeneration? Tertullian gives us the answer:

---

11 Henry Hart Milman, *The History of Christianity, From the Birth of Christ to the Abolition of Paganism in the Roman Empire*, Volume I (3 vols.) (London: John Murray, 1867), 60.

12 Alexander Hislop, *The Two Babylons* (Neptune, New Jersey: Loizeaux Brothers, Inc., 1959), 132.

13 Alexander Roberts and James Donaldson, eds., *Ante-Nicene Fathers, Latin Christianity: Its Founder, Tertullian*, Volume 3 (Peabody, Massachusetts: Hendrickson Publishers, 1999), 671.

> By the devil, of course, to whom pertain those wiles which pervert the truth, and who, by the mystic rites of his idols, vies even with the essential portions of the sacraments of God. He, too, baptizes some, that is, his own believers and faithful followers; he promises the putting away of sins by a laver (of his own); and if my memory still serves me, Mithra there (in the kingdom of Satan), sets his mark on the foreheads of his soldiers; celebrates also the oblation of bread, and introduces an image of a resurrection.[14]

Vos, Mullins, Milman, and Tertullian all agree on the essentials. The doctrine of baptismal regeneration predates the Christian church and is found among the pagan religions. Vos and Tertullian go one step further back in showing these views of the magical efficacy of religious rites have their source in the subtlety of the Devil. The Devil, in these pagan rites, has substituted magical efficacy for the power of the Holy Spirit. In his comments on the baptism of Simon Magus, Calvin rejects the magical potency of the sacraments and emphasizes the work of the Holy Spirit:

> It is quite plain from Simon's example that the grace, which is figured in baptism, is not conferred on all men indiscriminately when they are baptized. It is a dogma of the Papists that unless anyone presents the obstacle of mortal sin, all men receive the truth and the effect of the signs. So they attribute a magical potency to the sacraments, as they are beneficial without faith... In baptism we are washed from our sins, but Paul teaches that our washing is the work of the Holy Spirit (Titus 3:5).[15]

In his *Systematic Theology*, Douglas F. Kelly points out that Scripture condemned pagan religion as inspired by Satan:

> The New Testament saw Satan behind the gods of this world (2 Cor. 4:4 and Rev. 13:2), so when Moses warned the Israelites not to worship the gods of the Land they were entering, Satan was behind the whole polytheistic system.[16]

The Apostle Paul said the same kind of thing in 1 Corinthians

---

14 Ibid., 262.

15 David W. Torrance and Thomas F. Torrance, eds., John W. Fraser and W. J. G. McDonald, trans., *Calvin's Commentaries: The Acts of the Apostles, 1-13* (Grand Rapids, Michigan: Wm. B. Eerdmans Publishing Company, 1979), 233, 235.

16 Douglas F. Kelly, *Systematic Theology: Grounded in the Scripture and Understood in the Light of the Church*, Volume Two, *The Beauty of Christ: A Trinitarian Vision* (Fearn, Ross-Shire, Scotland: Christian Focus Publications, 2014), 325.

10:20: "No, but I say that the things which the Gentiles sacrifice, they sacrifice to demons and not to God; and I do not want you to be sharers in demons." Commenting on this verse, Charles Hodge wrote:

> Paul had just said that the heathen gods were nothing; to admit now that there were *deities* in the Grecian sense of the word *daimonion*, would be to contradict himself. We must understand the apostle, therefore, as saying, on the one hand, that the gods of the heathen were imaginary beings; and on the other, that their sacrifices were really offered to evil spirits. In what sense, however, is this true? The heathen certainly did not intend to worship evil spirits. Nevertheless they did it. Men of the world do not intend to serve Satan, when they break the laws of God in the pursuit of the objects of their desire. Still in doing so they are really obeying the will of the great adversary, yielding to his impulses, and fulfilling his designs. He is therefore said to be the god of this world. To him all sin is an offering and a homage. We are shut up to the necessity of worshipping God or Satan; for all refusing or neglecting to worship the true God, or giving to any other the worship that is due to him alone, is the worshipping of Satan and his angels. It is true therefore, in the highest sense, that what the heathen offer they offer to devils.[17]

What the Apostle Paul and Charles Hodge say about the heathen sacrifices must also be said about everyone who holds to a theory of the magical efficacy of sacraments. In their adoption of any magical view of sacramental efficacy, such people have unwittingly rejected the teaching of the Scripture about the sacraments and true worship. That leads them also to the rejection of the scriptural doctrine of salvation. There are only two religions, as Hodge wrote. One is true, the other is false. One is scriptural; the other is founded in paganism and inspired by Satan. Whoever adopts the pagan magical view of rites and sacraments is necessarily guilty of substituting heathen worship for the worship of God—whether intentionally or unintentionally.

Key Assessment: The theory of the magical efficacy of sacraments to penetrate the heart of the recipients has its roots in pagan religions and pagan philosophy.

In the matter of the sacraments, therefore, magical efficacy and the power of the Holy Spirit are juxtaposed. It is a fatal flaw of the propo-

---

17   Charles Hodge, *An Exposition of the First Epistle to the Corinthians* (Grand Rapids, Michigan: Wm. B. Eerdmans Publishing Company, 1969), 193.

nents of the Federal Vision that they hold to a view that replaces the work of the Holy Spirit with the magical working of the sacraments, a relic of paganism. It is beside the point that they define efficacy in such a vague way (i.e., that it is more than nothing but that it is less than permanently and always resulting in salvation), that it can be increased or decreased whenever necessary. By teaching that the sacraments, particularly baptism, have the power to convey new life, justification, forgiveness of sins and other graces temporarily, they have chosen a pagan magical definition and rejected the scriptural position.

Various Views of Baptismal Efficacy

The view that the sacraments have magical efficacy to confer grace is at the heart of the problem with the Federal Vision and the New Perspectives on Paul. For all the supposed differences between them, both of these theological movements assert that the benefits of Christ's redemption are conferred by water baptism. Protestant and Reformed confessions have always restricted the grace of the sacraments to the elect alone, but Peter Leithart says such graces belong to everyone who is baptized:

> All this the baptized is not only offered, but receives. All this he receives simply by virtue of being baptized.[18]

Again, Leithart says:

> Baptism confers grace *ex opere operato*. . . If grace is the favor of God manifested in the bestowal of favors, then baptism is and confers grace.[19]

The views of the proponents of the Federal Vision in both these areas are nearly identical to the position of the Council of Trent, quoted in the previous chapter, that sacraments can efficiently convey grace. The graces conveyed by baptism, according to the Catholic Catechism, are the forgiveness of sins, the new birth in the Spirit, purification from sin, adoption as a son of God, participation in the divine nature, and membership in the body of Christ.[20]

Yet, the views of the Federal Vision on baptismal efficacy vacil-

---

18 Record of the Case, Standing Judicial Commission, 2012-5, 508.
19 Ibid., 288.
20 *Catechism of the Catholic Church* (New York, New York: Doubleday, 1992), 353-4.

late between Pelagianism and the Semi-Pelagianism of the Council of Trent. When the Federal Vision over-emphasizes the objectivity of the sacraments, it veers towards Pelagianism. When it asserts, as Leithart does above, that sacraments must have the power to reach the inner man, it veers towards Semi-Pelagianism. The views of Pelagius on baptism were developed in his commentary on Romans, wherein he taught that baptism bestows grace[21], forgiveness of sins[22], good works[23], love for God[24], righteousness[25], crucifixion with Christ[26], sanctification[27], justification[28], burial with Christ, death to our sins, renunciation of our former life, and newness of life.[29]

The Federal Vision, Thomas Aquinas, the Papacy, and Pelagius all assert that baptism confers the benefits of Christ's redemption to every person baptized, but there are nuances of differences between

---

21 Theodore De Bruyn, Trans., *Pelagius' Commentary on St. Paul's Epistle to the Romans* (Oxford, England: Clarendon Press, 1993), 60. "*Through whom we received grace and apostleship* (Romans 1:5). Grace in baptism; apostleship when he was directed by the Holy Spirit (cf. Acts 13:2): for 'apostle' in Greek means 'sent' in Latin."

22 Ibid., 81. "*Having been freely justified by his grace* (Romans 3:24). Without the works of the law, through baptism, whereby he has freely forgiven the sins of all, though they are undeserving."

23 Ibid., pp. 83, 85. "*For we deem that a person is justified through faith without the works of the law* (Romans 3:28). Some misuse this verse to do away with works of righteousness, asserting that faith by itself can suffice [for one who has been baptized]. . . But by adding 'the works of the law' he indicates there is [also] a [work] of grace [which those who have been baptized ought to perform]."

24 Ibid., 85. "*Blessed is the one against whom the Lord has not reckoned sin* (Romans 4:8). But others say that when sins have been forgiven in baptism, love for God is increased, which covers a multitude of sins [and] finally keeps them from being counted against one as long as daily good works surpass past misdeeds (cf. 1 Pet. 4:8)."

25 Ibid., 95. "*For if by the sin of one person death reigned through one person, how much more shall those who have received an abundance of grace and of the gift and of righteousness reign in life through the one person Jesus Christ* (Romans 5:17). By which he has forgiven many sins; and an abundance of the gift of the Holy Spirit, because there are many gifts (cf. 1 Cor. 12:4); and also righteousness is given through baptism, and is not gained through merit."

26 Ibid., 97. "*Knowing this, that our old self was at the same time crucified* (Romans 6:6). Understand that through baptism you, who have been made a member of his body, were crucified with Christ (cf. Eph. 5:30)."

27 Ibid., 100. "*You have your benefit in sanctification, and have life eternal as the end* (Romans 6:22). This itself is already a benefit, that, having been sanctified by baptism, you are alive."

28 Ibid., 113. "*And those he predestined he also called, and those he called he also justified, and those he justified he also exalted* (Romans 8:30). Therefore, they are called to believe through the preaching, and are justified through baptism when they believe."

29 Ibid., 96 "He shows that we were baptized in this manner so that through the mystery we are buried with Christ, dying to our offences and renouncing our former life, so that just as [the Father] is glorified in the resurrection of the Son, so too on account of the newness of our way of life he is glorified by all, provided that not even the signs of the old self are recognizable in us."

them. Between the time of Pelagius and the Papacy during the Reformation, the Schoolmen took up Pelagius' heretical views on the sacraments. As Calvin wrote:

> The schools of the Sophists have taught with remarkable agreement that the sacraments of the new law (those now used in the Christian church) justify and confer grace, provided we do not set up a barrier of mortal sin. How deadly and pestilential this notion is cannot be expressed—and the more so because for many centuries it has been a current claim in a good part of the world, to the great loss of the Church.[30]

A few of the Sophists to whom Calvin was referring were Thomas Aquinas and Peter Lombard. Aquinas said that baptism confers forgiveness of sins, justification, incorporation into the passion and death of Christ, the washing of guilt, the crucifixion of the old man, the grace of the Holy Spirit, the fullness of virtue, a new birth into a spiritual life, inward enlightenment by God, good works and sanctification, and newness of life[31]. Yet, Aquinas, like the Federal Vision proponents, said baptism is ultimately effectual only for those who respond with sincerity, which left open the possibility of a baptized person falling from his state of grace. Thus, the grace of God is nullified by man's insincerity in the Thomist[32] system.

Calvin completely repudiated the sacramental views of the Schoolmen and Aquinas. His comments leave no doubt how dangerous he considered such a view:

> Of a certainty it is diabolical. For in promising a righteousness apart from faith, it hurls the soul headlong to destruction. Secondly, because it draws the cause of righteousness from the sacraments, it binds men's pitiable minds (of themselves more than enough inclined to earth) in this superstition, so that they repose in the appearance of a physical thing rather than in God Himself.[33]

Surely, proponents of the Federal Vision would retort that they do not believe in "a righteousness apart from faith," but they most certainly teach that baptism confers the benefits of Christ's redemp-

---

30 John T. McNeill, ed., Ford Lewis Battles, trans., *Calvin: Institutes of the Christian Religion*, Volume Two (Philadelphia: Westminster Press, 1960), 1289.

31 Thomas Aquinas, *Summa Theologica*, Translated by the Dominican Province (Forgotten Books, 2007), 124-138.

32 The school of thought that followed the teaching of Thomas Aquinas.

33 Calvin, *Institutes*, Volume Two, p. 1290, 1293, 1303, et. al.

tion even to those who have not yet believed unto eternal salvation. They teach that grace is conferred by baptism *before faith* and where true faith may never exist, which necessarily makes it "apart from faith." If it is before faith, it is necessarily apart from faith. That is the same position against which Calvin contended in the above quotes.

The views of the Schoolmen were developed from the sacramental views of the early church, particularly Pelagius, who taught that baptism imparts, objectively and externally, the graces of salvation. Yet none of these benefits is of any importance unless the baptized person continues to do good works until the end of his life. Prior to Pelagius, similar views were held by some early church leaders, the Judaizers, and the Pharisees.

Comparison Chart

The chart below compares the views of the Federal Vision (with Leithart as an example) with the views of Pelagius, Aquinas, and Rome:

Comparison of Views on Baptismal Efficacy

The Federal Vision and Peter Leithart	Roman Catholicism	Thomas Aquinas	Pelagius
New Life	New Birth	New Birth	New Life
Justification	Justification	Justification	Justification
Adoption	Adoption		Member of His body
Arrabon (Earnest) of Spirit	Life of Spirit	Grace of Holy Spirit	Gift of Holy Spirit
Sanctification	Sanctification	Sanctification	Sanctification
Divine Power	Participation in Divine Nature	Inward enlightenment by God	Love for God
Union with Christ	Union with Christ	Incorporation into Christ	
Spiritual Cleansing	Purification from sin	Washing of guilt	Crucified with Christ
Forgiveness of sins	Forgiveness of sins	Forgiveness of sins	Forgiveness of sins
Resurrection with Christ			Glorification with Christ

Westminster Confession of Faith

Against the Federal Vision view of the efficacy of baptism, the Westminster Confession of Faith 28.6 states:

> The efficacy of Baptism is not tied to the moment of time wherein it is administered; yet, notwithstanding, by the right use of the ordinance, the grace promised is not only offered, but really exhibited, and conferred, by the Holy Ghost, to such (whether of age or infants) as that grace belongeth unto, according to the counsel of God's own will.

These are two very different views of the order of salvation. The Federal Vision, the Papacy, Aquinas, and Pelagius hold that all the benefits of Christ, except perseverance, are conveyed to everyone who is baptized. The Westminster Standards teach that the efficacy of baptism is not tied to the moment it is administered, but that grace is conferred by the Holy Spirit according to the counsel of God's will to those who are the elect; which grace includes perseverance and all the other benefits of Christ's redemption and results infallibly in eternal salvation.

Development of the Sacramental Views of Pelagius

Pelagius developed his views on baptismal efficacy because he denied that the baptism of children is for the remission of sins. Thus, he devised another purpose for the sacrament. His solution was that baptism prepares children for the kingdom of heaven by giving them all the graces they need for eternity. Pelagius, therefore, did not reject all teaching about grace. He believed in God's common grace. He believed that God's grace was evident in creation, in the endowments He gave to man, in the law and in the gospel. Pelagius, however, did not believe grace is efficacious and saving. He asserted the free will of man in opposition to the saving, efficacious grace of God. In the place of saving grace, Pelagius developed his views of baptismal regeneration.

Yet, Pelagius believed that man does not need the work of the Holy Spirit in his heart to regenerate him. Regeneration was objective and external only in his view. Thomas Aquinas and the Council of Trent disagreed with Pelagianism at this point. Both Aquinas and Trent held that grace is subjective and internal. For instance, Aquinas wrote:

There is a two-fold element in the Law of the Gospel. There is the chief element, viz., the grace of the Holy Ghost bestowed inwardly.[34]

The Federal Vision, Aquinas, and the Council of Trent

Some Federal Visionists, particularly Peter Leithart, claim to find their views of baptism in Aquinas' writings. Yet, Aquinas believed in the inward grace of the Holy Spirit, and his views became the basis for the views of the Council of Trent. The Council of Trent in their Seventh Session, specifically the section "On the Sacraments in General," said:

> CANON VI.—If any one saith, that the sacraments of the New Law do not contain the grace which they signify; or, that they do not confer that grace on those who do not place an obstacle thereunto; as though they were merely outward signs of grace or justice received through faith, and certain marks of the Christian profession, whereby believers are distinguished amongst men from unbelievers; let him be anathema.

There are a couple of things that stand out in this quote from Trent. First, the Council clearly states that the sacraments confer the inward, internal, and subjective grace which they signify. Second, the Council repudiates the idea that the sacraments are merely "marks of Christian profession." Pelagius was guilty of this latter error, as quoted by Augustine.

Leithart's definition of baptismal efficacy differs from the Westminster Standards and the great Reformed theologians. He defines the efficacy of baptism in this way:

> Baptism is God's act, and it is as real and objective as the water on the baptized. Everyone who is baptized is claimed by Christ as His own. Baptism is not double, but the response to baptism is.[35]

Leithart's definition of "real," whether grace or relationship, in the context of baptismal efficacy must be understood as objective and external, as the above quote clarifies. It is not a real relationship as evangelical Christians define such. It is not a subjective relationship with grace being bestowed by God internally through the work of the Holy Spirit. Rather, it is real only in the sense that it objectively makes the baptized person a member of the visible church.

---

34 St. Thomas Aquinas, *Summa Theologica* in 3 Vols. Volume 1, Fathers of the English Dominican Province, trans., (New York, Boston, Cincinnati, Chicago, San Francisco: Benziger Brothers, 1947), 1103.

35 Record of the Case, Standing Judicial Commission, Case 2012-5, 202.

Federal Vision proponents derive their understanding of baptismal efficacy from St. Thomas Aquinas and the Medieval Scholastic scholars. Auburn Avenue Presbyterian Church in Monroe, Louisiana once had a statement on their website that for a correct doctrine of justification the church must go back to the time before the Reformation. During that period, the views of Aquinas held court and were later ratified by the Catholic Church at the Council of Trent. As Leithart said:

> Sacramental theology must be purged of mechanistic models and metaphors. Aquinas says that sacraments are like tools in the hands of God... In place of mechanistic categories, I have tried to think through issues of sacramental efficacy in personalist categories.[36]

The distinction between mechanistic and personalist categories of sacramental efficacy appears to mean that the sacrament "effects" something different for every person. That only further complicates the whole matter. The main point, though, is that Leithart, as a Federal Vision advocate, appeals to Aquinas for his views. Yet, Aquinas held that baptismal efficacy was subjective and internal. As Aquinas wrote in the *Summa Theologica*:

> The entire justification of the ungodly consists as to its origin in the infusion of grace.[37]

There are many similarities to Aquinas in the views of the Federal Vision, but there are some important distinctions. Aquinas considered himself a follower of Augustine, but his fundamental problem was that he departed from Augustine on the nature of the fall. He thought that the intellect of man was not affected by the fall and this led him to many errors concerning theology. Aquinas tried to combine pagan philosophy with Christian theology and a perusal of his masterpiece, *Summa Theologica*, reveals how frequently he appealed to Aristotle, Cicero, or other pagan philosophers for support of his views. In fact, Aquinas rarely appeals directly to the Scripture alone. In *Escape from Reason*, Francis Schaeffer puts his finger on the problem with Aquinas' theology:

---

36 Ibid., 187.

37 Aquinas, *Summa Theologica*, Volume 1, 1149-1150.

In Aquinas' view the will of man was fallen, but the intellect was not. From this incomplete view of the biblical Fall flowed all the subsequent difficulties. Man's intellect became autonomous. In one realm man was now independent, autonomous.

This sphere of the autonomous in Aquinas takes on various forms. One result, for example, was the development of natural theology. In this view, natural theology is a theology that could be pursued independently from the Scriptures.

From the basis of this autonomous principle, philosophy also became free, and was separated from revelation. Therefore philosophy began to take wings, as it were, and fly off wherever it wished, without relationship to Scriptures. . . Aquinas had opened the way to an autonomous philosophy, and once the movement gained momentum, there was soon a flood.[38]

Summary

For all of their emphasis on the objectivity of the covenant, it is interesting that Federal Vision proponents fall back into subjectivism on the matter of the efficacy of the sacraments. They take a magical efficacy view of the sacraments which has been perpetuated in creedal form by Catholicism and the Council of Trent. Such a view of the efficacy of the sacraments is essential to their system, as Leithart acknowledges. Yet, it is not a Christian position. It is a position that is tied to paganism and the devil's lie to Eve in the Garden of Eden. This view of the magical efficacy of the sacraments reveals another inconsistency in the Federal Vision system. They deny the true subjective grace of God while promoting a false subjectivism of the sacraments under the banner of restoring the objectivity of the covenant.

Conclusion

It is interesting, therefore, that both Pelagius and the Federal Vision in the chart above speak of "new life" being bestowed by baptism, while Aquinas and the Catholic Church speak of the "new birth." There is no scriptural distinction between those two terms but the Federal Vision certainly attempts to distinguish them, preferring to use the term new life. It is also interesting that both Pelagius and the Federal Vision believe that baptismal efficacy is external and objective only, while Aquinas and the Catholic Church believe it is also subjective and internal. The fact is that the Catholic Church from the Council

---

38 Francis A. Schaeffer, *Escape from Reason* (Downers Grove, Illinois: Intervarsity Press, 1968), 11-13.

of Trent onwards was basically Semi-Pelagian. They held to subjective and internal grace, but not efficacious grace. Herman Bavinck summarizes the true position concerning baptismal efficacy:

> True, essential Christian baptism is that which is administered to believers. Although baptism, like the external calling, still produces many a blessing even for unbelievers, its fruit and full power can only be enjoyed by believers. Objectively baptism, like the Word, remains the same. Those who in faith receive the Word and hence also those who in faith receive baptism really obtain the promises that God has attached to it. God remains true to himself and bestows salvation on everyone who believes. But faith is not everyone's possession. Ultimately the fruit of baptism is only enjoyed by those who are elect and therefore come to faith in God's time.[39]

The Federal Vision errs by making baptism efficacious for all the baptized before faith and even without saving faith in Christ. Its proponents mistake God's promises in baptism to be unconditional and they neglect the scriptural conditions of repentance and faith. They so objectify baptism that they deny the importance of the subjective work of the Spirit in the grace of regeneration and saving faith. Yet, they are confused even on this point. They assert that baptism confers a real relationship with Christ that can be lost. That leaves undefined whether that "real relationship" is subjective or only objective. The Federal Vision often vacillates on such matters, which is one of the main reasons their teaching is so confusing. Herman Bavinck's position is the correct one. Objectively, the promises to baptism remain the same, but those promises must be received by faith. Unbelievers may receive many temporary blessings from their baptism, but the reality of grace is reserved for the elect alone.

---

39 John Bolt, ed., John Vriend, trans., Herman Bavinck, *Reformed Dogmatics*, Volume 4: *Holy Spirit, Church, and New Creation* (Grand Rapids, Michigan: Baker Academic, 2008), 532.

-8-
The Federal Vision and Baptismal Regeneration

> "Baptism is the moment when we see the transition from death to life and a person is saved. . . This covenant sign and seal marks his conversion and his entrance into the church as the body of Christ. From the perspective of the covenant, he is united to Christ when he is baptized . . . Baptism marks the entrance into the kingdom of God and the beginning of life-long training as kingdom subjects. According to the Great Commission, conversion without baptism is an anomaly. A sinner is not really 'converted' until he is baptized. . . Christians are those who have been baptized. Unbelievers are those who have not been baptized."[1]

NORMAN SHEPHERD, FORMER PROFESSOR AT WESTMINSTER THEOLOGICAL SEMINARY IN PHILADELPHIA, PA, WHOSE THEOLOGICAL SYSTEM, SHEPHERDISM, HAS GREATLY INFLUENCED THE FEDERAL VISION

> "Baptism unites us to Christ and his church and thus in him gives us new life [Rom. 6:11; 2 Cor. 5:17 cited]. By our baptism we have been reborn, in this sense, having died with Christ, we have been raised with him."[2]

STEVE WILKINS, FEDERAL VISION PROPONENT

---

[1] Norman Shepherd, *The Call of Grace: How the Covenant Illuminates Salvation and Evangelism* (Phillipsburg, New Jersey: P&R Publishing Company, 2000), 94, 100, 101.

[2] Steve Wilkins, "The legacy of the Halfway Covenant," (Monroe, Louisiana, 2002 Auburn Avenue Presbyterian Church Pastors Conference lecture). Cited in Guy Prentiss Waters, *The Federal Vision and Covenant Theology: A Comparative Analysis* (Phillipsburg, New Jersey: P&R Publishing, 2006), 235.

Most of the Federal Vision proponents once claimed to hold to baptismal regeneration in some sense, but recently they have tried to distance themselves from baptismal regeneration theories while retaining the doctrines that undergird them. Some doctrine of baptismal regeneration is essential to the development of the Federal Vision system, as this chapter will show. Yet, those who signed "A Joint Federal Vision Profession" in 2007 appear to back away from any such doctrine with the following statement:

> We *deny* the common misunderstanding of baptismal regeneration—i.e. that an effectual call or rebirth is automatically wrought in the one baptized.[3]

At first glance, that statement seems to repudiate any baptismal regeneration view, but that is not what the signers of the "Profession" say. They deny holding to any view which says that every baptized person is the subject of an *effectual call or rebirth*. They deny that every baptized person receives the subjective grace of the Holy Spirit of regeneration and effectual grace. They also deny holding views such as the "common misunderstanding of baptismal regeneration."

Protestant and Catholic Theories of Baptismal Regeneration

In *Infant Baptism Scriptural and Reasonable*, Samuel Miller shows that there are actually two common theories of baptismal regeneration which have been held by some Protestants. The first theory is "that the inward grace of regeneration *always* accompanies the outward sign of baptism."[4] This first theory emphasizes the subjective experience of grace through the operation of the Holy Spirit.

The second theory is that "baptism is that rite which marks and ratifies the introduction of its subject into the visible kingdom of Christ; that in this ordinance the baptized person is brought into a new state or relation to Christ, and his sacred family; and that this new state or relation is designated in the scripture by the term *regeneration*, being intended to express an *ecclesiastical birth*, that is, being

---

3 "A Joint Federal Vision Profession", *Credenda Agenda*, Volume 19, Series 3, Special Edition, (2007): 12.

4 Samuel Miller, *Infant Baptism Scriptural and Reasonable: and Baptism by Sprinkling or Affusion the Most Edifying Mode* (Philadelphia: Presbyterian Board of Publication, 1835), 102.

born into the visible kingdom of the Redeemer."[5] This second theory emphasizes the objective sense of grace.

There are differences between these two theories, but there are also similarities. The first theory says the inward grace of regeneration is bestowed whenever baptism with water is performed. The second says that the regeneration which takes place at baptism is an ecclesiastical (or objective) regeneration only. Yet, both theories deny the efficacious grace of the Holy Spirit. The first theory says baptism bestows true subjective grace, but that grace is not efficacious. It depends on man's free will and, therefore, does not always result in eternal salvation. Effectual calling in the Scripture always leads to glory because it is the new birth of the Holy Spirit which cannot be lost. Neither the baptismal regeneration theories held by some Protestants (including the Federal Vision proponents) nor the theories held by Romanists or Eastern Orthodoxy teach that effectual calling is bestowed through baptism. Everyone who holds to any theory of baptismal regeneration believes that regeneration can be lost. Thus, it does not matter whether the regeneration is inward or ecclesiastical. The grace of regeneration can be lost either way. Neither position, according to its own beliefs, is guaranteed to result in salvation.

Most of the proponents of the Federal Vision hold views on baptism that are similar to the second theory of baptismal regeneration given by Miller above. Wilson, Leithart, Wilkins, and others claim to be interested in restoring the objectivity of the covenant. Their emphasis is on objective grace—not subjective grace. They assert that what baptism does is unite the baptized with the visible body of Christ, thereby giving him an ecclesiastical new birth. This second theory would seem to be less dangerous than the first in some ways, but it is still fraught with serious errors. Here again we quote from Miller:

> 1. It makes an unauthorized use of an important theological term. It is vain to say that after giving fair notice of the sense in which we use a term, no misapprehension or harm can result from the constant use of it in that sense. The plea is insufficient. If the sense in question be an unusual and especially unscriptural one, no one can estimate the mischief which may result from the use of it in that sense. . .
> 2. But there is a more serious objection. If men be told that every one who is baptized, is thereby regenerated—"born of God"—"born of

---

5 Ibid., 107.

the Spirit"—made a "new creature in Christ"—will not the mass of mankind, in spite of every precaution and explanation that can be employed, be likely to mistake on a fundamental point; to imagine that the disease of nature is trivial, and that a trivial remedy for it will answer; to lay more stress than they ought upon an external rite, and to make a much lower estimate than they ought of the nature and necessity of that holiness without which no man shall see the Lord?[6]

The assumption that "baptismal regeneration" confers a regeneration which cannot be lost is a misunderstanding of that doctrine. In neither of the two views of baptismal regeneration mentioned by Miller above is regeneration considered permanent. Thus, A. A. Hodge gives the proper definition:

> The Protestant advocates of Baptismal Regeneration. . . hold that baptism is God's ordained instrument of communicating the benefits of redemption in the first instance. That by baptism the guilt of original sin is removed, and the Holy Ghost is given, whose effects remain like a seed in the soul, to be actualized by the free-will of the subject, or neglected and hence rendered abortive. Every infant is regenerated when baptized. If he dies in infancy the seed is actualized in heaven. If he lives to adult age, its result depends upon his use of it.[7]

The doctrine of baptismal regeneration is that everyone who is baptized receives the benefits of Christ's redemption (whether objectively or subjectively), and *if* they persevere to the end they will be saved. Pelagius, Aquinas, Rome, and the Federal Vision proponents all hold to some theory of baptismal regeneration, whether objectively or subjectively. The grand difference between them is that both the Federal Vision and Pelagius hold to a theory of baptismal regeneration like Miller's second illustration above—a theory that emphasizes the objective sense of grace. On the other hand, both Aquinas and Rome (in the Council of Trent) hold to the first theory of baptismal regeneration mentioned by Miller—a theory that emphasizes the subjective experience of grace.

Francis Turretin ridicules the doctrine of baptismal regeneration in the nineteenth topic of his *Institutes of Elenctic Theology* with the following quotes:

---

6 Ibid., 107-8.

7 A. A. Hodge, *Outlines of Theology* (Grand Rapids, Michigan: Zondervan Publishing House, 1972), 627.

The sacraments are nowhere called vehicles or receptacles of grace, but are expressly said to be signs and seals of the covenant of grace.[8]

The sacraments cannot operate, or confer by an inherent power, what according to the institution of God they presuppose or demand beforehand in the subject.[9]

Turretin's argument is both simple and profound. The Federal Vision's teaching on baptismal efficacy has implications for the Lord's Supper also. Leithart's views are to baptism what transubstantiation is to the Lord's Supper. Either both "sacraments are holy signs and seals of the covenant of grace, immediately instituted by God, to represent Christ and His benefits" (WCF 27.1); or, both sacraments have power to efficaciously convey real grace to those who participate in them. The Federal Vision advocates assert that baptism conveys a real relationship with Christ to everyone who is baptized. The Catholic Church additionally contends that the Mass efficaciously conveys the real presence of Christ in the elements. One error necessarily leads to the other. Thus, Calvin refuted transubstantiation by a comparison to what does *not* happen in baptism:

> But this principle was hidden from them, that the bread is a sacrament only to persons to whom the word is directed; just as the water of baptism is not changed in itself.[10]
>
> Sacraments are nothing but instrumental causes of bestowing grace upon us, and are beneficial, and produce their effect only when they are subservient to faith.[11]

Likewise, Thomas Cranmer denied the Papist doctrine of the "real presence" of Christ in the Lord's Supper:

> No more truly is Christ corporally or really present in the due ministration of the Lord's Supper than He is in the due ministration of baptism.[12]

---

8 George Musgrave Giger, trans., James T. Dennison, ed., Francis Turretin, *Institutes of Elenctic Theology*, Volume 3 (Phillipsburg, New Jersey: P&R Publishing, 1997), 364.

9 Ibid.

10 John T. McNeill, ed., Ford Lewis Battles, trans., *Calvin: Institutes of the Christian Religion*, Volume 2 (Philadelphia: The Westminster Press, 1967), 1377.

11 Henry Beveridge, ed. and trans., *John Calvin: Tracts and Letters*, Volume 3: Tracts, Part 3 (Edinburgh, Scotland and Carlisle, Pennsylvania: The Banner of Truth Trust, 2009), 174.

12 John Edmund Cox, ed., *Writings and Disputations of Thomas Cranmer* (Cambridge, England: The University Press, 1844), 3.

John Murray, whom Federal Vision proponents mistakenly quote as favorable to some of their positions, commented on baptismal efficacy:

> As a rite instituted by Christ, baptism is not to be identified with the grace signified and sealed. This is apparent from the terms of institution (Matt. 28:19), and from the nature of baptism as seal. The existence of the grace sealed is presupposed in the giving of the seal. The tenet of baptismal regeneration reverses the order inherent in the definition which Scripture provides. The efficacy resides entirely in the pledge of God's faithfulness.[13]

Baptismal Regeneration and the Proponents of the Federal Vision

In Chapter 7 on baptismal efficacy, there were several quotes from Federal Vision proponents who teach new life in Christ is bestowed through baptism. N. T. Wright, the Church of England's popular former Bishop of Durham, takes a view of baptism which is in keeping with the baptismal heritage of many people, past and present, within that denomination. In one of his books, he wrote the following about baptism:

> In order to understand baptism, here and elsewhere, we have to say something about sacramental theology. I have come to believe that the sacraments are best understood within the theology of creation and new creation, and of the overlapping of heaven and earth, that I have been exploring throughout this book. The resurrection of Jesus has brought about a new state of affairs in cosmic history and reality. . . Thus the event of baptism—the action, the water, the going down and the coming up again, the new clothes—is not just a signpost to the reality of the new birth, the membership (as all birth gives membership) in the new family. It really is the gateway to that membership. . .
>
> The important thing, then, is that in the simple but powerful action of plunging someone into the water in the name of the triune God, there is a real dying to the old creation and a real rising into the new—with all the dangerous privileges and responsibilities that then accompany the new life . . . for many, baptism remains in the background, out of sight, whereas it should be the foundational event for all serious Christian living, all dying to sin and coming alive with Christ.[14]

---

13 *Collected Writings of John Murray*, Volume Two: "Select Lectures in Systematic Theology" (Edinburgh, Scotland and Carlisle, Pennsylvania: The Banner of Truth Trust, 1977), 375.

14 N.T. Wright, *Surprised by Hope: Rethinking Heaven, the Resurrection, and the Mission of the Church* (New York, NY: HarperCollins Publishers, 2008), 271-273.

Key Assessment: The Federal Vision denies baptismal regeneration in the sense of the bestowal of an inner grace that is efficacious to everyone baptized, but believes that baptism bestows an ecclesiastical new birth.

Wright does not distinguish between the elect and the non-elect, between believers and the merely nominal. He says that a real dying and a real rising happen to "someone" whenever that person is plunged into the water. His words are strikingly similar to what the proponents of the Federal Vision state about baptism also. Steve Wilkins, quoted at the beginning of this chapter, further describes what happens in baptism from his perspective:

> In baptism, we are transferred by the power of the spirit, from the old Adam, and the wrath and curse of God which rested upon the old man, into the new man, which is Christ Jesus. We are made new creatures in that sense, by the power of the Spirit, being restored to living communion with God.
>
> By baptism the Spirit joins us to Christ since he is the elect one and the Church is the elect people, we are joined to his body. We therefore are elect. Since he is the justified one, we are justified in him. Since he is the beloved one, we are beloved in him. . .
>
> Being brought from death to life, occurs *formally*, that is its *publicly signified and sealed*, at baptism.[15]

The Federal Vision advocates, therefore, teach that the purpose of baptism is to make us members of the kingdom of God and to unite us in a formal, objective relationship with God. For instance, Leithart said in his trial:

> Regeneration typically means in reformed theology, typically means a gift that's given only to the elect. And so I don't believe that new birth in that sense is given by baptism. But I think as new life within the context of the visible church is given by baptism. But I avoid the idea, I avoid terminology of regeneration in talking about baptism.[16]

While some people might think that we are twisting the statements of the adherents to the Federal Vision in an unwarranted way, they need to consider what Peter Leithart said about the work of the Holy Spirit:

---

15 Waters, *Federal Vision and Covenant Theology*, 236-7.

16 Record of the Case, Standing Judicial Commission of the Presbyterian Church in America, Case 2012-5, RE Gerald Hedman vs. Pacific Northwest Presbytery, 536.

> Moreover, the means the Spirit uses to bring us to fellowship with Christ come from the outside. The gospel comes as an external word (verbum ex auditu). . . The Word always comes to us in physical and therefore external form—marks on paper or vibrations in the air.[17]

Leithart leaves no doubt that his position is that the Spirit works externally—not internally. He believes in outward, external, objective grace. He does not believe in inward, internal, subjective grace.

In these statements and others, proponents of the Federal Vision (as well as N. T. Wright and Norman Shepherd) speak of new life in Christ and being born of God in ways contrary to the scriptural meaning of those words. The warning of Miller earlier in this chapter is important to remember. Also, Wilkins says baptism not only signifies and seals grace. He hedges by stipulating that this seal is formal and public, but he still connects the sealing of the ordinance with the outward act. The Scripture teaches that grace is sealed only when the Holy Spirit works efficaciously in the heart.

Baptismal Regeneration and the Church Fathers

It is a common misconception that almost all the church fathers held to baptismal regeneration. The idea is put forth that all those who deny such a *robust* view of the sacraments have departed from the historic Christian faith. But is that thesis correct? Did or did not the early church fathers believe in baptismal regeneration? Actually, there was always a difference in the views of church leaders. Some have held to baptismal regeneration theories and others have rejected it. Yet, a false doctrine does not become acceptable simply because an ancient class of theologians believed it. Scripture, not tradition, is the touchstone of truth.

One of the fathers, Augustine, Bishop of Hippo, is often accused of teaching this doctrine. There certainly are some of his statements on baptism which are unclear, but there are other places where he speaks with great perspicuity. In those clear instances, he unmistakably distinguishes between outward baptism and spiritual baptism. For instance, in a treatise on baptism written against the Donatists, Augustine made the following statements about baptism:

> Outward baptism may be administered, where inward conversion of the heart is wanting; and on the other hand, inward conversion

---

17 Peter J. Leithart, *The Baptized Body* (Moscow, Idaho: Canon Press, 2007), 120.

of the heart may exist, where outward baptism has never been received.[18]

It does not follow that whosoever has the baptism of Christ is also certain of the remission of his sins if he has this only in the outward sign, and is not converted with a true conversion of the heart, so that he who gives remission should himself have remission of his sins.[19]

He who imagines baptism to consist in the carnal form is not spiritual; neither can he obtain the celestial gift, who trusts that he can be changed by water, not by faith.[20]

The sacraments doe [sic] effect or worke [sic] that which they signify, only in the elect.[21]

Theodoret, Bishop of Cyrrus in Syria, wrote in A. D. 450:

> Grace sometimes precedes the sacrament, sometimes follows it, and sometimes does not even follow it.[22]

Jerome, Bishop of Jerusalem and a contemporary of Augustine, distinguished between true and false baptism, in the following quote:

> If they who have been baptized into Christ, have put on Christ, it is manifest that they who have not put on Christ were not baptized into Christ. . . If any hath received only that which is corporal and visible, viz: the Laver of water, he hath not put on Jesus Christ. For even Simon Magus received the externall washing, yet because he had not the Holy Ghost, therefore he did not put on Christ.[23]

Cyprian was elected Bishop of Carthage in A.D. 249 and martyred nine years later by Proconsul Galerius Maximus for refusing to sacrifice to pagan gods. He distinguished the true baptism of the Spirit from that which is without the Spirit as follows:

---

18 John Charles Ryle, *Knots Untied: Being plain statements on disputed points in Religion from the standpoint of an Evangelical Churchman*, (Cambridge, England: James Clarke & Co., Ltd., 1977), 127.

19 Philip Schaff, editor, *A Select Library of the Nicene and Post-Nicene Fathers of the Christian Church*, Vol. IV, St. Augustin: "The Writings Against the Manicheans and against the Donatists" (Grand Rapids, Michigan: Wm. B. Eerdmans Publishing Company, 1996), 494.

20 John Davenant, *An Exposition to the Epistle of St. Paul to the Colossians* (Lynchburg, Virginia: James Family Christian Publishers, 1979), 446.

21 Cornelius Burges, *Baptismall Regeneration of Elect Infants Professed by the Church of England, According to the Scriptures, the Primitive Church, the Present Reformed Churches, and Many Particular Divines Apart* (Oxford, England: I. Lichfield for Henry Curteyn, 1629), 133.

22 Ryle., *Knots Untied*, 126.

23 Burges, *Baptismall Regeneration of Elect Infants*, 131.

> Wherefore let them grant that, either the Spirit is present where they say true baptism is, or, that it is no true baptisme, where the Spirit is not; because baptisme cannot be without the Spirit.[24]

John Chrysostom was appointed Archbishop of Constantinople in A.D. 397 and died in exile ten years later. All Christians hold him in high esteem and he is considered a saint by both the Catholic and Orthodox churches. Chrysostom was a nickname which means "golden tongue," a moniker earned by his eloquence in preaching Christ. He made some statements about baptism which can easily be understood to teach baptismal regeneration wherein he emphasized more the acquirement of salvation than the application of it. For instance, he said:

> To have been born the mystical Birth, and to have been cleansed from all our former sins, comes from Baptism; but to remain for the future pure, never again after this to admit any stain belongs to our own power and diligence.[25]

Yet, such statements about the objective efficacy of baptism are offset by what he said in other places. Another statement about baptism is as profound as it is simple:

> In baptism the chief part is the Spirit, by which the water becomes effectual.[26]

In that quote, Chrysostom tied the efficacy of the water to the work of the Holy Spirit rather than making the water of baptism alwys efficacious in some sense—the latter being the fatal mistake of the Federal Vision. In another place, Chrysostom said:

> What anguish of heart doe I sustaine so often as I see some, even when they are ready to breath their last, runne unto baptisme, and yet never a whit the more purged by it.[27]

Ambrose, was the Archbishop of Milan and considered one of the four doctors of the early church. His influence was great in the fourth

---

24 Ibid., 118.

25 Philip Schaff, ed., *A Select Library of the Christian Church: Nicene and Post-Nicene Fathers*, "Chrysostom: Homilies on the Gospel of Saint John and the Epistle to the Hebrews," First Series, Vol. XIV, (Peabody, Massachusetts: Hendrickson Publishers, 1999), 37.

26 Burges, *Baptismall Regeneration of Elect Infants*, 122.

27 Ibid., 124.

century A. D., particularly on St. Augustine. His views on baptism are set forth in this quote:

> There are in Baptisme, three things, Water, Blood and the Spirit. Take away but one of these, and ye destroy the Sacrament. For what is water without the blood of Christ; or a common element, without the effect of the Sacrament?[28]

Cyril of Jerusalem (313-386) distinguishes between the effectual grace of the Holy Spirit and the mere operation of the water of baptism:

> Therefore, when you are about to descend into the water, do not think merely of the actual water, but look for its saving power through the effective operation of the Holy Spirit. . . If anyone has been baptized with water, without being counted worthy of the Spirit, he does not have the grace in its completeness.[29]

Gregory (335-395), Bishop of Nyssa and one of the three Cappadocian Fathers, rejected the idea that water bestows spiritual renovation and regeneration:

> Baptism is a purification of sins, a remission of transgressions, a cause of renovation and regeneration. . . It is not the water that bestows this bounty (for then it would be exalted above all creation), but the commandment of God and the intervention of the Spirit, which comes sacramentally to give us liberty. But water has a part to play, by giving an outward sign of the purification.[30]

These quotes from Augustine, Jerome, Theodoret, Ambrose, Chrysostom, Cyril of Jerusalem, and Gregory of Nyssa prove that many of the church fathers were not as prone to misunderstand the meaning of the sacraments as they have often been accused. Calvin quoted copiously from Augustine in defending the Consenus Tigurinus against the ideas of Joachim Westphal, which he would not have done if Augustine's views on the sacraments had been nearly identical with the views of the Council of Trent (as is often alleged).

---

28 Ibid., 126.

29 Henry Bettenson, editor and translator, *The Early Christian Fathers: A Selection from the Writings of the Fathers from St. Cyril of Jerusalem to St. Leo the Great* (London, New York, Toronto: Oxford University Press, 1974), 39.

30 Ibid., 160-161.

Baptismal Regeneration and Papists

Indeed, baptismal regeneration did not become the official doctrine of the Catholic Church until the Council of Vienne in 1311-2. The first decree of the Council established as the official Catholic doctrine that sanctifying grace is always conferred through baptism to both infants and adults. Prior to that Council, there had always been two different positions held by Catholic theologians concerning the efficacy of baptism. The first view was that which was held by Augustine, Ambrose, Chrysostom, Theodoret, Cyprian, Jerome, and others as documented in the quotes above. That view is in basic agreement with the view formulated in the Consensus Tigurinus, which prevailed in the Reformed symbols. The second and prevailing view at the Council of Vienne was the view of Pelagius, Hugo de St. Victor, Bonaventure, Alexander of Hales, Duns Scotus, Thomas Aquinas, and others. The Council of Vienne determined that the second view was the more likely of the two positions held by her theologians.

As late as 1250, Pope Innocent IV had still considered it an open question whether or not infants are conferred grace in baptism. His opinion was placed in the Canon Law of the Church of Rome and was referenced by the Council of Vienne:

> All are faithfully to profess that there is one baptism which regenerates all those baptized in Christ, just as there is one God and one faith. We believe that when baptism is administered in water in the name of the Father and of the Son and of the Holy Spirit, it is a perfect means of salvation for both adults and children. Yet, because, as regards the effect of baptism in children, we find that certain theologians have held contrary opinions, some saying that by baptism guilt is indeed remitted in infants but grace is not conferred, others on the contrary asserting that both guilt is remitted and the virtues and sanctifying grace are infused with regard to habit though for the time being not with regard to use, we, considering the general efficacy of Christ's death, which through baptism is applied in like manner to all the baptised, choose, with the approval of the sacred council, the second opinion, which says that sanctifying grace and the virtues are conferred in baptism on both infants and adults, as more probable and more in harmony with the words of the saints and of modern doctors of theology.[31]

Innocent IV clarified the main differences between the two views. The first view is that "by baptism guilt is indeed remitted in infants but

---

31 Council of Vienne, 1311-1312, Decree 1. Accessed at: http://www.legionofmarytidewater.com/faith/ECUM15.HTM on October 28, 2014.

grace is not conferred." The second view is that "both guilt is remitted and the virtues and sanctifying grace are infused." Though Augustine and the other fathers quoted above did not always speak as clearly as we could wish on the matter of baptism, they undoubtedly held to the first view referenced by the Council and not the second view. Otherwise, we would have to conclude that both Pope Innocent IV and the Council of Vienne were wrong for stating that there were two different views that had been held by the theologians of the church.

A century after the Council of Vienne (1311-1312), the Council of Ferrara (1438-1445) was called in an attempt to seek reconciliation with the Eastern Church, but it failed to heal the breach caused by the Great Schism. One of the statements of this Council was that the sacraments both "contain and confer grace," a view which was repeated by the Council of Trent a century later.

The Schoolmen of the Medieval Church were chiefly responsible for the development of the sacramental theories of the Church of Rome. They always referred first to Augustine in theological definitions, but they departed from his views in many ways. For instance, Aquinas said, along with Alexander of Hales, that "the sacraments justify and confer grace *ex opere operato*." That phrase means that where the symbol is, grace automatically operates. That is a view which Augustine never stated and with which he would not have agreed. It is contradictory of his other statements that the grace of baptism belongs only to the elect. Philip Schaff describes the methodology of the Schoolmen in devising their sacramental theories:

> In defining what a sacrament is—*quid est sacramentum*—the Schoolmen started with Augustine's definition that a sacrament is a visible sign of an invisible grace, but went beyond him in the degree of efficiency they ascribe to it. Beginning with Hugo, they assert in unmistakable language that the sacraments, or outward symbols, contain and confer grace—*continere et conferre gratiam*—the language afterwards used by the Council of Trent. They have a virtue in themselves.[32]

Schaff is undoubtedly correct in stating that the substance of Aquinas' statements on the sacraments were adopted by the Council of Ferrara in 1439 and the Council of Trent in 1560,[33] for even Catholic

---

32 Philip Schaff, *History of the Christian Church*, Volume V: *The Middle Ages* (Grand Rapids, Michigan: Wm. B. Eerdmans Publishing Company, 1981), 704.

33 Ibid., 701-2.

theologians acknowledge both points. For instance, Pope Leo XIII in 1879, made the following comment about Aquinas' influence on the Council of Trent:

> The Fathers of Trent made it part of the order of conclave to lay upon the altar, together with sacred Scripture and the decrees of the supreme Pontiffs, the *Summa* of Thomas Aquinas, whence to seek counsel, reason, and inspiration.[34]

Anyone who has read extensively in Aquinas' *Summa Theologica* has surely observed that he was more of a compiler and organizer than an original thinker. Aquinas attempted to combine Scripture with Aristotelian philosophy, an attempt which had been made by Pelagius and others before him, and held to Augustinianism imperfectly. He often began the discussion of some theological matter by reference to Augustine's views, but just as often started with a statement from Aristotle or one of the pagan philosophers. Contradictory theological positions were held by Aquinas, as by the other Schoolmen. For instance, many of them held to the efficacious grace and predestination of Augustine, but they also believed the sacraments conferred non-efficacious grace. There are ways in which the views of the Schoolmen were technically Semi-Pelagian. Sometimes they tried to synthesize the conflicting views of Augustinianism and Pelagianism into one harmonious position. There are other ways in which the Schoolmen simply held to two contradictory and opposite positions without ever reconciling them. Most of the Schoolmen were Augustinians, but their love of philosophy opened the door to free will and the doctrines of men.

James Atkinson, who edited *Luther's Early Theological Works* for the Library of Christian Classics series, tells us the way this dynamic tension worked itself out in the theology of the Schoolmen:

> Medieval theology always admitted in theory that a man's salvation depended ultimately on the prevenient grace of God and on this issue they never repudiated Augustine. But in its reverence for Aristotle it had to find a place for the action of man's free will. Scotus taught that the process of justification was an infusion of divine grace which creates a habit of the will towards a love of God and a love of man. This

---

34 *Aeterni Patris*, Encyclical of Pope Leo XIII, "On the Restoration of Christian Philosophy", accessed at: http://w2.vatican.va/content/leo-xiii/en/encyclicals/documents/hf_l-xiii_enc_04081879_aeterni-patris.html on June 26, 2015.

is appropriated by acts of the will which are meritorious, and these gradually change a sinner into a righteous person by setting him on this process. The obvious way to get the initial grace is by means of the sacraments which infuse grace. Grace is infused at Baptism and more and more in the Eucharist. Such is the process. But it is not unimpeded. It is warred against by sin which defeats the life-giving process of justification. Such is the human plight. Penance then, on this analysis, comes to occupy the place of the cardinal doctrine round which all these things hinge. Luther saw that this system had the effect (unintended) of depriving a man of the full meaning of the sacraments of Baptism and Holy Communion. With this doctrine of penance there was involved all the teaching of the distinction between *attritio* and *contritio*; the system of satisfactions imposed by the priestly hierarchy with all its mitigating scheme of indulgences and the revolting pecuniary traffic all too often involved; the treasury of merits; congruent and condign merit; Purgatory, disciplines and punishments. . . Its whole system was semi-Pelagian at heart and was based on human self-righteousness or works righteousness. The Church had lost the Augustinian doctrines of grace.[35]

The Schoolmen did not intend to throw out Augustinianism, which had been the accepted doctrine of the Church for 900 years before them, but by dallying with pagan philosophy they adopted a conflicting opinion which ultimately became the majority opinion. That false principle resulted in all the other repugnant doctrines of the Papal system—penance, indulgences, works righteousness, justification as both an infused principle and a process, and purgatory.

The Catholic Church chose the first theory on baptismal regeneration outlined by Samuel Miller at the beginning of this chapter as her own position with the Council of Trent. That theory of baptismal regeneration is more properly Semi-Pelagianism. It says that true subjective grace is given in the action of baptism, but it is grace which can be resisted and overcome by the will of man.

The essential belief, of both Papists and High Churchmen,[36] is that the fundamental blessings of salvation are conveyed through baptism to both adults and children alike, but those blessings are not perma-

---

35 James Atkinson, ed. and trans., *Luther: Early Theological Works* (Philadelphia: Westminster Press, 1962), 264.

36 The name of a party within the Church of England that held/holds to the same sacramental views as the Council of Trent concerning baptismal regeneration and baptismal efficacy. They are some of the Protestant advocates of this doctrine to whom Hodge was referring in his earlier quote. Their views are similar to the views advocated by the Federal Vision today.

nent until the baptized perseveres until the end. As Cunningham says:

> The Council of Trent expressly teaches,—viz., that baptism is the instrumental cause of justification, which with Romanists comprehend both forgiveness and regeneration,—that all adults receive when baptized, unless they put a bar in the way, these great blessings,—that all infants, being unable to put a bar in the way of the efficacious operation of the sacrament, receive in baptism the forgiveness of original sin and renovation of their moral natures,—and that no sin of unbaptized persons, not even the original sin of those who die in infancy, is forgiven without baptism.[37]

Baptismal Regeneration and High Church Protestants

Dr. Henry Philpotts, Bishop of Exeter, England from 1830-1869, "asserted, in a charge which he published in 1848, that several of the Confessions of the Reformed Churches—specifying 'the Helvetic, that of Augsburg, the Saxon, the Belgic, and the Catechism of Heidelberg'—agreed with the Church of Rome and the Church of England in teaching the doctrine of baptismal regeneration."[38] The Federal Vision proponents today have likewise attempted to clothe their views in legitimacy by asserting that baptismal regeneration views were taught in the above confessions, as well as many others, including the Westminster Confession of Faith. William Goode's reply to Philpotts in his book, *The Doctrine of the Church of England as to the Effects of Baptism in the Case of Infants*,[39] was "crushing and unanswerable," according to William Cunningham. Goode, who was Dean of Ripon, based his work on direct quotes from the founding fathers of the Church of England, thereby proving that they did not hold to the popish theories of baptismal regeneration. J. C. Ryle considered Goode's work as the very best book ever written on baptismal regeneration. In fact, it has never been answered and Philpotts himself subsequently retracted his errors with a sheepish attempt to excuse his mistakes on what he claimed were contradictory statements in those Reformed confessions.

The main purpose of Goode's book was to show that the framers of the Reformed confessions never taught baptismal regeneration,

---

37 William Cunningham, *The Reformers and the Theology of the Reformation* (London: The Banner of Truth Trust, 1967), 234.

38 Ibid., 241.

39 William Goode, *The Doctrine of the Church of England as to the Effects of Baptism in the Case of Infants* (London: J. Hatchard and Son, 1850).

and that such a view was not held by the leading founders of the Church of England. Goode asserted that theories of baptismal regeneration were based on a superficial knowledge of the theology of the Reformed confessions, including the Thirty-Nine Articles, and a false interpretation of some of their statements. Cunningham elaborates on Goode's purpose in writing his book:

> One leading argument which he employs, in order to establish this general position, is in substance this: No one who embraces the Calvinistic system of theology can consistently believe the high church doctrine of baptismal regeneration; the great body of the fathers and founders of the Church of England, the men who prepared her formularies, her articles and liturgy, in the reign of Edward, and established them, with scarcely any change and almost precisely as we now have them, in the reign of Elizabeth, were Calvinists; and, consequently, there can be no inconsistency between a reception of these formularies and a rejection of the Tractarian doctrine of baptismal regeneration.[40]

Goode's book is 571 pages long and is filled with copious quotes from all the great leaders of the Church of England, as well as such Reformers as Martin Bucer and Peter Martyr. Though not written in a popular style, it is absolutely devastating to the idea of baptismal regeneration.

Baptismal Regeneration and the Westminster Assembly

One of the most troubling aspects of the Federal Vision is its insistence that the Reformed creeds and the Westminster divines agree with its views on baptism or, at least, receive them as an acceptable interpretation of the Scripture. For instance, Rich Lusk, in an online article, "Baptismal Efficacy and the Reformed Tradition: Past, Present, and Future," attempts to prove that the Reformers "held a robust view of baptismal efficacy"[41] from which the modern Reformed churches have departed. Lusk's views of the Reformed symbols is not held by A. A. Hodge, who wrote in his excellent commentary on the Westminster Confession of Faith concerning baptismal regeneration:

---

40 Cunningham, *Reformers and the Theology of the Reformation*, 176.

41 Rich Lusk, "Baptismal Efficacy and the Reformed Tradition: Past, Present, and Future," accessed on July 29, 2015 at: http://www.hornes.org/theologia/rich-lusk/baptismal-efficacy-the-reformed-tradition-past-present-future.

> Romanists and Ritualists have inferred that the sign is inseparable from the grace signified, and that these spiritual effects are due to the outward ordinance. Hence the doctrine of baptismal regeneration. But it must be observed that the Scriptures do not assert these spiritual attributes of water baptism in itself considered, but of water baptism as the sign or emblem of baptism by the Holy Ghost. These spiritual attributes belong only to the baptism by the Spirit, and they accompany the sign only when the sign is accompanied by that which it signifies. It does not follow, however, that the sign is inseparable from the grace. The grace is sovereign; and experience teaches us that it is often absent from the sign, and the sign is least frequently honoured by the presence of the grace when it is itself most implicitly relied upon.[42]

There are three words used by the Westminster Standards concerning the sacraments: *signify*, *seal*, and *exhibit*. Of the three words, *exhibit* is probably the most important for this controversy concerning baptismal regeneration. William S. Barker, who was a defense expert witness at the trial of Peter Leithart, is certainly correct when he says that the seventeenth-century meaning of the word *exhibit* (from the Latin *exhibere*) was '*to convey.*' Yet, Barker missed the mark when he stated:

> There is a sense in which in baptism the sacrament not only signifies and seals but conveys something to the recipient of the sacrament.[43]

Is it true that "something" is always conveyed to "the recipient" of the sacrament of baptism? Was it the intention of the writers of the Westminster Standards to communicate that idea by using the term "exhibit" concerning the sacraments? One of the Scottish Commissioners to the Westminster Assembly was George Gillespie, who wrote the following words concerning the intended meaning of the word *exhibit* by the Westminster divines:

> I answer, That exhibition which they speak of, is not the giving of grace where it is not (as is manifested by the afore-quoted testimonies), but an exhibition to believers—a real, effectual, lively application of Christ, and of all His benefits, to every one that believeth, for the strengthening, confirming, and comforting of the soul. . . Our divines do not say that the sacraments are exhibitive ordinances, wherein grace is communicated to those who have none of it, to unconverted or unbelieving persons. . .

---

42 A. A. Hodge, *The Confession of Faith: A Handbook of Christian Doctrine Expounding the Westminster Confession* (London: The Banner of Truth Trust, 1961), 330.

43 Record of the Case, Standing Judicial Commission, 2012-5, 595.

> Protestant writers do not only oppose the *opus operatum* and the *causalitas physica* and *insita* but they oppose (as is manifest by the testimonies already cited[44]) all causality or working of the first grace of conversion and faith in or by the sacraments, supposing always a man to be a believer and within the covenant of grace before the sacrament, and that he is not made such, nor translated to the state of grace in or by the sacrament.[45]

Gillespie's statements are determinative of the sense in which the word *exhibit* was meant by the authors of the Westminster Standards.[46] They viewed the exhibition of the grace to be given only to those who were already recipients of the grace of the Holy Spirit. Nothing is exhibited in the sacrament which is not first conveyed to the soul through the work of the Spirit. In this respect, Barker's suggestion that "something" is conveyed in baptism to every "recipient" is contrary to the intended meaning of the word *exhibit* by the Westminster divines, as testified by one of its commissioners.

In his work on the Westminster Assembly, Robert Letham mentions that two other commissioners, Cornelius Burgess and Daniel Featley, taught that true grace is conferred to the elect alone, whether that grace is considered as initial or actual. As Letham says:

> For both Burgess and Featley, all elect persons are regenerate in the initial sense at baptism and in the actual sense at effectual calling. On the other hand, nonelect persons are not regenerate in the initial sense at baptism, nor are they in the actual sense either. However, since we do not know who the elect are, we are by the judgment of charity to judge all who are baptized are regenerate in the initial sense.[47]

This distinction between initial and actual regeneration was perhaps the view of only those two commissioners, Burgess and Featley. Federal Vision advocates, such as Rich Lusk, refer to both ministers as commissioners who held the "robust" view of baptism endorsed by the Federal Vision. Yet, both of them restricted the grace of baptism

---

44 In his work, *Aaron's Rod Blossoming*, Gillespie quoted from Calvin, Bullinger, Ursinus, Musculus, Bucer, Hommius, Aretus, Vossius, the Scottish Confession, the Synod of Dort, the Belgic Confession, Pareaus, and others to prove that baptismal regeneration is not and never was the view of Calvinists. See the next endnote.

45 George Gillespie, *Aaron's Rod Blossoming* (Harrisonburg, Virginia: Sprinkle Publications, 1985), 233.

46 Cf. also Cunningham, *Reformers and the Theology of the Reformation*, p. 280.

47 Record of the Case, Standing Judicial Commission, 2012-5, 222.

to the elect alone and denied that any nonelect persons ever received any baptismal grace. Nonetheless, Burgess received no small measure of criticism for his views by orthodox Calvinists of his day and wrote a book to clear himself of the suspicion of teaching heterodoxy. The title of that book was, *Baptismal Regeneration of Elect Infants Professed by the Church of England, According to the Scriptures, the Primitive Church, the Present Reformed Churches, and Many Particular Divines Apart*. The strongest part of Burgess' book is his assertion that baptismal regeneration is of elect infants only, and that such was the view of the Fathers, the Reformed creeds, and the greatest of the Reformed divines. The weakest part of his book is his attempt to distinguish between initial and actual regeneration. Initial regeneration is indefinable and impossible to support from the Scripture. Moreover, the Westminster Confession of Faith and other Reformed creeds never make such a distinction concerning "initial and actual" regeneration. Burgess' views were accepted as orthodox only because he limited regeneration to elect infants. If he had held a view that all infants receive some initial regeneration (or new life), Burgess' view would have been considered at least heterodox.

In his commentary on the Confession of Faith, A. A. Hodge wrote concerning this exhibition of grace:

> The sacraments were designed to "apply"—i.e., actually to convey—to believers the benefits of the new covenant. If they are "seals" of the covenant, they must of course, as a legal form of investiture, actually convey the grace represented to those to whom it belongs. Thus a deed conveys an estate, or the key handed over in the presence of witnesses the possession of a house from the owner to the renter. Our confession is explicit and emphatic on this subject. The old English word "exhibit," there used, does not mean to show forth; but in the sense of the Latin exhibere, from which it is derived, to administer, to apply. . .
>
> So that this grace-conferring virtue depends on two things: (1.) The sovereign will and power of the Holy Spirit. (2.) The lively faith of the recipient.[48]

Hodge, like Gillespie and Cunningham, unequivocally states that the sacraments convey grace only to those who are first recipients of the work of the Holy Spirit and have a lively faith in Christ for their salvation. The grace is conveyed to *believers*—it is not conveyed in order to initiate faith or as a spark of new life to those who are spiritually dead.

---

48 Hodge, *Confession of Faith*, 331-332.

There are several other Reformed theologians who take the same view as Gillespie, Hodge, and Cunningham. For instance, Robert Shaw, in his commentary on the Westminster Confession of Faith, wrote:

> That the sacraments themselves cannot confer saving grace is evident; for if they had this power in themselves, they would be equally effectual to all who receive them.[49]

In another place, Shaw also says:

> Socinians represent the sacraments as being merely solemn badges by which the disciples of Jesus are discriminated from other men.[50]

This same mistake about the sacraments is often made by the proponents of the Federal Vision and even by N. T. Wright. On the one hand, they exaggerate the efficacy of the sacraments. On the other hand, they diminish the sacraments, especially baptism, to being nothing more than a badge of membership for the covenant community.

Dr. John Davenant (1572-6141), Lord Bishop of Salisbury and a British delegate to the Synod of Dordt, wrote in his excellent commentary on Colossians:

> For, as in the baptism of adults previous faith is required, according to that declaration of our Saviour, Mar. XXI.16, He that believeth and is baptized shall be saved; and he that believeth not shall be damned; so, from those who are baptized in infancy, subsequent faith is required; which if they do not exhibit afterwards, they retain only the outward sanctification of baptism, the internal effect of sanctification they have not.[51]

J. C. Ryle, nineteenth-century Bishop of Liverpool, wrote concerning baptismal regeneration:

> I see fresh reasons for dreading the doctrine that all baptized persons are regenerate. . . . I see it interfering with every leading doctrine of the Gospel;—it encourages men to believe that election, adoption, justification, and the indwelling of the Spirit, are all conferred on them in

---

49 Robert Shaw, *The Reformed Faith: An Exposition of the Westminster Standards* (Inverness, Scotland: Christian Focus Publications, 1974), 281.

50 Ibid., 280.

51 Davenant, *Exposition of Colossians*, 446.

baptism;—and then, to avoid the difficulties which such a system entails, the fulness of all these mighty truths is pared down, mutilated, and explained away. . . I see it ultimately producing in some minds a mere sacramental Christianity,—a Christianity in which there is much said about union with Christ, but it is a union begun only by baptism and kept up only by the Lord's Supper,—a Christianity in which the leading doctrines that the Apostle Paul dwells on in almost all his Epistles, have nothing but a subordinate position.[52]

In the writings of Federal Vision men today, we see the paring down of scriptural truths. Baptism, they say, confers a real relationship with Christ, justification, new life, forgiveness of sins, and other benefits. But these graces conferred on all those baptized are not the same truths enumerated in Scripture. For the Federal Vision advocates, the relationship with Christ is not permanent. It is objective, rather than subjective. The other benefits of Christ are also objective. Justification is not once-for-all. The new birth is not the efficacious seed of God which results in eternal life. The forgiveness of sins does not result in all their sins being placed on the scapegoat never to be seen again. The benefits conferred in baptism, according to these proponents, are all subordinate to the obedience and perseverance of the baptized. Only through such obedience and perseverance can anyone baptized hope to gain salvation. Thus, the work of Christ for our salvation is diminished and the obedience of the so-called *faithful* is magnified in the Federal Vision system.

Summary
By denying the common misunderstanding of baptismal regeneration, the proponents of the Federal Vision think they have dismissed baptismal regeneration theories from their system altogether. The Federal Vision system rejects the idea that baptism bestows efficacious grace; rejects the subjective view of baptismal regeneration of Catholicism; adopts the objective view of baptismal regeneration, whether wittingly or unwittingly; and, thereby, more nearly aligns with Pelagianism on this point than with the Semi-Pelagianism of the Council of Trent. The history of Christian doctrine shows that baptismal regeneration was not the view of all the early church Fathers (as is often supposed), but was later codified as the official doctrine of the church by the Councils of Vienne (1311-12), Ferrara (1439), and

---

52 Ryle., *Knots Untied*, 123.

Trent (1560) through the influence of the Schoolmen, especially Aquinas. Such views of baptism were rejected by the Westminster divines who held that grace is exhibited or conveyed to the elect alone when they come to saving faith. Protestants, such as High Church Anglicans who hold to baptismal regeneration theories, are departing from the views of the Reformers.

Conclusion

One of the essential problems with the Federal Vision is that, in effect, its proponents deny the sealing function of the sacraments. They confuse the sign with the thing signified and ignore the sealing aspect, even when they mention the sealing aspect of the sacraments. The sacraments are seals in that they actually *exhibit* or *confer* the graces signified to all those for whom those graces are appointed; that is, to the elect of God. Thus, the language of the Scripture and the Westminster Confession of Faith which speaks so highly of the sacraments is actually speaking about the sealing function of them. The sacraments are not seals to those who do not have faith or never come to faith in Christ.

The historic Reformed and scriptural position on the sacraments is correctly articulated by Herman Bavinck:

> Faith alone apart from any sacrament communicates, and causes believers to enjoy, all the benefits of salvation. . . . Baptism can only signify and seal the benefits that are received by faith and thereby strengthen that faith.[53]

The sacraments perform their work in the hearts of the elect. In them alone, the grace signified is also sealed through faith alone. The failure of the Federal Vision to make these same distinctions about baptism lies at the root of all their errors.

---

53 John Bolt, ed., John Vriend, trans., Herman Bavinck, *Reformed Dogmatics*, Volume 4: *Holy Spirit, Church, and New Creation* (Grand Rapids, Michigan: Baker Academic, 2008), 515.

–9–
The Federal Vision and the Order of Salvation

"As I see it, the Federal Vision's central affirmation is this: *Without qualification or hedging, the church is the body of Christ.* Everything the Federal Vision says about baptism, about soteriology, about apostasy flows from that affirmation."[1]

PETER LEITHART, FEDERAL VISION PROPONENT

---

1 Peter J. Leithart, *The Baptized Body* (Moscow, Idaho: Canon Press, 2007), ix.

Soteriology embraces both the accomplishment and application of redemption. The accomplishment of salvation is the objective side of redemption and concerns the work of Christ for us. The application of salvation is the subjective aspect of redemption and concerns the work of the Holy Spirit in us. One of the great errors of the proponents of the Federal Vision is that they emphasize aspects of the objective side of redemption to the detriment of the subjective work of the Spirit. They are also guilty of various errors on the objective side of redemption such as denying the imputation of Christ's righteousness to believers, limiting justification to the forgiveness of past sins, making perseverance in grace uncertain, teaching that all who are baptized receive a covenantal election which is neither eternal nor unconditional, and replacing the efficacious grace of the Spirit with an inefficacious grace bestowed by baptism. Thus, the Federal Vision system rejects the *ordo salutis* of the Bible and propounds an unscriptural paradigm of salvation.

The quote at the beginning of this chapter is from Peter Leithart's book, *The Baptized Body*, wherein he clearly affirms the Federal Vision position despite denying at his trial that he is a Federal Visionist. There is no distinction in that system between those who are in the visible and invisible church; between those who are baptized with water and those who are truly baptized; between objective and subjective grace; and between the general call and the effectual call, etc. The Federal Vision system emphasizes outward and external grace, but fails to make the above distinctions. This chapter concerns the soteriology of the Scripture and the Reformed confessions. Soteriology always includes internal, supernatural, and subjective grace. Soteriology is the application of Christ's redemption to sinners by the Holy Spirit and results in eternal salvation in every instance. The Federal Vision system cannot be made to fit with the soteriology of the Scripture. The Federal Vision system makes every person in the visible church a recipient of every grace and benefit of Christ, except perseverance. Thus, it necessarily makes every individual sovereign in the matter of his or her own salvation. The Federal Vision is thereby a confused and confusing system of theology. Herman Bavinck defines the tension which causes this confusion in every system of nomism as follows:

> When we return to the starting point of Scripture for our understanding of the order of salvation, we encounter the difficulty that it tells us

two apparently contradictory truths: salvation is God's work and we must work out our salvation. We run the risk of Pelagian nomism, on the one hand, and antinomianism, on the other. Both fail to do justice to the work of Christ. Nomism blurs the line between Christianity and paganism and is present in pietistic as well as rationalistic forms. Antinomianism correctly stresses the full accomplished work of Christ but ignores the application of the work of salvation and thus in effect denies the personality and work of the Holy Spirit.[2]

The Federal Vision system is guilty of Pelagian nomism concerning the order of salvation. It is a denial that salvation, from beginning to end, is God's work. Instead, it stresses that we must work out our own salvation that will hopefully result in our final justification at the judgment. Interestingly, it also slips into the antinomian error of denying the work of the Holy Spirit in the application of salvation. As Bavinck notes, that error is a denial of the personality and work of the Holy Spirit.

In 1 Corinthians, the Apostle Paul said, "God is not the author of confusion" (1 Corinthians 14:33, KJV). Confusion in the church is not of God. God is the author of order. There is orderliness in salvation also. As John Murray said in his great classic, *Redemption Accomplished and Applied*:

> When we think of the application of redemption we must not think of it as one simple and indivisible act. It comprises a series of acts and processes. To mention some, we have calling, regeneration, justification, adoption, sanctification, glorification. These are all distinct, and not one of these can be defined in terms of the other. Each has its own distinct meaning, function, and purpose in the action and grace of God.[3]

Romans 8:29, 30—Election, Calling, Justification, and Glorification

There is an order in which this series of acts takes place in the salvation of every believer. That order is given to us by Scripture itself when we compare one passage with another. The classic passage on the order of salvation is Romans 8:29, 30, which says: "For those whom He foreknew, He also predestined to become conformed to the image of His Son, so that He would be the firstborn among many

---

[2] John Bolt, ed., John Vriend, trans., Herman Bavinck, *Reformed Dogmatics*, Volume 3: *Sin and Salvation in Christ* (Grand Rapids: Baker Academics, 2006), 489.

[3] John Murray, *Redemption Accomplished and Applied* (Grand Rapids, Michigan: Wm. B. Eerdmans Publishing Company, 1970), 79-80.

brethren; and these whom He predestined, He also called; and these whom He called, He also justified; and these whom He justified, He also glorified."

Salvation begins in eternity and ends in eternity. It begins in the foreknowledge and predestination of God before the foundation of the world. Its destiny is glorification for all eternity. Its goal is to conform believers to the image of Christ. Paul lists four specific and distinct acts in Romans 8 that are part of this order of salvation: predestination, calling, justification, and glorification. Predestination results in calling. Calling results in justification. Justification results in glorification. These acts represent an unbroken chain which connects God's eternal purpose before the foundation of the world with the ultimate destiny of all believers in glory. This golden chain of salvation limits the *ordo salutis* to the elect alone.

The first act is eternal predestination, based on God's foreknowledge, which is more than mere foresight. Pelagius misinterprets Romans 8:29, 30 by confusing foreknowledge with foresight:

> 29 *For those he foreknew*. The purpose according to which he planned to save by faith alone those whom he had foreknown would believe, and those whom he freely called to salvation he will all the more glorify as they work [towards salvation]. *He also predestined to be conformed to the image of his Son*. To predestine is the same as to foreknow. Therefore, those whom he foresaw would be conformed in life he intended to be conformed in glory.
>
> 30. *And those he predestined he also called, and those he called he also justified, and those he justified he also exalted*. Those he foreknew would believe he called. Now a call gathers together those who are willing, not those who are unwilling; or at any rate the discrimination is not against persons, but rather in time. He says this on account of the enemies of the faith, so that they may not judge God's grace to be fortuitous. Therefore, they are called to believe through the preaching, and are justified through baptism when they believe, and are glorified in charismatic powers in the resurrection to come.[4]

The result of Pelagius' twisted logic is that he makes salvation depend on man, rather than on God's grace. Predestination is thus conditioned on the foresight of those who believe; calling is inefficacious and applies only to those who are seen to be working towards sal-

---

4 Theodore DeBruyn, trans., *Pelagius' Commentary on St. Paul's Epistle to the Romans* (Oxford: Clarendon Press, 1993), 112-113.

vation; justification is through baptism when one believes; and, glorification is only for those who have met all these conditions. Thus, predestination is conditional, not unconditional, in Pelagius' system. John Murray gives the correct exegetical interpretation of Romans 8:29 in his commentary on that epistle:

> It should be observed that the text says "whom he foreknew"; whom is the object of the verb and there is no qualifying addition. This, of itself, shows that, unless there is some other compelling reason, the expression "whom he foreknew" contains within itself the differentiation which is presupposed. . . It means "whom he set regard upon" or "whom he knew from eternity with distinguishing affection and delight," and is virtually equivalent to "whom he foreloved". This interpretation, furthermore, is in agreement with the efficient and determining action which is so conspicuous in every link of the chain—it is God who predestinates, it is God who calls, it is God who justifies, and it is he who glorifies. Foresight of faith would be out of accord with the determinative action which is predicated of God in these other instances and would constitute a weakening of the total emphasis at the point where we should least expect it.[5]

Between these two positions represented by the commentaries of Pelagius and Murray on Romans, there can be no middle ground concerning the order of salvation. Monergism is on one side and synergism is on the other side. Augustinianism and Calvinism have always stressed the divine monergism that is clearly taught in Romans 8 and numerous other parts of Scripture; that is, that salvation is a work of the sovereign God alone. Pelagianism, Semi-Pelagianism, and Arminianism have always taught synergism; that is, that God predestines only on the basis of the foresight of faith; that humans are responsible for their salvation through the exercise of their own free will; and, that monergism is a violation of free will. People aligned with the Federal Vision try to have it both ways on the matter of the order of salvation. They claim to hold to predestination, but their theory of covenant election is patently synergistic. (We will further address their claim to hold to eternal predestination in detail in Chapter 12). They do not start with eternal predestination in their order of salvation for the covenant community, but with their view of baptismal efficacy which results in covenant election. They do not base their

---

5   John Murray, *The Epistle to the Romans*, Volume I, two volumes in one (Grand Rapids, Michigan: Wm. B. Eerdmans Publishing Co., 1968), 318-319.

theory on efficacious grace alone, but on baptismal efficacy which is, admittedly, often inefficacious even in their view. They claim to hold to one order of salvation, but they attempt to insert their theories of baptismal efficacy into Reformed soteriology. It would be easier for them to mix water and oil or to combine light and darkness than to unite the tenets of monergism and synergism into one seamless order of salvation.

Key Assessment: The Federal Vision's order of salvation for the covenant community begins with covenant baptism, not eternal predestination.

The *ordo salutis* is sometimes alleged to be a later innovation of the Reformed faith with which Calvin was unfamiliar[6]. While the *ordo salutis* certainly underwent fuller development by post-reformational scholars, Calvin unquestionably held to the basics of it. As he wrote in his commentary on Romans 8:30:

> Paul now employs a climax in order to confirm by a clearer demonstration how true it is that our conformity to the humility of Christ effects our salvation. In this he teaches us that our participation in the cross is so connected with our vocation, justification, and finally our glory, that they cannot in anyway be separated.[7]

Paul tells us in Romans 8:28 that we are "called according to His purpose." Murray further comments:

> This means that purpose provides the pattern or plan according to which calling takes place. Therefore purpose is prior to the calling, and, in this case, of course, eternally prior.[8]

The mind of God comprehended everything necessary for our salvation. There is a distinct order which is according to His eternal purpose and that order cannot be changed or varied. That order begins in time and space with what is denominated by Paul as "calling." We also know such calling by another term, effectual calling. Jesus said, "For many are called, but few are chosen" (Matthew 22:14). This

---

6 William Evans, *Imputation and Impartation: Union with Christ in American Reformed Theology* (Eugene, Oregon: Wipf and Stock Publishers, 2009), 52-53.

7 David W. Torrance and Thomas F. Torrance, eds., Ross MacKenzie, trans., *Calvin's Commentaries: The Epistle to the Romans and Thessalonians* (Grand Rapids, Michigan: Wm. B. Eerdmans Publishing Company, 1979), 180.

8 Murray, *Redemption Accomplished and Applied*, 170.

verse distinguishes between the outward call which goes out through the gospel and the inward call which is effectual unto salvation. Paul is obviously referring to the effectual call of God in Romans 8:29, 30 because he says calling results in justification and glorification. As Robert Haldane said concerning this phrase, "called according to his purpose," in verse 28:

> This is a further description or characteristic of God's people. They are called not merely outwardly by the preaching of the Gospel, for this is common to them with unbelievers, but called also by the Spirit, with an internal and effectual calling, and made willing in the day of God's power. They are called according to God's eternal purpose, according to which He knew them, and purposed their calling before they were in existence; for all God's purposes are eternal. It imports that their calling is solely according to grace; for when it is said to be a calling according to God's purpose, it is distinguished from a calling according to works. It imports that it is an effectual and permanent calling; for God's purposes cannot be defeated.[9]

Faith and Repentance

This basic outline of the order of salvation found in Romans 8 can be filled in by other passages of Scripture. The Scripture teaches in many places that justification is by or through faith. "For we maintain that a man is justified by faith apart from works of the law" (Romans 3:28. Cf. also Romans 1:17; 4:4, 5; 5:1; Galatians 2:16; 3:24). This would necessarily mean that faith precedes justification in the order of salvation. Yet, faith is never divorced from repentance in the Bible. They are twin graces that are always found together. Jesus said: "Repent and believe in the gospel" (Mark 1:15). Paul said his mission was to preach "repentance toward God and faith in our Lord Jesus Christ" (Acts 20:21) to both Jews and Greeks. Consider also Acts 3:19 and 26:20, both of which connect faith and repentance. Thus, the scriptural order of salvation then becomes: election, calling, faith and repentance, justification, and glorification.

Regeneration

Faith and repentance require an ability which the natural man does not have. The sinner is dead in his trespasses and sins (Ephesians 2:1); he has an evil, unbelieving heart (Hebrews 3.12); his heart is a

---

9 Robert Haldane, *An Exposition of the Epistle to the Romans* (MacDill AFB, FL: MacDonald Publishing Company, n.d.), 395.

heart of stone (Ezekiel 36:26); his mind and conscience are defiled and seared as with a branding iron (Titus 1:15; 1 Timothy 4:2). By nature, his mind is hostile to God and cannot please God (Romans 8:7, 8). A living faith cannot grow in the soil of such a heart. The natural man needs a new heart before he can believe. God promises that work of grace in Ezekiel 36:26, 27:

> Moreover, I will give you a new heart and put a new spirit within you and I will remove the heart of stone from your flesh and give you a heart of flesh. I will put My Spirit within you and cause you to walk in My statutes.

This new heart is a spiritual heart which replaces the heart of stone. It is the result of the work of the Holy Spirit. Jesus said to Nicodemus, "Truly, truly, I say to you, unless one is born again he cannot see the kingdom of God" (John 3:3). This new birth or regeneration necessarily precedes faith and repentance in the order of salvation. The expanded order of salvation then becomes: election, calling, regeneration, faith and repentance, justification, and glorification.

Union with Christ
There are four other acts or processes which it is necessary to include in a scriptural order of salvation. They are union with Christ, adoption, sanctification, and perseverance. Romans 8:9, 10 teach us that the Triune God dwells in us and we are united to the Godhead through the Spirit. As those verses say, "However, you are not in the flesh, but in the Spirit, if indeed the Spirit of God dwells in you. But if anyone does not have the Spirit of Christ, he does not belong to Him. If Christ is in you, though the body is dead because of sin, yet the spirit is alive because of righteousness." We are taught in those verses that it is the Spirit who dwells in us and this Spirit is the Spirit of God and the Spirit of Christ. Moreover, it is in this way that Christ dwells in us and we have our union with Him. As D. Martyn Lloyd-Jones says:

> This is one of the most amazing statements that we can ever encounter. What it means is that, because the Holy Spirit dwells in us, it is also true that the Lord Jesus Christ dwells in us, and it is also true to say that the Father dwells in us. . . . It is therefore true of all Christians.

> This is the ultimate doctrine, it is the highest peak of the Christian doctrine of salvation.[10]

Union with Christ is the pinnacle of salvation because our hearts become the abode of the Living God who dwells in us. As Murray writes:

> Union with Christ is the central truth of the whole doctrine of salvation. All to which the people of God have been predestined in the eternal election of God, all that has been secured and procured for them in the once-for-all accomplishment of redemption, all of which they become the actual partakers in the application of redemption, and all that by God's grace they will become in the state of consummated bliss is embraced within the compass of union and communion with Christ.[11]

This union is not merely an ecclesiastical union accomplished through water baptism as taught by the Federal Vision. It is not simply an external, objective grace of the objective covenant. It is the subjective indwelling of the Triune God—Father, Son, and Holy Spirit. It is the experience only of those who are true Christians and who are guaranteed never to apostatize because of their union with Christ. All of the application of redemption is bestowed on us through union with Christ. Thus, it is closely related to both effectual calling and regeneration. All those who are effectually called are regenerated and united with Christ. Yet, it is hard to determine the right place for union with Christ in the order of salvation. Union with Christ is not one act alone, but embraces the whole order of salvation in its application to the elect.

Adoption

Closely related to justification by faith is adoption. Ephesians 1:5 records, "He predestined us to adoption as sons through Jesus Christ to Himself." Our adoption sustains a very close relationship to our regeneration. There are two ways we become members of God's family—we are born into it and we are adopted into it. These two ways are not distinct but maintain the closest relationship each to the other. Everyone who is regenerated is also adopted. We are children of God both by regeneration and adoption. The Westminster Standards are

---

10   D. M. Lloyd-Jones, *Romans: An Exposition of Chapter 8:5-17, The Sons of God* (Grand Rapids, Michigan: Zondervan Publishing House, 1975), 59.

11   Murray, *Redemption Accomplished and Applied*, 170.

surely correct when they teach that adoption is "an act of God's free grace." We are adopted judicially, on a once-for-all basis. It is because our relationship with God once begun can never be severed that the Scripture teaches we are adopted into His family.

Sanctification

John Murray was certainly correct when he said, "Sanctification is a work of God in us. . . Sanctification is specifically the work of this indwelling and directing Holy Spirit."[12] Murray is often quoted by Federal Vision proponents because of his teaching of definitive sanctification, that union with Christ and regeneration effect a decisive break with sin. Yet, he always maintained that sanctification is also a lifelong process in every believer which requires them to put to death the old sin nature and to grow in grace. Because of our regeneration, our union with Christ, and the work of the Spirit in us, a decisive blow against sin has been delivered. Yet, sin has not been fully eradicated.

In his trial, Peter Leithart made the following comment about definitive sanctification:

> Sanctification, when it's used definitively, typically has to do with our standing before God as worshipers of God.[13]

If sanctification, definitive or otherwise, affects our standing before God, then it is not a work of the Spirit in us, but an act of God for us. And Leithart confirms that is exactly what he thinks it is in another part of the record of his trial:

> But the definitive sanctification, the deliverdict is a monergistic act of God.[14]

By "deliverdict," Leithart means both a deliverance from sin and a verdict against it. He has, thus, coined a new word which is unique to his writings. His use of this new word is to convey his idea that sanctification, particularly definitive sanctification, and justification are to be melded together.

---

12 Ibid., 141.

13 Record of the Case, Standing Judicial Commission of the Presbyterian Church in America, Case 2012-5, RE Gerald Hedman vs. Pacific Northwest, 482.

14 Ibid., 521.

As Leithart again says:

> Hence, I concluded that the Bible, and Paul in particular, sometimes use the language of "justification" to describe what Murray called "definitive sanctification," the once-for-all deliverance from Sin and Death.[15]

Leithart also confuses justification and sanctification in the following quote:

> In several articles, I have argued that in some passages of Scripture, the language of "justification" is used to describe an act of deliverance.
> Since being under the dominion of sin is one of the consequences of our sin, justification liberates from this dominion.[16]

In other places, Leithart also refers to justification as a deliverdict. Thus, he defines both justification and definitive sanctification as deliverdicts. He also accuses Reformed theology of going beyond Scripture in distinguishing too sharply between justification and sanctification. In the above quotes, he has essentially defined sanctification and justification as the same act. Justification is a decisive break with sin and so is definitive sanctification for him. Justification is an ongoing process of living obedience to God and so is sanctification in his view. It is a misreading of Leithart, and other Federal Vision proponents, to accuse them of holding to the Catholic position on justification. Catholicism, ever since the Council of Trent, has taught that we are justified through the work of God's Spirit in renewing us. In the section on justification, Canon XI of the Council of Trent says:

> If any one saith, that men are justified, either by the sole imputation of the justice of Christ, or by the sole remission of sins, to the exclusion of the grace and *the charity which is poured in their hearts by the Holy Ghost*, and is inherent in them; or even that the grace, whereby we are justified, is only the favor of God, let him be anathema.[17]

The work of God's Spirit in us is one of subjective grace and that is the doctrine of Catholicism. Yet, the emphasis of the advocates of the Federal Vision is on objective grace which makes it nearer to Pelagianism than the Semi-Pelagianism of the Council of Trent.

---

15 Ibid., 209.

16 Ibid.

17 Philip Schaff, ed., David Schaff, rev., *The Creeds of Christendom: With a History and Critical Notes*, Volume II: *The Greek and Latin Creeds* (Grand Rapids, Michigan: Baker Book House, 1983), 113.

While it is true that Leithart refers to definitive sanctification as a monergistic act of God, this monergistic act takes place at baptism, according to his views. Every baptized person is given the same gifts by God, and the difference is in the way the baptized person responds to that gift. As Leithart said in another place:

> Baptism is God's act, and it is real and objective as the water on the baptized. Everyone who is baptized is claimed by Christ as His own. Baptism is not double, but the response to baptism is. Some will respond with faith in the promise delivered in baptism, and with loyal adherence to the Lord who claims them. Others will respond with varying degrees of treachery. Both, though, are baptized, and the traitor's end is all the worse because he rejected gifts God gave him.[18]

Despite calling sanctification God's monergistic act, Leithart repudiates monergism in this place and others. That is a common theme of the Federal Vision proponents. For Leithart, it is the response of the person baptized that makes the difference, not the gift or grace of God. Augustine dealt with the same issue in his controversy with Pelagius and continually quoted to him 1 Corinthians 4:7—"What do you have that you did not receive?" That single verse convinced Augustine that it is God's sovereign grace alone which makes us to differ. Thereby, he rejected and opposed Pelagius' view that the difference is in the response of the individual. The Federal Vision proponents make the same mistake as Pelagius made when they assert, as Leithart does, that the response to baptism is what makes us to differ.

Perseverance

The Scriptures teach twin truths about the doctrine of perseverance that cover both the divine and human sides of the equation. First, believers are preserved by the Lord from falling away from salvation. For instance, it is taught that believers are "protected by the power of God through faith for a salvation ready to be revealed" (1 Peter 1:5) and "that He who began a good work in you will perfect it until the day of Christ Jesus" (Philippians 1:6). That is the divine side. Second, we are taught that "it is the one who has endured to the end who will be saved" (Matthew 10:22) and "we have become partakers of Christ if we hold fast the beginning of our assurance firm until the end" (Hebrews 4:14). True faith is faith that endures, faith that perseveres. Yet,

---

18 Record of the Case, Standing Judicial Commission, 2012-5, 202.

none of us could persevere without the preserving grace of God. On the other hand, no believer can fail to persevere since he is indeed upheld by Christ. Thus, perseverance is certain in the Scripture and the Reformed confessions when both sides of this issue are considered.

The Westminster Standards teach the same *ordo salutis* as the Scripture: predestination, effectual calling, regeneration, faith and repentance, justification, adoption, sanctification, perseverance, and glorification. These are all guaranteed to every one of the elect and form an unbroken continuum which results in eternal salvation.

The Federal Vision's Order of Salvation

The *ordo salutis* of the Federal Vision for the covenant community does not start with God's eternal predestination. Neither does it start with effectual calling. Their whole theory of salvation would fall apart if their advocates started with either one of those actions of God. Yet, it is impossible to combine the eternal predestination / unconditional election of the Scripture with their view of a conditional, covenant election. One necessarily excludes the other. It is impossible to combine the effectual calling / efficacious grace of the Scripture with their view of baptismal efficacy / inefficacious grace. Nevertheless, Federal Vision proponents such as Peter Leithart certainly attempt to combine these two very different streams of soteriology into one, as seen in the following quote:

> Does this leave me with a "parallel soteriological system to the decretal system of the Westminster Standards"? No more than the New Testament does, because the New Testament speaks both of people who are "in Christ" and cut off, and of people who are "in Christ" and can never be lost. As I understand the New Testament, this does not imply two parallel "soteriological systems." There are not two streams of salvation. There is only one. The elect have been in the stream since eternity and are, from their personal incorporation into Christ, in the stream.
>
> The reprobate may move in and then out of the same stream.[19]

In that quote, Leithart asserts that the reprobate move in and then out of the same stream of salvation as the elect. He thinks thereby that he maintains that there is only one stream of salvation, one order of salvation. Yet, no Reformed confession has ever held that the reprobate are ever truly in the stream of salvation. Leithart's views

19 Ibid., 198.

require him to define the stream of salvation as the visible church, in distinction from the invisible church. Yet, the true stream of salvation is composed only of those who are elect in Christ from the foundation of the world.

Scripture cannot accommodate Leithart's theory of the order of salvation. Romans 8:29, 30 is very specific that the elect and only the elect are in the golden chain of salvation. Only those elected are called; only those called are justified; and, only those justified are glorified.

Yet, here is the Federal Vision's order of salvation which is gathered from the various statements its proponents have made about baptism in earlier chapters or in chapters that will follow:

- Baptismal efficacy / (inefficacious grace)
- Covenant election through baptism (temporary for many)
- New life (an ecclesiastical change of status)
- Justification by baptism (not permanent for all)
- Adoption by baptism (not permanent for all)
- Sanctification by baptism
- Faith as a response to baptism (not permanent for all)
- Justification by faith (temporary until the final verdict at the judgment)
- Perseverance (some, not all, persevere)
- Apostasy (which is not always permanent)
- Final Justification (for those alone who persevere in covenant faithfulness)
- Glorification (for those only who are finally justified)

Summary

In the Federal Vision system, covenant election is the result of baptism, whereas the unconditional and eternal election of the Scripture precedes every other grace that God bestows. The Federal Vision proponents, such as Leithart, say they believe in effectual calling according to the Westminster Standards, and deny that they believe in parallel orders of salvation—one for the elect and another for the reprobate. Yet, their whole system is a denial of efficacious grace. Where would eternal predestination and effectual calling fit in the above order of salvation? They cannot go before baptismal efficacy / covenantal election without totally destroying the whole system. They cannot go before faith because the Federal Vision teaches that some have true faith and then apostatize. They cannot go before the second justification because there is no guarantee that such will persevere and be finally justified. They have to go after perseverance and final justification and before glorification. In other words, the divine decree would have to be a decree to save those who are foreseen to persevere and to be finally justified. We could ask similar questions about all the other steps of salvation in the ordo salutis. The order of salvation of the Federal Vision is actually an order of salvation for some and an order of damnation for others. They combine election and reprobation in the same ordo salutis.

Conclusion

There is no possible way that the Federal Vision system can be melded together with the Scripture and the Westminster Standards into one order of salvation. The Federal Vision's supposed order of salvation is actually hyper-synergism, and cannot be reconciled with the monergism of God's free grace and His order of salvation. Their system is so confused that covenant election comes after the sacrament of baptism which is the symbol and seal of salvation for the elect according to the Scripture and the Westminster Standards. Theirs is an order of salvation in which the caboose is pulling the train.

-10-

The Federal Vision and Theonomy

"Central to the theory and practice of Christian ethics, whether personal or social, is every jot and tittle of God's law as laid down in the revelation of the Older and New Testaments. The Christian is obligated to keep the whole law of God as a pattern of sanctification, and in the realm of human society the civil magistrate is responsible to enforce God's law against public crime."[1]

GREG BAHNSEN, FORMER PROFESSOR AT REFORMED THEOLOGICAL SEMINARY IN JACKSON, MS

---

1 Greg L. Bahnsen, *Theonomy in Christian Ethics* (Nutley, New Jersey: The Craig Press, 1977), xiii.

Historic Christianity and the Federal Vision

In 1975-6, a new theological movement called "theonomy" burst onto the scene of the Reformed world through the teaching of a first-year professor, Dr. Greg Bahnsen, at Reformed Theological Seminary (RTS) in Jackson, Mississippi. Bahnsen's first year as an instructor at RTS paralleled my senior year at that institution. One of the classes he taught was on "theonomy" and we read proof sheets of his forthcoming book, *Theonomy in Christian Ethics*[2], for our discussions and instruction. No class during my three years at RTS ever evoked such a wide-range of reactions as did that class. All of the other professors at RTS took issue with Bahnsen's basic thesis and prepared a paper in opposition to it. The Board of Trustees quickly became concerned with Bahnsen's teaching, with the result that his tenure at RTS was very brief. Like many students at that time, I was initially attracted to theonomy before rejecting it.

Key Assessment: Almost all of the Federal Vision proponents are / were theonomists or have been influenced by theonomy. The Federal Vision teaching is the doctrine of theonomy applied to the covenant.

Theonomy is a compound word from two Greek words—theos (God) and nomos (law). Theonomy purports to be simply the application of God's law to all of life. Yet, it is actually a unique and new twist on God's law. While the Reformed faith has always held to the continuing validity of the moral law and the fulfillment of the ceremonial laws in Christ, theonomy insists on the continuing validity of the civil or judicial law. Bahnsen's basic position is the "abiding validity of the law in exhaustive detail." He taught that every jot and tittle of the law was still normative in the Christian era. That position contradicts the Westminster Confession of Faith 19.4, which says:

> To them also, as a body politic, He gave sundry judicial laws, which expired together with the State of that people; not obliging any further now than the general equity thereof may require.

Of course, Bahnsen went to great lengths in his book and his classroom lectures to try to prove that the "general equity" required keeping the judicial laws in exhaustive detail. As he said:

> Central to the theory and practice of Christian ethics, whether personal or social, is every jot and tittle of God's law as laid down in the rev-

---

2 This book was not published until 1977.

elation of the Older and New Testaments. The Christian is obligated to keep the whole law of God as a pattern of sanctification, and in the realm of human society the civil magistrate is responsible to enforce God's law against public crime."[3]

There is a consensus in the Reformed community concerning the necessity of Christians to live in obedience to the moral law. Likewise, almost no one disagrees with Bahnsen that the ceremonial laws have been fulfilled in Christ. The disagreement is over the continuing validity of the civil laws in modern society. As R. Scott Clark succinctly writes:

> The Westminster Divines used the word "expired" to describe the civil and ceremonial laws and there is a flat contradiction between theonomic conviction of the "abiding validity" of the civil laws and the reformed view that they are "expired."[4]

Theonomy is an important aspect of the errors of the Federal Vision because it is one of its primary theological underpinnings. There are certainly other theologians who have influenced the Federal Vision, but the influence of theonomy cannot be overlooked. Not all theonomists agree with the Federal Vision movement and, perhaps not all those in the Federal Vision are theonomists. Yet, there is a great deal of overlap between those who hold to theonomy and to the Federal Vision.

One of the more well-known theonomists who holds to the Federal Vision is James Jordan. As a seminarian, he assisted Bahnsen in preparing his book on theonomy for publication. Many of the men in the Federal Vision today have been influenced by him and invite him to their churches for conferences. Peter Leithart, Jeffrey Meyer, and Greg Lawrence have all acknowledged their debt to Jordan for their understanding of the Scripture. Other men like John Barach, Steve Schlissel, Steve Wilkins, Rich Lusk, Tim Gallant, Andrew Sandlin, Michael Schneider, and Randy Booth are Federal Vision advocates who either have held to theonomy or still do. These men have greatly influenced the younger generation of ministers who are drawn to this heresy.

---

3 Bahnsen, *Theonomy*, xiii.

4 R. Scott Clark, "Theonomy and the Federal Vision," September 1, 2007. Accessed at: http://rscottclark.org/2007/09/theonomy-and-the-federal-vision/ on October 24, 2014.

The Two Strands of Theonomy

There are two intertwined strands to theonomy. One strand is civil and involves the reconstruction of society according to the civil or judicial laws of the Old Testament. This strand is known as Christian Reconstructionism. When most people think of theonomy, they imagine this strand as representative of the whole. But there is another strand to theonomy which emphasizes the application of the law to the covenant community. This strand is not as prominent as the civil aspect of theonomy, but it is definitely outlined in Bahnsen's book. The difference between these two strands is the difference between society and the church. The goal is the same in both; only the starting point is different. As Clark writes:

> Theonomy and the Federal Vision are not identical but they are twins. The FV wants to regenerate the culture through sacerdotalism, e.g., through baptismal union with Christ whereby all baptized persons are, ex opere operato (Rich Lusk, a proponent of the FV, has spoken this way—on this see *Covenant, Justification, and Pastoral Ministry*), and temporarily, historically, conditionally united to Christ. Both visions are aimed at the restoration of Christendom. One is primarily ecclesiastical and the other primarily civil. These common attitudes, interests, and approaches, however, help explain why so many theonomists have been attracted to the FV and vice versa.[5]

Many people who become theonomists are first attracted to the goal of the reconstruction of society according to the laws of the Bible. In a fallen world, that illusory hope can be very enticing, even intoxicating, which explains why even some non-Reformed ministers have adopted theonomy. A number of them adopt theonomy as an addendum to an otherwise evangelical, gospel centered theology. It is my conviction from personal conversations with him that even Bahnsen viewed theonomy that way.

Bahnsen's Agreement with Evangelical Theology

The following quotes from his book show the basic evangelical bent of Bahnsen's theology:

(1) Bahnsen taught that our redemption is in Christ, in His atonement, which must be applied to us by the work of the Spirit in order to save us:

---

5 Ibid.

Theonomy is not a scheme for personal self-justification. God's grace, expressed in the accomplished and applied redemption of Jesus Christ, alone can save us.[6]

(2) He distinguished the law from the redemptive grace of God in the gospel:

Using the law as a means of salvation is highhanded flattery and disdain for God's grace.[7]

(3) Unlike most Federal Vision proponents and the followers of the New Perspectives on Paul, as taught by N. T. Wright, Bahnsen viewed the Judaizers in the Scripture as trusting in a works-based scheme of salvation:

Paul also opposed Judaistic legalism; many of the disparaging comments he makes about law-keeping are directed against the Judaizers who abused God's law by making it a way of justification.[8]

(4) He affirms the second and third uses of the law, that is, that it reveals the sinful condition of mankind and is a rule for the obedience of Christians:

The law does *not* save a man, but it *does* show him *why* he needs to be saved and *how* he is to walk after he is saved.[9]

(5) He would have repudiated the final justification theories of the Federal Vision and the New Perspectives on Paul because he believed that keeping the law can never be a condition for justification:

Christ's perfect obedience to the law of God secures our release from the necessity of personally keeping the law as a condition of justification.[10]

(6) Bahnsen taught that the law was a pattern for sanctification, but not justification. Yet, law was more comprehensive than the moral law in his view:

Scripture uniformly views the law as a standard of righteousness after

---

6 Bahnsen, *Theonomy*, 35.
7 Ibid., 90.
8 Ibid., 121.
9 Ibid., 127.
10 Ibid., 128.

which we should pattern our sanctification and Christian life, but *justification* is *never* by our obedience to the law.[11]

(7) Most Federal Vision proponents deny that the active obedience of Christ is imputed to believers. They generally restrict imputation to the passive obedience of the sufferings of Christ in His atonement. Bahnsen taught that both the active and passive righteousness of Christ are imputed to believers for their salvation:

> The extent of Christ's righteous obedience is seen in the fact that He both actively obeyed the prescriptive as well as passively obeying the penal requirements of the law, the former in order to qualify as a substitute, the latter in order to atone for sin. Having obeyed the law in its moral requirements in order that His perfect righteousness might be imputed to us, He came under the law's curse and condemnation so that our transgressions could be forgiven.[12]

(8) And again, he says:

> Therefore, although *our own* obedience to the law cannot be used as a way of justification, we are saved by the *imputed* obedience of the messiah (1 Cor. 1:30; Phil. 3:9), an obedience to *both* the prescriptive and penal requirements of God's law.[13]

(9) Bahnsen also was careful to distinguish between justification and sanctification contrary to many in the Federal Vision who conflate these two distinct graces:

> It is the perfect obedience of God's Son that is imputed to the Christian in justification, and sanctification can be understood as a progressive growth toward the personal realization of that level of righteousness which has been imputed to the believer.[14]

(10) The Joint Federal Vision Profession gives a very confused and confusing statement about regeneration. Yet, Bahnsen asserted very clearly that regeneration is the work of the Holy Spirit:

> Scripture says that the Holy Spirit regenerates us in order that we who were once disobedient and spiritually dead might live in accord with God's law.[15]

---

11 Ibid., 135.
12 Ibid., 152.
13 Ibid., 153.
14 Ibid., 161.
15 Ibid., 175.

(11) And finally, Bahnsen clearly taught justification by faith alone and his assessment of the book of Galatians is contrary to the views of the Federal Vision and N. T. Wright's New Perspectives on Paul:

> The fundamental concern of the book of Galatians is the gospel of justification by faith alone.[16]

In the above quotes, Bahnsen made several statements that are contradictory of the views of the Federal Vision and he denied that our works contribute to our justification, while never agreeing with the doctrine of a final justification.[17]

Bahnsen's View of the Judicial Laws

Yet, there is another strand of theonomy that introduces a new view of the law. Reformed theologians have generally taken the view which is expressed in the Westminster Standards that the moral law has permanent validity, but that the ceremonial and civil laws have expired. The Scripture itself indicates a difference between the three types of law—moral, ceremonial, and judicial. The moral law was written on tablets of stone, indicating permanency. Both the ceremonial and civil laws were written on vellum which, over time, passes away. Theonomy teaches that all of God's judicial laws have continuing validity in exhaustive detail. No Reformed confession has ever taken that view of the judicial laws.

Through this insistence on the continuing validity of all the judicial laws in exhaustive detail, theonomy also has flattened the distinction between the law and the gospel. That is an error which eventually results in a works righteousness scheme of salvation; but works righteousness is contrary to the entire argument of Paul in Galatians, especially Galatians 3:15-18. In that section, Paul shows that the promise of salvation through Christ predated the law by 430 years. It is interesting that Bahnsen makes no comment on Galatians 3:17, despite his copious remarks on numerous other verses of Scripture. Yet, Calvin comments on that verse:

---

16 Ibid., 499.

17 In 1977, I specifically asked Bahnsen about the passages of Scripture which teach that there will be a judgment according to works and his answer was in line with classical Reformed theology as represented by Cornelis Venema and others. His position at that time was contrary to the interpretation given to those passages, such as Romans 2, by the proponents of the Federal Vision and the New Perspectives on Paul.

> Paul blots out all the false doctrines taught by seducers who sought to mix the law and the gospel together. He is revealing that now all these things are superfluous, that is to say, sacrifices, circumcision and suchlike. That is not to argue that we cannot profit by reading what is contained in the law: no, but the practice of it has been abolished.[18]

Paul's argument in Galatians 3:15-18 is that the promise has permanent validity because it predated the law. If the law had been first, it would have the higher and more permanent position. As Calvin further elaborates:

> Now Paul asks, "Which is more ancient—the free promise of salvation or the law?" We are aware of the difference between them. Now if the law were the more ancient, it must hold firm, because God never changes and is not subject to variation. However, if the free promise came first and was made before the law was decreed, then we must conclude that God has not changed his mind, nor withdrawn his original promise. He would not have desired the abolition of this covenant, for such would been a withdrawal of his kindness and mercy. . . Paul tells us that the free promise was given before the law. It therefore follows that the law does not change anything about the promise; its nature and its force remain intact.[19]

Calvin's reasoning is that if the law had been given prior to the promise, then the promise would have been withdrawn and abolished when Christ came. The other side of that line of thought is that the ceremonial and judicial laws have now been withdrawn and abolished. Of course, Calvin is not implying that the moral law has been abolished. The moral law is permanent, as Francis Turretin shows:

> Hence arises a manifold difference between the moral law and others both in origin (because the moral is founded upon natural right and on this account is known by nature; but the others upon positive right and on this account are from free revelation) and in duration. The former is immutable and eternal; the latter mutable and temporary. In regard to object, the one is universal embracing all; the others particular applying only to the Jews (the civil, indeed, inasmuch as it regarded them as a distinct state dedicated to God; the ceremonial, however, referring to their ecclesiastical state and state of minority and infancy). In regard to use, the moral law is the end of the others, while the others are subservient to the moral.[20]

---

18 Kathy Childress, trans., John Calvin, *Sermons on Galatians* (Edinburgh, Scotland and Carlisle, Pennsylvania: The Banner of Truth Trust, 1997), 288.

19 Ibid., 290.

20 James T. Dennison, Jr., ed., George Musgrave Giger, trans., Francis Turretin, *Institutes of the*

The Federal Vision and Theonomy

Turretin's view on the law is common among Reformed theologians. By making all three types of law—moral, ceremonial, and civil—permanent with abiding validity in exhaustive detail, theonomy has reversed the scriptural position set forth in Galatians. Instead of being temporary, the ceremonial and civil laws would become permanent. It then becomes almost impossible to define in what ways those laws have continuing validity today. Some, like R. J. Rushdoony, think that even the dietary laws are binding on Christians today since those laws were not part of the sacrificial laws which point to the atonement of Christ. Yet, the larger problem is that this emphasis on the abiding validity of all the Old Testament laws necessarily reduces the importance of the gospel. It establishes a conflict in the hearts of everyone who imbibes theonomy which can only be resolved when either the law or the gospel becomes the dominant principle. For many theonomists, the law prevails and they become proponents of the Federal Vision. For other theonomists, the conflict is unresolved and the battle is unremitting. Some ultimately reject theonomy altogether and cling to the gospel.

There is some debate whether R. J. Rushdoony and Greg Bahnsen would be in the Federal Vision if they were alive today. David Bahnsen has stated his father would be in favor of the Federal Vision. Bahnsen's principles of theonomy and his Reformed soteriology were certainly in dynamic conflict. Eventually he might have chosen one or the other as the ruling theology in his life. While it is doubtful that he would have thrown away his pet theory of theonomy, he also knew theology too well to easily cast off evangelical and Reformed soteriology. In my opinion, it is likely that he would have held to both without allowing either one to dominate the other. It is easier to surmise what Rushdoony would have done. Rushdoony wrote the foreword to Bahnsen's book on theonomy and made a statement that represented a decidedly Federal Vision interpretation of faith:

> True faith means law-obedience, and obedience spells power and blessing.[21]

In that statement, Rushdoony goes beyond what Reformed theology has always said about faith producing fruit. He equates faith with

---

Elenctic Theology, Volume 2 (Phillipsburg, New Jersey: P&R Press, 1994), 146.
21 Rousas J. Rushdoony, "Foreword" in Bahnsen, *Theonomy*, xi.

law-obedience. It is not difficult to see how such a definition of faith could soon become known as "covenant faithfulness" as in "true faith means covenant faithfulness."

There are several theonomists who hold theonomy as an addition to evangelical theology. They believe in the gospel and justification by faith alone. They preach evangelical doctrines regularly and are in complete disagreement with the Federal Vision at that point. Some of them are among the most vociferous critics of the Federal Vision and accuse it of being a heresy. Such theonomists are in agreement with one strand of theonomy—the strand which concerns civil society. Theonomy, to them, means that true Christians are responsible to keep the moral and judicial laws as a rule for their obedience and that they should work to get just laws into their society. Such theonomists deny that the principles of theonomy are to be applied to the doctrine of the covenant. Guy Prentis Waters, however, shows that the Federal Vision and theonomy are based on the exact same hermeneutical principle:

> We have seen that the hermeneutic employed by many FV proponents resonates with theonomic conceptions of the covenantal continuity. For all of theonomy's care to emphasize its espousal of the necessity of personal regeneration, of biblical preaching, and of personal piety, the published writings of theonomist writers have generally emphasized the outward, the external and the corporate. It is this emphasis that has occasioned FV proponents' recasting of biblical religion along predominately outward, external, and corporate lines.[22]

Not all theonomists emphasize the outward, the external, and the corporate in their writings, but many of them do. Not all theonomists apply their hermeneutical principle to the doctrine of the covenant. Yet, the tendency of theonomy is certainly towards a "recasting of biblical religion along predominately outward, external, and corporate lines." Those theonomists who do not move in that direction are being inconsistent with their basic principles. They have two competing systems of theology within their hearts and minds. Yet, as Christ taught, no man can serve two masters. He will either love the one and not the other or he will serve the one and not the other.

---

22 Guy Prentiss Waters, *The Federal Vision and Covenant Theology: A Comparative Analysis* (Phillipsburg: P&R, 2006), 296.

The Federal Vision and Theonomy

Bahnsen's View of the Objectivity of the Covenant

In *Theonomy in Christian Ethics*, Bahnsen made several statements which laid the foundation for the development of the Federal Vision theology. For instance, he emphasized the objectivity of baptism and the sacraments apart from any mention of the subjective work of the Spirit:

> Similar words must be spoken with reference to Christian baptism. We who were buried with Christ in baptism are spiritually circumcised, signifying the cutting off of the sinful human nature (Col. 2:11-13); being raised with Christ we must seek those things which are above, in accord with godly holiness (Col. 3:1-17). The washing of baptism should have the effect of cleansing and sanctifying us (Eph. 5:25 f.) or else the baptism is meaningless for us. Our baptism must have the effect of causing us to walk in newness of life (Rom. 6:3 f.), which means that sin (the transgression of the law) should no longer reign in our lives (Rom. 6:5-13).[23]

Bahnsen stressed the effect that the washing of baptism *should* have in our lives. He totters between saying what the washing of baptism does and what it should do. He says that baptism spiritually circumcises us, raises us with Christ, and should have the effect of cleansing, sanctifying, giving us newness of life, and breaking the reign of sin in our lives. Bahnsen does not go as far as the Federal Vision proponents concerning water baptism, but neither does he emphasize the work of the Holy Spirit in the sacraments. Reformed theologians have always said that these graces are ours only through real baptism, the baptism of the Spirit. Bahnsen's position on baptism laid the foundation for the Federal Vision proponents adopting objective, external, and mediate views of the sacraments.

In another passage, Bahnsen emphasized obedience to the commandments as necessary to being built up in the means of grace and rightly partaking of the Lord's Supper:

> None of the means of grace can have the result of building us up in the faith if we do not strive to be obedient to the commandments of God. Disobedience to the law makes our prayer abominable, prevents us from understanding the word, makes us unworthy partakers of the Lord's supper, and is a forsaking of our covenant obligation in baptism.[24]

---

23 Bahnsen, *Theonomy*, 181.

24 Ibid.

Bahnsen's statement is altogether too legalistic and non-evangelical, putting too much emphasis on obedience to the exclusion of saving faith and the work of the Holy Spirit. In comparison, Larger Catechism #171 stresses evangelical graces as being the root of preparing us to come to the Lord's supper:

> They that receive the sacrament of the Lord's Supper are, before they come, to prepare themselves thereunto, by examining themselves of their being in Christ, of their sins and wants; of the truth and measure of their knowledge, faith, repentance, love to God and the brethren, charity to all men, forgiving those that have done them wrong; of their desire after Christ, and their new obedience; and by renewing the exercise of those graces, by serious meditation, and fervent prayer.

There are several statements in Bahnsen's book which lay the foundation for the erroneous position on perseverance which is prevalent in the Federal Vision. The Scripture and the Reformed confessions always speak of perseverance as a certainty for believers. Bahnsen and the Federal Vision define perseverance as a work which the members of the covenant community must perform in order to remain in good standing and to continue to be blessed. Perseverance defined in that way is not certain. It is at most a hypothetical possibility and a responsibility. Yet, certain perseverance is the teaching of Scripture and such perseverance is guaranteed by God's preserving grace. Here is what Bahnsen said about perseverance:

> Under the New Covenant, no less than the Older, continued blessing rests upon perseverance of the saints (Col. 1:22 f.; Heb. 3:14; 6:11f.; Phil. 3:13f.; etc.).[25]

The passages referenced by Bahnsen actually teach that God's saints will persevere because of the work of grace in their lives. For instance, Philippians 3:11 says, "I press on that I may lay hold of that for which I was laid hold of by Christ Jesus." Christ first laid hold of Paul and the Apostle's perseverance must be seen in that context. Certain perseverance is based on God's preserving grace which is prior to and greater than man's perseverance. Certain perseverance is guaranteed by God's grace.

In another passage, Bahnsen writes about the necessity of persevering obedience:

---

25 Ibid., 188.

> Continued blessing for Adam in paradise, Israel in the promised land, and the Christian in the kingdom has been seen to be dependent upon persevering obedience to God's will as expressed in His law.[26]

In this passage, Bahnsen makes no distinction between the persevering obedience to the law by Adam in paradise, Israel in the Promised Land, and Christians today. Yet, Adam did not have the grace of certain perseverance that is given to all believers in Christ. If he had possessed certain perseverance as believers possess it, then he could not have fallen into sin. As the Shorter Catechism #13 says:

> Our first parents, *being left to the freedom of their own will*, fell from that estate wherein they were created, by sinning against God. (Italics added for emphasis.)

The believer is never left entirely to the freedom of his own will in the matter of his perseverance, as Adam was. The grace of perseverance is a gift of God and the additional gift of God's preserving protection is afforded every believer. Adam in paradise did not have those graces, and was no match for the subtlety of the Devil in his day of trial. The perseverance of the believer cannot be equated with the trial of Adam in the Garden. By doing so, Bahnsen set the stage for wrong views by the Federal Vision on salvation, the law, the covenant of works, and perseverance.

The possibility of losing our covenant blessings through disobedience is enunciated by Bahnsen in another quote:

> If a man disobeys God's law, he has broken covenant with God, and his covenant sign loses its value; this is just as true under the New Covenant as under the Older.[27]

It is not difficult to see how Bahnsen's view has morphed into the view by several Federal Vision proponents that unfaithfulness to the covenant causes covenant members to lose their elect standing in Christ, etc. Yet, God's covenant promises are not conditioned on the obedience of the members of the covenant; otherwise they would surely fail. As Calvin comments on Jeremiah 32:40:

26 Ibid., 203.
27 Ibid., 188.

> Thus he again shows that perseverance, no less than the commencement of acting rightly, is the gift of God and the work of the Holy Spirit... It hence then follows, that the whole course of our life is directed by the Spirit of God, so that the end no less than the beginning of good works ought to be ascribed to his grace.[28]

Concerning the law both before and after the fall, Bahnsen says:

> The law, both *prior* to and *after* the fall, is gracious. *Subsequent* to *salvation* the law shows us how to *respond* to God's grace and love.[29]

In the context of this quote, Bahnsen emphasizes that the law reveals the redemptive work of Christ, but his caricature of the law's work is too optimistic. He does not distinguish between the grace of God before the fall and after the fall, particularly its effect on the unbelieving conscience. In comparison, Calvin represented the law very differently:

> Because observance of the law is found in none of us, we are excluded from the promises of life, and fall back into the mere curse. For since the teaching of the law is far above human capacity, a man may indeed view from afar the proffered promises, yet he cannot derive any benefit from them. Therefore this thing alone remains: that from the goodness of the promises he should the better judge his own misery, while the hope of salvation cut off he thinks himself threatened with certain death. On the other hand, horrible threats hang over us, constraining and entangling not a few of us only, but all of us to a man. They hang over us, I say, and pursue us with inexorable harshness, so that we discern in the law only the most immediate death.[30]

What then are Bahnsen's fundamental flaws with respect to the law? His emphasis on being obedient to the law in exhaustive detail brings about a possible conceit that such obedience is actually possible for the believer. The whole of Scripture testifies otherwise, as Calvin so eloquently stated above. The moral law is the rule for the obedience of the believer, but no Christian can perfectly fulfill it. To the unbeliever, the law is a fearful threat of impending doom.

---

28 John Calvin, *A Commentary on Jeremiah*, Volume IV (Edinburgh, Scotland and Carlisle, Pennsylvania: The Banner of Truth Trust, 1989), 217.

29 Bahnsen, *Theonomy*, 235.

30 Ford Lewis Battles, trans., John T. McNeill, ed., *Calvin: Institutes of the Christian Religion*, Volume 1, The Library of Christian Classics, Volume XX (Philadelphia: The Westminster Press, 1967), 352.

Thus, Bahnsen is guilty of two errors in his work on theonomy. First, he established a new paradigm for the law by connecting the believer's obedience to the whole Old Testament law in exhaustive detail. Second, he emphasized obedience to the law so strenuously that he often comes close to the dangerous Pelagian spectrum of errors. Pelagius, as we have seen, taught that mankind could live in obedience to God's requirements. *Theonomy in Christian Ethics* often makes it seem like the believer can actually fulfill all of God's laws. There is very little emphasis in theonomy on the threatening aspect of the law which Calvin described above. Concerning the law, Pelagius taught:

> But we do praise God as the Author of our righteousness, in that He gave us the law, by the teaching of which we have learned how we ought to live.[31]

Pelagius, likewise, almost completely discounted the threatening aspects of the law and saw the law as a gracious act of God which revealed the way the righteous should live.

Summary
The theonomic teaching of Greg Bahnsen is a system that is in dynamic conflict with itself. Bahnsen combined evangelical doctrines with an insistence that the whole Old Testament law in exhaustive detail must be obeyed. Yet, an evangelical interpretation of the law says that the law cannot be kept perfectly by fallen creatures, even when redeemed by God's free grace in Christ. Theonomy makes it seem that Christians can fulfill the law. That error places the scheme of theonomy within the spectrum of the Pelagian heresies. It was Pelagius who taught that the law revealed how we ought to live. The result is that the law is diminished by those who think they can keep it. The law becomes formal, outward, and objective. It is also reduced to the level of our ability to obey it. Thus, the theonomic system of Bahnsen has resulted in the covenant nomism of the Federal Vision which neither requires nor expects that the law will be kept perfectly and perpetually.

---

31 Philip Schaff, ed., *Nicene and Post-Nicene Fathers*, Volume V, (Grand Rapids: Wm. B. Eerdmans Publishing Company, 1971), 88.

Conclusion

The melding together of sacerdotalism and theonomy is not an entirely new phenomenon in the history of the church, either. Philip Schaff writes concerning the monk, Damiani:

> Damiani became the leader of the strict monastic party which centred at Cluny and labored, from the sacerdotal and theocratic point of view, for a reformation of the clergy and the church at a time of their deepest degradation and corruption.[32]

Despite his assertion of justification by faith alone, Bahnsen blurs the issue in the following quote:

> Quite clearly we are justified by faith—that is, by *living* faith, and "faith without works is dead" (Jas. 2:16).[33]

It is not difficult to see how defining justification in terms of a "living faith" can easily become defining justification in terms of a faith that is covenantally faithful. In that way, the emphasis is placed on the kind of faith that justifies; rather than the object of faith, the person and work of the Lord Jesus. That easily becomes the heresy of Pelagianism and Rome. Whenever a leader of a movement speaks with confusion rather than clarity, the followers of that movement will be more attracted to the confusing aspects than to the clear aspects. They will go even further in their confusion than their teacher. Thus, Bahnsen's confusion concerning justification by faith alone and the law has inescapably resulted in his disciples becoming even more confused. Bahnsen's adoption of several aspects of the objectivity of the covenant has resulted in his disciples adopting erroneous views of the sacraments. It is not a coincidence that the revival of sacerdotalism has grown out of the theonomic camp.

The most interesting point, though, is that the Federal Vision is a theory of covenant nomism or neonomianism. Their theory is similar to the views of neonomianism. Neonomianism believes that Christ has made a *new law* that is significantly easier to follow than the Mosaic law. Federal Vision proponents such as Rich Lusk disagree with the Westminster Confession of Faith that the law re-

---

32 Philip Schaff, *History of the Christian Church*, Volume IV, (Grand Rapids, Michigan: Wm. B. Eerdmans Publishing Company, 1980), 789.

33 Bahnsen, *Theonomy*, 162.

quires personal, perpetual, and perfect obedience. Such a theory is akin to neonomianism and is in dynamic conflict with the stated principles of theonomy. Theonomy says that the law is still valid in exhaustive detail. Neonomianism says that the law has been relaxed to make it easier to obey. So which is it? Is the law still valid in exhaustive detail or has the law been relaxed? The Federal Vision has no answer to that question.

-11-

The Federal Vision and the Reformed Symbols

> "I do not believe that my conclusions are outside the Reformed tradition, but I recognize that I have been pushing various boundaries on this issue... The Reformed tradition has been 'narrow' in its grasp of justification, and that it is 'too rigid' in distinguishing justification and sanctification... There is a long history in the Reformed tradition of referring to the final, favorable judgment on the righteous as a 'justification.'"[1]
>
> PETER LEITHART, FEDERAL VISION PROPONENT

> "We have allowed our theological system to become a filter through which we read the Word of God."[2]
>
> STEVE WILKINS, FEDERAL VISION PROPONENT

---

[1] Record of the Case, Standing Judicial Commission of the Presbyterian Church in America, Case 2012-5, RE Gerald Hedman vs. Pacific Northwest Presbytery, 186, 209, 211.

[2] Steve Wilkins, "Introduction," in *The Federal Vision* (Monroe, Louisiana: Athanasius Press, 2005), 12.

The purity of the gospel as expounded in the Reformed symbols such as the Westminster Confession of Faith, the Canons of Dort, the Heidelberg Catechism, and others is at issue in this doctrinal controversy with the Federal Vision. No Presbyterian and Reformed creeds, confessions, or catechisms either explicitly or implicitly teach the Federal Vision's scheme of salvation. Papist and Orthodox symbols teach similar views on baptismal efficacy, justification, and other doctrines, but those symbols differ with the Federal Vision on the matter of subjective grace. Thus, the Federal Vision is even more purely Pelagian than the Council of Trent (Roman Catholic) and the Confession of Dositheus (Orthodox). When Reformed creeds are referenced in support of the Federal Vision position, they are misread, misunderstood, or misquoted.

It is typical for Federal Vision proponents to support their views by reference to the teaching of anyone within the broader Reformed community over the past five hundred years who has ever said anything similar to their positions. Apparently, that is their unstated definition of the Reformed tradition. First, they pit Scripture against the Reformed creeds, as the Orthodox Presbyterian Church correctly alleged in 2004. Second, they appeal to the views of ministers, whether heterodox or heretical in their doctrine, as proof of their own supposed Reformed bona fides. They rule almost nothing in or out of the Reformed tradition, particularly in the areas of sacramentology and soteriology. Yet, almost every heresy which has ever existed has also been taught by someone within the broader Reformed tradition over the past five hundred years. Thus, there has to be a better definition of the Reformed tradition, and there is. The definitive elements of the Reformed tradition can rightly be gathered only from the expressions of it in the various Reformed creeds. Thus, Philip Schaff wrote in his *The Harmony of the Reformed Confessions*:

> The Reformed Confessions are Protestant in bibliology, oecumenical or old catholic in theology and Christology, Augustinian in anthropology and the doctrine of predestination, evangelical in soteriology, Calvinistic in ecclesiology and sacramentology, and anti-papal in eschatology.[3]

There is a generic consensus among the various Reformed creeds and confessions. The same system of doctrine is found in all of them

---

3 Philip Schaff, *The Harmony of the Reformed Confessions: As Related to the Present State of Evangelical Theology* (New York: Dodd, Mead, and Company, 1877), 10.

which is the true Reformed tradition. Yet, there is great dissimilarity among the various views of many Reformed ministers, past and present. The true Reformed tradition must be found in the Reformed symbols—not in the personal views of Reformed ministers. Otherwise, there is no Reformed tradition unless it also includes almost every heresy known to the church.

Proponents of the Federal Vision frequently use anecdotal illustrations to buttress their assertions about the correct interpretation of Scripture. This has been a favorite tactic of ministers who hold to Federal Vision views while serving in evangelical, Reformed denominations. Both Steve Wilkins and Peter Leithart resorted to this tactic when they were being tried or examined by their respective presbyteries. Both claimed validity for their positions whenever they could find any Reformed minister, however obscure, that taught one or another point similar to their scheme of salvation. On other occasions, Federal Vision proponents will claim that the Reformed symbols themselves are in support of their basic positions. Some of their references to various sections of those Reformed symbols prove nothing; other items actually prove harmful to their position—such as where one part of the symbols qualifies another part contrary to the sense that the Federal Vision proponents attach to it. Yet, no statement in any of the Reformed symbols, rightly understood, ever supports the doctrines taught by the Federal Vision system.

The Reformed Symbols

There are certainly statements in all the Reformed symbols that can be twisted contrary to their context and intended meaning. Some of those statements can beguile the misguided in ways that are favorable to the Federal Vision. At the 2002 Pastors' Conference in Monroe, Louisiana, Steve Wilkins cherry-picked statements from several of the Reformed symbols and read them to the gathered pastors in an attempt to prove that the Federal Vision view of baptismal efficacy was also the view of the Reformers. From various reports of that session, there was an excitement which ran through the audience as the attendees felt they had been given the key to interpreting the symbols. The Defense for Peter Leithart at his trial, referred to certain statements from the Consensus Tigurinus (written in 1549 by Calvin to bring unity among the Reformed ministers on the sacraments, especially the Lord's Supper) as supposed "proof" that the Consensus, among other Reformed symbols, took a high view of the efficacy of the sacraments, particularly baptism. In the trial documents, they quoted the fifth through the twentieth statements of the Consensus Tigurinus and highlighted the ninth statement, which reads:

> IX. THE SIGNS AND THE THINGS SIGNIFIED ARE DISTINCT. Therefore although we draw a distinction, as we must, between signs and the things signified, yet we do not disjoin the truth from the signs. But we acknowledge that all who embrace in faith the promises there offered receive Christ spiritually with his spiritual gifts, and even those who for a long time have been partakers of Christ continue and renew their commitment.[4]

It is puzzling why Federal Vision proponents would ever think that the ninth article of the Consensus Tigirinus is favorable to their position. A careful reading of that article teaches that Christ and His gifts are offered and received only by those who have faith in Him before coming to the sacrament. For that reason, Charles Hodge could write concerning this symbol:

> The Consensus Tigurinus is the most carefully prepared and guarded statement of the doctrine of the Reformed Church which has come down from the age of the Reformation. . . Article nineteen teaches that the benefits signified by the sacraments may be obtained without their use. Paul's sins were remitted before he was baptized. Cornelius received the Spirit before he received the external sign of regeneration. In the twentieth article it is taught that the benefit of the sacrament is not confined to the time of their administration. God sometimes regenerates in their old age those who were baptized in infancy or youth.[5]

Hodge also referred to the ninth article quoted above as being consistent with the statements in the rest of the Consensus. Of course, we are not left to depend on Hodge's assessment of the Consensus Tigurinus for our understanding of that symbol. Calvin himself has given us an exposition of the articles:

> What would these worthy men have here? Would they have God to act by the Sacraments? We teach so. Would they have faith to be exercised, cherished, aided, confirmed by them? This too we assent. Would they

---

4 Record of the Case, Standing Judicial Commission, 2012-5, 133.

5 Charles Hodge, *Systematic Theology*, Volume III (Grand Rapids, Michigan: Wm. B. Eerdmans Publishing Company, 1970), 580-581

have the power of the Holy Spirit to be exerted in them, and make them available for the salvation of God's elect? We concede this also. The question turns upon this—should we ascribe all the parts of our salvation entirely to God alone, or does he himself by using the Sacraments transfer part of his praise to them. . . When we say, that the signs are not available to all indiscriminately, but to the elect only, to whom the inward and effectual working of the Spirit is applied, the thing is too clear to require a lengthened statement. For if any one wishes to make the effect common to all, he is not only refuted by the testimony of Scripture, but by experience.[6]

Calvin distinguishes his view of sacramental efficacy by several things. First, he says that salvation is ascribed to God's grace alone and not to the efficacy of the sacraments apart from the work of the Spirit. Second, Calvin says the sacramental signs "are not available to all indiscriminately, but to the elect only." Third, the sacraments are a seal of the "inward and effectual working of the Spirit" in the hearts of the elect. Concerning the idea that the efficacy of the sacraments is common to all who participate in them, Calvin says that such a view "is not only refuted by the testimony of Scripture, but by experience." Moreover, Calvin says the sacraments seal the inward and effectual work of the Spirit, whereas the Federal Vision says the sacraments confer external, objective grace. In the same exposition of the Consensus Tigurinus, Calvin further elaborates:

> The effect of the spiritual blessings which the sacraments figure, is given to believers without the use of the sacraments. As this is daily experienced to be true, and is proved by passages of Scripture, it is strange if any are displeased with it.[7]

Calvin later wrote a little tract called, *The Best Method of Obtaining Concord*, to set forth the views upon which the Reformed pastors agreed concerning the sacraments. In that tract, he stated:

> The grace or virtue of the Spirit is not inclosed by the external signs, because they do not profit all equally or indiscriminately, nor does the effect also appear at the same moment; but that God uses the Sacrament as to him seems good, so they help forward the salvation of the elect, and instead of conferring anything on others rather turn to their destruction. That, in short, the Sacraments are of no avail unless they

---

[6] Henry Beveridge, ed. and trans., *John Calvin: Tracts and Letters*, Volume 2: Tracts, Part 2 (Edinburgh, Scotland and Carlisle, Pennsylvania: The Banner of Truth Trust, 2009), 229-231.

[7] Ibid., 236.

are received in faith, which is a special gift of the Spirit, not depending on earthly elements, but on the operation of the same Spirit. External helps are only added to meet the weakness of our capacity.[8]

There are several statements in this tract that show Calvin's view on the sacraments, and the views of the other Reformation leaders, were diametrically opposite of the views of the Federal Vision. Calvin makes it clear that the sacraments do not "confer anything" on those who are not the elect, but instead work to their destruction. Calvin states that the Reformers were agreed on these points. There is simply no way that the Federal Vision proponents can twist Calvin's words to favor their position. The Reformers agreed that the sacraments are effective only through the operation of the Holy Spirit to those who have true faith inasmuch as they alone are the elect of God. All others receive the sacraments to their damnation and destruction. Of course, this is exactly what Paul warns in 1 Corinthians 11:27, 29:

> Therefore whoever eats the bread or drinks the cup of the Lord in an unworthy manner, shall be guilty of the body and blood of the Lord. . . For he who eats and drinks, eats and drinks judgment to himself if he does not judge the body rightly.

Calvin's view of the efficacy of the sacraments is in line with the other great Reformed symbols. For instance, Questions 70 and 72 of the Heidelberg Catechism on holy baptism, say:

> Q 70. What is it to be washed with the blood and Spirit of Christ?
> A. It is to have the forgiveness of sins from God, through grace, for the sake of Christ's blood, which he shed for us in his sacrifice on the cross; and also to be renewed by the Holy Ghost, and sanctified to be members of Christ, that so we may more and more die unto sin and live unto righteousness.
> Q. 72. Is, then, the outward washing of water itself the washing away of sins?
> A. No; for only the blood of Jesus Christ and the Holy Spirit cleanse us from all sin.

Philip Schaff was by no means rash or imprudent in his judgments and can never be accused of taking a fringe position. He has summarized the teaching of the Reformed confessions concerning the sacraments as follows:

---

8 "The Best Method of Obtaining Concord" in Calvin, *Tracts and Letters*, Volume 2, 573-4.

> The opus operatum theory, the necessary connection of water with moral regeneration and all mechanistic conceptions of the real presence, whether in the form of transubstantiation or consubstantiation, are rejected.
>
> > Here lies the serious doctrinal difference between the Calvinistic and Lutheran symbols. The former make spiritual regeneration independent of water baptism, so that it may either precede or succeed it or coincide with it, according to divine pleasure. . . . The latter teach unconditional baptismal regeneration.[9]

Schaff states unequivocally that all the Reformed symbols reject the baptismal regeneration theories of the Lutheran and Catholic churches. In the Reformed symbols, spiritual regeneration is independent of water baptism and can happen before, during, or afterwards, according to God's sovereign grace. The Federal Vision teaches that baptismal regeneration of a particular kind, an ecclesiastical new life, takes place at every baptism. They teach that a baptized person is given objective grace and formally united with the church, but deny the bestowal of subjective grace. In so doing, they mistakenly think they have avoided the error of Catholicism which is Semi-Pelagian on the sacrament of baptism. By limiting grace to that which is objective, the Federal Vision takes a more purely Pelagian position, whether wittingly or unwittingly.

Many people erroneously think that the doctrinal symbols of the Anglican communions teach baptismal regeneration, but Schaff asserts otherwise:

> The Church of England teaches in her formularies the Calvinistic theory of the sacraments in general, and of the Lord's Supper in particular; but in the baptismal service of the Book of Common Prayer, she clearly teaches baptismal regeneration without qualification, and in practice she gives larger scope to the sacramentarian principle.[10]

Neither the doctrinal standards of the Church of England, nor its leading ministers up to the time of William Laud, Archbishop of Canterbury from 1633-1640, had ever taught baptismal regeneration. The sacerdotal corruption of that denomination was in contradiction of her doctrinal formularies.

---

9 Schaff, *Harmony of the Reformed Confessions*, 15.
10 Ibid., 16.

Reformed Tradition

Federal Vision proponents, such as Peter Leithart, claim that their sacramental views are within the Reformed tradition and buttress their claim with quotes from various ministers within the broader Reformed church. Sometimes, those sources are quoted accurately, and other times they are not. Many of the ministers and theologians quoted as examples of the Reformed tradition, such as Richard Baxter or Louis LeBlanc or Pierre Jurieu and others, are either not well-known or are not first-rate theologians. In no other discipline or science would the second-rate and third-rate men be held up as examples of what the tradition should be.

One probable reason why the Federal Vision proponents make the interpretation of Scripture subservient to the views of ministers within their definition of the Reformed tradition is that they can always find support for their views somewhere in the teaching of someone ordained at some time or another in a Reformed church. That definition of tradition is their friend. On the other hand, the Reformed symbols are strictly opposed to all the foundational doctrines of the Federal Vision. There is no support in either Scripture or the Reformed symbols for the Federal Vision doctrines on justification by covenant faithfulness, the covenants, assurance, final justification, the sacraments, apostasy, grace, baptismal efficacy, regeneration, etc.

At the time of the Protestant Reformation, both sides in the controversy appealed to tradition, in addition to the teaching of Scripture, in support of their views. Both sides could also find support for their views in tradition because there are two very different Christian traditions within the history of the church. One tradition is based on the foundation of the apostles and prophets, with Christ being the chief cornerstone. That tradition of scriptural doctrine is carried forth, albeit imperfectly, from the foundation of the New Testament church to our own day, and is based on the Reformation principle, Sola Scriptura (Scripture alone). The other tradition goes back to the Pharisees and the Judaizers, being characterized by ceremonialism (sacramentalism) and works salvation (nomism of various sorts, including what is today called "covenant faithfulness"). The first tradition is known as Augustinianism and / or Calvinism. The second tradition is known as Pelagianism, Semi-Pelagianism, and Arminianism. The first tradition places Scripture above tradition. The second tradition places tradition above Scripture and is guilty of the same error for which Christ rebuked the Pharisees (Matthew 15:3-6). These two very different traditions have sometimes become intermingled in the minds and hearts of some ministers within the broader Reformed community. Yet, the inconsistencies of such ministers within the broader Reformed community do not make their views a part of the true Reformed tradition. Only someone who holds to the view that tradition is of greater importance than Scripture would ever think that way. The true Reformed tradition holds to Scripture alone above all else. The Reformed symbols are then viewed as subordinate standards, subservient to Scripture. The appeal to the views of other ministers is not for the purpose of establishing correct doctrine, but for the purpose of showing that the true scriptural doctrine has been held by some in all ages of the church.

Interestingly, the Reformed tradition is never defined by the Federal Vision proponents in any place that I can find. Yet, they continually appeal to this undefined Reformed tradition. The history of the Reformed churches includes numerous heresies. Are all those heresies also a part of the Reformed tradition since they were held by one or another minister at one time or another by men within the broader Reformed tradition? Is Barthianism an acceptable position within the Reformed tradition? Why or why not? Is neonomianism a part of the Reformed tradition? What about Sandemanianism or antinomianism? What about Arminianism or Socinianism? We could go on and on. Nonetheless, the Federal Vision proponents and their defendants remain undeterred. For instance, an expert witness at the trial of Peter Leithart testified as follows:

> I fear the time when we feel one particular interpretation of the standards is the only possible one. And we begin to rule out those who are still within the Reformed tradition that might have a slightly different interpretation of one issue or another.[11]

This expert witness mixes the Reformed symbols and the Reformed tradition together as one, without defining them. Of course, we are to maintain unity in essentials and liberty in non-essentials, but the essentials are defined by the Reformed symbols—not by some vague, undefined Reformed tradition.

One of the Federal Vision proponents, Peter Leithart, revealed at

---

11 Record of the Case, Standing Judicial Commission, 2012-5, 268-9.

his trial his own difficulty in defining his theological position in terms of either the Reformed symbols or the Reformed tradition:

> There are very few actual statements of the Confession that I disagree with.[12]
>
> I wanted to come up with a new way of talking about baptism and think about baptism for my own sake that would make 1 Peter 3, which has already been mentioned, seem like a very natural way to talk about baptism.[13]
>
> I do not believe my conclusions are outside the Reformed tradition, but I recognize that I have been pushing various boundaries on this issue.[14]
>
> I'm happy to have my views scrutinized and if in the judgment of the court, they're outside the bounds of the Westminster Confession that's one of the, one of my answers that I'm looking for the court to make that determination.[15]
>
> I guess I am still a Lutheran. . . . I grew up a Lutheran and I guess I still am.[16]

Leithart sometimes uses the Reformed tradition and the Westminster Confession as interchangeable terms and at other times he clearly distinguishes between them. A minister in a Reformed denomination does not subscribe to an undefined or ill-defined Reformed tradition, but to a specific Reformed symbol. Confusing the two things is harmful to the truth.

In the quotes above, Leithart made it clear that there were at least some statements of the Westminster Confession with which he disagrees. One of those statements would obviously be the whole matter of baptism, for he declared that he wanted to find "a new way of talking about baptism." He then mixed the undefined "Reformed tradition" with the Westminster Confession of Faith by saying that he did not think his views were outside the Reformed tradition, but he wanted the court to determine if they were outside the Westminster Confession of Faith. His views could very well be within someone's definition of the Reformed tradition, while remaining in blatant conflict with the Westminster Confession of Faith. Problems

12 Ibid., 496.
13 Ibid., 470.
14 Ibid., 186.
15 Ibid., 538.
16 Ibid., 526.

of this nature will continue to plague Reformed churches until her courts define the Reformed tradition as the essentials of the Reformed symbols.

Summary

There is no doubt that many of the views of the Federal Vision have been held by various ministers or theologians within the broader Reformed church. That fact does not place their views within the Reformed tradition, though. The Reformed tradition is rightly expressed within the various Reformed creeds. Those creeds are a faithful interpretation of the Scriptures and are amazingly consistent with one another, as Schaff clearly states. When the Federal Vision advocates appeal to the Reformed tradition while rejecting the doctrines taught by the Reformed symbols, they are being disingenuous. The Reformed tradition is comprised of those doctrines, especially soteriology and sacramentology, that are clearly taught in all the Reformed symbols.

Conclusion

The Federal Vision proponents often pretend to simply hold to the Scripture as their creed. This idea was exposed as a fraud by Edmund Burke in an eighteenth-century speech on the Acts of Uniformity:

> The subscription to Scripture is the most astonishing idea I have ever heard, and will amount to just nothing at all. Gentlemen so acute have not, that I have heard, ever thought of answering a plain obvious question: What is that Scripture, to which they are content to ascribe?. . . The Bible is a vast collection of different treatises: a man who holds the divine authority of one may consider the other as merely human. What is his canon? The Jewish—St. Jerome's—that of the Thirty Nine Articles—Luther's? Therefore to ascertain Scripture you must have one article more; you must define what Scripture is which you mean to teach. There are, I believe, very few who, when Scripture is so ascertained, do not see the absolute necessity of knowing what *general doctrine* a man draws from it, before he is sent down, authorized by the State, to teach it as pure doctrine, and receive a tenth of the produce of our lands. The Scripture is no one summary of doctrines regularly digested, in which a man could not mistake his way. It is a most venerable, but most multifarious collection of the records of the divine economy. . . If we do not get some security for this, we not only permit, but we actually pay

for, all the dangerous fanaticism which can be produced to corrupt our people, and to derange the public worship of the country. We owe the best we can (not infallibility, but prudence) to the subject: first sound doctrine, then ability to use it.[17]

Every Reformed creed or confession recognizes Scripture, not tradition, as the final arbiter in every matter of faith and practice. There is no disconnect between holding to Scripture and formulating doctrinal creeds. Creeds have always been the response of the church during times of doctrinal discord. They state unequivocally what is believed by the church concerning the doctrines at stake. The Federal Vision advocates want to move Reformed churches in a different direction. They tell us on the one hand that they believe in the Westminster Standards or the other Reformed symbols, but they contend that the Scripture pushes them in a different direction concerning their disputed views. If they cannot support their views from clear passages of Scripture, they appeal to uninspired men in support of their views—even men who have taught things judged by the church to be heterodox or, in some instances, heretical. Meanwhile, they contradict the clear teaching of the Reformed symbols on the doctrines of salvation. In so doing, they prove that their views are outside of the true Reformed tradition which is rightly found only in the Reformed symbols. In reality they have a system of doctrine which they are imposing on the Scripture, and they support it by reference to tradition—even as the Papists do; even as the Pharisees did.

---

17 William G. T. Shedd, *Theological Essays* (Minneapolis, Minnesota: Klock & Klock Christian Publishers, Inc., 1981), 338-9.

-12-
The Federal Vision and Unconditional Election

"Covenantal election and individual election to salvation aren't actually that far apart. We can distinguish them perhaps, but we cannot, and we may not divide them completely. What is the connection? The connection has to do with God's promise, God's speech to us. God has promised every covenant member that he or she is elect in Christ."[1]

JOHN BARACH, FEDERAL VISION PROPONENT

"In other words, baptism's efficacy unto salvation is conditioned ultimately on God's decree, but proximately on our response."[2]

RICH LUSK, FEDERAL VISION PROPONENT

---

1 Guy Prentiss Waters, *The Federal Vision and Covenant Theology: A Comparative Analysis* (Phillipsburg, New Jersey: P&R Publishing, 2006), 118.

2 Rich Lusk, *Paedofaith: A Primer on the Mystery of Infant Salvation and a Handbook for Covenant Parents* (Monroe, Louisiana: Athanasius Press, 2005), 58. By making efficacy unto salvation depend on "our response," Lusk negates the unconditional nature of God's election.

In his work, *Calvinism and Evangelical Arminianism*, John L. Girardeau (1825-1898), a Southern Presbyterian minister, stated that both theological systems hold that election represents a definite number of individuals who are chosen to eternal life. In the Arminian system, that definite number is a result of God's foreknowledge that certain people would believe and persevere in holiness to final salvation. Yet, God's foreknowledge is still of a definite number who attain eternal life. The grand difference between Calvinism and Arminianism on election, therefore, lies in a different direction. As Girardeau says:

> The main difference between the two doctrines, that in regard to which the stress of the controversy between them takes place, is concerning the question of the conditionality or the unconditionality of election.[3]

Key Assessment: The Federal Vision teaches the conditional election of all those who are baptized which is a view that is in dynamic conflict with the scriptural doctrine of unconditional election by God's grace alone.

The advocates of the Federal Vision espouse both a conditional election and an unconditional election. They generally refer to unconditional election as decretal election and to conditional election as covenant election (which results from baptism). This inconsistency in their beliefs is best summarized by J. Gresham Machen who wrote concerning liberalism in the early 1900s:

> There is sometimes a salutary lack of logic which prevents the whole of a man's faith being destroyed when he has given up a part. But the true way to examine a spiritual movement is in its logical relations; logic is the great dynamic, and the logical implications of any way of thinking are sooner or later to be worked out.[4]

There are many people who apparently are unwilling to question the Reformed *bona fides* of the Federal Vision adherents as long as they affirm (whether consistently or inconsistently) that they believe in the doctrine of election. In *Hedman vs. Pacific Northwest Presbytery*, the representatives of presbytery argued before the Standing Judicial Commission of the Presbyterian Church in America that Peter

---

3 John L. Girardeau, *Calvinism and Evangelical Arminianism: Compared as to Election, Reprobation, Justification, and Related Doctrines* (Harrisonburg, Virginia: Sprinkle Publications, 1984), 46.

4 J. Gresham Machen, *Christianity and Liberalism* (Grand Rapids, Michigan: William B. Eerdmans Publishing Company, 2009), 146.

Leithart is Reformed because he professes to hold to the doctrine of election. That assessment is too simplistic. In a section on the doctrinal views of the Pharisees, Alfred Edersheim revealed that Jewish sect vacillated between absolute predestination bordering on fatalism and making everything dependent on man's will:

> While the pharisees thus held the doctrine of absolute predestination, side by side with it they were anxious to insist on man's freedom of choice, his personal responsibility, and moral obligation. Although every event depended upon God, whether a man served God or not was entirely his own choice. As a logical sequence of this, fate had no influence as regarded Israel, since all depended on prayer, repentance, and good works.[5]

If the Federal Vision is a revival of the theological errors of the Judaizers and the Pharisees, it should not be surprising that the propagators of it vacillate between predestination and free will in the same manner as that ancient party. The vacillation of the Federal Vision advocates is manifested in their doctrine of covenant election which effectively negates God's eternal decree. For them, whether a person ultimately serves God or not is a matter of his or her own choice or perseverance, even as the Pharisees were accustomed to believe. No modern Reformed author would ever tout the Pharisees as being within the Reformed tradition, notwithstanding their espousal of absolute predestination. There is more to being Reformed than mere lip service to the most well-known doctrine of the Reformed faith. So, why should the Federal Vision proponents be classified as Reformed when they inconsistently hold to predestination after the example of the ancient Pharisees?

The Federal Vision and Election

It is certainly illogical and inconsistent for the advocates of the Federal Vision to hold to both conditional and unconditional election. Yet Federal Vision advocate, John Barach, attempts to connect so-called covenantal election with decretal election in the quote at the beginning of this chapter. Barach affirms that covenantal election bestows the privilege of incorporation into Christ on all the baptized. His view is that all those who are in covenant with Christ through bap-

---

5 Alfred Edersheim, *The Life and Times of Jesus the Messiah* (Peabody, Massachusetts: Hendrickson Publishers, 1995), 221.

tism are addressed by Paul and other apostles as the elect. Yet, Barach acknowledges that not all who are covenantally elect will prove to be eternally and unconditionally elect. In Barach's system, a member of the covenant can move back and forth from election to reprobation, depending on that person's covenant obedience or disobedience. Such a view connects election with covenantal obedience in an ongoing process and makes election conditional. As Guy Waters says:

> In summary, Barach embraces two distinct but overlapping doctrines of election. He affirms both decretal election and what he calls covenantal election. Decretal election for Barach has little practical value. He prefers to speak of covenantal election. Covenantal election, as Barach expresses it, bears remarkable similarities to the Arminian doctrine of conditional election. It is in this sense, notwithstanding his profession of the Reformed doctrine of (decretal) election, that we may say that Barach's overall doctrine of election is Arminian or at least semi-Arminian.[6]

Barach's view of covenantal election, like the view of others in the Federal Vision, is a corporate election to certain privileges (church membership, incorporation into Christ in a formal sense, etc.), but not the unconditional election of certain individuals to eternal life. Such a view of election has been the typical Arminian interpretation of the Scripture verses which refer to election. For instance, the Arminian commentator, James MacKnight, said concerning Romans 9:11:

> The Apostle, according to his manner, cites only a few words of the passage on which his argument is founded, but I have inserted the whole in the commentary, to show that Jacob and Esau are not spoken of as individuals, but as representing the two nations springing from them—"Two nations are in thy womb," etc.—and that the election of which the Apostle speaks is not an election of Jacob to eternal life, but of his posterity to be the visible Church and people of God on earth, and heirs of the promises in their first and literal meaning.[7]

Election for MacKnight is national, ecclesiastical, and visible, but not necessarily eternal. The covenantal election of Barach has all the essential aspects of the definition of election given by

---

6 Waters, *Federal Vision and Covenant Theology*, 120.

7 James Henley Thornwell, *The Collected Writings of James Henley Thornwell*, Volume 2: *Theological and Ethical* (Edinburgh, Scotland and Carlisle, Pennsylvania: The Banner of Truth Trust, 1974), 128.

MacKnight. Such covenantal election is corporate election of all those baptized, not individual election; it is election to privileges, not election to eternal life; it is election to the visible church, not the invisible church. That definition of election is and always has been the definition of both Arminians and Pelagians. For instance, Herman Bavinck astutely summarizes the weakness of the Pelagian system on predestination:

> Pelagianism seeks to vindicate itself at the point of "predestination to an efficacious grace." Reality teaches us that not everyone who hears the gospel receives it with a true faith. Why this difference? Pelagianism tells us that the grace that is granted to all is sufficient by itself; and that now the human will decides whether that grace will be and remain efficacious or not. In the Pelagian scheme of things, therefore, there is really no decree anymore after that of the universal offer of grace. From this point on, everything is left to humans to decide. God has done his part. He gave the opportunity (posse) and humans possess the power of decision (velle). But not a single Christian confession has ventured to adopt this Pelagian position. To some extent they have all taught an efficacious decree, a gift of faith, and hence have distinguished a second decree in the counsel of predestination. The question still remained, however: To whom is the "efficacious," "habitual," "infused" grace, that is true faith, actually given?[8]

Yet, Barach is not alone in this definition of election. Consider the words of Steve Wilkins concerning election:

> The elect are those who are faithful in Christ Jesus. If they later reject the Savior, they are no longer elect—they are cut off from the Elect One and lose their elect standing. But their falling away doesn't negate the reality of their standing prior to their apostasy. They were really and truly the elect of God because of their relationship with Christ.[9]

The relationship with Christ to which Wilkins refers is an ecclesiastical relationship which can be lost. He insists that this relationship is real, involving real communion and union with Christ, despite the fact that such an elect person can apostatize. By making covenant election a relationship which can be lost, Wilkins has necessarily made such election conditional. His view of election de-

---

8 John Bolt, ed., John Vriend, trans., Herman Bavinck, *Reformed Dogmatics*, Volume 2: *God and Creation* (Grand Rapids, Michigan: Baker Academic, 2004), 381.

9 Steve Wilkins, "Covenant, Baptism, and Salvation" in Steve Wilkins and Duane Garner, eds., *The Federal Vision* (Monroe, Louisiana: Athanasius Press, 2004), 58.

pends on covenant faithfulness and perseverance to the end. That is essentially the definition of election held by Arminians. Thornwell rightly states:

> The question between us and the Arminians respects simply the cause of election in the Divine mind—whether the decree is wholly unconditional, depending upon the mere good pleasure of God's will, or whether it is suspended upon a foresight of faith and perseverance in the creature.[10]

Election in the Scripture
There are numerous passages of Scripture that teach unconditional election and predestination. In fact, this doctrine is part of the warp and woof of all Scripture and is often implied even where it is not explicitly taught. It is not possible to consider all the different passages that teach election, but we would refer to the following verses as proof texts for this doctrine: Exodus 33:19; Deuteronomy 10:14, 15; Psalm 33:12; Psalm 65:4; Matthew 22:14; John 15:16; Acts 13:48; Romans 8:28-30; 9:11-13; 1 Corinthians 1:27-29; Ephesians 1:4, 5; 2:10; Philippians 1:29; 1 Thessalonians 1:4, 5; 2 Thessalonians 2:13, 14; 2 Timothy 2:10; 1 Peter 1:1, 2; 2:8, 9; 2 Peter 1:5-11; and Revelation 13:8; 17:8. Election or predestination is part of the broader doctrine of God's sovereignty over all things, and is taught throughout the Scripture.

Romans 9 is one of the clearest passages on God's unconditional election, but also one of the most contested passages by both Arminians and Pelagians. In that passage, Paul addresses the very objections that are often made against the doctrine of unconditional election. The Israelites had the covenants, the adoption as sons, the glory, the law, and the promises. Yet, they did not believe in the Christ who was descended from their flesh. How are we to understand their failure to believe? Was the covenant conditioned on their response, as Lusk teaches above? The Federal Vision's conditional doctrine of covenant election is predicated on the same assumption that Paul rejects in Romans—i.e., that everyone who is in the outer covenant is also in the inner covenant. As Charles Hodge says:

> The seed, or natural descendants of Abraham, are not all his children in the true sense of the term; i.e., like him in faith, and heirs of his prom-

---

10 Thornwell, *Collected Writings*, Volume 2, 125.

ise. So, in Gal. iii. 7, Paul says, "They which are of faith, the same are the children of Abraham."[11]

The failure of those in the Federal Vision to distinguish between those who are true members of the covenant and those who are not is one of their fundamental problems. They make no distinction between those who are objectively in the covenant and those who are subjectively in the covenant, as we shall see later in this chapter. Yet, Paul distinguishes between those who are children according to the flesh and those who are children according to the promise in Romans 9:8. Haldane clarifies this point in his commentary on that verse:

> All this indicated the distinction that existed in the nation of Israel, between those who, notwithstanding their being born in the line of Israel, were the seed of Abraham merely by carnal descent, and not the children of God by a spiritual regeneration. Only these last were the children of promise, as Isaac was, who were all one in Christ Jesus, and therefore in the highest sense Abraham's seed, and "heirs according to the promise," Gal. iii. 29—heirs of all the spiritual blessings secured to Abraham by promise.[12]

Some covenant children today are members according to the flesh only, even as many Israelites were. They are not true members of the covenant. Their failure is not that they do not persevere, but that they have never experienced regeneration. They have never become truly united with Christ. When the Federal Vision adherents refuse to distinguish between these two groups who are both within the outer covenant, they inevitably must deny essential truths of the gospel. One of those essentials of the faith is regeneration by the Spirit, which was considered by the Puritans to be one of the three R's of salvation—ruin by the fall, redemption through Christ, and regeneration by the Spirit. If regeneration is denied, then people are left to save themselves by their own determination. They must keep looking to Christ. They must persevere. They must work out a righteousness that will pass God's judgment in the final day. Yet, Paul says that the matter is simpler than that. Some are merely fleshly members of the covenant and others are true members through regeneration by the Spirit.

---

11 Charles Hodge, *Commentary on the Epistle to the Romans* (Grand Rapids, Michigan: William B. Eerdmans Publishing Company, 1972), 305.

12 Robert Haldane, *An Exposition of the Epistle to the Romans* (MacDill AFB, Florida: MacDonald Publishing Company, n.d.), 451.

It is impossible to integrate a conditional election with the teaching of Paul in Romans 9. Jacob is chosen and Esau is rejected before either of them had done anything good or bad. The Federal Vision says that covenant election becomes permanent through persevering faith and that it depends on our response to God's promises. That view is undercut by D. Martyn Lloyd-Jones who said:

> If it depended on anything in us, if our salvation and our ultimate glorification at any point or in any way were dependent upon us or upon anything that we have done or can do or ever will do, it would certainly fail. But, says Paul, it does not depend upon us. In order that the purpose of God according to election might stand, God chooses Jacob and not Esau before either of them was born, and before either of them had done anything good or evil.[13]

The Reformed doctrine of election has always been defined as unconditional. It does not depend on anything in man, foreseen or otherwise. Thus, Paul can state in Romans 9: 16, "So then it does not depend on the man who wills or the man who runs, but on God who has mercy."

Election in the Westminster Standards

The doctrine of the Westminster divines on unconditional election is the same in substance as can be found in all the Reformed symbols. There are two things that are particularly taught—first, that God predestined whatsoever comes to pass; second, God's predestination is not based on foresight of anything as a condition of that election. In other words, it is completely unconditional. The Westminster Confession of Faith, Chapter 3. 1, 2 says:

> God from all eternity did, by the most wise and holy counsel of his own will, freely and unchangeably ordain whatsoever comes to pass. . . . Although God knows whatsoever may or can come to pass upon all supposed conditions; yet hath he not decreed any thing because he foresaw it as future, or as that which would come to pass upon such conditions.

A. A. Hodge, in his incomparable commentary on the Westminster Confession of Faith, defines the positions of those who hold to conditional and unconditional election, respectively:

---

13 D. Martyn Lloyd-Jones, *Romans, An Exposition of Chapter 9: God's Sovereign Purpose* (Edinburgh, Scotland: The Banner of Truth Trust, 1991), 126.

> The Arminian holds that God, foreseeing from all eternity who will repent and believe, elects those individuals to eternal life on that condition of faith and repentance thus certainly foreknown.
>
> The Calvinist holds that God has elected certain individuals to eternal life, and all the means and conditions thereof, on the ground of his sovereign good pleasure. He chooses them to faith and repentance, and not because of their faith and repentance. That God does choose individuals to eternal life is certain.[14]

Covenant election, as held by the Federal Vision system, is contrary to the election of the Westminster Standards and all the Reformed symbols. The Federal Vision teaches that all who are baptized are also elected in Christ and will be saved if they persevere in faithfulness to their covenant vows. In their system, perseverance is a condition that depends on the response of man and makes the election conditional. David Dickson rejects this theory of conditional election, which is not new by any means, for the following reasons:

> Because the grace of regeneration, justifying faith, effectual calling, and perseverance to the end are given to the elect and to them only, according to the eternal decree of God, and therefore are effects, not causes or pre-required conditions, of election (Rom. 8:39; Acts 13:48; Matt. 24:24; 2 Tim. 1:9; John 15:16; Eph. 1:3-5; Matt. 13:11; Rom. 11:6-7).[15]

By making perseverance the condition for covenant election to result in eternal salvation, the Federal Vision has necessarily yoked God's eternal decrees to the response of humans. If God's election is based on that response, then God's election is conditional; not unconditional. Contrarily, if God's election is unconditional, then perseverance is a part of his decree and is certain. Despite the casuistry of Lusk, Wilkins, Barach, and others in the Federal Vision, it is impossible to have an unconditional election before the foundation of the world that is conditioned in any sense on some human response.

Election in the Arminian and Pelagian Schemes
Arminianism and Pelagianism hold to the same view on the matter of God's eternal election. Pelagius, in his commentary on Romans 9:10, said:

---

14 A. A. Hodge, *The Confession of Faith* (London: The Banner of Truth Trust, 1961), 70.

15 David Dickson, *Truth's Victory Over Error: A Commentary on the Westminster Confession of Faith* (Edinburgh, Scotland and Carlisle, Pennsylvania: The Banner of Truth Trust 2007), 29.

> Jacob and Esau too, were separated in God's sight before they were born on account of their [subsequent] faith, so that God's purpose for choosing the good and resisting the evil existed already in foreknowledge. So too, then, he has now chosen those whom he foreknew would believe from among the Gentiles, and has rejected those whom he foreknew would be unbelieving out of Israel.[16]

Wilkins and the other Federal Vision proponents never mention foresight or foreknowledge of faith as a condition for election, but they unanimously condition covenant election on perseverance. Their position must necessarily be that God chooses those for eternal life who are foreseen as persevering. Foresight of perseverance is a necessary presupposition for a system that combines both eternal election and covenantal election. Yet perseverance is certain for all the elect. Thus, there is no purpose in telling those who are supposedly covenantally elect through baptism that they will be saved *if* they persevere. They need the gospel of God's free grace in Christ preached to them rather than to be burdened with a works scheme of salvation. If perseverance is uncertain (which it is in the Federal Vision's covenant election scheme), then foresight of perseverance would be required for God to know who the eternally elect are. Unconditional election and covenant election cannot be melded together without one taking priority over the other. Certain perseverance and uncertain perseverance cannot be melded together without one taking priority over the other. The Federal Vision gives the first priority to covenant election and uncertain perseverance. Yet, the Scripture and all Reformed confessions state that certain perseverance is granted to all the elect, and only the elect, in God's eternal decree of unconditional election.

Reformed confessions to the contrary, Rich Lusk wrote the following concerning covenantal election:

> I suggest "viewing election through the lens of the covenant" is one helpful way of conceptualizing what Paul is doing in these texts such as these [Eph. 1 and Acts 20:28-30; Rom. 8 and 11:17f.]. Paul is treating the generally, or corporately, elect, as specially elect until and unless they prove otherwise. True corporate election may not issue forth in final salvation, as the nation of Israel shows (cf. Dt. 7, Rom. 9-11). Apostasy is a real possibility for all covenant members, and is to be warned against. But corporate election is the context in which special election

---

16 Theodore DeBruyn, trans., *Pelagius' Commentary on St. Paul's Epistle to the Romans* (Oxford: Clarendon Press, 1993), 116.

The Federal Vision and Unconditional Election

is worked out. There is indeed an election with [within?—GPW] an election (cf. Rom. 9:6), but for pastoral purposes, the two can and must be collapsed into one another.[17]

In that quote, Lusk goes beyond simply advocating a conditional covenantal election, but also says that apostasy is a real possibility for the entire elect community. Such a view would nullify both unconditional election and certain perseverance altogether. Apostasy is not a real possibility for those who are unconditionally elected, effectually called, and given the grace of perseverance. A real possibility of apostasy of the "elect" is logically possible only if election is conditional. This view of covenant election sounds very much like the Arminian position on election as stated by Bishop Richard Whately:

> We may conclude that no Christian is elected to eternal life absolutely, but only to the knowledge of the gospel, to the privileges of the Christian church, to the offer of God's Holy Spirit, and to the promise of final salvation on condition of being a faithful follower of Christ.[18]

If election is made to depend on the actions of the individual, then God's eternal predestination and election are secondary to the will of man. God's predestination must await the final acts of the individual. That is why the doctrine of final justification is not only a denial of the gospel, but also a denial of God's sovereign grace.

In the Federal Vision's view of covenant election, the New Testament references to the elect are interpreted as being true for all those who are objectively in the covenant. Wilkins, among others, says that all who are baptized comprise the elect. He and others argue that references by the apostles to the elect in their epistles were only references to covenant election since they could not know if all their hearers were truly regenerate. It is true that some of those to whom the apostles wrote did fall away from the faith, as John acknowledges in 1 John 2:19, but that does not nullify the promises or the grace of God. The apostles wrote about the experiences of God's redeeming grace which all saints receive inasmuch as the great majority of their hearers were true Christians. For that reason, 1 Peter 1:2-5 says that election includes the effects of true grace, obedience, sanctification by

---

17 Waters, *Federal Vision and Covenant Theology*, 115.

18 R. C. Reed, *The Gospel as Taught by Calvin* (Jackson, Mississippi: Reformed Theological Seminary and Presbyterian Reformation Society, n.d.), 60.

the Spirit, being born again, a living hope (which is infallible assurance), an imperishable inheritance reserved in heaven, and protection by the power of God against falling away from salvation. As Calvin comments on these verses:

> Although he assigns an election in the first place to the gratuitous favour of God, at the same time he would have us know it by the effects, for there is nothing more dangerous or more absurd than to overlook our calling and to seek for certainty of our election in the hidden foreknowledge of God, which is a very deep labyrinth. Therefore to obviate this danger, Peter supplies the best correction. Although in the first place he would have us consider the counsel of God, the cause of which is solely in Himself, yet he recalls to us the effect, by which he sets forth and bears witness to our election. That effect is the sanctification of the Spirit, that is, effectual calling, when faith which is born of the inward operation of the Spirit is added to the outward preaching of the Gospel.[19]

Calvin's exposition of these verses in 1 Peter completely contradicts the position of the Federal Vision advocates on election as well as other doctrines. Those holding to the Federal Vision so objectify the covenant that they deny that election can be known by the effects that it produces in the lives of the elect. We will have opportunity to return to this matter in Chapter 18, on assurance. It is important to note the differences between the way the Federal Vision proponents interpret passages about the elect in the Bible and the standard interpretations of Reformed theologians. The Federal Vision emphasizes the objective relationship with Christ of all who are baptized, and says that the mystery of election cannot be known for certain. The words of J. C. Ryle, quoted earlier in the book, are relevant at this point. Wrong views on baptism invariably affect a person's views on justification, sanctification, election, perseverance, and other doctrines. As a result, the Federal Vision has sacrificed the doctrine of eternal predestination on the altar of its view of baptismal efficacy. Its proponents have replaced unconditional election with the doctrine of conditional election. Conditional election is the most essential part of its system of theology and it is a denial of efficacious grace or effectual calling. The Federal Visionists may still give lip service to

---

19 William B. Johnston, trans., *Calvin's Commentaries, The Epistle of Paul the Apostle to the Hebrews and The First and Second Epistles of St Peter* (Grand Rapids, Michigan: William B. Eerdmans Publishing Company, 1970), 230.

unconditional election (at least in part), but it is evident that every Scripture doctrine for them must be squeezed into the mold of baptismal efficacy and covenant election.

The Arminian position on election, as summarized by John Owen in the following quote, is very similar to what the Federal Vision teaches:

> There is a complete election, belonging to none but those who are dying; and there is another, incomplete, common to all that believe: as the good things of salvation are incomplete which are continued whilst faith is continued, and revoked when that is denied, so election is incomplete in this life, and revocable.[20]

Again, Owen further states the Arminian position in the following words:

> There are three orders of believers and repenters in the Scripture, whereof some are beginners, others having continued for a time, and some perseverants. The first two orders are chosen *vere*, truly, but not *absolute prorsus*, absolutely, but only for a time,—so long as they will remain as they are; the third are chosen finally and peremptorily: for this act of God is either continued or interrupted, according as we fulfill the condition.[21]

Pelagius was more consistent than the advocates of the Federal Vision are when, in his comments on Romans 8:29, he made everything dependent solely on God's foreknowledge of man's response to the gospel:

> The purpose according to which he planned to save by faith alone those whom he freely called to salvation he will all the more glorify as they work [towards salvation].... To predestine is the same as to foreknow. Therefore, those he foresaw would be conformed in life he intended to be conformed in glory.... Those he foreknew would believe he called.[22]

Bavinck rightly understood that the primary objection of Pelagianism to predestination is revealed when eternal salvation is made dependent on God's grace, rather than on the free will of man. Thus, he assessed that system:

---

20 William Goold, ed., *The Works of John Owen, Volume X* (London: The Banner of Truth Trust, 1967), 56.

21 Ibid.

22 DeBruyn, trans., *Pelagius' Commentary on St. Paul's Epistle to the Romans*, 112.

> Pelagianism, however, does not yet marshal its full strength when it opposes the general and special providence of God. To some extent it even recognizes this doctrine. But it comes out fighting especially when the eternal state of rational creatures, the particular decree of predestination, is at issue. Now, predestination is only a particular application of the counsel or providence of God. . . . Pelagianism has traded predestination for foreknowledge and described foreordination as the decree of God in which he determined either eternal blessedness or eternal punishment for people, depending on whether he foresaw their persevering faith or their undying unbelief.[23]

The Federal Vision, likewise, conditions baptismal efficacy and covenant election on persevering faith. In this way, unconditional election is made subservient to covenant election. While the Federal Vision proponents have not yet given up the doctrine of unconditional election, they have practically given up what is the most important aspect of that doctrine—efficacious grace. In their writings, they hold to both unconditional election and conditional election. It is not logically possible to hold to both, but such is the inconsistency of mankind as Machen illustrated in the quotation earlier in this chapter. In our assessment of the Federal Vision, we must examine the movement by its logical relations, and not by the inconsistencies of those who hold it. It is necessary, for consistency's sake, that anyone who holds to unconditional and eternal election must also hold to efficacious grace. Unconditional election necessarily results in eternal salvation in every instance, or else it is not the election of the Scriptures. Unconditional election always includes all the saving benefits of Christ, including perseverance, or else it is not the same doctrine taught in the Bible. It is precisely at these points that the logical inconsistencies of the Federal Vision are exposed. Its proponents believe in the unconditional election of some to eternal life and the conditional, or covenantal, election of all who are baptized. Moreover, the Federal Visionists assert that unconditional election may be distinguished (perhaps), but cannot be divided. The Federal Vision advocates might appear to believe in a two-track system of election, but in reality they do not. Their "unconditional" election is intertwined with covenantal election in such a way that the two cannot be separated or divided. In the end, as Lusk stated, they believe election and baptismal efficacy are both conditioned on God's

---

23 Bavinck, *Reformed Dogmatics*, Volume 2, 377.

eternal decree and man's response. In such a system, man's response ultimately trumps God's election.

The other doctrines of the Federal Vision are logically consistent only with conditional election—not unconditional election. The doctrine of baptismal efficacy is inconsistent with efficacious grace and unconditional election. If God's efficacious grace is given to someone, that person will persevere and will be saved for eternity. Thus, the Federal Vision proponents who affirm unconditional election are in the position of having to hold also to conditional election—two principles that are as opposite as Augustinianism and Pelagianism. Some would scoff that no one could hold to two such disparate systems of salvation. Yet, William Cunningham shows that such inconsistency is exactly what Rome was guilty of before the Reformation:

> Before the Reformation, the Church of Rome could not be said to be either Calvinistic or Arminian, that is, she had not formally and officially committed herself to either side in the great controversy. She had always professed great respect for the opinions of Augustine, and for the decisions of the African Synods and the Council of Orange in the Pelagian controversy; and she had never, as a church, formally and officially given any doctrinal decision inconsistent with that profession. Thus far she might be said to be Calvinistic. But on the other hand, it is certain, that doctrines of a Pelagian and semi-Pelagian cast had been long sanctioned by a very large majority of her most influential authorities, and especially by many of the schoolmen; so that, before the Reformation, Pelagianism might be said to pervade nearly the whole of the ordinary teaching of the church, though it had never been formally sanctioned as authoritative and binding. In these circumstances, the Church of Rome could not with propriety be said to be either Augustinian or Pelagian, although, in somewhat different senses and aspects, both designations might be applied to her.[24]

The Federal Vision proponents individually might still hold to unconditional election in a certain sense, but the Federal Vision system is predicated on conditional election. Conditional election is necessary to that system in order to maintain its other doctrines—such as, baptismal efficacy, covenant election, the real danger of the apostasy of all true believers, final justification, and others.

---

24 William Cunningham, *The Reformers and the Theology of the Reformation* (London: The Banner of Truth Trust, 1967), 187-8.

Election and the Medieval Church

Before the Reformation, there were many in the Church of Rome who openly taught the doctrine of predestination, such as Augustine, Thomas Aquinas, Duns Scotus, and others. Aquinas, in particular, held to both the doctrines of election and baptismal efficacy, which makes certain of his views similar to those of the Federal Vision. Yet, Aquinas also believed that baptismal efficacy bestowed internal, subjective grace which could be resisted. When the Council of Trent deliberated in reaction to the Reformation, it did not formally discuss any of the leading aspects of the doctrine of predestination in Rome's controversy with the Reformers. Catholics were, thus, left to either hold to election or deny it.

The doctrines of original sin, divine grace, and eternal predestination were afterwards popularized in the Catholic Church by Cornelius Jansen (1585-1638) until the Bull Unigenitus was issued by Clement XI in 1713 which put an end to the toleration of the Jansenists. Yet, Augustinianism is still permitted to exist in Catholicism today under two main branches: the Augustinian Canons and the Augustinian Hermits. Thus, it is still true today that Catholicism can be called both Augustinian and Pelagian in different senses and aspects, but the predominant theology of the Catholic Church is at least Semi-Pelagianism.

Summary

Most of those who teach the Federal Vision scheme of salvation have remnants of Reformed theology in their core beliefs, primarily because of their background in Reformed churches. Yet, Reformed theology is only an aspect of their beliefs and not at all the dominant aspect. Unconditional election is no longer their dominant belief. That distinction belongs to conditional election, as expressed in their numerous statements to that effect. Their view of conditional, covenant election makes perseverance uncertain for all, apostasy a possibility for all the elect, and nullifies the unconditional election of the Scripture. Conditional election is not the doctrine of Reformed theology, but is the doctrine of Arminianism, Semi-Pelagianism, and Pelagianism.

Conclusion:

Francis Turretin summarizes the differences between unconditional and conditional election as follows:

> We must either ascend with the Scriptures to God discriminating among men by his own gift or descend with Pelagius to man discriminating himself by his own free will (for there can be no middle way).[25]

While it seems unimaginable to some to accuse the Federal Visionists of an Arminian or Pelagian doctrine of election, it is impossible to find their views in either the Scripture or the Christian confessions. They hold to covenant election that is conditional in contradiction to the Scripture and the great Reformed creeds. They make election dependent on the response of the individual. Conditional election is not a Reformed position. Conditional election is the position of Pelagianism and Arminianism. There is no middle position and the Federal Vision is wrong when it tries to meld unconditional election and conditional election into one seamless position.

---

25 James T. Dennison, Jr., ed., George Musgrave Giger, trans., Francis Turretin, *Institutes of Elenctic Theology*, Volume 1, First through Tenth Topics (Phillipsburg, New Jersey: P&R Publishing, 1992), 361.

-13-
The Federal Vision and Union with Christ

> "In baptism we are brought covenantally and publicly out of union with Adam and into union with Christ. . . . In this relationship, one has, in principle, all the blessings and benefits in the heavenly places delivered over to him as he is 'in Christ'. . . Baptism is like an adoption ceremony."[1]
>
> RICH LUSK, FEDERAL VISION PROPONENT

> "Baptism, then, as the sign and seal of this reality [i.e., union with Christ in his death, burial, resurrection, our partaking of the Holy Spirit]. . . By baptism the Spirit joins us to Christ since he is the elect one and the Church is the elect people, we are joined to his body. We therefore are elect."[2]
>
> STEVE WILKINS, FEDERAL VISION PROPONENT

---

[1] Shane Lems, "The Federal Vision and Union with Christ", November 15, 2013. Accessed at: http://theaquilareport.com/the-federal-vision-and-union-with-christ/ on October 22, 2014.

[2] Guy Prentiss Waters, *The Federal Vision and Covenant Theology: A Comparative Analysis* (Phillipsburg, New Jersey: P&R Publishing, 2006), 236.

One of the witnesses for the Defense at the trial of Peter Leithart made the following assessment of his theology:

> On the question of imputation, Dr. Leithart indicated to me that he was opposed to imputation being viewed as an independent act, something in the abstract, rather than in connection with union with Christ.[3]

The connection of imputation and union with Christ is not disputed by Reformed theologians. It is a fundamental truth taught in the Scripture and has been held by the greatest theologians throughout church history. As John Owen says:

> The foundation of the imputation asserted is union. Hereof there are many grounds and causes, as hath been declared; but that which we have immediate respect unto, as the foundation of this imputation, is that whereby the Lord Christ and believers do actually coalesce into one mystical person. This is the Holy Spirit inhabiting in him as the head of the church in all fulness, and in all believers according to their measure, whereby they become members of his mystical body.[4]

The Federal Vision and Union with Christ

Our primary question concerning imputation and union is this: What does the Federal Vision mean by union with Christ? The various statements of the Federal Vision advocates indicate that, for them, union with Christ is formal, but not spiritual. It is external, but not internal. It is objective, but not subjective. All the members of the visible church have this formal, external, objective union with Christ. Such union with Christ in their system is not restricted to the members of the invisible church and often proves to be temporary. However, a formal, external, visible, objective, temporary union is simply not the union with Christ of which the Scripture speaks. In reply to Lusk, Wilkins, Leithart and others in the Federal Vision, union with Christ cannot be limited to an external, objective, temporary union. Rather, it is a vital, spiritual, internal, mystical, permanent union.

The difficulty for the Federal Vision in addressing these concerns is underscored by various statements from "A Joint Federal Vision Profession." First, the signers state unequivocally that union with Christ through baptism is formal:

---

3 Record of the Case, Standing Judicial Commission of the Presbyterian Church in America, Case 2012-5, RE Gerald Hedman vs. Pacific Northwest Presbytery, 666-7.

4 William Goold, ed., *The Works of John Owen*, Volume V (London: The Banner of Truth Trust, 1967), 209.

> We *affirm* that God formally unites a person to Christ and to His covenant people through baptism into the triune Name, and that this baptism obligates such a one to lifelong covenant loyalty to the triune God, each baptized person repenting of his sins and trusting in Christ alone for salvation. Baptism formally engrafts a person into the Church, which means that baptism is into the regeneration, that time when the Son of Man sits upon His glorious throne (Matt. 19:28).[5]

Even this statement raises concerns and reveals inconsistencies. How can this union with Christ be formal only if it also engrafts a person into the church and baptizes him into the regeneration of all things when Christ sits on His glorious throne? The inconsistency in their position is further highlighted by the following statement from that same "Profession":

> We *affirm* that apostasy is a terrifying reality for many baptized Christians. All who are baptized into the triune Name are united with Christ in His covenantal life, and those who fall from that position of grace are indeed falling from grace. The branches that are cut away from Christ are genuinely cut away from someone, cut out of a living covenant body. The connection that an apostate had to Christ was not merely *external*.[6]

So, "A Joint Federal Vision Profession" asserts that union with Christ is formal, but not merely external. Such a distinction is without meaning. It is undefined and indefinable. If union with Christ is not "merely external," it also cannot be defined as formal only. Do the words used mean that union with Christ is spiritual and internal? Such an idea would complicate the matter even further for the Federal Visionists.

Finally, "A Joint Federal Vision Profession" blurs the distinction between the visible and invisible church in the section on "The Visible and Invisible Church." That section does not define the church as either visible or invisible, but asserts:

> We further affirm that the visible Church is the true Church of Christ, and not an "approximate" Church.[7]

---

5 "A Joint Federal Vision Profession," *Credenda Agenda*, Volume 19, Series 3, Special Edition, (2007): 5.

6 Ibid., 9

7 Ibid., 12.

Historic Christianity and the Federal Vision

If the visible church is the true church and not an approximate church, then what is the invisible church? Is the invisible church identical with the visible church? If the visible church is not identical with the invisible church, then how do they differ? These are legitimate questions which are left unanswered by the statements of the Federal Vision proponents. J. C. Ryle, who faced similar heresies in the nineteenth century, put his finger on the problem:

> They make no distinction between the visible Church which contains "evil as well as good," and the invisible Church which is composed of none but God's elect and true believers. They apply to the one privileges, and blessings, and promises which belong to the other. They call the visible Church, with its crowds of ungodly members, and baptized infidels, "the mystical body of Christ, the Bride, the Lamb's wife, the Holy Catholic Church," and the like. . . All these glorious titles do not properly belong to any visible Church, but to the mystical company of God's elect.[8]

The problem with the affirmations and denials the Federal Vision proponents make is that they conflict with their own paradigm of trying to restore the objectivity of the covenant. They emphasize the objectivity of the covenant, but the subjectivity of the covenant through God's redeeming grace is present throughout the Scripture. How can they maintain strictly the objectivity of the covenant without permitting the subjectivity of God's promises? For instance, how can they affirm that those branches that are cut away from the vine truly fall from grace and are cut out of a living covenant body that enjoys real fellowship with Christ? Their solution is to say that such union is not *merely external*. So, does that mean those covenant members have an *internal* relationship with Christ and can fall from true grace? The Federal Vision proponents then respond that the union of such apostates was only formal. They continually alternate their position between objectivity and subjectivity; between formal and spiritual; between external and internal; and, between visible and invisible. They define their positions in whatever way is necessary to prevent the appearance of contradiction. Then they resort to the opposite position when that becomes necessary. They are stuck on their own form of dialectical reasoning by which they synthesize things that in the Scripture clearly differ.

---

8 John Charles Ryle, *Old Paths: Being Plain Statements on Some Weightier Matters of Christianity* (Cambridge and London, England: James Clarke & Co., LTD., 1972), 502.

Their tactic is not surprising. It has been the tactic of heretics from the founding of the church. Samuel Miller, in an introductory essay to Thomas Scott's *The Articles of the Synod of Dort*, made the following observation:

> When heresy arises in an evangelical body it is never frank and open. It always begins by skulking, and assuming a disguise. Its advocates, when together, boast of great improvements, and congratulate one another on having gone greatly beyond the "old dead orthodoxy," and on having left behind many of its antiquated errors: but when taxed with deviations from the received faith, they complain of the unreasonableness of their accusers, as they "differ from it *only in words*." This has been the standing course of errorists ever since the apostolic age. They are almost never honest and candid as a party, until they gain strength enough to be sure of some degree of popularity.[9]

Anyone familiar with the history of theology can attest to the truthfulness of Miller's assessment. Arius, Pelagius, Arminius, Amyraut, the Unitarians, Albert Barnes, Karl Barth, and many others, have all contended that they were only making improvements to the faith.

Various Statements on Union with Christ

One of the chief problems with the Federal Vision is a wrong definition of what union with Christ is. Rich Lusk gives a typical Federal Vision definition of union with Christ as follows:

> Baptism is like an adoption ceremony. The adopted child is brought into a new relationship, given a new name, new blessings, a new future, new opportunities, a new inheritance—in short, a new life. And yet these blessings, considered from the standpoint of the covenant rather than the eternal decree, are mutable. The child is a full member of the family and has everything that comes with sonship. But, if he grows up and rejects his Father and Mother (God and the church), if he refuses to repent and return home when warned and threatened, then he loses all the blessings that were his. It would not be accurate to say that he never had these things; he did possess them, even though he never experienced or enjoyed some of them ("Do I Believe In Baptismal Regeneration?" n.d.).[10]

---

9 Thomas Scott, *The Articles of the Synod of Dort* (Harrisonburg, Virginia: Sprinkle Publications, 1993), 16-17.

10 Lems, "The Federal Vision and Union with Christ".

Peter Leithart put it this way when discussing baptism and union with Christ in a blog post called "Infant Baptism" (Aug. 6, 2004):

> Apostasy is possible. It is possible to be united to Jesus Christ, receive His Spirit, and then fall from that gracious condition and back into the world (John 15; 1 Cor. 10; 2 Pet. 2).[11]

A quote from John Barach, one of the signers of the Joint Profession, further illustrates the inevitable dichotomy they hold with respect to union with Christ:

> There is an objective covenant made with believers and their children. Every baptized person is in covenant with God and is in union then with Christ and with the Triune God. The Bible doesn't know about a distinction between being internally in the covenant, really in the covenant, and being externally in the covenant . . . every baptized person is in Christ and therefore shares in his new life.[12]

Barach's statement begs several questions. Why does he refer to an objective covenant made with believers and their children if the Bible does not make distinctions between the internal and external? If the Bible does not make such a distinction, then why does even the "Joint Federal Vision Profession" make it? Why did Barach sign a document that says, among other things, that "membership in the one true Christian Church is visible and objective"? How can there be a distinction between visible and invisible, and between objective and subjective, but not a distinction between external and internal? The Federal Vision proponents use these very distinctions when it serves their purpose, and ridicule the use of them when it serves a different purpose.

A greater problem for the Federal Vision with respect to union with Christ is this question: What is the basis for such union? The Scripture teaches that this union depends on two things: the work of Christ for believers, and the work of the Spirit in believers. As A. A. Hodge wrote:

> The first aspect of this union is its federal and representative character, whereby Christ, as the second Adam (1 Cor. XV.22), assumes in the covenant of grace those broken obligations of the covenant of works which the first Adam failed to discharge, and fulfills them all in behalf of his "sheep," "they whom the Father has given him."

---

11 Ibid.

12 Waters, *Federal Vision and Covenant Theology*, 133.

The second aspect of this union is its spiritual and vital character.[13]

Hodge's summarization of the two aspects of salvation is consistent with what is taught in the Westminster Confession of Faith 7. 2, 3. These sections of the Confession teach that the federal representation of Christ requires saving faith of those ordained unto eternal life and promises the Holy Spirit to make them willing and able to believe. Yet, the Federal Vision denies the spiritual and vital character of this union by defining union apart from saving faith and the internal work of the Holy Spirit. Its proponents assert that all the baptized are in union with Christ before they believe, and even if they never believe. The Federal Vision also denies the federal and representative character of this union for those who are alone the true sheep of Christ. Instead, the Federal Vision makes union with Christ depend on the sign of the covenant, baptism, rather than the covenant itself. Yet, the answer to the Westminster Larger Catechism Question #66 says:

> The union which the elect have with Christ is the work of God's grace, whereby they are spiritually and mystically, yet really and inseparably, joined to Christ as their head and husband, which is done in their effectual calling.

Such union with Christ is as permanent as the perseverance of the saints. It is forever. It is not a union accomplished by baptism. Rather, this union is accomplished only through effectual calling. In his commentary on Hebrews 3:14, John Owen writes:

> Now, our union with Christ, our participation of him, consists in the inhabitation of the same Spirit in him and us; and the first work of the Spirit given unto us, bestowed upon us, is to form Christ in us, whereby our union is completed... In this forming of Christ in us we are made partakers of all grace and holiness in the principle and root of them, for therein doth this image of God in Christ consist. Now, this proceeding from our union, the latter is, and must be, before it in order of nature, and so be the rule, measure, and cause of all that ensues.[14]

---

13 A. A. Hodge, *Outlines of Theology* (Grand Rapids, Michigan: Zondervan Publishing House, 1972), 482.

14 W. H. Goold, ed., John Owen, *An Exposition of the Epistle to the Hebrews*, Volume IV (Grand Rapids, Michigan: Baker Book House, 1980), 147-148.

A few pages later in that same commentary, Owen shows how the believer's union with Christ is the basis of every other grace of the Christian:

> It is the cause of all other graces that we are made partakers of; they are all communicated unto us by virtue of our union with Christ. Hence is our adoption, our justification, our sanctification, our fruitfulness, our perseverance, our resurrection, our glory. . . Our union with him is the ground of the actual imputation of his righteousness unto us; for he covers only the members of his own body with his own garments, nor will cast a skirt over any who is not "bone of his bone, and flesh of his flesh." And so he is "of God made unto us righteousness," 1 Cor. i.30.[15]

As with all the Reformed creeds, Owen connects all our graces together in an unbroken chain from election to justification to adoption to perseverance to glory. The Federal Vision contradicts Reformed theology and the Scriptures by separating both perseverance and glory from the other graces.

John 15 and Union with Christ

One of the key passages disputed by the Federal Vision proponents concerning union with Christ is John 15:1-6. The typical Federal Vision approach to this passage is to say that even the branches which do not bear fruit have a true relationship with Christ. As Norman Shepherd in his book, *The Call of Grace*, comments on John 15:

> If this distinction (outward and inward branches) is in the text, it is difficult to see what the point of the warning is. The outward branches cannot profit from it, because they cannot in any case bear genuine fruit. They are not related to Christ inwardly and draw no life from him. The inward branches do not need the warning, because they are vitalized by Christ and therefore cannot help but bear good fruit.[16]

Shepherd's approach is to deny the distinction between outward and inward branches by asserting that it would make the warning pointless. William Hendriksen's interpretation of John 15:1-6, especially verses 2 and 6, is the right approach:

> The two groups have in common their close contact with Christ and the Gospel. Speaking in terms of the metaphor, both groups were *in*

---

15 Ibid., 149-150.

16 Norman Shepherd, *The Call of Grace: How the Covenant Illuminates Salvation and Evangelism* (Phillipsburg, New Jersey: Presbyterian & Reformed Publishing Company, 2000), 89-90.

The Federal Vision and Union with Christ

the vine. That this relation of having been in the vine (or, dropping the metaphor, in Christ) does not have to refer to the spiritual, saving union with Christ is easy to see. Not all those who are in the covenant are of the covenant. Not all those who were baptized into Moses were saved (1 Cor. 10:1-5). That in speaking of men who have at one time been in him, but subsequently forsook him, Jesus had in mind not a merely hypothetical possibility but an oft-repeated situation in actual life. . .

In no sense whatever do such passages as 15:2 and 15:6 suggest that there is a falling away from grace, as if those who were once actually saved finally perish. This allegory plainly teaches that the branches which are taken away and burned represent people who never once bore fruit, not even when they were in Christ. Hence they were never true believers; and for them the in-the-vine relationship, though close, was merely outward.[17]

Steve Wilkins, commenting on this passage in John 15, gives a Federal Vision interpretation of this passage by denying the distinction between external and internal union with Christ:

> The distinction of "external" and "internal" union seems to be invented and is not in the text. All the branches are truly and vitally united to the vine. All can and should be fruitful. . .
>
> They have a real, objective, blessed relationship with God which must be preserved.[18]

Once again, a Federal Vision proponent denies the distinction between internal and external, but maintains the distinction between objective and subjective with no explanation of how those terms differ. Can a person be internally in relationship with Christ without being subjectively in relationship with Him? What is the purpose of restoring the objectivity of the covenant if there is no distinction between internal and external? How can a person have an internal relationship with Christ and lose his salvation? No answers have ever been provided by the Federal Vision to these questions and none ever will be.

---

17   William Hendriksen, *The Gospel of John* (Edinburgh, Scotland and Carlisle, Pennsylvania: The Banner of Truth Trust, 1976), 295-6.

18   Steve Wilkins and Duane Garner, eds., Steve Wilkins, "Covenant, Baptism, and Salvation" in *The Federal Vision* (Monroe, Louisiana: Athanasius Press, 2004), 63-64.

Historic Christianity and the Federal Vision

Key Assessment: The Federal Vision defines union with Christ as a formal and objective relationship which is conferred through baptism to all those who receive that rite. The Federal Vision denies that union with Christ is a spiritual and subjective union conferred by the Holy Spirit to believers alone.

Union with Christ is first of all a spiritual relationship through the Holy Spirit. 1 John 4:13 says, "By this we know that we abide in Him and He in us, because He has given us of His Spirit." There is a mutual abiding of believers in Christ and Christ in believers. This union conveys the Holy Spirit and all the benefits of Christ's redemption. It is a vital union which is sustained by the life of Christ in the believer. As Galatians 2:20 says, "I have been crucified with Christ; and it is no longer I who live, but Christ lives in me; and the life which I now live in the flesh I live by faith in the Son of God, who loved me and gave Himself for me."

This union with Christ, in part, is a legal or federal union. As A. A. Hodge says:

> All of our legal or covenant responsibilities rest upon Christ, and all of His legal or covenant merits accrue to us.[19]

It is interesting that a theological system which contends for the restoration of the objectivity of the covenant and the federal relationship of all the baptized in that covenant would also make the error of denying the most important aspects of that federal union with Christ. Yet, that is exactly what the Federal Vision proponents do when they deny that the legal (or covenant) responsibilities of believers rest upon Christ and His covenant merits are, in a legal and forensic sense, given to believers. The Federal Vision asserts that such benefits of Christ are given to all the baptized which do not necessarily result in eternal salvation. Yet, they deny the federal relationship with Christ which actually guarantees such salvation to the elect of God. They deny that Christ, as our federal head, assumed the legal obligations to fulfill the law in our behalf and that His perfect righteousness is *imputed* to believers. They deny that our justification is complete in Christ, our federal head, which negates any necessity for us to be justified on the basis of the totality of our

---

19 A. A. Hodge, *Outlines of Theology* (Grand Rapids, Michigan: Zondervan Publishing House, 1972), 484.

whole lives. These matters will be explored more fully in later chapters. Yet, these errors strike at the heart of the true union believers have with Christ as their federal head. By denying these truths, the Federal Vision proves once again that it is not a true vision of federal theology, but a vision of sacramental theology. Therein, they are guilty of the same type of error concerning union with Christ that Arminianism and Pelagianism make concerning the atonement. The possibility of salvation is widened to include all the baptized, but the actuality of salvation is narrowed to include only those who persevere in faithfulness. In their system, union with Christ does not permanently convey the saving benefits of Christ

Summary
Reformed theology has always taught that all the blessings of the covenant are bestowed on the elect through union with Christ, but such union is a true, spiritual union arising from the federal relationship which the elect have with the Redeemer. The Federal Vision has so objectified the covenant that the union of which they speak is a formal, outward union. Their union is not a true, spiritual union. Thus, the Federal Vision advocates deny the distinction between the visible and invisible church by making union with Christ dependent solely on water baptism.

Conclusion
In the Scripture, union with Christ is as indissoluble as the promise of salvation. For the Federal Vision proponents, union with Christ is dissoluble and guarantees nothing. It is dissoluble by apostasy or failure to persevere unto the end. Their union with Christ is made dependent on baptism rather than true saving faith. In contrast to the Federal Vision's false definition of union with Christ, William Cunningham gave the Protestant definition of such union:

> The Protestant doctrine, upon the other hand, is, that the only thing on which the possession by men individually of spiritual blessings,—of justification and sanctification,—is made necessarily and invariably dependent, is union with Christ; and that the only thing on which union to Christ may be said to be dependent, is faith in Him: so that it holds true, absolutely and universally, that wherever there is faith in Christ, or union to Christ by faith, there pardon and holiness,—all necessary spiritual blessings,—are communicated by God and received by men,

even though they have not actually partaken in any sacrament or external ordinance whatever.[20]

According to Cunningham, union with Christ is dependent on saving faith, and such union imparts to the believer all the spiritual blessings of Christ apart from the sacraments. This view of union with Christ is contrary to the view set forth by the Federal Vision proponents. Thus Herman Bavinck said concerning union with Christ and the benefits of Christ:

> There is no sharing in the benefits of Christ unless we share in his person, because benefits cannot be separated from the person, the benefits are not deposited in a merely human person, or a priest, or in a church (i.e. the sacraments) . . . the treasury of the blessings of Christ has been deposited nowhere but in Christ . . . there is no fellowship with the person of Christ without sharing with his person. . . Christ himself and all his benefits belong to the church through the Holy Spirit.[21]

John Flavel, in his book *The Method of Grace in the Gospel Redemption*, argues that the effectual application of redemption to believers is conveyed through the mystical union between Christ and His saints:

> The reality of the believer's union with Christ, is evident from the imputation of Christ's righteousness to him for his justification. . . Indeed Peter cannot be justified by the righteousness of Paul; but both may be justified by the righteousness of Christ imputed to them; they being members, jointly to one common Head. . . The saints union with Christ is not a physical union. . . Nor is it an essential union, or union with the divine nature, so as our beings are thereby swallowed up and lost in the Divine being. . . The union I here speak of, is not a federal union, or an union by covenant only. . . Though this union neither makes us one person nor essence with Christ, yet it knits our person most intimately and nearly to the person of Christ. . . The mystical union is wholly supernatural, wrought by the power of God. . . There are only two ligaments betwixt Christ and the soul, viz. the Spirit on his part, and faith on ours.[22]

---

20 William Cunningham, *Historical Theology*, Volume II (London: The Banner of Truth Trust, 1969), 124.

21 Herman Bavinck, *Our Reasonable Faith: A Survey of Christian Doctrine* (Grand Rapids, Michigan: Wm. B. Eerdmans Publishing Co., 1956), 399-400.

22 John Flavel, *The Works of John Flavel*, Volume 2 (London: The Banner of Truth Trust, 1968), 36, 38, 39.

There are several truths which are emphasized in this quote. First, Flavel says that imputation is through union with Christ and, thereby, the righteousness of Christ is imputed to believers which results in their justification. Second, this union is neither physical, nor essential. It is not a change of the essence of the believer whereby he is swallowed up in the Divine being. The subject of the *essence* of the believer was addressed in detail in Chapter 2 on "The Federal Vision and Regeneration." Third, this union is not a federal union. There is a federal relationship between Christ and His people as a result of God's covenants, but union with Christ is more than a mere federal representation. That statement by Flavel, if pondered carefully, undercuts the entire scaffolding of the Federal Vision system. True union with Christ is not merely federal or objective or external as the Federal Vision proposes. Instead, it is vital, internal, and subjective. Fourth, this union is mystical and supernatural, depending on the work of the Spirit in the soul of the believer and saving faith. Thus, the union with Christ of which the Federal Vision speaks is not the union of the Scriptures and the great Reformed creeds.

-14-
The Federal Vision and Justification by Faith Alone

"Biblically, again, the case is fairly simple. Does the New Testament ever claim that works are, in any sense, necessary for justification? Romans 2:16, again, claims that the 'doers of the law are justified.' That is a controversial passage, but it shows that works and justification are legitimately linked. James 2 is even clearer. Again, this is a controversial passage, but whatever the specific sense of James 2, he explicitly states that we are 'justified by works and not by faith alone' (v. 24)."[1]

PETER LEITHART, FEDERAL VISION PROPONENT

"This statement [Romans 2:13—DR] is not a theoretical proposition concerning some meritorious method of being righteous before God. The presuppositions undergirding Paul's statements include facts that the Law is 'obeyable,' that truly responding to the Law (the Word) in faith does justify, and that such justification is not an exclusively Jewish possession."[2]

STEVE SCHLISSEL, FEDERAL VISION PROPONENT

"Works of faith filled obedience, in a secondary way, cause our final justification and salvation. Works are the means through which we come into possession of eternal life. The path of obedience is the way we must trod [sic—DR] if we are to be justified at the last day."[3]

RICH LUSK, FEDERAL VISION PROPONENT

---

[1] Record of the Case, Standing Judicial Commission of the Presbyterian Church in America, Case 2012-5, RE Gerald Hedman vs. Pacific Northwest Presbytery of the Presbyterian Church in America, 213.

[2] Steve Wilkins and Duane Garner, eds., Steve Schlissel, "Justification and the Gentiles," in *The Federal Vision* (Monroe, Louisiana: Athanasius Press, 2004), 260.

[3] E. Calvin Beisner, ed., Rich Lusk, "A Response to 'The Biblical Plan of Salvation'," in *The Auburn Avenue Theology, Pros and Cons: Debating the Federal Vision* (Fort Lauderdale, Florida: Knox Theological Seminary, 2004), 128.

The seventeenth-century Reformed theologian, Johann Heinrich Alsted, wrote words which have often been attributed to Luther:

> The article of justification is said to be the article of the standing or falling church.[4]

I have not found any place where Luther wrote those exact words, but he certainly agreed with that position. He also expressed himself similarly in various places, particularly in the Smalcald Articles of 1537. Calvin and all the Reformers agreed with Luther on the necessity of this article of faith. One of the later Reformed theologians, Antonius Walaeus, wrote:

> The topic of justification in theology is easily foremost and for us the most saving. If it be obscured, adulterated, or overturned, it is impossible for purity of doctrine to be retained in other loci or for the true Church to exist.[5]

One of the key differences, but by no means the only difference, between the Federal Vision and the historic Protestant faith concerns justification by faith alone. The proponents of the Federal Vision generally have two ways to respond to these differences. First, they sometimes affirm that they believe in justification by faith, conveniently leaving "alone" out of their statement. Second, if pressed concerning the deletion of "alone," they will assert they do indeed believe in "justification by faith alone," but their meaning is different than the classical understanding of the phrase. In either instance, they qualify "justification by faith alone" as justification by covenant faithfulness. Such a definition of faith is a fundamental and radical change of the scriptural way of salvation. Faith is not the same as faithfulness. True faith will lead to faithfulness, but faithfulness is not equivalent to faith. Faithfulness is equivalent to obedience. As an example, Peter Leithart testified at his trial:

> I heartily affirm that Abraham was justified apart from works and before circumcision, and I heartily agree, and have always taught, that

---

4 Johann Heinrich Alsted, *Theologica didactica, exhibens locos communes theologica methodo scholastica*, (Hanover, Germany: C. Eifrid, 1618), 417.

5 Ernst Bizer, ed., G. T. Thompson, trans., Heinrich Heppe, *Reformed Dogmatics* (Grand Rapids, Michigan: Baker Book House, 1978), 543.

sinners are justified when we receive Christ, and His righteousness, by faith alone.[6]

Leithart's statement begs the question how he can hold to justification by faith alone and also hold to justification by baptismal grace; or, how he can hold to both justification by faith alone and final justification. Not surprisingly, Leithart contradicts his statement on "justification by faith alone" in the following quote:

> Second, the Protestant doctrine has been too rigid in separating justification and sanctification, more rigid certainly than Scripture itself... I argue below that, when examined under a military-conflictual metaphor rather than solely under the imagery of the "courtroom," justification and definitive sanctification are not merely simultaneous, nor merely twin effects of the single event of union with Christ (though I believe that is the case). Rather, they are the same act. God's declaration that we are justified takes the form of deliverance from sin, death, and Satan. God declares us righteous by delivering us from all our enemies, or, to use the language of 1 Kings 8, God "justifies by giving to the righteous according to his righteousness," by keeping His covenant promises with those counted righteous.[7]

It is interesting that in an article in which Leithart claims to be giving biblical perspectives on the doctrine of justification, he uses a metaphor which has no foundation in the Bible. He defines justification in terms of "a military-conflictual [sic] metaphor" which necessarily denies the forensic nature of the doctrine. The Bible nowhere defines justification in that way. This is typical Federal Vision doublespeak. Federal Vision proponents first say that they believe in justification by faith alone. Then, they redefine justification to include sanctification and covenant faithfulness. Finally, they affirm that justification is based on personal righteousness.

Justification by Faith Alone in the Scripture

Justification by faith alone is obscured, adulterated, and overturned at the present time by the Federal Vision proponents such as Leithart, Schlissel, Lusk, Wilkins, and others. The true doctrine of the gospel is at stake in this controversy. Therefore, the first thing we must consider

---

6 Record of the Case, Standing Judicial Commission, Case 2012-5, 93.

7 Peter Leithart, "Judge Me, O God: Biblical Perspectives on Justification," in Steve Wilkins and Duane Garner, eds., *The Federal Vision* (Monroe, Louisiana: Athanasius Press, 2004), 211-212.

in this chapter is this question: Does the Bible teach that sinners are justified by faith alone?

There are certain key verses of Scripture that are the battleground for this dispute between the Federal Vision and the historic Protestant faith over justification by faith alone. It is acknowledged that the Scripture nowhere uses the phrase "justification *by faith alone*." Yet, the near equivalent to that standard formulation is given in one of those key verses, Romans 3:28.

1. Romans 3:28—"For we maintain that a man is justified by faith apart from the works of the law."

The phrase "apart from works of the law" is what is intended by those who assert that justification is through faith alone. As Robert Haldane commented on this verse:

> This passage asserts not merely that men are justified without *perfect* obedience to any law, but without *any* obedience of their own. It may likewise be remarked, that believers will not be acquitted at the last day on account of their works, but will be judged according to their works. Our God does not justify any according to their works, but freely by His grace.[8]

Writing in the early nineteenth century, Haldane elaborated on themes which are pertinent in the present controversy with the Federal Vision. Haldane specifically says that the judgment according to works which every believer will undergo is not a *final justification* or a *final acquittal* based on works. Judgment and justification are two different things.

Many people reduce the scriptural teaching about justification to a simple denial of the works of morality (good works), but Romans 3:28 specifically says that we are "justified by faith apart from the works of the law." That phrase is a comprehensive term which includes all the works of the law—moral and ceremonial. Circumcision was the sign of the Abrahamic covenant before the law was given at Mount Sinai, but it was also included in the law as a requirement for all male sons (Leviticus 12:3). Romans 3:28 sets the stage for Paul's argument in Romans 4:9-15 that Abraham received the righteousness through faith before receiving the sign of circumcision. Circumcision

---

8 Robert Haldane, *An Exposition of the Epistle to the Romans* (MacDill AFB, Florida: MacDonald Publishing Company, n.d.), 155-156.

is a work of the law and assumes that the one circumcised will be obedient to the law. As Charles Hodge states:

> The Jews believed that circumcision secured its benefits, not only as a seal of the covenant, but from its own sanctifying power. This was only one aspect of the doctrine of salvation by works, against which the sacred writers so earnestly protested. . . The doctrine of salvation by rites was, in the view of the Apostles, a much lower form of doctrine, more thoroughly Judaic, than the doctrine of salvation by works righteousness.[9]

Hodge makes an important point in light of the denial by the Federal Vision advocates that they teach salvation by works. By connecting salvation with the rite of baptism, they are necessarily teaching salvation by works; and, a much lower form of salvation by works at that. Their form of doctrine is thoroughly Judaic; it is the ancient heresy of the Judaizers. Whenever justification is connected with circumcision or baptism, the lowest form of works righteousness is taught.

There are examples of both types of works righteousness in the Scripture. The Judaizers connected ceremonial works with moral works at the Council at Jerusalem: "It is necessary to circumcise them and to direct them to observe the Law of Moses" (Acts 15:5). Circumcision assumed and demanded that the one circumcised would be obedient to the law (Galatians 5:3). The rich young ruler focused on the moral requirements of the law when he asked Jesus, "Good teacher, what shall I do to inherit eternal life?" (Mark 10:17). Paul, before his conversion, trusted in his circumcision on the eighth day as part of his hope of righteousness before God. The Scriptures frequently teach that the circumcision of the flesh is nothing (Deuteronomy 10:16; 30:6; Jeremiah 4:4; 9:25; Romans 2:28, 29; 1 Corinthians 7:19; and Galatians 5:6; 6:15) without a heart that has also been circumcised. Justification is neither through ceremonial works nor moral works of righteousness. Both are works of the law and have no part in our justification which is by faith alone.

James D. G. Dunn, a New Perspectives on Paul scholar, made the mistake of trying to distinguish between ceremonial works and moral works in his comment on Romans 3:28. He said that Paul was prohibiting ceremonial works, but not moral works:

---

9 Charles Hodge, *Systematic Theology*, III (Grand Rapids, Michigan: Wm. B. Eerdmans Publishing Co., 1970), 602.

His denial that justification is from works of law is, more precisely, a denial that justification depends on circumcision or on observation of the Jewish purity and food taboos. . . . "Works of the law" are nowhere understood here, either by his Jewish interlocutors or by Paul himself, as works which earn God's favour, as merit-amassing observances. They are rather seen as badges: they are simply what membership of the covenant people involves, what mark out the Jews as God's people.[10]

Yet, John Murray, in his comment on Romans 3:28, describes why all works are excluded in the matter of justification by faith:

The only answer is the specific quality of faith as opposed to that of works. Justification by works always finds its ground in that which the person is and does; it is always oriented to that consideration of virtue attaching to the person justified. The specific quality of faith is trust and commitment to another: It is essentially extraspective and in that respect is the diametric opposite of works. Faith is self-renouncing; works are self-congratulatory. Faith looks to what God does; works have respect to what we are.[11]

In his commentary on Romans, W. G. T. Shedd refutes the Romanist doctrine of making justification dependent on infused righteousness or personal sanctification:

The Romanist attempt to produce justification by sanctification, to obtain the pardon of sin upon the ground of either internal or external obedience, is not an adaptation of means to ends. It is like an attempt to quench thirst with bread, instead of water. The true correlate to guilt is atoning sacrifice, and to substitute anything in the place of it, however excellent and necessary in other respects the substitute may be, must be a failure.[12]

When either Romanists or the Federal Vision proponents assert that justification is based on the total life of a person, they are confusing the issue, as Shedd astutely observes. The justification of a sinner can only be through an atoning sacrifice, to which all the Scripture abundantly testifies. Works can never justify because there is no atoning sacrifice in them.

---

10   James D. G. Dunn, *Jesus, Paul and the Law* (Louisville: Westminster John Knox, 1990), 191, 194.

11   John Murray, *The Epistle to the Romans* (Grand Rapids, Michigan: Wm. B. Eerdmans Publishing Co., 1968), 123.

12   William G. T. Shedd, *A Critical and Doctrinal Commentary on the Epistle to the Romans* (Grand Rapids, Michigan: Zondervan Publishing House, 1967), 87.

It is interesting that even a modern Roman Catholic scholar acknowledges that Romans 3:28 teaches justification by faith alone. Friar Brendan Byrne of the Jesuit Theological College in Melbourne, Australia, wrote on these verses in his commentary on Romans:

> The following thesis-type statement of the principle of justification by faith apart from the works of the law (v. 28) has been highly significant in the history of the interpretation, becoming the watchword of the Reformation movement, which (rightly) understood Paul's simple qualification "by faith" (pistei) to have the sense of "by faith alone."[13]

Byrne's comments would seem to unequivocally affirm his support, as a Catholic priest, for the doctrine of justification by faith alone. Yet, Catholicism holds to sacramental grace and justification by baptism which are works of the law, as Hodge pointed out. So, it is not surprising that Byrne takes back his support for justification by faith alone in a supplemental note on Romans 3:28:

> The justification in question is always the eschatological justification but, granted that the believer already stands under the eschatological action of God, the present reference is valid.[14]

What that eschatological justification is to Byrne will be made plainer in the section on Romans 2:13. Yet, his emphasis on eschatological justification is similar to what the Federal Vision says about salvation, and vice versa. It is also similar to Pelagius' comment on Romans 3:28 that is in keeping with the nomism expressed by the Federal Vision proponents. Pelagius states:

> But in this verse we are treating he is speaking about that person who in coming to Christ is saved, when he first believes, by faith alone. But by adding "the works of the law" he indicates there is [also] a [work] of grace [which those who have been baptized ought to perform].[15]

Pelagius held to essentially the same views on justification and faith as the Federal Vision adherents. In his commentary on Romans 4:5, 6, Pelagius made the following comment:

---

13 Daniel J. Harrington, ed., Brendan Byrne, *Romans* (Collegeville, Minnesota: The Liturgical Press, 1996), 137.

14 Ibid., 139.

15 Theodore DeBruyn, ed. and trans., *Pelagius' Commentary on St. Paul's Epistle to the Romans* (Oxford: Clarendon Press, 1993), 83.

> When an ungodly person converts, God justifies him by faith alone, not for the good works he did not have. One's initial faith is credited as righteousness to the end that one may be absolved of the past, justified for the present, and readied for the future works of faith.[16]

Pelagius says that God justifies by faith alone *for the present*, but this is only to the end that such a person is *readied for the future works of faith*. His words are open to two different interpretations. Does he mean that the future works evidence the reality of true faith (which has always been the Protestant position) or does he mean that they complete our justification? In other parts of the commentary, Pelagius affirms that the life of Christ saves us if we imitate it;[17] that forgiveness is only for past sins, not future ones;[18] that believers are able to live sinless lives.[19] The Pelagian system is based on works salvation, not grace. Therefore, works are always a part of the faith which justifies in his system. The above quote from Pelagius is almost identical to the following words of Federal Vision advocate Peter Leithart:

> In all of this, it is crucial to remember continually that justification, however defined, is by faith. And in part that means that our justification/vindication is not completely and fully revealed before the Last Judgment. We are justified in the present, but in another sense we await final public vindication.[20]

In those words, Leithart opines that justification *by faith* necessarily means that justification is not completed until the final judgment. That is contrary to how justification by faith alone has always been interpreted by Reformed theologians and the Reformed symbols. It is important, therefore, to understand that affirming justification by faith alone is not a magical statement which guarantees that a person's view is correct. It is necessary for one to also repudiate the place of works in contributing to justification.

---

16 Ibid., 85.

17 Ibid., 92.

18 Ibid., 123.

19 Ibid., 96, 99.

20 Record of the Case, Standing Judicial Commission of the Presbyterian Church in America, Case 2009-6, Bordwine, Rogland, and Stellman vs. Pacific Northwest Presbytery, 24.

The Federal Vision and Justification by Faith Alone

2. Romans 2:13—"For it is not the hearers of the law who are just before God, but the doers of the law will be justified."

The similarity of the Federal Vision and Roman Catholicism on Romans 2:13 is our next consideration in this chapter. Like Schlissel's quote at the beginning of this chapter, Leithart also references Romans 2:13 in the following words:

> Yes, we do have the same obligation that Adam (and Abraham, and Moses, and David, and Jesus) had, namely, the obedience of faith. And, yes, covenant faithfulness is the way to salvation, for the "doers of the law will be justified" at the final judgment.[21]

Leithart, Schlissel, and other Federal Vision advocates state that covenant faithfulness is "the way to salvation" and is consistent with *doing the law* in order to be justified. Byrne similarly affirms justification by works in his comment on Romans 2:13:

> But the *principle* of justification (judgment) according to works stands and believers still have to come before the judgment seat of God to be assessed on the way they have preserved and lived out the righteous status graciously granted them through faith.[22]

N. T. Wright, Bishop of Durham, makes a similar comment on Romans 2:13:

> Justification, at the last, will be on the basis of performance, not possession.[23]

Norman Shepherd, who succeeded John Murray at Westminster Theological Seminary, says concerning this verse:

> The Pauline affirmation in Romans 2:13, "the doers of the Law will be justified," is not to be understood hypothetically in the sense that there are not persons who fall into that class, but in the sense that faithful disciples of the Lord Jesus Christ will be justified.[24]

We could multiply the quotes from Federal Vision authors con-

---

21 Ibid., 34.

22 Harrington, ed., Byrne, *Romans*, 89.

23 N.T. Wright, *The Letter to the Romans* in *The New Interpreter's Bible*, 12 vols. (Nashville: Abingdon, 2002), 10:440.

24 Norman Shepherd, "Thirty-four Theses on Justification in Relation to Faith, Repentance, and Good Works," presented to the Philadelphia Presbytery of the Orthodox Presbyterian Church, November 18, 1978. Thesis 20.

cerning Romans 2:13, but it would only be more of the same. Federal Vision proponents all see this verse as teaching a final justification by works which vindicates them defining salvation as being through faith plus works or a working faith or faithful obedience or covenant faithfulness, etc. Their goal, apparently, is to counter any tendency to antinomianism.

Shepherd's interpretation of Romans 2:13 wrests it out of context. From Romans 1:18- 3:20, Paul proves that both Jews and Gentiles are guilty before God. He concludes by stating in Romans 3:20—"Because by the works of the Law no flesh will be justified in His sight; for through the Law comes the knowledge of sin." The Gentiles were guilty by the light of nature which they suppressed in unrighteousness. The Jews were guilty, despite having the Law, because God only justifies the doers of the Law; not the hearers of it. Lest anyone think that the Apostle was teaching a method of justification through keeping the Law, Paul unequivocally says that no one will be justified in God's sight through that means. The Federal Vision commits the cardinal mistake of interpretation by ignoring the larger context of Romans 2:13. As someone has well said, "A text without a context is a pretext." Thus, they make Romans 2:13 contradict Romans 3:20-4:25.

Charles Hodge is only one of numerous commentators who give the correct interpretation of Romans 2:13:

> In obvious allusion to the opinion, that being a Jew was enough to secure heaven, the apostle says, It is not the hearers but *the doers of the law* that are justified. He is not speaking of the method of justification available for sinners, as revealed in the gospel, but of the principles of justice which will be applied to all who look to the law for justification. If men rely on works, they must have works; they must be doers of the law; they must satisfy its demands, if they are to be justified by it. For God is just and impartial; he will, as a judge administering the law, judge every man, not according to his privileges, but according to his works, and the knowledge of duty which he possessed. On these principles, it is his very design to show that no flesh can be justified.[25]

Calvin, likewise, interprets Romans 2:13 as disqualifying anyone from being justified on the basis of works:

> We do not deny that absolute righteousness is prescribed in the law, but

---

25 Charles Hodge, *Commentary on the Epistle to the Romans* (Grand Rapids, Michigan: Wm. B. Eerdmans Publishing Co., 1972), 54.

since all men are convicted of offence, we assert the necessity of seeking for another righteousness. Indeed, we can prove from this passage that no one is justified by works. If only those who fulfil the law are justified by the law, it follows that no one is justified, for no one can be found who can boast of having fulfilled the law.[26]

In flagrant contradiction of the context, Wright, Shepherd, Leithart, Schlissel, Lusk, and numerous other Federal Vision or New Perspectives proponents interpret Romans 2:13 as teaching that the basis for justification at the last day, the Day of Judgment, will be works. They assert that justification in that day will be based on the totality of a person's life of faithful obedience to the law. Such a view necessarily makes justification to be based on works. Yet, Paul in Romans 3:20 says no one will be justified by the works of the Law. By taking this wrong position, the Federal Vision underestimates the holiness of God's law and overestimates man's ability to comply with the strictness of God's demands.

3. James 2:14-26

The third key passage for the Federal Vision in trying to twist the Scriptures to teach justification based on works is James 2:14-26. People who deny justification by faith alone have always seized on what they perceive to be a conflict between Paul and James concerning the doctrine of justification. Particularly, they quote James 2:24, "You see that a man is justified by works and not by faith alone." Thus, Rich Lusk says that James has in view the same kind of justification as Paul—"forensic, soteric justification" and that "in some sense, James is speaking of a justification in which faith and works combine together to justify."[27] In our consideration of this passage, we first acknowledge that both Romans 4:9 and James 2:23 quote from Genesis 15:6 to support their positions. The main question is this: Do Paul and James contradict each other?

The Lutheran commentator, R. C. H. Lenski, sums it up well:

> Paul and James deal with different kinds of works. Paul deals with works of law which have nothing to do with true gospel faith, which are

---

26 David W. Torrance and Thomas F. Torrance, eds., Ross Mackenzie, trans., John Calvin, *The Epistles of Paul to the Romans and to the Thessalonians* (Grand Rapids, Michigan: Wm. B. Eerdmans Publishing Company, 1979), 47.

27 http://www.hornes.org/theologia/rich-lusk/future-justification-to-the-doers-of-the-law accessed on June 30, 2015.

the boast of all Pharisees and all work-righteous men, who think that they are able to save themselves by such works, at least to aid Christ in saving them. Trust in works of law is the direct opposite of faith in Christ alone. James deals with gospel works, which ever evidence the presence of gospel faith, which, like this faith, glorify Christ alone, without which all claim of having true faith is spurious, a self-delusion. Both James and Paul attribute salvation to a living faith (Mark 16:16; John 3:16), but Paul lays stress on what must be removed if a man is to have and to retain this faith, James on what dare not be absent when a man has and wants to retain his faith. Paul roots out what destroys and excludes faith; James stimulates sluggish faith. The two are in perfect agreement; in the ethical parts of all his epistles Paul, too, calls for the fruits of faith.[28]

It has always been the position of the Reformers and their children that faith alone can justify us, but true faith is never alone. True faith always has good works to evidence it. Paul lays emphasis on the first position in proving that we are justified by faith apart from the works of the law. James lays emphasis on the second part of the Reformers' position that true faith is never alone.

The Early Church Fathers on Justification by Faith Alone
One of the leading arguments by the Federal Vision proponents against the Reformers' doctrine of justification by faith alone is that it represented a fundamental change from the doctrine of the Medieval Church and earlier Christian leaders. They assume, therefore, that the united testimony of the Medieval Church is in their favor and they appeal to it for support.

It is certainly true that some of the Apostolic Fathers did not make clear and unmistakable statements in favor of what are called the doctrines of grace. Those doctrines are generally called the evangelical truths—ruin by the fall, redemption by Christ, and regeneration through the Spirit. They include justification by faith alone in the atonement of Christ. The Apostolic Fathers usually resorted to quotes from Scripture without explaining in what sense they understood those verses. Yet, the opposition to Pelagianism which prevailed in the fifth century confirms that the Apostolic Fathers had not defected from the doctrines of grace nearly as much as is generally believed. As William Cunningham wrote:

---

28 R. C. H. Lenski, *The Interpretation of The Epistle to the Hebrews and The Epistle to James* (Minneapolis, Minnesota: Augsburg Publishing House, 1966), 577-8.

Augustine, the great defender of the truth against Pelagius and his followers, while appealing to the early writers in support of the doctrines which he had established from Scripture, and which he has the distinguished honor of having first developed in a connected and systematic way, admitted that many of them had spoken without due care and precision upon these points, but contended that in the main they concurred in his opinions. It is very certain that they were not Pelagians, for they almost universally admitted that there was a corruption of man's moral nature introduced and spread among mankind by the fall, which Pelagius denied. That they were wholly free from what was afterwards called semi-Pelagianism, or that they held fully and explicitly the Augustinian or Calvinistic system, is not by any means so clear.[29]

Nonetheless, there were certain of the Apostolic Fathers who expressed themselves in favor of justification by faith alone. One of those was Clement of Rome who wrote an early letter to the Corinthian church. Clement said:

> We are not justified through ourselves: that is to say, we are not justified, either through our own wisdom, or our own understanding, or our own piety, or, lastly, through works which we have done in holiness of heart.[30]

Ignatius, the disciple of John, made the following statement early in the second century:

> To me, Jesus Christ is in the place of all ancient muniments. For his cross and his death and his resurrection and the faith which is through him are my unpolluted muniments: and in these, through your prayers, I am willing to have been justified.[31]

The venerable Polycarp, martyred for the faith at the age of eighty-six, was also a disciple of John. He wrote:

> Knowing that through grace you are saved, not from works, but by the will of God, through Jesus Christ.[32]

Justin Martyr was a convert to Christianity about thirty years after

---

29 William Cunningham, *Historical Theology: A review of the principal doctrinal discussions in the Christian Church since the Apostolic Age*, Volume I (London: The Banner of Truth Trust, 1969), 180.

30 George Stanley Faber, *The Primitive Doctrine of Justification Investigated*, (London: R. B. Seeley and W. Burnside, 1837), 82.

31 Ibid., 86.

32 Ibid., 87.

the death of the Apostle John and wrote during the early part of the second century:

> For no longer, by the blood of goats and of sheep or by the ashes of a heifer or by the oblations of flour, are they purified: but by Faith, through the blood of Christ and his death, who died on this very account.
>
> It was not by reason of circumcision that Abraham was testified of God to be righteous, but on account of faith. For before he was circumcised it was said of him: Abraham believed in God: and it was imputed unto him for righteousness.[33]

The authorship of *The Epistle to Diognetus* is uncertain. Some conjecture that it was Justin Martyr and others that it was Pantaenus, the master of Clement of Alexandria. Whoever wrote it made the following comments concerning our justification:

> For what else but His righteousness would have covered our sins? In whom was it possible for us lawless and ungodly men to have been justified, save only in the Son of God? O the sweet exchange, O the inscrutable creation, O the unexpected benefits; that the iniquity of many should be concealed in One Righteous Man, and the righteousness of One should justify many that are iniquitous! Having then in the former time demonstrated the inability of our nature to obtain life, and having now revealed a Saviour able to save even creatures which have no ability, He willed that for both reasons we should believe in His goodness and should regard Him as nurse, father, teacher, counsellor, physician, mind, light, honour, glory, strength and life.[34]

Irenaeus, a native of Smyrna and Bishop of Lyons, wrote concerning justification by faith:

> The Lord was not unknown to Abraham, whose day he desired to see; neither was the Father of the Lord unknown to him; for he had learned from the Word of the Lord, and believed him. Wherefore also, by the Lord, it was imputed unto him for Righteousness. Faith, which is to God, justifieth a man.[35]

Clement of Alexandria labored at the end of the second century and the beginning of the third. He spoke unequivocally in favor of justification by faith alone:

---

33 Ibid., 89.

34 J. R. Harmer, ed., J. B. Lightfoot, *The Apostolic Fathers* (Grand Rapids, Michigan: Baker Book House, 1973), 256-257.

35 Faber, *Primitive Doctrine of Justification*, 94.

Abraham was justified, *not* from works, but from faith. After the end of life, therefore, it is no profit to men even though now they shall have performed good works, unless they have faith.[36]

While other examples could be given, the last person we will quote from the early church period is Athanasius who stood firm against the Arian heresy which almost overran the church. Athanasius said about justification:

Not through these, but from faith, a man is justified; as also was Abraham.[37]

Though the statements of the early church fathers were not as clear as the later statements of the Reformers, there is certainly ample evidence to prove they believed that justification was by faith, not works; that our sin is imputed to Christ and His righteousness to us; that His death on the cross was the means of securing our justification; and, that original sin prevents everyone from being able to merit salvation.

The Medieval Church on Justification by Faith Alone

From the time of Augustine onwards, there were various Christian leaders who made definite statements in favor of justification by faith alone. There was also a great and horrible declension concerning this doctrine as a result of the inroads of Pelagianism. The doctrine of justification by faith alone was corrupted at a very early period and this corruption was further championed by the Scholastics who paved the way for the fully developed doctrine of Rome. The leading Scholastic theologian in this development of Romanism was Thomas Aquinas, whose theological system was virtually ratified by the Council of Trent and with it Semi-Pelagianism was officially adopted by the Catholic Church. Yet, the doctrine of justification by faith alone was not totally lost even during the Medieval Church.

St. Basil the Great (329-379), bishop of Caesarea Mazaca in Cappadocia, who is recognized by both the Eastern Orthodox and Catholic churches, said:

This is the true and perfect glorying in God when a man is not lift-

---

36 Ibid., 96.
37 Ibid., 100.

ed up on account of his own righteousness, but has known himself to be wanting in true righteousness, and to be justified by faith in Christ alone.[38]

Aurelius Ambrosius, or St. Ambrose (340-397), Bishop of Milan, Italy, said:

There is no need, therefore, of the Law, since through faith alone, an ungodly man is justified.[39]

Origen, who was guilty of theological errors on other points, nevertheless wrote concerning this doctrine:

Through faith, without the works of the Law, the thief was justified.[40]

Jerome (347-420), Bishop of Jerusalem at the time of Pelagius, elaborated on this doctrine:

When an ungodly man is converted, God justifies him through faith alone, not on account of good works, which he possessed not; otherwise, on account of his ungodly deeds, he ought to have been punished.[41]

Chrysostom (347-407), John of Damascus, said:

For, certainly, it is the righteousness of God, when we are justified, not by works (for, in that case, it were needful that no stain should be found), but by grace, where sin is made to vanish away.[42]

St. Augustine says:

He begins from faith, in order to make it clear that, not good works, preceding Justification, show what man hath merited, but that good works, following after Justification, show what man hath received.[43]

St. Anselm, Archbishop of Canterbury from 1093 to 1109, said:

Dost thou believe that thou canst not be saved but by the death of

---

38 James Bannerman, *The Doctrine of Justification: An Outline of its History in the Church and of its Exposition from Scripture* (London: The Banner of Truth Trust, 1961), 108.
39 Ibid.
40 Ibid., 109.
41 Ibid.
42 Ibid.
43 Ibid., 110.

Christ? Go to, then, and whilst thy soul abideth in thee, put all thy confidence in this death alone—place thy trust in no other thing—commit thyself wholly to this death,—cover thyself wholly with this alone,—cast thyself wholly on this death, —wrap thyself wholly in this death.[44]

Bernard of Clairvaux (1090-1153), who has been called the theologian of the cross, wrote:

> Whoever, feeling compunction for his sins, hungers and thirsts after righteousness, let him believe in Thee who "justifies the ungodly;" and thus, being justified by faith alone, he shall have peace with God.[45]

Reformation Debates on Justification by Faith Alone

The tactics of the Federal Vision with respect to justification by faith alone are reminiscent of the way the Papists confused the issue at the time of the Reformation. As Calvin comments on Galatians 5:6, "But faith working by love":

> There would be no difficulty in this passage, had the Papists not dishonestly twisted it to uphold the righteousness of works. When they want to refute our doctrine that we are justified by faith alone, they seize upon this weapon: "If the faith that justifies us be that which works by love, faith alone does not justify." I reply they do not understand their own babbling; far less what we teach. It is not our doctrine that the faith which justifies us is alone. We maintain that it is always joined with good works. But we contend that faith avails by itself for justification.[46]

The Federal Vision confuses these two theological terms—justification and judgment—and thereby makes eternal salvation dependent on works. Their view is not new, but is typical of the Papist position. For instance, the theological faculty of the University of Paris (the Sorbonne) compiled a statement of articles which they decreed all religious instructors were to teach. In the fourth article, "Of Justification by Works," they stated:

> Moreover, a sinner is not justified by faith alone, but also by good

---

44 Ibid.

45 Ibid., 111.

46 David W. Torrance and Thomas F. Torrance, eds., T. H. L. Parker, trans., John Calvin, *The Epistles of Paul to the Galatians, Ephesians, Philippians and Colossians* (Grand Rapids, Michigan: Wm. B. Eerdmans Publishing Company, 1972), 96.

works, which are so necessary, that without them no adult can obtain life.[47]

In support of their view, the faculty referred first to 'philosophic reason' and then to various first principles (but not to Scripture) before clearly stating their position:

We are condemned on account of bad works; therefore we are justified on account of good works.[48]

In his antidote to these articles of faith, Calvin quoted copiously from Scripture before augmenting his position by reference to the views of Augustine, Bernard, and Basil the Great. Calvin's reference to their views indicates clearly that he considered all three of them to be in agreement with justification by faith alone.

Yet, there were some Papists during the days of the Reformation who were very subtle and deceitful on the matter of a sinner's justification by faith. One of them was James Sadolet, Bishop of Carpentras, France, and soon to be a Cardinal. Sadolet wrote a letter to the citizens of Geneva on March 18, 1539, during the period that Calvin was removed from the pastorate of St. Peter's Church, in an effort to woo that city back to Romanism. In part of that letter, Sadolet pretended to believe in justification by faith alone, stating:

> Moreover, we obtain this blessing of complete and perpetual salvation by faith alone in God and in Jesus Christ. When I say faith alone, I do not mean, as those inventors of novelties do, a mere credulity and confidence in God, by which, to the seclusion of charity and other duties of a Christian mind, I am persuaded that in the cross and blood of Christ all my faults are unknown; this, indeed, is necessary, and forms the first access which we have to God, but it is not enough... When we say, then, that we can be saved by faith alone in God and Jesus Christ, we hold that in this very faith love is essentially comprehended as the chief and primary cause of our salvation.[49]

Though Sadolet claims that salvation is obtained by faith alone in God and Christ, he says that such faith—which he calls "a mere credulity and confidence in God"—is the first access to God, but it is insufficient to justify. Rather, he defines faith as comprehending love "as the chief and primary cause of our salvation." Thus, Sadolet turns the

---

47 Henry Beveridge, ed., *John Calvin: Tracts and Letters*, Volume I, Tracts, Part I (Edinburgh, Scotland and Carlisle, Pennsylvania: The Banner of Truth Trust, 2009), 80.
48 Ibid.
49 Ibid., 9-10.

scriptural definition of salvation on its head. Instead of God's love for sinners being the fountainhead of our salvation, he makes our love for God the "primary cause."

Sadolet's letter is beguiling and cunning. He refers to the Reformers as men who were dissatisfied with their low station in the Catholic Church which spirit of dissatisfaction caused their sedition and schism in tearing the spouse of Christ to pieces. He portrays them as confessing to God on the day of judgment the reason for their holding to the doctrine of justification by faith alone as follows:

> That we should trust to faith alone, and not also to good works, to procure us righteousness and salvation—seeing, especially, that thou hadst paid the penalty for us, and by thy sacred blood wiped away all faults and crimes, in order that we, trusting to our faith in thee, might thereafter be able to do, with greater freedom, whatsoever we listed.[50]

Sadolet makes two errors in this hypothetical confession of the Reformers. First, he has them putting their trust in "faith alone." Trust in faith is not the same thing as trust in Christ. All the Reformers were very clear on that fundamental issue. Trust in faith is actually nothing other than trust in works. Under such a scheme, it is not Christ who saves through faith, but faith saves without Christ. Second, Sadolet accuses the Reformers of antinomianism—a common, though mistaken, charge. He has them confessing to God their sole reason for believing in salvation by faith alone is so that they can do whatever they want with complete freedom.

In his response to Sadolet's letter, Calvin contends that the true meaning of justification is that:

> Man is reconciled in Christ to God the Father, by no merit of his own, by no value of works, but by gratuitous mercy.[51]

In the next paragraph, Calvin disagrees with Sadolet's definition of faith:

> But faith, you say, is a general term, and has a larger signification. I answer, that Paul, whenever he attributes to it the power of justifying, at the same time restricts it to a gratuitous promise of the divine favour,

50 Ibid., 18.
51 Ibid., 42.

and keeps it far removed from all respect to works. Hence his familiar inference—if by faith, then not by works. On the other hand—if by works, then not by faith.[52]

In defining faith as covenant faithfulness, N. T. Wright, Peter Leithart, Steve Wilkins and others in the Federal Vision/New Perspectives on Paul make the same mistake concerning justification by faith alone that Papists, Cardinal Sadolet, and Pelagius have made. Justification for them is not through the merits of Christ alone, but also through the works of man—regardless how those works are defined.

Summary
The Federal Vision advocates speak confusedly concerning the doctrine of justification. Sometimes, they assert that they hold to justification by faith alone, but they take positions that are in dynamic conflict with the Scripture, the Reformed symbols, and the way the greatest theologians of the church have viewed the doctrine both before and since the Reformation. The Federal Vision's emphasis on both justification by water baptism and final justification make it clear that they do not believe in a once-for-all forensic justification through faith in Christ alone.

Conclusion
The doctrine of justification by faith alone is taught in Scripture, was the chief doctrine of the Protestant Reformers, and has been held by great church leaders both before and since the Reformation. Some people look vainly for unanimity among the early church or medieval church leaders concerning this doctrine. Yet, there has never been unanimity concerning justification by faith alone, whether before or after the Protestant Reformation. The issue is not whether *all* have believed in justification by faith alone in any particular period of church history. The salient point is that this doctrine has been maintained by faithful witnesses in all periods of church history. The Reformers did not skip over the whole history of the church up to their time and wrongly interpret the meaning of Paul's teaching, as those holding to the Federal Vision and the New Perspectives on Paul allege. Justification by faith

---

52 Ibid., 42-43.

alone and justification by faith plus works have both been taught by various branches of the church throughout all her history. The issue cannot be determined by tradition or references to the opinions of uninspired men. The touchstone of truth is Scripture. The Reformers and the Reformed creeds stand with Scripture in ascribing our justification to faith alone in the finished work of Christ alone by God's grace alone.

-15-
The Federal Vision and Imputation

"The notion of [Jesus'] thirty-three years of Torah-keeping being imputed to me is problematic. . . These works were not accumulating points that would be credited to Jesus' people; rather, they were vocation fulfilling acts that prepared the way for the 'one Man's righteous act,' namely his death on the cross. . .

"The active obedience itself, then, is not saving in itself. Rather, it's the precondition of his saving work in his death and resurrection." [1]

RICH LUSK, A FEDERAL VISION PROPONENT

---

[1] Calvin Beisner, ed., Rich Lusk, "A Response to 'The Biblical Plan for Salvation'" in *The Auburn Avenue Theology, Pros and Cons: Debating the Federal Vision* (Fort Lauderdale, Florida: Knox Theological Seminary, 2004), 140.

The doctrine of imputation in classic Reformed theology includes three things: the imputation of Adam's sin to all his descendants, the imputation of the believer's sin to Christ, and the imputation of the whole obedience of Christ (both active and passive) to the believer. The meaning of both the Hebrew and Greek words interpreted as "impute" is "to count, to reckon, to be counted, to be reckoned, to be charged to" someone. It means to reckon or count something to a person, whether or not it actually belongs to him. The meaning of the word, *impute*, is very important for a correct understanding of this doctrine. As James Buchanan wrote:

> Most of the leading errors on the subject of Justification may be traced to obscure or defective views in regard to the nature or import of imputation, and have arisen from supposing—either that it consists in the infusion of moral qualities, in which case Justification is confounded with Sanctification—or that, in so far as imputation may be distinguished from such infusion, it is founded, at least, on the moral qualities which thus became inherent, in which case Justification has for its immediate ground a personal, and not a vicarious, righteousness.[2]

While the word imputation is used infrequently in Scripture, the idea is present in several passages where the word itself is not mentioned. We will examine some of those Scriptures later in this chapter. Most of the proponents of either the Federal Vision or the New Perspectives on Paul limit the imputation of Christ's obedience to His passive obedience only—that is, His suffering and death. They deny that the righteousness of Christ, His active obedience, is imputed to believers. In the quote above, Lusk calls the imputation of Christ's active obedience (what he refers to as Jesus' Torah-keeping) "problematic." The Federal Vision proponents adopt both of the errors mentioned above by Buchanan at one time or another. First, their doctrine of final justification denies the imputation of Christ's righteousness and grounds justification on personal righteousness. Yet, personal righteousness is always subjective in nature, whether viewed from the Augustinian or Pelagian perspectives. It is either the work of subjective grace through the Holy Spirit or it is the subjective faithfulness of the individual. In that respect, the Federal Vision's emphasis on the objectivity of the covenant is once again betrayed by their own version of subjectivism. Second, the Federal Vision's interpretation of defini-

---

2 James Buchanan, *The Doctrine of Justification* (London: The Banner of Truth Trust, 1961), 337.

tive sanctification confuses justification with sanctification similar to the following statement of the Council of Trent:

> If anyone shall say, that men are justified either by the sole imputation of the righteousness of Christ, or by the sole remission of sin, to the exclusion of that grace and charity which is shed abroad in their hearts by the Holy Spirit, and which inheres in them, or shall say that grace whereby we are justified is merely and only the favor of God: let him be accursed.[3]

In the Scripture, the three imputations—Adam's sin to all his posterity, our sins to Christ, and Christ's righteousness to believers—are so intimately connected that the denial of one will eventually lead to the denial of the other two. Thus, saving faith in Christ requires us to assent to the idea of imputation even if the term is unfamiliar to us. For instance, a sinner in coming to Christ must acknowledge three things essential to saving faith: that he is a sinner by nature (the imputation of Adam's sin), that Christ has died for his sins (the imputation of Christ's passive righteousness), and that God accepts and accounts him as perfect through Christ alone (the imputation of Christ's active obedience). The denial by the Federal Vision of the imputation of Christ's righteousness to believers is, therefore, not an intramural debate of little concern. It is a denial of one of the three foundational legs of the gospel. When the imputation of Christ's righteousness is denied, then His life of obedience becomes primarily an example for our own obedience. He profits us only by imitation, not by imputation, and our final justification is based on the totality of our lives, according to this system. That theory of final justification (which denies the imputation of the active obedience of Christ) limits the imputation of the passive obedience of Christ to past sins only; whereas the true doctrine is that Christ has died for all the sins of His people. Both those positions inevitably lead to a denial of the imputation of Adam's sin to his descendants in some degree or another. As the Puritan author, Thomas Watson, astutely observed:

> The Pelagians of old held, that Adam's transgression is hurtful to posterity by imitation only, not by imputation. But the text, "In whom all have sinned," confutes that.[4]

---

3 William G. T. Shedd, *A History of Christian Doctrine*, Volume II (Edinburgh: T. & T. Clark, 1877), 325.

4 Thomas Watson, *A Body of Divinity* (London: The Banner of Truth Trust, 1970), 143.

George Smeaton, in *The Apostle's Doctrine of the Atonement*, says:

> The antithesis between our own righteousness and that which is called the righteousness of God is different. It is between that which is subjective (our own) and that which is objective (God's).[5]

Thus, interestingly, the Federal Vision position is a repudiation of objective righteousness in favor of subjective righteousness. In this instance, the Federal Visionists are inconsistent with their own first principles. There are, indeed, both objective and subjective aspects of salvation. Both aspects are necessary for our salvation. The Federal Vision always misses the mark by emphasizing the wrong work of salvation at the wrong time. This mistake is endemic to the whole system. When they should emphasize the subjective work of the Spirit in working faith in the hearts of God's people, Federal Vision proponents emphasize the objectivity of the covenant in water baptism; when they should emphasize the objectivity of God's grace in the imputation of Christ's righteousness to believers, they emphasize the subjective righteousness of the individual as the ultimate ground of his justification. Such errors are neither small nor immaterial.

Romans 5:12-21

It is necessary at the outset, therefore, to establish the fact that Adam's sin is indeed imputed to all his posterity. The whole system of the Federal Vision depends on a reframing of the doctrine of sin which permits people to fulfill the law for their own righteousness. The work of Christ is limited to forgiveness of sins and an example for our obedience. In his comments on Romans 5, Federal Visionist, Peter Leithart, patently denies that the active obedience of Christ is even a part of Paul's argument in that passage:

> One could argue that verse 18 is a proof text against the imputation of active obedience, since it roots justification not in a series of acts of obedience during the life of Jesus but in a single act of righteousness in His death on the cross.[6]

---

5 George Smeaton, *The Apostles' Doctrine of the Atonement* (Grand Rapids, Michigan: Zondervan Publishing House, 1957), 113.

6 Record of the Case, Standing Judicial Commission of the Presbyterian Church in America, Case 2012-5, RE Gerald Hedman vs. Pacific Northwest Presbytery, 217.

Thus, Leithart limits the imputation of Christ's obedience to his death—not his life. John Murray, though, disagrees with such an interpretation of Romans 5:18 and further clarifies his point in his comments on both verses 18 and 19:

> If the question be asked how the righteousness of Christ could be defined as "one righteous act", the answer is that the righteousness of Christ is regarded in its compact unity in parallelism with the one trespass, and there is good reason for speaking of it as the one righteous act because, as the one trespass is the trespass of the one, so the one righteousness is the righteousness of the one and the unity of the person and of his accomplishment must always be assumed.[7]

Later in that commentary, Murray further elaborates:

> Undoubtedly it was in the cross of Christ and in the shedding of his blood that this obedience came to its climactic expression, but obedience comprehends the totality of the Father's will as fulfilled by Christ.[8]

Romans 5:12-21 is one of the great passages of Scripture concerning the themes of the federal headships of Adam and Christ, the principle of imputation, and the objective side of salvation. Thus, it is bewildering when a system that claims to restore the objectivity of the covenant opposes the clear teaching of Scripture by rejecting the objective, forensic imputation of Christ's righteousness to His people. The Federal Vision is a misnomer because it is antagonistic to true federal theology. Instead of basing justification on "the totality of the Father's will as fulfilled by Christ" (which is objective), its advocates make it dependent on the totality of the life of the individual (which is subjective). Such inconsistency and contradiction is to be found throughout their whole system.

Centuries before the Federal Vision system was devised, Pelagius denied both the imputation of Christ's righteousness to believers and the imputation of Adam's sin to his posterity in his commentary on Romans 5:

> Adam became only the model for transgression, but Christ [both] forgave sins freely and gave an example of righteousness.[9]

---

7   John Murray, *The Epistle to the Romans*, Vol 1, Two volumes in one, (Grand Rapids, Michigan: Wm. B. Eerdmans Publishing Co., 1971), 201-2.

8   Ibid., 205.

9   Theodore De Bruyn, trans., *Pelagius' Commentary on St. Paul's Epistle to the Romans*, (Oxford,

> Just as by the example of Adam's disobedience many sinned, so also many are justified by Christ's example.[10]
>
> If Adam's sin injured those who have not sinned, then also Christ's righteousness profits those who do not believe.[11]

In those comments, Pelagius manifests the logical connection between the denial of the imputation of Jesus' righteousness to believers, and the denial of the imputation of Adam's sin to all his descendants. If Christ's righteousness is not imputed to us, He is merely an example for our righteousness, even as Adam's sin was a bad example for us. One denial inevitably leads to the other. As Pelagius further comments on Christ's righteousness in his Romans commentary:

> *How much more, having been reconciled, shall we be saved in his life.* If we have been saved by Christ's death, how much more shall we glory in his life, if we imitate it.[12]

> *Therefore just as through one person sin came into the world, and through sin death.* By example or by pattern. Just as through Adam sin came at a time when it did not yet exist, so in the same way through Christ righteousness was recovered at a time when it survived in almost no one.[13]

The history of Christian doctrine reveals that errors about imputation always lead back to some form of Pelagianism. This scene has been played out many times before. In that regard, Bernard of Clairvaux proved himself to be a much better theologian than the Federal Vision proponents by connecting all three imputations in the following quote:

> When one sins, all are held to be guilty; shall the innocence be counted only for the one who is innocent? The sin of the one produced death for us all; shall the righteousness of the one restore life to one only? Is God's justice more able to condemn than to restore? Is Adam more powerful for evil than Christ for good? Will Adam's sin be imputed [imputabitur] to me and Christ's righteousness not pertain to me? Has

---

England: Clarendon Press, 1993), 95.

10 Ibid.

11 Philip Schaff, ed., Peter Holmes and Robert Ernest Wallis, trans., Saint Augustin, *Anti-Pelagian Writings*, Volume V of *A Select Library of the Nicene and Post-Nicene Fathers of the Christian Church* (Grand Rapids, Michigan: Wm. B. Eerdmans Publishing Company, 1978), 245.

12 De Bruyn, *Pelagius' Commentary on Romans*, 92.

13 Ibid.

the disobedience of the former ruined me, while the obedience of the latter will be of no benefit to me?[14]

He bore the punishment of our sin [peccati meritum] and gave us his righteousness by paying the debt of death and restoring life. . . Death has been put to flight by death in Christ, and Christ's righteousness is imputed [imputatur] to us.[15]

The contrast throughout Romans 5:12-21 is between the imputation of Adam's sin which results in condemnation and the imputation of Christ's righteousness which results in justification of life. The Scripture clearly states that "through the obedience of the One *the many will be made righteous.*" Yet, the Federal Vision theory would turn that verse around to say "through the obedience of the One *the many are forgiven.*" The denial of the imputation of Christ's active obedience limits imputation to forgiveness of sins only. Yet, the clear teaching of Scripture in Romans 5 and other passages is against such a position.

2 Corinthians 5:21
The Federal Vision also denies the most important objective truths of the covenant—particularly, the assumption by Christ of our covenant responsibilities to the works of the law. Such a view is contradicted by 2 Corinthians 5:21- "He made Him who knew no sin to be sin on our behalf, so that we might become the righteousness of God in Him." There is a curious inconsistency in the Federal Vision theology which proves it is wrong. Concerning the interpretation of 2 Corinthians 5:21, Smeaton writes:

> In the same sense in which Christ was made sin—that is, objectively and by imputation—in that sense are His people made the righteousness of God.[16]

A true understanding of the objectivity of the covenant demands that the people of God are made the righteousness of God through the imputed righteousness of Christ to them. By denying the imputation of Christ's righteousness, advocates of the Federal Vision are inconsistent with their own emphasis on the objectivity of the covenant.

---

14 Anthony N. S. Lane, *Bernard of Clairvaux: Theologian of the Cross* (Collegeville, Minnesota: Liturgical Press, 2013), 71.

15 Ibid., 70.

16 Smeaton, *Apostles' Doctrine of the Atonement*, 113.

This point is clarified by Philip E. Hughes comment on 2 Corinthians 5:21:

> It should be noted, further, that, just as Paul does not say that Christ was made sinful, but sin, for us, so also he does not say that in Him we are made righteous, as though henceforth untouched by sin, but *righteousness*, indeed, even more expressly, the righteousness *of God*—that righteousness, namely, which being, of God, is complete and inviolable forevermore. It is, in a word, the sinner's *justification* of which the Apostle is speaking, whereby our trespasses are reckoned to Christ and the absolute and spotless perfection of His righteousness is reckoned to us, with the consequence that "there is now no condemnation to them that are in Christ Jesus" (Rom. 8:1). Justification, indeed, does not preclude sanctification, whereby the believer increasingly becomes that which judicially he already is; on the contrary, justification presupposes sanctification; and the two become one at last in the consummating experience of glorification. But meanwhile they must be kept distinct, since the former is instantaneous and complete, while the latter is gradual and progressive. And both are in Christ our Righteousness.[17]

Charles Hodge, commenting on the same verse, shows that the way in which Christ was made sin for us was by being a sin offering; in dying in our place. As he said:

> The only sense in which we are made the righteousness of God is that we are in Christ regarded and treated as righteous, and therefore, the sense in which he was made sin, is that he was regarded and treated as a sinner. His being made sin is consistent with his being in himself free from sin; and our being made righteous is consistent with our being in ourselves ungodly. In other words, our sins were imputed to Christ, and his righteousness is imputed to us.[18]

John Calvin likewise commented on this passage:

> How can we become righteous before God? In the same way Christ became a sinner. For He took, as it were, our person, that He might be the offender in our name and thus might be reckoned a sinner, not because of His own offences but because of those of others, since He Himself was pure and free from every fault and bore the penalty that was our due and not His own. Now in the same way we are righteous in Him, not because we have satisfied God's judgment

---

17 Philip Edgcumbe Hughes, *Paul's Second Epistle to the Corinthians* (Grand Rapids, Michigan: Wm. B. Eerdmans Publishing Co., 1971), 214.

18 Charles Hodge, *An Exposition of the Second Epistle to the Corinthians* (Grand Rapids, Michigan: Wm. B. Eerdmans Publishing Co., 1970), 148-9.

by our own works, but because we are judged in relation to Christ's righteousness which we have put on by faith, that it may become our own.[19]

Zechariah 3:1-5

The most beautiful illustration of the two parts of justification in the Old Testament is found in Zechariah 3:1-5. In that passage, Satan accuses Joshua, the high priest, of his unfitness to be a priest due to the filthy garments he is wearing; whereas, the law required priests to wear holy garments, for glory and beauty. The angel of the Lord tells those surrounding Joshua to remove the filthy garments from him and to clothe him with festal robes and a clean turban. In removing the filthy garments, the angel tells Joshua, "See, I have taken your iniquity from you and will clothe you with festal robes" (Zechariah 3:4b). The filthy garments represented his sin and the festal robes represented the righteousness that was given to him or imputed to him. There was a perfect exchange which completely mirrors the work of Christ for our salvation. Sin is taken away and righteousness is given. Thomas V. Moore commented on this passage:

> Then to show that it was not their righteousness but another's that was the ground of their acceptance, and that it was not to encourage them in sin, but to remove it, the divine angel commanded, v. 4, that these filthy garments (the symbol of sin) should be removed, and, festal robes (the symbol of imputed righteousness) should be put on him, thus setting forth the great and consoling doctrine of a gratuitous justification because of the merits of the Redeemer.[20]

PCA minister, Richard Phillips, makes a similar comment on this passage in his excellent commentary on Zechariah:

> The angel of the Lord did not infuse righteousness—or anything else—into Joshua. He did not give him grace over a certain period of time in which he could clean up his own act. Instead, the Scripture depicts an imputed righteousness, a glorious garment that is the gift of God, bestowed by abounding grace apart from merit and prior to any improvement in the individual. What the angel bestowed was not a righteousness achieved by Joshua but the righteousness of another—what

---

19 T. A. Smail, trans., David W. Torrance and Thomas F. Torrance, eds., John Calvin, *The Second Epistle of Paul to the Corinthians and the Epistles to Timothy, Titus and Philemon* (Grand Rapids, Michigan: Wm. B. Eerdmans Publishing Co., 1964), 81-2.

20 Thomas V. Moore, *A Commentary on Zechariah* (London: The Banner of Truth Trust, 1968), 65.

Philippians 3:9

The final Scripture we will consider is Philippians 3:9 in which Paul contrasts his former life as a Pharisee with his present faith in Christ. That verse says, "And may be found in Him, not having a righteousness of my own derived from the Law, but that which is through faith in Christ, the righteousness which comes from God on the basis of faith." Buchanan's comments on this verse are insightful:

> The two righteousnesses are not only distinct, but different; and not only different, but directly opposed, and mutually exclusive, considered as grounds of Justification; insomuch that he who is justified by one, cannot possibly be justified by the other. If the righteousness of man be sufficient, the righteousness of God is superfluous; if the righteousness of God be necessary, the righteousness of man can have no place. Nor can any conciliation or compromise be effected between them, so as to admit of their being combined in one complex ground of acceptance; for they represent two methods of Justification which are irreconcilably opposed,—the one by grace, the other by works.[22]

The only possible way to understand what Paul means in Philippians 3:9 is through the imputation of Christ's righteousness to believers. Paul contrasts personal righteousness according to the law with the alien righteousness of Christ imputed to those who receive it through faith. The righteousness whereby Paul is found in Christ cannot be and is not his own works of righteousness. Christ's righteousness is not a mere example to us of how to live righteously, but it becomes the righteousness of every believer.

The Westminster Assembly and Imputation

There are some scholars who assert that the Westminster Standards do not require belief in the imputation of Christ's active obedience. They say that the Westminster divines reached a consensus concerning the imputation of Christ's righteousness which permitted those members, particularly Richard Vines and Thomas Gataker, to agree to its language while denying that the active obedience of Christ is im-

---

21 Richard D. Phillips, *Zechariah*, (Phillipsburg, New Jersey: P&R Publishing, 2007), 70-1.

22 Buchanan, *Doctrine of Justification*, 330.

puted to believers. One such contemporary author is William Barker who wrote on this very point:

> The Westminster Divines, in such controversies, sought to be clear and faithful to Scriptural language, yet to allow for shades of difference within a generic Calvinism.[23]

Yet, Barker also acknowledged that the Westminster Standards still clearly teach the imputation of the active obedience of Christ to believers. Thus, he opined only that the Westminster divines allowed for differences on this point. James R. Daniel Kirk is another contemporary author who concluded that the deletion of the word "whole" in the final version of chapter eleven of the Westminster Confession of Faith indicates that there was allowance for "a range of views with respect to the precise nature of Christ's righteousness."[24] Westminster Confession of Faith 11.1 says:

> Those whom God effectually calleth, he also freely justifieth; not by infusing righteousness into them, but by pardoning their sins, and by accounting and accepting their persons as righteous; not for anything wrought in them, or done by them, but for Christ's sake alone; nor by imputing faith itself, the act of believing, or any other evangelical obedience to them, as their righteousness; but by imputing the *[whole]* obedience and satisfaction of God unto them, they receiving and resting on him and his righteousness, by faith; which faith they have not of themselves, it is the gift of God. (The word whole is in italics and enclosed in brackets to indicate that it was removed in the final version of this section.)

Those who claim that the deletion of the word "whole" in the final version indicates that the Assembly consciously accommodated views that denied the imputation of Christ's righteousness to believers are making an argument based on silence that is contradicted both by this section and other parts of the Westminster Standards. This section of the Confession clearly states that evangelical obedience is not imputed to the believer for his righteousness. Yet, those who deny the imputation of Christ's righteousness—such as Richard Baxter, Albert Barnes, N. T. Wright, and the Federal Vision proponents—invariably

---

23 William S. Barker, *Puritan Profiles: 54 Influential Puritans at the Time When the Westminster Confession of Faith was Written* (Fearn, Scotland: Mentor/Christian Focus Publications, 1996), 176.

24 James R. Daniel Kirk, "The Sufficiency of the Cross," *Scottish Bulletin of Evangelical Theology* (2006), 37-38.

teach that one's own evangelical obedience *is* imputed to them as their righteousness. It would have taken more than the mere deletion of the word "whole" for the Westminster Assembly to accommodate that view. Thus, Jeffrey K. Jue in "The Active Obedience of Christ and the Theology of the Westminster Standards: A Historical Investigation"[25] concluded that there is no evidence that the Westminster divines reached a consensus to accommodate those who denied the imputation of the active obedience of Christ. Indeed, as Jue says:

> Placing the doctrine of justification within the Westminster Standards as a whole reveals a distinct and consistent theological system that does not comport with the system of theology presented by Vines and Gataker, which includes their "passive obedience only" doctrine of justification.[26]

Other members of the Westminster Assembly pushed back from the positions of Vines and Gataker concerning Christ's active obedience. Peter Smith, a Westminster Assembly commissioner from Barkway, Hertfordshire, England, interpreted Romans 5:12-21 as follows:

> By the "righteousness of the one" must be understood the active obedience of Christ, & the reason is because the word is frequently taken, especially in the Old Testament, for the morall law . . . Ther is a communication in the workes of Christ, his active and passive obedience.[27]

In fact, the Westminster Assembly's Larger and Shorter Catechisms very clearly state that it is both the obedience and satisfaction that is imputed to believers. The answer to the Shorter Catechism Question #33 says:

> Justification is an act of God's free grace, wherein he pardoneth all our sins, and accepteth us as righteous in his sight, only for the righteousness of Christ imputed to us, and received by faith alone.

The Larger Catechism #70 is even more direct in attributing justification to the imputation of Christ's righteousness:

> Justification is an act of God's free grace unto sinners, in which he pardoneth all their sins, accepteth and accounteth their persons righteous

---

25 K. Scott Oliphant, editor, *Justified in Christ: God's plan for us in Justification* (Fearn, Scotland: Christian Focus Publications, 2007), 99-130.

26 Ibid., 128.

27 Ibid., 122.

in his sight; not for anything wrought in them, or done by them, but only for the perfect obedience and full satisfaction of Christ, by God imputed to them, and received by faith alone.

The Larger Catechism specifically rejects the heresies of both the Council of Trent ("anything wrought in them") and Pelagius ("or done by them"), while affirming that the perfect obedience of Christ is imputed to believers as their righteousness in Christ and is received by faith alone. Since the Catechisms (1647) were written after the Confession was completed (1646), the argument that the Westminster divines arrived at a consensus to accommodate the views of Twisse, Gataker, and Vines and to allow for the denial of the active obedience of Christ cannot be seriously entertained. In the Westminster Confession of Faith Chapter 11, sections 1 and 2, the words "obedience and satisfaction," and "obedience and death" must be taken to mean the active and passive obedience of Christ. Any attempt to make the Westminster Confession mean something else is an argument based on silence in light of the clear teaching of the Assembly's catechisms on the imputation of Christ's righteousness.

Imputation of Christ's Righteousness in Other Reformed Symbols

Other Reformed creeds, both before and after the Westminster Confession of Faith, emphasize that justification is through the whole righteousness of Christ. For instance, the Belgic Confession of 1561 said:

> However, to speak more clearly, we do not mean that faith itself justifies us, for it is only an instrument with which we embrace Christ our Righteousness. But Jesus Christ, imputing to us all his merits, and so many holy works, which he hath done for us and in our stead, is our Righteousness.[28]

The French Confession of 1559 also emphasized what we denominate as the active and passive righteousness of Christ:

> We therefore reject all other means of justification before God, and without claiming any virtue or merit, we rest simply in the obedience of Jesus Christ, which is imputed to us as much to blot our sins as to make us find grace and favor in the sight of God.[29]

---

28 Philip Schaff, ed., David S. Schaff, rev., *The Creeds of Christendom*, Volume III, *The Evangelical Protestant Creeds* (Grand Rapids, Michigan: Baker Book House, 1983), 408.

29 Ibid., 370.

The answer to question #60 of the Heidelberg Catechism (1563) also affirms that both the active and passive obedience of Christ are imputed to the believer:

> God, without any merit of mine, of mere free grace, grants and imputes to me the perfect satisfaction, righteousness, and holiness of Christ, as if I had never committed nor had any sin, and had myself accomplished all the obedience which Christ has fulfilled for me, if only I accept such benefit with a believing heart.[30]

The Second Helvetic Confession of 1566, written by Heinrich Bullinger, is very clear concerning the imputation of both our sins to Christ and His righteousness to us, as seen in Chapter 15, section 3:

> To speak properly, then, it is God alone justifieth us, and that only for Christ, by not imputing unto us our sins, but imputing Christ's righteousness unto us.[31]

The Savoy Declaration of 1658 states in Chapter 11, section 1 that both the active and passive obedience of Christ are imputed to believers. The London Confession of Faith in 1689 and the Philadelphia Confession of Faith of 1688 adopted the exact language of the Savoy Declaration concerning the active and passive obedience of Christ. Moreover, even the Thirty-Nine Articles of the Church of England of 1562 stated:

> We are accounted righteous before God, only for the merit of our Lord and Saviour Jesus Christ by Faith, and not for our own works or deservings.[32]

The Lutheran Formula of Concord also affirms the imputation of Christ's righteousness to believers:

> For he bestows and imputes to us the righteousness of the obedience of Christ; for the sake of that righteousness we are received by God into favor and accounted righteous.[33]

Generic Calvinism as expressed in the various Reformed creeds

---

30 Ibid., 326.

31 Peter Hall, *The Harmony of Protestant Confessions: Exhibiting the Faith of the Churches of Christ, Reformed After the Pure and Holy Doctrine of the Gospel* (Edmonton, Alberta, Canada: Still Waters Revival Books, 1992), 149.

32 Schaff, *Creeds*, Volume III, 494.

33 Ibid., 116.

both before and after the Westminster Assembly is very clear that imputation includes both our sins to Christ and His righteousness to us. No Reformed creed, including the Westminster Standards, ever denies the imputation of Christ's righteousness to believers. There is a unanimous consensus in the Reformed symbols concerning the imputation of Christ's righteousness to the believer that undercuts any attempt to interpret the Westminster Confession of Faith in opposition to this doctrine.

Richard Baxter's Neonomianism

Richard Baxter, the author of such great works as *The Saints' Everlasting Rest*, *A Call to the Unconverted*, and *The Reformed Pastor*, served the church well in the area of practical theology, but was greatly deficient in the area of systematic theology. Baxter agreed with the views of Hugo Grotius (1583-1645), a Dutch jurist who laid the foundation for international law, that God did not require the law to be satisfied by Christ, but changed it into a new law with easier terms. This new law became known as Neonomianism. Baxter himself was aware that his theology would cause others to accuse him of heresy as he noted in his *Aphorisms of Justification*:

> I know this is the Doctrine that will have the loudest Out-cries raised against it; and will make some cry out, *Heresy, Popery, Socinianism!* and what not! For my own part, the Searcher of Hearts knoweth, that not singularity, Affectation of Novelty, nor any Good-will to Popery, provoketh me to entertain it: But that I have earnestly sought the Lord's Direction upon my knees, before I durst adventure on it.[34]

Baxter needed to do more than earnestly seek the Lord's directions on his knees. He needed to base everything on the only touchstone of faith—the infallible Word of God. His failure to do so led him to take a position denying the imputation of Christ's righteousness to believers. Rather, his position was that the believer's own works are the righteousness which meet the demands of God's new covenant. As he wrote:

> As it is beyond Doubt that Christ will then justify Men according to their Works: So 'tis evident, that this is not only to discover the Sincerity of their Faith; but that it is also, as they are Parts of that evangelical

---

34 Richard Baxter, *An Extract of Mr. Richard Baxter's Aphorisms of Justification* (Newcastle upon Tyne, England: John Gooding, 1745), 31.

Righteousness, which is the condition of their Justification.[35]

Thus, Baxter conceived that justification was based partly on Christ's satisfaction for our sins and partly on our own works. Such a legal strain, in its reaction to Antinomianism, "at a later stage showed itself to be full-blown Moderatism."[36] This tendency of legalism towards Moderatism or Liberalism has also been noted by Packer and Machen. Baxter's work was both a reaction against antinomianism and an effort to remove the supposed advantages of the Papists in the matter of justification. One of those advantages of the Papists, according to Baxter, was the insistence by Protestants on the imputation of Christ's righteousness to believers. The result of neonomianism was "so much of a return to Roman doctrine [that] it looked as if in the last resort Paul must be saved from himself."[37] As Macleod observes:

> This reaction was found not only in the High Church Sacramentarian school of the Anglicans, which was Arminian in its cast of thought, but also in that wing of Nonconformity which held itself most aloof from the extreme of an Antinomian tendency.[38]

VARIOUS ERRORS CONCERNING IMPUTATION

1. Limiting Justification to Pardon

The Westminster Standards (Westminster Confession of Faith 11:1; Larger Catechism Q # 70; Shorter Catechism Q # 33) teach that there are two parts of justification; pardon and acceptance. Pardon is more aligned with the passive obedience of Christ and acceptance with the active obedience. The ground of our acceptance is through Christ alone—not through our own works. The Federal Vision proponents reduce justification to pardon for sin only with acceptance being contingent on God's future verdict that their lives have been righteous. For instance, Leithart leaves out our acceptance through the righteousness of Christ when he defines justification:

---

35 Ibid., 33.

36 John MacLeod, *Scottish Theology in Relation to Church History Since the Reformation* (Edinburgh, Scotland and Carlisle, Pennsylvania: The Banner of Truth Trust, 1974), 111.

37 Ibid., 139.

38 Ibid., 140.

The Federal Vision and Imputation

Justification is, you're justified from sin. Sin is being pictured as an external enslaving power. And that's what we're delivered from."[39]

It is interesting that Leithart also reduces sin to an "external enslaving power," whereas the Scripture describes it as a matter of the heart first of all. When sin is externalized, the natural result is that it is defined in terms of actions only. That is a very Pelagian construction of sin. If sin is externalized, then it also means that the heart of man does not need a spiritual renovation. Thus, the way is opened for the Federal Vision's theory of a final justification based on one's personal obedience. Yet, final justification is unnecessary since a scriptural definition of justification also includes our acceptance in Christ. As Jonathan Edwards said:

> God doth in the sentence of justification pronounce a sinner perfectly righteous, or else he would need a further justification after he is justified.[40]

Albert Barnes, who was convicted of heresy in 1837 by the General Assembly of the Presbyterian Church in America, similarly reduced justification to pardon and dismissed acceptance through the imputation of Christ's righteousness:

> It is not that *his* righteousness becomes ours. This is not true; and there is no intelligible sense in which that can be understood. But it is God's plan for *pardoning* sin, and for *treating us* as if we had not committed it.[41]

Sometimes it is wrongly alleged that Calvin limited justification to pardon and did not consider the matter of the imputation of righteousness of Christ to the believer. Those who make such assertions are guilty of quoting the great Reformer out of context. In his commentary on Romans, Calvin made the following statement about chapter 8, verse 30:

> Justification might quite well be extended to include the continuation of the divine favour from the time of the calling of the believer to his death. But because Paul uses this word throughout the Epistle for the unmerited imputation of righteousness, there is no necessity for us to

---

39   Record of the Case, Standing Judicial Commission, Case 2012-5, 520.

40   James Wood, *Old and New Theology* (Philadelphia: Presbyterian Board of Publication, 1845), 149.

41   McLeod, *Scottish Theology*, 143.

depart from this meaning.[42]

Then again in his *Institutes of the Christian Religion*, Calvin said:

> On the contrary, justified by faith is he who, excluded from the righteousness of works, grasps the righteousness of Christ through faith, and clothed in it, appears in the God's sight, not as a sinner, but as a righteous man.[43]

2. Limiting Imputation to the Verdict or Effects

In one of his statements, Leithart reduced the imputation of either the active or passive obedience to the effects or the verdict only:

> There is no "independent" imputation of the active obedience of Christ, nor even of the passive obedience for that matter; we are regarded as righteous, and Christ's righteousness is reckoned as ours, because of our union with Him in His resurrection. What is imputed is the verdict, *not the actions of Jesus*.[44]

That is an old error. The New Divinity theologians, Albert Barnes and Charles Finney, made the same distinction about imputation, to which Archibald Alexander replied as follows:

> Some have attempted to evade the doctrine [of the imputation of Christ's righteousness], by alleging that not the righteousness of Christ, but its effects are imputed to us. They who talk thus do not seem to understand what they say. It must be by the imputation of the righteousness that the good effects are derived to us; but the imputation of the effects cannot be. What we are inquiring after is the reason why these blessings become ours. It cannot be on account of our own righteousness; it must be on account of the righteousness of Christ. How does this righteousness avail to obtain for us pardon and justification and peace with God? The answer is by imputation; that is, it is set down to our credit. God accepts it on our behalf; yea, he bestows it upon us. If there is any such thing as imputation, it must be of the righteousness of Christ itself, and the benefits connected with salvation flow from this imputation. The righteousness of Christ can only justify us, by being imputed to us.[45]

---

42 David W. Torrance and Thomas F. Torrance, eds., Ross MacKenzie, trans., *Calvin's Commentaries: The Epistle to the Romans and Thessalonians* (Grand Rapids, Michigan: Wm. B. Eerdmans Publishing Company, 1979), 182.

43 John T. McNeill, ed., Ford Lewis Battles, trans., *Calvin: Institutes of the Christian Religion*, Volume I (Philadelphia: The Westminster Press, 1967), 726-7.

44 Record of the Case, Standing Judicial Commission, Case 2012-5, 79.

45 Wood, *Old and New Theology*, 152-153.

Faustus Socinus and his followers, the Socinians, also asserted that imputation is limited to the effects or benefits. Whereas the Papists taught an infused righteousness instead of an imputed righteousness, John Owen noted that the Socinians denied such imputation:

> The Socinians, who expressly oppose the imputation of the righteousness of Christ, plead for a participation of its effects or benefits only.[46]

Thus, the Federal Vision advocates have unwittingly taken up the mantle of Socinianism by reducing imputation to the effects or benefits or verdict of Christ. In their overemphasis on the objectivity of the covenant, they have deftly avoided the errors of Rome, but they have been captured by the errors of Pelagius and Socinus instead.

3. Asserting Jesus Had to Obey the Law for Himself

Under direct examination at his trial, Leithart further summarized his position concerning Jesus' obedience:

> What I've described—what I've described as the prosecution has quoted is based on Romans 4:25 that Jesus' resurrection is his own justification before the Father. Jesus is raised from the dead as a declaration to the world that this is the righteous son of the Father.[47]

This is the position of Norman Shepherd and others in the Federal Vision/ New Perspectives on Paul camp. Yet, Romans 4:25 says: "He was delivered over because of our transgressions, and was raised because of our justification." Jesus was raised for *our* justification—not for *His* justification. By making Jesus' resurrection about His own justification, the Federal Vision also says that Jesus was responsible to obey the law for Himself just like other men. For instance, Leithart says:

> Yes, we do have the same obligation that Adam (and Abraham, and Moses, and David and Jesus) had, namely the obedience of faith.[48]

That is a position taken by Charles G. Finney, who also denied the imputation of Christ's righteousness and said Jesus was obligated to obey the law:

---

46 William H. Goold, ed., *The Works of John Owen*, Volume V (London: The Banner of Truth Trust, 1967), 174.

47 Record of the Case, Standing Judicial Commission, Case 2012-5, 478-479.

48 Ibid., 78-79.

> Jesus Christ was bound to obey the law for himself and could no more perform works of supererogation or obey on our account than anybody else.[49]

Yet, the Scripture is clear that Jesus voluntarily obeyed the law for us and laid down His life for us. (Cf. John 10:18; Psalm 40:6-8.) If Jesus was "obligated" to obey the law, then He did not do it willingly, voluntarily, and with authority over his death. As David Dickson says:

> The Son of God incarnate becomes voluntarily, a very capable, discreet, ready, and obedient servant to the Father for us.[50]

A. A. Hodge gives the true position concerning the voluntary nature of Christ's atonement:

> Christ, although a man, was a divine person, and therefore never personally subject to the Adamic covenant of works. He was essentially righteous, but he was *made under the law* as our representative, and his obedience under the *voluntarily assumed conditions of his earthly life* was purely vicarious.[51]

Faustus Socinus, and the Socinians, held the same position as Leithart and Finney concerning the voluntary nature of Christ's sacrifice, as John Owen writes:

> He [Socinus] supposeth, that if all he did in a way of obedience, was due from himself on his own account, and was only the duty which he owed unto God for himself in his station and circumstances, as a man in this world, it cannot be meritorious for us, nor any way imputed to us.[52]

For Socinus, this false principle became the channel by which he denied the divinity of Christ. Owen proved Christ could not have been "under the law" to obey it for Himself, since He is both God and man.[53] Christ assumed human nature for His people—not for Him-

---

49 Lewis Cheeseman, *Differences between Old School and New School Presbyterians* (Rochester, New York: Erastus Darrow, 1848), 57.

50 David Dickson, *A Commentary on the Psalms* (Edinburgh, Scotland and Carlisle, Pennsylvania: The Banner of Truth Trust, 1995), 223.

51 A. A. Hodge, *Outlines of Theology*, (Grand Rapids, Michigan: Zondervan Publishing House, 1972), 415.

52 Wood, *Old and New Theology*, 137.

53 W. H. Goold, ed., *The Works of John Owen*, Volume V (London: The Banner of Truth Trust, 1967), 253-257.

self. He obeyed the law for His people—not for Himself. Nonetheless, the Socinians twisted scriptural terms to their own sense. As James Buchanan says concerning the Socinians:

> While they hold a sinner's justification to be his own personal repentance and reformation, they taught, nevertheless, that, in their own sense of the terms, he is "justified freely by grace,"—that he is "justified by faith,"—that he is justified by means "of the death of Christ,"—and that his faith, repentance, and obedience are not the meritorious or procuring causes of his pardon and acceptance, but simply the conditions on which the enjoyment of these blessings depends.[54]

Proponents of the Federal Vision deny the imputation of Christ's righteousness while contending that a sinner is justified by grace or through faith. The only basis for gratuitous salvation is the imputation of both Christ's active and passive obedience, but the Federal Vision denies the imputation of Christ's righteousness. Thereby, they join league with such heresies as those promoted by Catholicism, Pelagius, Socinus, Barnes, Finney, and others.

Summary
One of the doctrines that the Federal Vision most virulently opposes is the imputation of Christ's righteousness or His active obedience. In so doing, the Federal Vision advocates place their position outside the Reformed tradition of the Reformed symbols. Though there were a few members of the Westminster Assembly who denied the imputation of Christ's active obedience, their views were not adopted by the Assembly. All the Reformed creeds and confessions clearly teach the imputation of Christ's righteousness to believers. Moreover, this doctrine is clearly taught in several Scripture passages.

Conclusion
Calvinism, in its creeds and through its greatest theologians, has always upheld the three imputations of Scripture—Adam's sin to his posterity, our sins to Christ, and Christ's righteousness to believers. There are those in the broader Reformed community who have differed from these views, but their opinions have universally been rejected by Reformed judicatories and have never been incorporated in the

---

54 Buchanan, *Doctrine of Justification*, 177.

Reformed creeds. Scriptural soteriology depends on a correct understanding of imputation. Whenever and wherever the imputation of Christ's righteousness to the believers is denied, it has led to heretical opinions concerning salvation. The Scripture, the Reformed creeds, and the greatest Reformed theologians are all opposed to the limiting of imputation to Christ's passive obedience only or to the *effects* of Christ's active obedience—without the imputation of the same.

-16-

The Federal Vision and Covenant Faithfulness

> "However, after the exile, Judaism drifted into greater and greater nomism and prepared itself for the coming Messiah by scrupulous attention to the Law's demands. The result was Pharisaic pride, on the one hand, and despair for the sinner on the other. In this context, Jesus announced the good news of God's reign: forgiveness of sins by the gift of grace. The kingdom was for all who were poor in spirit, not just for Jews who kept the law."[1]
>
> HERMAN BAVINCK

---

1 John Bolt, ed., John Vriend, trans., Herman Bavinck, *Reformed Dogmatics*, Volume 3: *Sin and Salvation in Christ* (Grand Rapids, Michigan: Baker Academics, 2006), 485.

Integral to both the Federal Vision and the New Perspectives on Paul is the doctrine of covenant faithfulness or covenantal nomism[2], particularly as it is developed by E. P. Sanders. In this writer's opinion, many evangelical and Reformed theologians have conceded too much to Sanders' work on second temple Judaism, *Paul and Palestinian Judaism: A Comparison of Patterns of Religion*. Sanders argues that second temple Judaism after their return from captivity had changed significantly, whereby they held to a paradigm of salvation initiated by grace, but completed by obedience. Sanders called this pattern of religion "covenantal nomism." Cornelis Venema comments on Sanders' meaning of covenantal nomism:

> Covenantal nomism is, accordingly, Sanders' term for the pattern of religion within Judaism that regards "getting in" as a consequence of God's gracious initiative and "staying in" as a consequence of the person's resolute commitment to God and obedience to his law.[3]

There are some interesting things about Sanders' thesis. First, he teaches that Judaism underwent a change after the Jews' return from captivity, but he does not tell us what influenced this change. According to the scholars quoted in Chapter 7, "The Federal Vision and Baptismal Efficacy," this change came about because the Jews in captivity were influenced by pagan magical views of rites and sacraments. Second, Sanders' book attempts to set the framework for the New Testament teaching on justification, especially Galatians, in light of the covenant nomism of second temple Judaism.

The Federal Vision and Covenant Nomism

Sanders' paradigm of Jewish religion after the captivity is a view held by proponents both of the Federal Vision and the New Perspectives on Paul. In fact, they both generally agree with this paradigm as the way of salvation for today. Thus, they assert that the Reformers misunderstood the Apostle Paul's objection to a works-based salvation in Galatians and Romans. Sanders defines what he means by covenantal nomism as follows:

---

2 Nomism means law keeping.

3 Cornelis Venema, *The Gospel of Free Acceptance in Christ* (Edinburgh, Scotland and Carlisle, Pennsylvania: The Banner of Truth Trust, 2006), 154.

The view that one's place in God's plan is established on the basis of the covenant and that the covenant requires as the proper response of man his obedience to its commandments, while providing means of atonement for transgression.[4]

The New Perspectives on Paul proponent, N. T. Wright, is quick to add that this paradigm of grace completed by good works or covenant faithfulness is not Pelagianism. Too many evangelical scholars are eager to agree with him. Yet, this paradigm of grace completed by works is the same paradigm of salvation that Paul warned against in Galatians 3:3, "Are you so foolish? Having begun by the Spirit, are you now being perfected by the flesh?" In Paul's hypothetical question, the grace of the Spirit would be temporary only and His persevering grace would be denied. Otherwise, Paul would not accuse them of trying to be "perfected by the flesh." Rather, their salvation would be perfected by the Holy Spirit indwelling them. It is either by the flesh or it is by the Spirit, but it cannot be by both. As William Hendriksen commented on Galatians 3:3:

> By placing *Spirit* and *flesh* so near to one another. . . the difference between the two receives the proper emphasis. The active presence of *the Spirit* spells the indwelling of Christ; hence, rebirth, the implantation of the seed of true faith, the sense of forgiveness and sonship, and the further gifts of illumination, liberty, joy, assurance of salvation, power against Satan, answered prayers, effective witness bearing, etc. It produces gifts both outward and inward. . . On the other hand, *the flesh* is the absence of Christ's indwelling. It indicates anything apart from Christ on which one bases his hope for salvation. The Galatians were beginning to renounce Christ as the all-sufficient Savior. Having begun in the Spirit they were now tending to place their confidence in fleshly means—such as trusting in the advice of the Judaizers, hence also in legal works, strict observance of ceremonies, circumcision, etc.[5]

Thus, the paradigm of salvation of the proponents of the New Perspectives on Paul and the Federal Vision is the same paradigm as the Judaizers and Pelagians and all other moralists / legalists. Their paradigm says salvation is begun by the objective work of Christ and com-

---

4   E. P. Sanders, *Paul and Palestinian Judaism: A Comparison of Patterns of Religion* (Philadelphia: Fortress Press, 1977), 75.

5   William Hendriksen, *Exposition of Galatians* (Grand Rapids, Michigan: Baker Book House, 1974), 114.

pleted by their own faithfulness or obedience; it is begun by outward grace and completed by fleshly obedience. That is Pelagianism, even though it is frequently not recognized as such. For instance, Venema mistakenly states concerning the Reformers in his excellent book, *The Gospel of Free Acceptance in Christ*:

> Accordingly, when the Reformers of the sixteenth century opposed the doctrine of justification in the medieval Roman Catholic Church, they did not oppose (let alone claim to oppose) it because it was Pelagian, as writers of the new perspective intimate. The Reformers, including Calvin and Luther, objected to the teaching that sinners are justified by God *partly* on the basis of his grace in Christ and *partly* on the basis of their willing cooperation with this grace, which includes good works that increase the believer's justification and merit further grace.[6]

Many modern Reformed scholars have agreed with Venema, but his statement that the Reformers never referred to the Roman Catholic Church as being Pelagian is certainly incorrect. The evidence that the Reformers, including Calvin and Luther, did indeed accuse the Catholic Church of being Pelagian is overwhelming and will be presented in Chapter 22. Before the Council of Trent, the Catholic Church had not decided whether to be Augustinian or Pelagian, but the Reformation forced her to make a decision. The Council of Trent was part of the Counter-Reformation and was an attempt by the Catholic Church to answer the Reformers on the question of justification by faith alone. Trent tried to strike a middle position on all the great questions involved and, therefore, was Semi-Pelagian in its conclusions. Yet, Trent did not complete its work until 1563, forty-six years after the Reformation had begun. It is proper to call the Roman Catholic Church ever since Trent a Semi-Pelagian denomination, but that was not true of her when the Reformation began. And the first-generation Reformers rightly referred to her as Pelagian.

Covenant Nomism and Pelagianism

The person who understood Pelagianism the best was the Bishop of Hippo, St. Augustine. Most modern scholars define Pelagianism as being a graceless system in which a man pulls himself up by his bootstraps. Thus, when Sanders or Wright or the Federal Vision

---

6 Venema, *Gospel of Free Acceptance*, 157.

proponents speak of salvation being initiated by grace, it is immediately assumed that their systems are Semi-Pelagianism at worst.. However, Pelagius did not deny all grace, which every person who has ever read Augustine's Anti-Pelagian writings certainly realizes. Pelagius limited grace, but did not deny it. Augustine observed that Pelagius limited grace to the forgiveness of sins, the illumination of the Holy Spirit, the teaching of the law, and the example of Christ. Consider the following quote from Pelagius:

> God helps us by His teaching and revelation, whilst He opens the eyes of our heart; whilst He points out to us the future, that we may not be absorbed in the present; whilst He discovers to us the snares of the devil; whilst He enlightens us with the manifold and ineffable gift of heavenly grace.[7]

There are numerous quotes from Pelagius' writings which reveal that he believed in grace of a certain kind. His system was not totally graceless. Even though he stated that all men have free will, he taught that God's grace assists a person's free will through the law and the teaching. Thus, he *limited* grace to that which is external and objective. It would be helpful for everyone interested in these issues to read Augustine's works on the subject. Concerning Pelagius' description of grace above, Augustine wrote:

> And what else is this than placing God's grace in "the law and the teaching"? Hence, then it is clear that he acknowledges that grace whereby God points out and reveals to us what we are bound to do; but not that whereby He endows and assists us to act, since the knowledge of the law, unless it be accomplished by the assistance of grace, rather avails for producing the transgression of the commandment.[8]

In other places, Augustine shows that Pelagius defines grace as including the forgiveness of sins[9] and the example of Christ,[10] but not the vivifying work of the Holy Spirit which alone gives us the power

---

[7] Philip Schaff, ed., Peter Holmes and Robert Ernest Wallis, trans., *Saint Augustin's Anti-Pelagian Writings*, Nicene and Post-Nicene Fathers, Volume 5 (Grand Rapids, Michigan: Wm. B. Eerdmans Publishing Company, 1978), 220.

[8] Ibid. 220.

[9] Ibid., 231.

[10] Ibid.

to live a godly life.[11] Thus, Pelagius also believed that salvation was initiated by grace of a sort, but must be maintained by individual faithfulness. In Chapter 3, "The Federal Vision and Grace", it was established that the primary distinctive of Pelagianism is its emphasis on the outward, objective grace of God in opposition to the inward, subjective grace.

It is often taught that Pelagianism and Semi-Pelagianism are different in that the former denies the necessity of grace altogether while the latter recognizes that grace is necessary to cooperate with people's free will. Actually, Pelagianism and Semi-Pelagianism are alike in their denial of efficacious grace, their affirmation of the freedom of man's will, and their affirmation of the necessity of God's grace in salvation (according to their definition of grace). Pelagianism, though, limits God's grace to objective things—the law and teaching, the example of Christ, and the forgiveness of sins—while Semi-Pelagianism teaches the necessity of the inward, subjective grace of God. Yet, both Pelagianism and Semi-Pelagianism teach that God's grace can be resisted; this is a large part of the errors of those systems. Concerning Pelagius' view of the necessity of grace at all times, Augustine wrote:

> Although he [i.e. Pelagius] makes that grace of God whereby Christ came into the world to save sinners to consist simply in the remission of sins, he can still accommodate his words to the meaning, by alleging that the necessity of such grace for every hour and for every moment and for every action of our life, comes to this, that while we recollect and keep in mind the forgiveness of past sins, we sin no more, aided not by any supply of power from without, but by the powers of our own will as it recalls to our mind, in every action we do, what advantage has been conferred upon us by the remission of sins.[12]

In that quote, Augustine shows that Pelagius affirmed the necessity of grace, in his limited definition of the term, for all of life—every hour, every moment, and every action. What Pelagius denied was that God's grace is internal, subjective, and efficacious. This is a different picture of Pelagianism than is often painted by modern authors. Pelagius so limited grace that he effectively denied it. Yet, he always referred to its necessity in the limited way in which he taught it.

Semi-Pelagianism, likewise, denies that grace is efficacious, but

11 Ibid., 192.
12 Ibid., 218.

The Federal Vision and Covenant Faithfulness

comes closer to the truth. For instance, John Cassian (A.D. 360-435), an ascetic monk and theologian best remembered for his mystical writings, attempted to synthesize Augustinianism and Pelagianism. His teaching was condemned by the Council of Orange in A.D. 530 as being Semi-Pelagian. In *The Conferences of John Cassian*, he asserts the necessity of God's inward grace:

> From which we clearly infer that the initiative not only of our actions but also of good thoughts comes from God, who inspires us with a good will to begin with, and supplies us with an opportunity of carrying out what we rightly desire: for "every good gift and every perfect gift cometh down from above, from the Father of lights," who both begins what is good, and continues and completes it in us.[13]

Therein, Cassian affirms that grace reaches to the initiative of our actions, the thoughts, the good will, and the opportunities to carry out our desires. Such grace is not merely example or teaching, but reaches to the inner spring of a person's life. If Cassian had stopped at that point, he would have been on firm ground, but he did not. In another part of the *Conferences*, Cassian stated:

> And by this testimony we can clearly see what we ought to ascribe to free will, and what to the design and daily assistance of the Lord, and that it belongs to divine grace to give us opportunities of salvation and prosperous undertakings and victory: but that it is ours to follow up the blessings God gives us with earnestness or indifference.[14]

Cassian was trying vainly to reconcile free grace and free will. Man has liberty, but not ability apart from God's efficacious grace. Augustine emphasized free grace; Pelagius emphasized free will; and Cassian sought to synthesize the two. Yet, Cassian placed too much emphasis on free will, which was to be expected. He ascribed to the will the power to either follow up God's grace with earnestness or to resist it with indifference.

Thus, the following chart shows the differences between Pelagianism, Semi-Pelagianism, Augustinianism-Calvinism, and the Federal Vision:

---

13 Philip Schaff and Henry Wace, eds., *Nicene and Post-Nicene Fathers*, Volume 11, "Sulpitius Severus, Vincent of Lerins, John Cassian," Second Series (Peabody, Massachusetts: Hendrickson Publishers, Inc., 2004), 423.

14 Ibid., 329.

Believe in:	Objective Grace	Subjective Grace	Efficacious Grace
Pelagianism	Yes, with limitations	No	No
Semi-Pelagianism	Yes, with limitations	Yes, with limitations	No
Augustinianism-Calvinism	Yes	Yes	Yes
Federal Vision	Yes, with limitations	No	No

This chart shows that the Federal Vision, according to its own stated views, lines up more nearly with Pelagianism. Of course, the Federal Vision proponents try to have it both ways. They both affirm and deny efficacious grace, but their unique theories require the denial of efficacious grace. They remain officially non-committal to the necessity of supernatural regeneration in their "Joint Profession," but they cannot have it both ways. Their emphasis on objective grace alone is a denial of subjective grace and supernatural regeneration. The Scripture and the Reformed faith require that we believe in objective, subjective, and efficacious grace together.

All of this is relevant because of the paradigm of Sanders (as well as Wright, the New Perspectives on Paul, and the Federal Vision), that second temple Judaism believed that one gets in the covenant by grace, but maintains that status by covenantal faithfulness. That paradigm is closer to Pelagianism than Semi-Pelagianism. For instance, the Council of Trent, the most Semi-Pelagian creed in the history of the church, states that grace is internal and subjective:

> The disposition, or preparation, is followed by Justification itself, which is not remission of sins merely, but also the sanctification and renewal of the inward man, through the voluntary reception of the grace, and of the gifts, whereby man of unjust becomes just, and of an enemy a friend, that so he may be *an heir according to hope of life everlasting.*[15]

There are three things about that statement which stand out. First, the Council makes justification consist in the sanctification and renewal of the inward man. Second, the Council clearly affirms that

---

15 Philip Schaff, *The Creeds of Christendom: with a History and Critical Notes*, Volume II (Grand Rapids, Michigan: Baker Book House, 1983), 94.

grace is inward and subjective. Third, the Council makes grace dependent upon the voluntary reception of such by the individual which exalts free will to an unscriptural position. John Cassian certainly agreed with both the second and third points, but the Federal Vision does not agree with the second point. Its vision of restoring the objectivity of the covenant is opposed to inward and subjective grace. Thus, whether wittingly or unwittingly, the Federal Vision's paradigm of salvation lines up more closely with Pelagianism.

Covenant Nomism and Works Righteousness

Many people reduce the scriptural teaching about justification to a simple denial of the works of morality (good works), but Romans 3:28 specifically says that we are "justified by faith apart from the works of the law." That phrase is a comprehensive term which includes all the works of the law—moral and ceremonial. Circumcision was the sign of the Abrahamic covenant before the law was given at Mount Sinai, but it was also included in the law as a requirement for all male sons (Leviticus 12:3). Romans 3:28 sets the stage for Paul's argument in Romans 4:9-15, that Abraham received the righteousness through faith before receiving the sign of circumcision. Circumcision is a work of the law and assumes that the one circumcised will be obedient to the law. For instance, William Cunningham wrote in *Historical Theology*:

> The natural enmity of the human heart to the principles and plans of the divine procedure in regard to the salvation of sinners . . . has appeared in two different forms: first, a tendency to rely for the forgiveness of sin and the enjoyment of God's favour upon what men themselves are, or can do; and, secondly, a tendency to rely upon the intervention and assistance of other men or creatures, and upon outward ordinances. Heathenism exhibited both; and the corrupted Judaism of our Saviour's days,—the prevailing party of the Pharisees,—exhibited both. The Sadducees of the apostolic days, and the Socinian and the rationalistic, or the semi-infidel, forms of professed Christianity in modern times, have exhibited only the first of these tendencies, in different degrees of grossness, on the one hand, or plausibility, on the other; while Popery, like heathenism and corrupted Judaism, exhibits, a combination of both.[16]

---

16 William Cunningham, *Historical Theology: A review of the principle doctrinal discussions in the Christian Church since the Apostolic Age*, Volume II (London: The Banner of Truth Trust, 1969), 121.

Legalism always assumes at least one of these forms of works salvation and often assumes both. Legalism is a denial of the Gospel whereas antinomianism is a denial of the law. The ancient Sadducees, who were the archetypes of rationalism and liberalism, agreed with the Pharisees about salvation through works of morality but parted from them concerning salvation by religious rites and ceremonies. The Federal Vision, by emphasizing nomism and sacramentalism, assumes both forms of works salvation. It teaches that salvation is bestowed according to works of moral righteousness (covenantal nomism) and according to works of sacramental / ceremonial righteousness (baptism in particular). The Judaizers also always believed in both forms of works salvation—as did Pelagius, as does Rome, etc.

Works salvation, or legalism, has always been the greatest plague to the true gospel in the history of the church. Some branches of the church have tended toward the sacramental aspect of works—Catholicism, Orthodoxy, and to a lesser extent, Lutheranism and Anglicanism.

In Philippians 3:5, 6, Paul sets forth both sacramental works and moral works as the basis for his former hopes of salvation. He says, "circumcised the eighth day . . . as to the righteousness which is in the law found blameless." His hope before coming to faith in Christ was in both the ceremony of circumcision and his moral righteousness. Commenting on these verses, John Daillie said:

> He names circumcision the first, because it was the first and most necessary sacrament of the Jewish people, the seal of the Mosaic covenant, the livery, mark, and glory of an Israelite, which separated him from all the nations of the world, and was the principal subject of controversy between the apostle and the false teachers, who, above, all things, contended for it, and esteemed it essentially necessary to justification. . .
>
> And this was precisely the error in which Paul himself had formerly been, when in the school of the Pharisees; believing, like them, that circumcision, sacrifices, abstinence, ablutions, and other ceremonies of the law, were really expiatory for sin, and merited the favor of God, having been instituted by Moses for that end.[17]

When nomists of any brand, whether Pelagians or Romanists or Neonomians or the Federal Vision, assert that justification is based on the total life of a person, they are confusing the issue. The justifi-

---

17 John Daillie, *An Exposition of Philippians* (MacDill AFB, Florida: Tyndale Bible Society, n.d.), 180, 192.

cation of a sinner can only be through an atoning sacrifice, to which all the Scripture abundantly testifies. Works can never justify because there is no *atoning* sacrifice in them. Thus, John Calvin, in his book against Pighius, wrote:

> On the possibility or impossibility of keeping the law there is no reason for him to put us in contention with the Fathers. For when we maintain that it is impossible for man to keep the law, we have two things in mind: first, that the perfection which is there demanded of us far exceeds our natural strength; and secondly, that no one has ever existed who has rendered in full the righteousness demanded by the law.[18]

Covenant Nomism and the Westminster Standards

The Westminster Standards teach that the difference between the covenant of works and the covenant of grace is at the soteriological level. The basic problem in denying the distinction between the covenant of works and the covenant of grace is that justification is then based on covenant faithfulness, which the Westminster Standards say is impossible. Thus, Augustine quotes the Pelagians as follows:

> But we do praise God as the Author of our righteousness, in that He gave us the law, by the teaching of which we have learned how we ought to live.[19]
>
> We confess that even the old law, according to the apostle, is holy and just and good, and that this could confer eternal life on those that kept its commandments, and lived righteously by faith, like the prophets and patriarchs, and all the saints.[20]

This last statement of the Pelagians sounds almost identical to Leithart's statement earlier in this book where he said, "And, yes, covenant faithfulness is the way of salvation, for the 'doers of the law will be justified' at the final judgment."[21] The Pelagians taught that covenant faithfulness ("lived righteously by faith") is the way of salvation. In point of fact, Pelagius taught that the law and the gospel have

---

18 A. N. S. Lane, ed., G. I. Davies, trans., John Calvin, *The Bondage and Liberation of the Will* (Grand Rapids, Michigan: Baker Books, 1996), 51.

19 Philip Schaff, ed., *Nicene and Post-Nicene Fathers*, Volume V, (Grand Rapids: Wm. B. Eerdmans Publishing Company, 1971), 88.

20 Ibid., 420.

21 Record of the Case, Standing Judicial Commission of the Presbyterian Church in America, Case 2009-6, Bordwine, Rogland, and Stellman vs. Pacific Northwest Presbytery, 34.

essentially the same effect in leading us to heaven. In Pelagius' mind, there was no antithesis between law and gospel, such as the covenant of works / covenant of grace distinction. For Pelagius, grace is law; the New Testament is law.[22] Christ is not the Savior for Pelagius, but an example to be followed. The law is an example of God's will for our lives and the law requires obedience, as Pelagius says:

> First, then, get to know God's will, as contained in his law, so that you may be able to do it, since you can be certain you are a Christian only when you have taken the trouble to keep all God's commandments.[23]

Both Federal Visionists (such as Leithart) and the Pelagians fail to take serious account of the strict and perpetual requirement of the law which condemns us all (for example, Galatians 3:10).

Nomism of various types has been taught in every branch of the church throughout church history. The Federal Vision's scheme of covenantal nomism is almost identical to Pelagius' views on baptismal efficacy, final justification, the conflation of justification and sanctification, law and grace, and perseverance. Such covenantal nomism, according to Herman Bavinck, necessarily shrinks the gospel:

> Nomism (Pelagianism in its various forms and degrees) not only collides with the decrees of God, but also fails to do justice to the person and work of Christ. To the degree that in the acquisition of salvation it expands the activity of humans, it shrinks that of Christ. It is clear, certainly, that if faith, repentance, and perseverance are in whole or in part within the powers of human beings and their work; if the decision concerning one's actual salvation ultimately, when it comes to the crunch, lies in human hands, then Christ can at most have acquired the *possibility* of our being saved.[24]

Thus, Westminster Confession of Faith 19.6 says:

> Although true believers be not under the law, as a covenant of works, to be thereby justified or condemned; yet it is of great use to them, as well as to others; in that, as a rule of life informing them of the will of God, and their duty, it directs and binds them to walk accordingly.

---

22 Robert F. Evans, *Pelagius: Inquiries and Reappraisals* (London: Adam & Charles Black, 1968), 106.

23 B. R. Rees, *The Letters of Pelagius and His Followers* (Rochester, New York: Boydell Press, 1991), 160.

24 John Bolt, ed., John Vriend, trans., Herman Bavinck, *Reformed Dogmatics*, Volume 3 (Grand Rapids, Michigan: Baker Academic, 2008), 566.

Covenant nomism makes the law into a covenant of works for one's justification or condemnation, a position that is contrary to the Scriptures and all the Reformed confessions. As A. A. Hodge commented on the above section of the Westminster Confession:

> That since the fall no man is able to attain to righteousness and eternal life through obedience to the law.[25]

If covenant faithfulness is the path to salvation, as the Federal teaches, then both righteousness and eternal life can be attained through obedience to the law. Yet, that view is in dynamic conflict with the Scripture and the great Reformed confessions.

Summary

The Federal Vision's emphasis on covenant faithfulness as the way to salvation is a denial of the Gospel. Nomism, as Bavinck stated, is Pelagianism in its various forms and degrees. It collides with the decrees of God, as Chapter 12 proved, and it fails to do justice to the Person and work of Christ. Covenant nomism is another name for works salvation and conflicts with justification by faith alone. It is a doctrine that the Jews learned during the period of their captivity.

Conclusion

Augustine made it clear that faith in Christ becomes unnecessary if a person can be saved by keeping the law or by covenant faithfulness (which are essentially the same thing). As he wrote in his book *On Nature and Grace*:

> For my part I have to say what the apostle said in regard to the law: "Then Christ died in vain." For if he said this about the law, which only the nation of the Jews received, how much more justly may it be said of the law of nature, which the whole human race has received, "If righteousness come by nature, then Christ died in vain, then human nature cannot by any means be justified and redeemed from God's most righteous wrath—in a word, from punishment—except by faith.[26]

In a letter to his friend, Boniface, Augustine analyzes what happens when salvation is by nomism:

---

25 A. A. Hodge, *The Confession of Faith* (London: The Banner of Truth Trust, 1961), 257.
26 Schaff, ed., *Augustin: Anti-Pelagian Writings*, Volume 5, 122.

> Our religion distinguishes the just from the unjust, not by the law of works, but by the law of faith, without which the works which seem good turn to sin.[27]

Salvation by covenant faithfulness, as the Federal Vision teaches it, makes the atonement of Christ irrelevant. Christ died in vain in such a system. Yet, there are other difficulties with all the nomistic theories of salvation. Bavinck underscores what those things are:

> The trade in indulgences was not an excess or an abuse but the direct consequence of the nomistic degradation of the gospel.[28]

The covenant nomism theories of the Federal Vision will lead the church back into the blind superstition which made possible the sale of indulgences to a credulous public in the period before the Reformation. If salvation is by covenant faithfulness or works of any kind, then people will naturally think they can do things to earn it or to purchase it.

---

27 Henry Beveridge, ed. and trans., John Calvin, *Tracts and Letters*, Volume 3: Tracts, Part 3 (Edinburgh, Scotland and Carlisle, Pennsylvania: The Banner of Truth Trust, 2009), 150.

28 Bavinck, *Reformed Dogmatics*, Volume 3, 519.

-17-
The Federal Vision and Apostasy

> "All who are baptized into the triune Name are united with Christ in His covenantal life, and so those who fall from that position of grace are falling from grace. The branches that are cut away from Christ are genuinely cut away from someone, cut out of a living covenant body. The connection that the apostate had to Christ was not merely external."[1]
>
> A JOINT FEDERAL VISION PROFESSION

---

[1] *A Joint Federal Vision Profession* accessed at: http://www.federal-vision.com/resources/joint_FV_Statement.pdf, on October 20, 2014

It was John Trapp, one of the greatest commentators on Scripture, who wrote about the seventeenth century in which he lived:

> It were far easier to write a book of apostates in this age than a book of martyrs.[2]

It is impossible to read the Bible or to live in this world without seeing numerous examples of those who have apostatized from the faith. In the trial of Peter Leithart, the Defense used the anecdotal illustration of Charles Templeton to buttress their theory that people can truly fall away from faith in Christ. Templeton, like Billy Graham, was a renowned evangelist who rose to fame in the 1940s and was considered by some to be a greater hope for reaching the world with the gospel than even Graham himself. Yet, Templeton apostatized, renounced the faith, and became an atheist. Shortly before his death in 2001, he wrote a book, *Farewell to God*, which represented his break with Christianity.

A more recent example of such inexplicable apostasy would be the case of Frank Schaeffer, son of the great twentieth-century theologian, Francis Schaeffer, founder of L'Abri in Switzerland. Frank Schaeffer has had an interesting, transformative journey in rejecting the evangelical faith of his parents. Initially, he left evangelicalism for Eastern Orthodoxy. He now refers to himself as an atheist who believes in God, prays every day, and attends church. Schaeffer's example hits home with Reformed evangelicals because his father was a minister in the Reformed Presbyterian Church, Evangelical Synod, and then the Presbyterian Church in America.

What are we to think of such anecdotes? First, we must remember that anecdotes are not facts of principle, but they are facts of life. They are life stories. Anecdotes are often great illustrations of some truth of Scripture, but they are never a substitute for Scripture. Second, these anecdotes about Templeton and Schaeffer do not answer the important questions concerning their lives. Were they genuine Christians who fell away from the faith or were they merely among those who came close to the truth without ever truly believing? We will have to look in another direction to answer those questions. Anecdotes tease us with possibilities, but cannot answer the questions they raise.

---

2 I. D. E. Thomas, comp., *The Golden Treasury of Puritan Quotations* (Chicago: Moody Press, 1975), 20.

The Federal Vision and Apostasy

It is at this point that the Federal Vision displays a flawed definition of both grace and apostasy. The proponents of the Federal Vision differ with Reformed theology concerning apostasy. They hold that it is possible for a true believer to fall from grace which is a denial of efficacious grace. In the words quoted from "A Joint Federal Vision Profession" at the beginning of this chapter, the signers of that document said:

> All who are baptized into the triune Name are united with Christ in His covenantal life, and so those who fall from that position of grace are falling from grace. The branches that are cut away from Christ are genuinely cut away from someone, cut out of a living covenant body. The connection that the apostate had to Christ was not *merely* external.[3]

That same "Profession" also affirms that those who were chosen before the foundation of the world to final salvation cannot apostatize. Yet, that caveat raises more questions than it answers. What does this "Profession" mean by the word grace? Is it redemptive grace or common grace? What is the nature of the supposed "genuine" relationship these apostates had with Christ? Was it a saving relationship or only a formal, ecclesiastical relationship? If the connection the apostate had to Christ was not *merely* external, as this "Profession" asserts, then what was it? The only other option is that it was subjective and internal, the very things the Federal Vision denies about baptism, the covenant, grace, covenant election, and other aspects of the doctrines of salvation. It is not surprising that the Federal Vision defines the relationship of the apostate as more than *merely* external, but less than efficacious. It is a system of theology in a constant state of flux.

Perhaps the most succinct definition of apostasy ever was given by the Puritan minister, Timothy Cruso (1656-1697), in these words:

> Apostasy is a perversion to evil after a seeming conversion from it.[4]

The Federal Vision drops "seeming" from its definition of apostasy. Its proponents define apostasy as a real falling from grace by someone who has had a real relationship with Christ. Moreover, apostasy according to the Federal Vision is never final or irremediable until the

---

3 *A Joint Federal Vision Profession*, accessed on October 20, 2014.
4 Thomas, *Golden Treasury of Puritan Quotations*, 20.

end of life. Any system based on nomism or legal righteousness can never rule someone in or out of eternal salvation until the very end. Interestingly, the position of the Federal Vision concerning apostasy places its system of thought squarely in line with Catholic theology on the matter.

Hebrews 6:1-12

Several passages of Scripture that touch on the subject of apostasy have been hotly debated by Calvinists on the one hand and Pelagians or Arminians on the other hand. In every instance, the Federal Vision proponents champion the Pelagian, Semi-Pelagian, or Arminian interpretation of those passages in opposition to the Reformed position. In Hebrews 6:4-6, the author of that epistle describes how close to a saving relationship with Christ some professors of faith had come before falling away to utter damnation. He says concerning those who "have fallen away, it is impossible to renew them to repentance" (Hebrews 6:6). John Brown comments on this verse:

> By "falling away," we are plainly to understand what is commonly called apostasy. This does not consist in an occasional falling into actual sin, however gross and aggravated; nor in the renunciation of some of the principles of Christianity, even though these should be of considerable importance; but in an open, total, determined renunciation of all the constituent principles of Christianity, and a return to a false religion, such as that of the unbelieving Jews or heathens, or to determined infidelity and ungodliness.[5]

In Hebrews 6:9, the author describes genuine converts in a different way: "But, beloved, we are convinced of better things concerning you, and things that accompany salvation." Those better things that accompany salvation indicate clearly that there are temporary operations of the Holy Spirit that do *not* accompany salvation? Those temporary operations were mentioned by the author of Hebrews in verses 4 to 6 of the sixth chapter. Yet, Steve Wilkins and Auburn Avenue Presbyterian Church in Monroe, Louisiana dismiss the Reformed interpretation of Hebrews 6 with the following statement:

> The question raised does not concern the nature of the grace received in the past (i.e. real regeneration vs. merely common operations of the

---

5 John Brown, *Hebrews* (London, England and Carlisle, Pennsylvania: The Banner of Truth Trust, 1972), 289.

Spirit), but whether or not the one who has received this grace will persevere. Thus, the solution to Heb. 6 is not developing two psychologies of conversion, one for the "truly regenerate" and one for the future apostate, and then introspecting to see which kind of grace one has received. This is a task beyond our competence. The solution is to turn from ourselves and to keep our eyes fixed on Jesus, the Author and Finisher of our faith.[6]

Wilkins and the AAPC thereby discount the distinction between supernatural regeneration and the common operations of the Spirit. What kind of grace accompanies salvation if it is not efficacious grace that bestows real regeneration? Thus, their position on apostasy also results in a redefinition of grace which denies the distinction between common grace and special grace. Otherwise, the Federal Vision proponents would be compelled to admit that not every baptized person receives everything Christ has to offer. They would also have to admit that there are differences between the elect and the reprobate that are as great as the differences between light and darkness. Such admissions would destroy the foundation of the Federal Vision system. Yet, the differences between the elect and temporary believers are brought out by Robert Rollock (1555-1599), a second-generation Scottish Reformer, in the following statement:

> Out of this therefore, it follows that the temporiser is also a hypocrite, seeing that he is not sincere, and that the temporary faith is hypocritical, seeing it is not sincere.[7]

At his trial, Peter Leithart wrongly referenced Rollock as one who was in support of the Federal Vision's view of temporary benefits or the common operations of the Spirit. Leithart asserted that such temporary benefits bestow a real relationship to Christ that can be lost and he claimed that Rollock agreed with him. Yet, Leithart should have read the very next sentence of Rollock's work which is quoted above. Rollock clearly states that "temporisers" are hypocrites and insincere. Insincere hypocrites cannot find salvation by persevering in a temporary faith that is hypocritical and insincere. Hypocrisy is still hypocrisy and insincerity is still insincerity, no matter how much

---

[6] Guy Prentiss Waters, *The Federal Vision and Covenant Theology: A Comparative Analysis* (Phillipsburg, New Jersey: P&R Publishing, 2006), 156. This quote from a "Summary Statement of AAPC's Position on the Covenant, Baptism, and Salvation" is found on this page.

[7] William M. Gunn, ed., "A Treatise of God's Effectual Calling," in *The Select Works of Robert Rollock*, Volume 1 (Edinburgh, Scotland: The Woodrow Society, 1844), 210.

perseverance is added to them. A temporary faith is devoid of God's efficacious and saving grace. Thus, the Federal Vision advocates have backed their position into a corner by denying the distinction between real regeneration and the common operations of the Spirit. They have only two choices. First, they can deny all distinctions between temporary faith and saving faith. Second, they can abandon their whole system as being hopelessly contradictory and inconsistent. They have chosen the first option with all its glaring inconsistencies and contradictions of Scripture.

Graces which Accompany Salvation

The primary charge which Hebrews 6:1-12 makes against apostates is that they do not bear fruit because they do not have the things that accompany salvation. Instead, they produce thorns and thistles—but not fruit (Hebrews 6:7, 8). In John 15:1-6, Christ makes the same charge of fruitlessness. Christ cursed the fig tree for the same reason—it bore no fruit. In Isaiah 5:1-8, God makes the same indictment of fruitlessness against His covenant people. Thus, Jesus said, "Either make the tree good and its fruit good or the tree bad and its fruit bad, for the tree is known by its fruit. . . Every good tree bears good fruit, but the bad tree bears bad fruit. . . You will know them by their fruits." What are the fruits which the apostle says proves that they have those things which "accompany salvation"? He lists the three great fruits in Hebrews 6:10-12—faith, hope and love. "God is not unjust so as to forget. . . the *love* which you have shown toward His name. . . we desire that each one. . . realize the full assurance of *hope*. . . imitators of those who through *faith* and patience inherit the promises." Faith, hope and love are called the great trilogy of graces. Whoever is devoid of them is not a true Christian. Paul said, "But now faith, hope, and love, abide these three; but the greatest of these is love" (1 Corinthians 13:13). These are "the things that accompany salvation" which the apostates never had. They never had true faith in Christ; they never had a sincere love of God or of His children; they never had a true hope of eternal life with Christ. 1 John 4:7 says concerning love: "Beloved, let us love one another, for love is from God; and everyone who loves is born of God and knows God." Dante's oft-quoted saying in his *Divine Comedy*, "Hope is the mother of all disappointments," is wrong. True hope is never disappointed. In the latter part of chapter six, the author of Hebrews says concerning hope: "This hope we have as an anchor of the soul, a hope sure and steadfast and one which enters within the veil" (Hebrews 6:19).

1 John 5:16, 17

1 John 5:16, 17 says, "There is a sin leading to death, I do not say that he should make request for this. All unrighteousness is sin, and there is a sin not leading to death." On this passage, Calvin commented:

> From the context we may infer that it is not what they call a partial fall, or the transgression of a single commandment, but apostasy, men alienating themselves completely from God. For the apostle adds afterwards that God's children do not sin, that is, they do not forsake God and give themselves wholly to Satan as his slaves. It is not surprising if such a defection is mortal. For God never so deprives His own of the grace of the Spirit but that they keep some spark of godliness. Therefore, they must be reprobate and given up to destruction who so fall as to reject all fear of God.
>
> If anyone asks whether the door of salvation is shut against their repentance, the answer is plain. As they are given over to a reprobate mind and are destitute of the Holy Spirit, they can do nothing but with obstinate minds rush always to the worse, adding sins to sins. Moreover, as the sin of blasphemy against the Spirit always brings such a defection with it, there is no doubt but this is indicated here.[8]

The Federal Vision is in a hard position. In asserting that true recipients of grace can apostatize, they deny efficacious grace, certain perseverance, unconditional election, assurance of salvation, and many other great truths of the Scripture. Unless they can prove that true Christians can apostatize, their whole system unravels. What value is there in telling those who are baptized that they have been given everything that Christ has to give if indeed there are things that accompany salvation they have not received in baptism? That would destroy the Federal Vision system. If apostasy is a possibility for those who are really joined to Christ, as the Federal Vision asserts, then it undermines the assurance of salvation. As Bavinck says:

> When Scripture expressly states that it is impossible to restore to repentance those who are in view in these texts (Heb. 6:4; 10:26; 2 Peter 2:20;

---

8 David W. Torrance and Thomas F. Torrance, eds., T. H. L. Parker, trans., *Calvin's Commentarie: The Gospel According to St. John 11-21 and The First Epistle of John* (Grand Rapids, Michigan: Wm. B. Eerdmans Publishing Company, 1961), 311.

1 John 5:16), it cannot be denied that the reference is to a sin that carries with it a judgment of hardening and that makes repentance impossible. And of such a sin—also according to the confession of those who hold to the impossibility of a falling away—there is only one, namely, the sin against the Holy Spirit. Now if this is true, then the doctrine of the falling away of saints leads to the conclusion that either the sin of blaspheming the Holy Spirit can be committed also, or even perhaps only, by those who are born again, or the above texts lose all their evidential value against the doctrine of the perseverance of the saints.[9]

If those who are truly born again can commit the sin against the Holy Spirit, then the doctrine of the perseverance of the saints is not true. Perseverance would merely be possible but not certain. Yet, if those who apostatize are not true Christians, then there is no such doctrine as the falling away of the saints. The Federal Vision is caught between two conflicting positions by asserting that those who apostatize were and are the recipients of true grace.

Matthew 12:31, 32
A doctrine closely related to apostasy is the sin against the Holy Spirit, or the unpardonable sin. Bavinck's quote above referred to it. Jesus mentions it in Matthew 12:31, 32: "Therefore I say to you, any sin and blasphemy shall be forgiven people, but blasphemy against the Spirit shall not be forgiven. Whoever speaks a word against the Son of Man, it shall be forgiven him; but whoever speaks against the Holy Spirit, it shall not be forgiven him, either in this age or in the age to come." The blasphemy of the Spirit is couched in such language in the Scripture that it is difficult to determine exactly what it is. In fact, there are several Scripture passages which warn against a sin which is beyond forgiveness. Givens B. Strickler, the nineteenth-century Southern Presbyterian minister, once wrote about this sin:

> Indeed, at first view there would seem to be a number of such sins. . . But while there is but one sin that is unto death, it is plain that that one sin presents itself in the Scriptures under a number of different forms. . . The fact seems to be that God has intentionally left the nature of this sin so obscure that it cannot be accurately defined; and that He has done so for at least two reasons. . . One is that we have no right to

---

9 John Bolt, ed., John Vriend, trans., Herman Bavinck, *Reformed Dogmatics*, Volume 4, *Holy Spirit, Church, and New Creation* (Grand Rapids, Michigan: Baker Academic, 2008), 268.

know just what this sin is. We have no right to know just where it is on the line of sinful progress... The other reason why they do not tell us is such knowledge, if given, would be grossly abused.[10]

Calvin's comments on Matthew 12:31, 32 are also worth repeating:

> For blasphemy against the Spirit is a certain sign of reprobation. Hence it follows that whoever fall into it have been given a reprobate spirit. For just as we deny that it is possible for anyone truly born again of the Spirit to cast himself into such a horrifying crime, so on the contrary we must hold that those who do fall into it never rise again. In this way God avenges contempt of His grace: He hardens the hearts of the reprobate so that they never desire to repent.[11]

Calvin, like all evangelical authors, makes a clear distinction between those truly born again of the Spirit and those who are guilty of this blasphemy of the Spirit in his comments on Hebrews 6:6 and other places. Those who have a true relationship with Christ can never commit this horrible sin. Those who are guilty of such blasphemy have a reprobate spirit and can never repent of this sin. The Federal Vision is out of accord with Christ, the Scriptures and the Reformed Faith on this matter for they do not believe apostasy is unforgivable.

Every apostate commits the unpardonable sin because it is impossible to renew him to repentance. Without repentance, he can never be forgiven. Thus, Jesus says the one who commits the unpardonable sin will never be forgiven. Yet, the unpardonable sin is broader than apostasy. Jesus warned the hardened Pharisees about the unpardonable sin. They had neither been enlightened; nor had they tasted of the heavenly gift; nor had they ever been made partakers of the Holy Spirit; nor had they ever tasted the good word of God. They were in a different situation than the people to whom the author of Hebrews wrote. The Pharisees sinned against the Holy Spirit by rejecting the signs and wonders worked by Jesus in their midst. Yet, they never professed Christ so they also never apostatized. Thus, the blasphemy of the Holy Spirit is the broad sin of which apostasy is a part. The Federal Vision fails to make this distinction. In his comments on King

---

10   G. B. Strickler, *Sermons* (New York: Fleming H. Revell Company, 1910), 193-197.

11   David W. Torrance and Thomas F. Torrance, eds., T. H. L. Parker, trans., *Calvin's Commentaries: A Harmony of the Gospels*, Volume II (Grand Rapids, Michigan: Wm. B. Eerdmans Publishing Company, 1972), 47.

Saul, Federal Vision proponent, Rich Lusk, repudiates the scriptural teaching that true believers can never commit this sin:

> Saul received the same initial covenantal grace that David, Gideon, and other saved men received, though God withheld from him continuance in that grace... [he] really did taste of God's mercy and love; he really did possess the Holy Spirit and the new creation life the Spirit brings; he really was adopted into God's family and really lived a godly, exemplary life for a time. But he failed to persevere.[12]

Lusk's comments imply that the primary difference between apostates and true believers is the matter of perseverance. His position is a denial of three things: the certainty of perseverance, effacious grace, and unconditional election.

Falling from Grace in Catholic and Arminian Doctrine

The possibility of true believers falling from grace has been a doctrine of the Catholic Church since at least the Council of Trent and in many sections of the Church even before then. Concerning the Decree on Justification, taken up in the sixth session, the Council of Trent made the following statement about losing grace:

> CANON XXIII. If any one saith, that a man once justified can sin no more, nor lose grace, and that therefore he that falls and sins was never truly justified; or, on the other hand, that he is able, during his whole life, to avoid all sins, even those that are venial,—except by a special privilege from God, as the Church holds in regard of the Blessed Virgin; let him be anathema.

The position of the Federal Vision is more similar to this statement of the Council of Trent than even *The Five Arminian Articles of the Remonstrants* (1610). For instance, the fifth article of the Remonstrants said:

> But whether they are capable, through negligence, of forsaking again the first beginnings of their life in Christ, of again returning to this present evil world, of turning away from the holy doctrine which had delivered them, of losing a good conscience, of becoming devoid of grace, that must be more particularly determined out of the Holy Scripture, before we ourselves can teach it with the full persuasion of our minds.[13]

---

12 Waters, *Federal Vision and Covenant Theology*, 158.

13 Philip Schaff, ed., David S. Schaff, rev., *The Creeds of Christendom: With a History and Critical*

Therein, the Remonstrants left the matter undetermined as to the possibility of the truly regenerate falling from grace. Yet, both Trent and Rich Lusk, in his quote about Saul above, unequivocally assert that apostasy is possible for those who have experienced a real conversion to God. Reformed theology has always rejected the possibility of true believers losing their salvation. Such a doctrine contradicts the perseverance of the saints which is a key doctrine in Reformed theology. Thus, concerning the difference between the elect and the reprobate, Calvin writes:

> Moreover, the efficacy of the Call I mentioned must be understood to consist in that not only is the grace of God offered to us, but our will is formed to embrace it. For between the Elect and the Reprobate there is this difference, that while God addresses both by the voice of man, he specially teaches the former inwardly by his Spirit. The ministry of man, I say, is common to both, but the inward grace of the Spirit is peculiar to the Elect. Hence the words of Christ, "Whoso hath heard and learned of the Father cometh unto me." (John vi. 45.)
>
> Unless these points are put beyond controversy, though we may ever and anon repeat like parrots that we are justified by faith, we shall never hold the true doctrine of Justification.[14]

Trent attacked the doctrine of certain perseverance in its section concerning justification. Calvin, on the other hand, shows that a true understanding of justification by faith requires us to hold to efficacious grace, the inward work of the Spirit in the hearts of the elect. That inner grace of the Spirit always results in the perseverance of the saints. The great doctrines of salvation hang together or fall together. The elect receive an inner call of the Spirit which transforms their will to believe in Christ. They are justified by faith and God's grace is effectual to the very end. They can never fall away from Him because of His grace to them.

Apostasy is Beyond Repentance

In a passage referenced earlier, Hebrews 6:6 says, ". . . it is impossible to renew them again to repentance." This same truth is taught in other places of the Scripture—2 Peter 2:20-22; 1 John 2:19; Hebrews

---

Notes, Volume III, *The Evangelical Protestant Creeds* (Grand Rapids, Michigan: Baker Book House, 1983), 548-549.

14 Henry Beveridge, ed. and trans., *John Calvin: Tracts and Letters*, Volume 3: Tracts, Part 3 (Edinburgh, Scotland and Carlisle, Pennsylvania, The Banner of Truth Trust, 2009), 254.

3:12; and Matthew 13:20, 21, to reference a few of them. This sin is the blasphemy of the Spirit—Mark 3:28-30. Apostasy is not simply falling into sin, even great sins. Christ says all manner of sins will be forgiven, except for one. Proverbs 24:16 says—"A righteous man falls seven times and rises again, but the wicked stumble in calamity." On the other hand, Esau "found no place for repentance, though he sought for it with tears" (Hebrews 11:17). It is the promise of the gospel that everyone who sincerely seeks for Christ will find Him. The Scripture says, "You will seek Me and find Me when you search for Me with all your heart" (Jeremiah 29:13). These apostates had many blessings—five are enumerated in Hebrews 6:4-6. They were enlightened, tasted of the heavenly gift, made partakers of the Holy Spirit, tasted the good word of God, and tasted the powers of the age to come.

King Saul in the Old Testament was one who had the Spirit of prophecy come on him with power which caused the crowds to ask, "Is Saul also among the prophets?" (1 Samuel 10:11). Lusk says Saul truly received grace and truly lived a godly life for a period. That is a position consistent with the Federal Vision system's view of apostasy. But is it true to Scripture? Did Saul truly have the Spirit of adoption as a son of God by faith? Was Saul a godly man, like David, if only for a short period of his life? If so, when was that period that Saul lived a godly life? Perhaps, Lusk and other Federal Vision advocates would point to 1 Samuel 10:9 which says "God changed his [Saul's—DR] heart" at the time of his choice to be the King of Israel. If that was the Spirit of adopting grace, then Saul would truly be an example of a saint that fell from grace. Matthew Henry's comments on that passage are insightful:

> It became a proverb, commonly used in Israel, when they would express their wonder at a bad man's either becoming good, or at least being found in good company, Is Saul among the prophets? Note, Saul among the prophets is a wonder to a proverb. Let not the worst be despaired of, yet let not an external show of devotion, and a sudden change for the present, be too much relied on; for Saul among the prophets was Saul still.[15]

The change in Saul was external and temporary. This was quickly

---

15 *Matthew Henry's Commentary on the Whole Bible,* Vol. III (Old Tappan, New Jersey: Fleming H. Revell Company, n.d.),

apparent in his administration as King. He was not a man after God's own heart when he sacrificed the burnt offering at Gilgal contrary to Samuel's directions. He was not a man of faith when he trembled in fear at the threats of Goliath. He was not a man of God when the evil spirit came on him and caused him to rave in madness. He was not one who lived a godly life when he tried to pin David to the wall with a spear or chased him across every mountain ridge or ravine. Saul was so close to the kingdom of God, but so far away. When he wanted counsel, he went to the witch at Endor instead of to God. If Saul is the best supposed illustration of someone who truly received grace only to fall from it, then the Federal Vision's position on apostasy is in serious trouble. No one in the Bible, whether in the Old or New Testaments, is a better illustration than Saul of the difference between gifts and grace. Saul, like all who believe only temporarily, was insincere and hypocritical.

Saul is not alone in having the gift of prophecy, but being devoid of saving grace. Christ foretold that many would come to Him on the Judgment Day saying that they had prophesied in His name and cast out many demons (Matthew 7:21-23). His response to them will be: "I never knew you; Depart from Me, you who practice lawlessness." Yet, Lusk raises the possibility of an apostate returning to covenant faithfulness:

> Yes! If someone apostatizes and is cut off from the covenant community in excommunication, that person is always free to repent and return to the church and the Lord. Indeed we must recognize that one purpose of excommunication is to restore the wayward brother (1 Cor. 5, 1 Tim. 1:19-20). We see at least one such apostate repenting and returning to the church in Paul's Corinthian correspondence. Mt. 12.31ff, Heb. 6:4-6 and 1 John 5:16 have sometimes been used to deny the freedom of apostates to return. But this is a misreading of these passages.[16]

Lusk reduces apostasy to scandal or immorality, whereas the Scripture places the seat of apostasy in a determination to resist the Spirit and reject the gospel. Lusk equates apostasy with the discipline of excommunication as though membership in the visible church is the same thing as a true relationship with Christ. Yet, Augustine is certainly correct when he says:

---

16 Waters, *Federal Vision and Covenant Theology*, 159-160.

They were not sons even when they were in profession and name sons.[17]

In many ways, the positions of the Federal Vision are taken from the writings of Thomas Aquinas. There are differences between the Federal Vision system and Thomism, particularly with respect to subjective grace. On apostasy, Aquinas wrote:

> Apostasy denotes a backsliding from God. This may happen in various ways to the different kinds of union between man and God... A man may also apostatize from God by rebelling in his mind against the Divine commandment: and though this man may apostatize in both the above ways, he may still remain united to God by faith.[18]

Aquinas' position is almost unbelievable. He says that a person may apostatize "by rebelling in his mind", but still remain united to God by faith. Aquinas equates apostasy with backsliding. Believers may backslide, but only the unregenerate can apostatize. Whether he backslides or rebels against God's commandments in his mind, he has still not fallen so as to be unable to be recovered, according to Aquinas. Such a position conflicts with the clear teaching of Scripture.

The Federal Vision proponents try to have it both ways. They claim they believe in eternal election, but they deny what is most essential about that doctrine—God's efficacious, internal, subjective grace through the Spirit which is given to the elect alone. They assert that all the baptized are externally in covenant with God and all of them receive the same graces, whether they are unconditionally elect or not. The difference then becomes that some people persevere and others do not. As Steve Wilkins wrote concerning apostasy:

> The apostate forsakes the grace of God that was given to him by virtue of his union with Christ... That which makes apostasy so horrendous is that these blessings actually belonged to the apostates—though they only had them temporarily, they had them no less truly. The apostate doesn't forfeit "apparent blessings" that were never his in reality, but real blessings that were his in covenant with God.[19]

---

17 James T. Dennison, ed.; George Musgrave Giger, trans., Francis Turretin, *Institutes of Elenctic Theology*, Volume 2 (Phillipsburg, New Jersey: P&R Publishing, 1994), 606.

18 St. Thomas Aquinas, *Summa Theologica*, Volume II, Translated by the Fathers of the English Dominican Province (New York, Boston, Cincinnati, Chicago, San Francisco: Benziger Brothers, Inc., 1947), 1228.

19 Steve Wilkins and Duane Garner, eds., Steve Wilkins, "Covenant, Baptism, and Salvation" in *The Federal Vision* (Monroe, Louisiana: Athanasius Press, 2004), 62.

Wilkins' position on apostasy is supported by the following statements from Doug Wilson:

> Apostasy is a real sin in real time. It is important for us to settle in our minds at the outset what an apostate falls away *from*. In short, he falls from Christ, he falls from grace (Gal. 5:4). But what does this mean? In the text quoted above, he has been *enlightened* (an early Church expression for baptism), he has *tasted* the heavenly gift, he has been made a *partaker* of the Holy Spirit, and so on. There is a certain kind of reality to this experience that is assumed. The cut-away branch has no fruit (which is why it was cut away)—but it has had sap (which is why it had to be cut away).[20]

The similarity of the Federal Vision position with the Arminian position on apostasy is brought out by Francis Turretin's words concerning the latter:

> The Arminians (in order to defend the apostasy of the saints) uphold the mutability of election. Thus they make it twofold: one incomplete and not decisive (peremptoriam) (of those who will believe), which can be revoked and made void by the inconstancy of men who fall away from faith; the other, however, complete and decisive (of those persevering and dying in faith), which is immutable.[21]

The Federal Vision advocates make the same error as the Remonstrants (Arminians) when they speak of two elections, one conditional and the other unconditional. They resolve the matter of apostasy by exalting the free will of humanity, whether wittingly or unwittingly, and making salvation dependent upon *uncertain* perseverance. Thus, they place their theological position outside of the Scripture and the Reformed creeds.

Summary

The position of advocates of the Federal Vision on apostasy is clear and unequivocal. They assert that it is possible for those who have truly received grace—the same grace as all others who have been baptized—to fall away from that state of grace. They dismiss the clear statements of Scripture which teach otherwise (cf. Hebrews 6:1-12). They use people like King Saul as a supposed illustration of someone who was truly godly for a period of time. They hold to two elections,

---

20 Waters, *Federal Vision and Covenant Theology*, 150.
21 Turretin, *Institutes of Elenctic Theology*, Volume 1, 365.

one conditional and the other unconditional, as the key to understanding why some baptized church members persevere and others do not. They teach that true saints can fall from grace. Their position is not the position of the Scripture and the Reformed creeds. It is the position of the Arminians and Pelagians. On this point, they are clearly outside the boundaries of the Reformed faith.

Conclusion

The Federal Vision confuses the external and internal, the objective and subjective. It tries to deny those distinctions even as it denies the difference between the visible and invisible church. Yet, no system of theology can successfully deny such distinctions. Thus, the inconsistencies and contradictions of the Federal Vision are revealed in its various confusing statements. Turretin's comments are noteworthy:

> Thus the apostle distinguishes "being in the church" as to external profession and the ecclesiastical body; and "being of the church" as to internal communion and the mystical body of Christ (which belongs to the elect alone).[22]

---

22   Ibid., 606.

–18–
The Federal Vision and Assurance of Salvation

"For we know that if the earthly tent which is our house is torn down, we have a building from God, a house not made with hands, eternal in the heavens."

(2 CORINTHIANS 5:1)

"But how do you know that promise is really for you and not just for other people in the church, people who've advanced further in their sanctification or who've had some special experience that convinced them of God's love? The answer is that you've had that special experience. You've been baptized."[1]

JOHN BARACH, FEDERAL VISION PROPONENT

"We cannot get assurance unless we're convinced that God declares me His beloved child in the water of baptism."[2]

PETER LEITHART, FEDERAL VISION PROPONENT

---

1 Guy Prentiss Waters, *The Federal Vision and Covenant Theology: A Comparative Analysis* (Phillipsburg, New Jersey: P&R Publishing, 2006), 134.

2 Tim Bayly, "Peter Leithart: 'No Baptism, No Justification'," *The Aquila Report*, December 2, 2014. Accessed at: http://theaquilareport.com/peter-leithart-no-baptism-no-justification/ on December 3, 2014.

The assurance of salvation is a doctrine clearly taught in the Scripture and it is fundamental to a right understanding of the gospel. The Apostle John gives four tests of assurance in his first epistle: faith, love, righteousness, and the indwelling of the Holy Spirit. Romans 8:16 also emphasizes that assurance is based on the witness of the Spirit. These various tests or proofs for assurance are commonly reduced to just three: saving faith, the witness of the Spirit, and the bearing of fruit. The answer to Westminster Larger Catechism Question 80 mentions those three tests for assurance:

> Such as truly believe in Christ, and endeavor to walk in all good conscience before him, may, without extraordinary revelation, by faith grounded upon the truth of God's promises, and by the Spirit enabling them to discern in themselves those graces to which the promises of life are made, and bearing witness with their spirits that they are the children of God, be infallibly assured that they are in the estate of grace, and shall persevere therein unto salvation.

Key Assessment: The Federal Vision makes baptism the primary source for the assurance of salvation and tells members of the visible church to look to their baptism for such assurance.

Of these three tests for assurance, saving faith is the most important in the same sense that love is greater than faith and hope. There can be no assurance apart from faith in Christ. As Hebrews 11:1 says: "Faith is the *assurance of things hoped for*, the conviction of things not seen." Yet, the Federal Vision substitutes faith *in baptism* for faith alone in Christ, as Barach's quote above clearly shows. The exclusive emphasis of the Federal Vision on objective grace, according to their definition of it, leads to a denial of all subjectivity in the matter of assurance. Objective grace is the work of Christ for our salvation and includes, among other doctrines, both the imputation of His active obedience to believers and their once-for-all justification by faith alone. The Federal Vision generally denies both of those doctrines and, as a result, their definition of objective grace is limited. Therefore, we must first consider what the Scriptures teach about assurance.

Romans 8:16

True assurance of salvation must embrace both the work of Christ for us and the work of the Spirit in us. While there is an overly subjective emphasis among some Christian groups, the subjective side of salvation and assurance cannot be denied without peril. The Scripture itself emphasizes the subjective side of assurance. For instance, Paul says in Romans 8:16, "The Spirit Himself testifies with our spirit that we are children of God." Charles Hodge said concerning this passage:

> *Beareth witness to*, means *confirms* or *assures*. "The Sprit of God produces in our spirit the assurance that we are children of God." How this is done we cannot fully understand, any more than we can understand the mode in which he produces any other effect in our mind. The fact is clearly asserted here, as well as in other passages. See Rom. v. 5, where the conviction that we are the objects of the love of God, is said to be produced "by the Holy Ghost which is given unto us." See 2 Cor. i. 22, v. 5; Eph. i. 13, iv. 30; and in 1 Cor. ii. 4,5; 1 John ii. 20, 27, and other passages, the conviction of the truth of the gospel is, in like manner, attributed to the Holy Spirit. From this passage it is clear that there is a scriptural foundation for the assurance of salvation. Those who have filial feelings towards God, who love him, and believe that he loves them, and to whom the Spirit witnesses that they are the children of God, cannot doubt that they are indeed his children. And if children, they know they are his heirs, as the apostle teaches in the following verses.[3]

In those words, Hodge mentions several things which are subjective in nature as being proofs to the believer that he is a child of God—the conviction produced by the Holy Spirit that we are objects of His love, the conviction of the truth of the gospel through the Holy Spirit, filial feelings towards God, the love for God, and the assurance that God loves us. All of these subjective experiences are supported by Romans 8:16 and several other passages in the Bible mentioned by Hodge. A denial of the subjective aspect of assurance is patently unscriptural and ultimately leads to a denial of assurance altogether. Thus, D. Martyn Lloyd-Jones could say concerning Romans 8:16:

> This is, beyond any question, one of the most glorious statements concerning Christian experience found anywhere in the Bible from beginning to end. Nothing is more important from the standpoint of enjoy-

---

3 Charles Hodge, *Commentary on the Epistle to the Romans* (Grand Rapids, Michigan: Wm. B. Eerdmans Publishing company, 1972), 267.

ing our great salvation. If it can be said that any one verse constitutes the hallmark of the evangelical Christian, I would say that it is this one. It has always been dear to the hearts of evangelical Christians ever since the Protestant Reformation, for there is no other verse which shows so clearly the difference between Protestantism and Roman Catholicism as this particular verse. . .

The Spirit by a direct operation on our minds and hearts and spirits gives us an absolute certainty and assurance of our sonship.[4]

Ephesians 1:13, 14

One of the passages mentioned by Hodge which also teaches the internal testimony of the Holy Spirit as a ground of assurance is Ephesians 1:13, 14: "In Him, also after listening to the message of the truth, the gospel of your salvation—having also believed, you were sealed in Him with the Holy Spirit of promise, who is given as a pledge of our inheritance, with a view to the redemption of God's own possession, to the praise of His glory." Paul says the Holy Spirit is a pledge from God of our inheritance. The Holy Spirit gives an internal assurance to every believer that God will keep His promise of eternal salvation. That pledge is the Spirit Himself. As John Calvin said in his sermon on these verses:

> All the trials, then, which shake us show clearly enough that we do not profit as we ought to do by the gospel. And, therefore, God on his part is pleased to empower it by his Holy Spirit, and to print it so certainly in our hearts that we may be steadfast and the same steadfastness may not be beaten down by all that the devil can do or devise to overthrow our faith. . .
>
> For we can take up all the reasons of this world and yet we shall never be assured as fully and perfectly as we ought to be that God will be merciful to us and defend us in the midst of all the dangers of this world. . .
>
> We may also gather from St. Paul's words that we have weapons with which to meet the foe and strive well, and that although our enemy is mighty and sturdy, yet he will never overcome us, so long as we take advantage of what is said here, namely, that God's Spirit seals the truth and the certainty of the promises of the gospel in us.[5]

Calvin's statements in that sermon make it clear that he un-

---

[4] D. Martyn Lloyd-Jones, *Romans: An Exposition of Chapter 8:5-17, The Sons of God* (Grand Rapids, Michigan: Zondervan Publishing House, 1975), 285, 301.

[5] John Calvin, *Sermons on The Epistle to the Ephesians* (Edinburgh, Scotland and Carlisle, Pennsylvania: The Banner of Truth Trust, 1973), 74-75.

derstood assurance is not always full and complete. The Devil assaults us and uses many weapons against us. Nonetheless, we who believe have a greater weapon that confirms and assures us. We have the Holy Spirit of promise who is a seal to us of the certainty of God's promises in the gospel. Calvin says God empowers us through the Holy Spirit and thereby gives us assurance.

Hodge commented on this passage as follows:

> It is because the Spirit is an earnest of our inheritance, that his indwelling is a seal. It assures those in whom he dwells of their salvation, and renders that salvation certain. Hence it is a most precious gift to be most religiously cherished.[6]

In his commentary on Ephesians 1:13, 14, Geoffrey B. Wilson observes this inward witness in connection with assurance:

> But as this seal cannot be seen, its presence may be known only by the characteristic effects [John 3:8]. So believers are authenticated as the children of God by the inward witness of the Spirit [Rom 8.16]. And it is because they are sealed by a living Person who can be grieved by sin, that they may lose for a time this subjective assurance of their salvation, even though they remain objectively sealed unto the day of redemption [4.30].[7]

In those comments, Wilson brings together both the subjective and objective aspects of assurance. No believer is assured *because* of subjective experiences, but true assurance must include the subjective experience through the indwelling of the Spirit. Eternal salvation, along with the assurance of salvation, is secured by the objective work of Christ in His atonement for our sins and the imputation of His righteousness, but its realization is through the ministry of faith. While saving faith always includes an element of assurance, it is only the Spirit who can work new life and saving faith in our hearts. Thus, the internal witness of the Spirit can never be denied without undermining the whole doctrine of assurance.

---

6 Charles Hodge, *Commentary on the Epistle to the Ephesians* (Old Tappan, New Jersey: Fleming H. Revell Company, n.d.), 65.

7 Geoffrey B. Wilson, *Ephesians: A Digest of Reformed Comment* (Edinburgh, Scotland and Carlisle, Pennsylvania: The Banner of Truth Trust, 1978), 30-31.

1 John 5:13

There are several passages in 1 John where the subject of assurance is mentioned. The clearest passage, though, is 1 John 5:13, which says, "These things I have written to you who believe in the name of the Son of God, so that you may know that you have eternal life." It would be wrong to deduce that John's readers did not have the assurance of their salvation before he encouraged them to *know* that they have eternal life. It is common in the epistles for the apostles to encourage their readers to continue to do what they were already doing. Paul encouraged the Philippians to work out their salvation with fear and trembling even as they had always obeyed. Often the epistles endorse things that are already true of believers. 1 John 5:13 is certainly one of those occasions. As Calvin commented on this verse:

> There should be daily progress in faith; and so he says that he was writing to those who already believed, so that they might believe more firmly and certainly, and thus enjoy a full confidence of eternal life. Hence, the use of teaching is both to initiate the ignorant in Christ and also to confirm more and more those who know Him. Therefore we must pay heed to our duty of learning, that our faith may increase throughout our life. For there are still many remnants of unbelief in us, and our faith is so weak that what we believe is not yet really believed without more confirmation.[8]

While 1 John 5:13 is the Beloved Disciple's crowning statement on assurance, it is certainly not his only one. In other places, he connects assurance with keeping God's commandments through the indwelling of the Spirit (3:24); with the love of the brethren (3:14) and the love of God (4:17); and, with faith in Christ (4:15). John often intermingles these three things together in such a way that one cannot be a true test of assurance without the presence of the others. For instance, 1 John 4:20 says, "If someone says, 'I love God,' and hates his brother, he is a liar." Or, 1 John 2:4 says, "The one who says, 'I have come to know Him,' and does not keep His commandments, is a liar, and the truth is not in him." In the last verse, he combines obedience to the commandments with belief in the truth as tests of assurance.

In this way, the Scripture avoids the errors both of antinomianism and of legalism in the matter of assurance. Assurance is inconsistent

---

8 David W. Torrance and Thomas F. Torrance, eds., T. H. L. Parker, trans., *Calvin's Commentaries: The Gospel According to John 11-21 and The First Epistle of John* (Grand Rapids, Michigan: Wm. B. Eerdmans Publishing Company, 1961), 307.

with an ungodly life, so the antinomian will be deficient in assurance. Legalism is not the foundation of assurance either. Once again, Calvin sheds light on this matter in his comments on 1 John 2:4:

> How does he prove that those without godliness who boast that they have faith are liars? From its contrary. For he has already said that the knowledge of God is efficacious. For God is not known by the naked imagination, but he reveals Himself inwardly to our hearts by the Spirit. Moreover, since many hypocrites boast they have faith, the apostle condemns all such falsehood. For what he says would be superfluous unless many made a false and vain impression of Christianity.[9]

It is certainly true that the witness of the Spirit and the good works of the believer can never be the ultimate ground of our assurance. Thus, A. N. S. Lane is correct when he writes:

> For Calvin the ground of assurance does not lie within ourselves. It is not our faith or our works or our experience of the Holy Spirit. These can play a secondary role as a confirmation of or an aid to our assurance. But the primary ground of assurance is objective. It is the Gospel, the mercy of God, the free promise of justification in Christ. I know that God is my gracious Father because of his love for me, shown in Christ and declared in his Word. The ground of assurance lies not within ourselves but rather in the promises of God, in Christ. "Confidence of salvation is founded upon Christ and rests on the promises of the gospel."[10]

Ultimately, there can be no dichotomy between the objective and subjective sides of assurance. They work together. They cannot be separated. They are like the statements that are made about justification. Justification is by faith alone, but the faith that justifies is never alone. It is always accompanied by fruits of salvation. Assurance is grounded in Christ alone, but such assurance is never apart from the internal, subjective witness of the Spirit and the evidence of fruit in the believer's life. The Apostle John made those points abundantly clear in his first epistle. Calvin rightly emphasizes this last paradigm of assurance in his comments on 1 John 3:19:

> Why then does the apostle say that *we shall assure our heart before God*? In these words he tells us that faith does not exist apart from a

---

9 Torrance, *Calvin's Commentaries*, 246.

10 A. N. S. Lane, "Calvin's Doctrine of Assurance Revisited", in D. W. Hall, ed., *Tributes to John Calvin: A Celebration of his Quincentenary* (Phillipsburg, New Jersey: P&R Publishing, 2010), 277.

good conscience. Not that assurance comes from it or depends on it; but because we are truly, and not falsely, assured of our union with God only when He manifests Himself in our love by the efficacy of His Holy Spirit. For we must always consider what the apostle is dealing with. Since he condemns a feigned and false profession of faith, he says that there can be no genuine assurance before God unless His Spirit produces in us the fruit of love. All the same, although a good conscience cannot be separated from faith, none should conclude from this that we must look to our works for our assurance to be firm.[11]

It is interesting that the Federal Vision denies that assurance can include such subjective matters as the witness of the Spirit or the fruit of the believer as secondary contributors. Rather, its proponents emphasize the objective ground of assurance apart from any subjective assistance. Strangely, a system that holds to a final justification based on works denigrates assurance that is based secondarily on the fruits of faith. For instance, Wilkins ridicules such questions as:

> Was our repentance genuine? Have we truly believed in the Lord Jesus or have we deceived ourselves? The implication that we must look deep within for our assurance of salvation is mistaken and sure to result in deeper confusion. . . Our assurance cannot be based on what we see within ourselves but Christ himself. . . Our salvation is based upon His faithful work and faithfulness *not* upon our own works or experience no matter how genuine they might be.[12]

Superficially, Wilkins seems to be saying something similar to what Robert Murray McCheyne once said, "For one look at yourself, take ten looks at Christ."[13] But the relationship between the statements of Wilkins and McCheyne is only superficial. McCheyne believed in justification by faith alone; Wilkins does not. McCheyne believed that Christ is "the Lord our righteousness" (Jeremiah 23:6) whose righteous robe is imputed to believers in the gospel; Wilkins and the Federal Vision advocates do not. McCheyne did not believe that Christ's life—i.e., his active righteousness—is merely an example to us of how to live in obedience to God and hopefully attain final justification; the denial by the Federal Vision of the imputation of Christ's righteousness to believers means that Christ's life is merely an example to us.

---

11 Torrance, *Calvin's Commentaries*, 278.

12 Waters, *Federal Vision and Covenant Theology*, 139.

13 Andrew A. Bonar, *Memoir and Remains of R. M. McCheyne*, (London: The Banner of Truth Trust, 1966), 279.

Moreover, McCheyne did not deny the need for believers to look at themselves; whereas as Wilkins does. In a letter to an unnamed person, McCheyne makes the following comments:

> Christ is the glorious One who stood for many. His perfect garment is sufficient to cover you. You had no hand in His obedience. You were not alive when He came into the world and lived and died; and yet, in the perfect obedience, you may stand before God righteous. This is all my covering in the sight of a holy God. I feel infinitely unholy in myself; in God's eye, like a serpent or a toad; and yet, when I stand in Christ alone, I feel that God sees no sin in me, and loves me freely. The same righteousness is free to you. It will be as white and clean on your soul as on mine.[14]

For McCheyne, the imputed righteousness of Christ is the robe which covers believers and gives us assurance that we have a right standing before God. Wilkins and the others who hold to the Federal Vision do not believe in the imputation of Christ's righteousness. Therefore, the assurance they teach is not based on the fullness and freeness of the gospel. It is, at best, a moment-by-moment assurance based on a dim hope that our baptism will prove to be true and that we will persevere until the end. In reality, that is no assurance at all.

Moreover, McCheyne's encouragement for others to look to Christ was not based on a denial of subjective grace, as is the case with Wilkins and others in the Federal Vision. McCheyne encouraged looking to Christ alone for salvation and for assurance because he was well aware of the sinfulness of the human heart, especially his own heart. On the other hand, the errors of the Federal Vision work together in denying, point-by-point, the everlasting gospel. Their position on assurance is another example whereby they point people away from the true foundation of assurance in Christ's whole righteousness, active and passive, and they encourage them to trust in their baptism instead.

Catholicism on Assurance

The views of the Federal Vision on assurance are thereby neither Protestant nor Reformed. There is no passage of Scripture that grounds assurance in baptism. There is no Reformed symbol, creed, or confession that teaches their views. Unsurprising-

---

14 Ibid., 279-280.

ly, the Federal Vision's doctrine of assurance is almost identical to what the Church of Rome teaches. Assurance of salvation, as Lloyd-Jones said, is an essential doctrine of evangelical Christianity. There has always been a fundamental difference between the Reformed Churches and the Papacy concerning this doctrine. The Reformed position has always been that assurance of salvation is good, while the Papists have taken the opposite view. Cardinal Robert Bellarmine, perhaps the greatest Catholic theologian during the Counter-Reformation, once wrote:

> The greatest of all Protestant heresies is assurance.[15]

Bellarmine was simply echoing the view taken by Rome in the Council of Trent when he emphasized the sacraments—rather than the finished work of Christ—as the ground of assurance. As he wrote in his *Spiritual Writings* concerning the mass:

> Finally, by this food the will is filled with the grace of most certain hope and most ardent love.[16]

Bellarmine's position was that the Mass bestows a 'most certain hope' on its participants which must be continually fed by the sacrament. Such sacramental assurance is not the infallible assurance of faith taught in Westminster Confession of Faith 17.2. Sacramental assurance replaces the testimony of the Spirit with the water of baptism (Federal Vision) or the food of the mass (Roman Catholicism). It is not a new invention or discovery, but is as old as circumcision itself. Before his conversion to Christ, Paul trusted in his circumcision, as he recounted in Philippians 3:5, "Circumcised the eighth day." The Pharisees boasted of their circumcision and made it their hope of salvation. Assurance based on sacramental grace is an essential doctrine in the Catholic Church. Thus, Thomas Aquinas wrote in *Summa Contra Gentiles* concerning the connection between the sacraments and salvation:

> Since, however, the death of Christ is, so to say, the universal cause of human salvation, and since a universal cause must be applied singly to each of its effects, it was necessary to show men some remedies through

---

15 Sinclair Ferguson, *In Christ Alone* (Orlando, Florida: Reformation Trust, 2008), 149.

16 John Patrick Donnelly and Ronald J. Treske, trans. and eds., Robert Bellarmine, *Spiritual Writings* (Mahwah, New Jersey: Paulist Press, 1989), 346.

which the benefit of Christ's death could somehow be conjoined to them. It is of this sort, of course, that the sacraments of the Church are said to be.[17]

It was on the basis of this sacramental grace that Aquinas developed his doctrine of the possibility of assurance, which he called the "hope of a wayfarer." Such hope is not infallible and may prove to be false in the end, but it is based on grace received in the sacraments. Aquinas' thoughts on assurance were codified as Catholic doctrine by the Council of Trent in Canons XIV and XVI to their sixth session, wherein they wrote:

> XIV. If anyone saith, that man is truly absolved from his sins and justified, because that he assuredly believed himself absolved and justified; or, that no one is truly justified but he who believes himself justified; and that, by this faith alone, absolution and justification are effected: let him be anathema.
> XVI. If anyone saith, that he will for certain, of an absolute and infallible certainty, have that great gift of perseverance unto the end,—unless he have learned this by special revelation: let him be anathema.

Key Assessment: Both Catholicism and the Federal Vision hold to a moment-by-moment doctrine of assurance in which the sacraments are the source of their hope.

The hallmark of Catholic doctrine on assurance is that it is at best a hope, but not an infallible assurance. Like Pelagianism and Semi-Pelagianism, Catholicism holds to a moment-by-moment assurance at best. Catholics deny the certainty of assurance which is the cornerstone of all the Reformed creeds. Therefore, George Smeaton assessed Catholic doctrine concerning assurance as follows:

> On the ROMISH THEORY, which transmutes the gospel into a new law, the system of ethics never escapes from the legal bondage, and is never ushered into liberty; for it discourages all assurance of salvation.[18]

---

17 Charles J. O'Neil, trans., Thomas Aquinas, *Summa contra Gentiles*, (Garden City, NY: Image Books, 1957), 4:56,1.

18 George Smeaton, *The Doctrine of the Holy Spirit* (Edinburgh, Scotland and Carlisle, Pennsylvania: The Banner of Truth Trust, 1974), 245.

The Federal Vision on Assurance

Like the Catholic Church, the Federal Vision proponents emphasize the sacraments, particularly baptism, as the best ground for assurance. For instance, Steve Schlissel says:

> Everyone who is baptized is to be regarded as belonging to Christ with obligations to live in accordance with the covenant in which he has been placed by the grace of God.[19]

John Barach ties assurance to baptism in the following quote:

> All God's salvation—from election to glorification—is found in Christ. And when you were baptized, God promised to unite you to Jesus Christ. That's what it means to be baptized into Christ. You're united to Jesus and all His salvation is for you.[20]

Barach is saying that assurance is not based on some special experience that only a few people receive. He asserts, both here and at the beginning of this chapter, that the special experience is baptism itself which conveys the totality of salvation in Christ, from election to glorification. Looking to Christ for salvation in that context is tantamount to trusting in baptism. Steve Wilkins makes a similar statement about baptism and assurance:

> All the things that you and I are rightly concerned about, externalism, presumption, things we see all around us, the covenant prevents that when it's preached in its fullness. We belong to Christ. Baptism is the infallible sign and seal of this, and now we must learn to live faithfully and never depart from him. In regard to our assurance, we are pointed away from ourselves, and what we think we perceive to be true inwardly of us, *which no one can know*. And pointed to Christ, the only ground of assurance.[21]

What is interesting about this quote from Wilkins is that he first bases assurance on baptism which he calls an infallible sign and seal of salvation. Yet, baptism does not always result in eternal salvation. Assurance based on baptism too often proves to be presumption or false assurance. He then supplements this *infallible* baptismal assurance with the necessity of living faithfully to

---

19 Waters, *Federal Vision and Covenant Theology*, 128.

20 Ibid., 134.

21 Ibid., 140.

Christ and never departing from him. But that is not certain either. Finally, he bases assurance on "Christ, the only ground of assurance." We dealt earlier in this chapter with what Wilkins means by that statement. Trusting in Christ is tantamount to trusting in baptism for Wilkins and other Federal Vision proponents because baptism bestows all the benefits of Christ's salvation to every one who is baptized in their system.

Another Federal Vision advocate, Doug Wilson, tries to ground assurance in objective truth while attempting to avoid any subjectivism. For instance, he says that what is needed is an "objective assurance . . . found in real faith responding to an objective gospel."[22] Wilson strives to avoid the slippery slope of tying assurance to any effort to peer into the secret counsels of God. Yet, it must be emphasized that Reformed theology has never tied assurance to God's secret counsels. The emphasis has always been in the other direction. God's secret counsels are made manifest by saving faith, by the witness of the Spirit, and by the subjective work of the Spirit in the lives of believers, which produce genuine fruits of saving faith. Yet, Wilson fails in his effort to divorce objective assurance from subjective marks, as Waters shows:

> In his chapter on assurance, Wilson sets forth various marks whereby a Christian may be assured of salvation. They include "holding fast to Jesus Christ," "the gift of the Spirit," "love for the brothers," "understand[ing] spiritual things," "obedien[ce]," and "chasten[ing] for disobedience." These marks, we may observe, clearly embrace subjectively and inwardly as well as outwardly discernable realities.[23]

These marks whereby a Christian may be assured are set forth in Wilson's book, *Reformed is Not Enough: Recovering the Objectivity of the Covenant*.[24] His inconsistency on the matter of assurance is telling and reveals the difficulty in trying to make the objective and the subjective antithetical in the matter of assurance of salvation. Yet, Wilson is apparently unaware of his own inconsistency as a quote from his lecture at the 2002 Auburn Avenue Presbyterian Church Pastors' Conference clearly shows:

---

22 Ibid., 143.

23 Ibid.

24 Douglas Wilson, *"Reformed" Is Not Enough: Recovering the Objectivity of the Covenant* (Moscow, Idaho: Cannon Press, 2002), 126-129.

God is kind to those who continue, he is severe with those who fall. But the falling is defined by God's holy law. Falling is not defined by morbid introspection. That's not where we find the definition of falling. When you, if you want to search inward, if you want to look inward, you can always find more than enough to hang you. There is no assurance looking inward, assurance always comes from looking out, look to God, look to his promises, look to Christ on the cross, look at what God has said, you look away, you don't look in.[25]

Of course, the great question is this: How can anyone look to Christ for salvation at all unless the Holy Spirit has worked within his or her heart? The great dividing line in all of theology is at the point of God's grace vivifying the human spirit. The Federal Vision proponents place their theological system in the orbit of Pelagianism when they deny the subjective aspect of salvation, assurance, and grace. Thus, Richard A. Muller comments concerning Calvin's doctrine of assurance:

> For Calvin, the issue is knowing not merely the objective datum of Christ's sufficient satisfaction but also knowing that we have been "received by Christ into his care and protection," that we truly "hear his voice," and as members of his "flock" are enclosed "within his fold." There is, in other words, and must be a subjective apprehension of Christ's benefits in order for the objective work of satisfaction to be a basis for assurance.[26]

The alienation of the objective and subjective grounds of assurance is a false dichotomy. Joel Beeke is on target when he writes in his excellent work on assurance, *The Quest for Full Assurance*:

> Subjective experience must always be rooted in the objective promise. Secondary grounds of assurance have validity only when subjective experience relies on the objective promises, for the subjective is nothing more than the application to the believer's consciousness of the objective. Consequently, like the objective ground, subjective grounds must never be separated from faith, the blood of Christ, the Holy Spirit, the covenant of grace, and the Word of God.[27]

---

25 Waters, *Federal Vision and Covenant Theology*, 143-144.

26 Richard A. Muller, *Calvin on the Reformed Tradition: On the Work of Christ and the Order of Salvation* (Grand Rapids, Michigan: Baker Academic, 2012), 252.

27 Joel R. Beeke, *The Quest for Full Assurance: The Legacy of Calvin and His Successors* (Edinburgh, Scotland and Carlisle, Pennsylvania: The Banner of Truth Trust, 1999), 129.

Summary

With respect to the doctrine of assurance, the Federal Vision is guilty of trying to separate strands of truth which hang together or fall together. Its proponents attempt to avoid the error of being overly introspective and subjective, but they run into the potential errors of self-deceit and carnal presumption. They teach all the baptized to look to their baptism as their assurance of God's favor. What is that type of assurance but healing the wounds of sin superficially? One of their cardinal errors is a wrong doctrine of the ministry of the Holy Spirit who binds together into one all the different strands of assurance. Where the Spirit of God is operating on the hearts of people, there will be true assurance based on both the objective and subjective grounds of the Gospel.

Conclusion

While there are some nuances of dissimilarity among Reformed theologians concerning assurance, there are many more similarities. Particularly, the Reformed position is the same as the Scriptural references, at the beginning of this chapter, which emphasize the witness of the Spirit and the fruits of saving faith as secondary grounds of assurance. The persistent denial by the Federal Vision proponents of the secondary grounds of assurance puts them at odds with the history of Reformed theology, places them in violation of their ordination vows (if they have subscribed to a Reformed confession such as the Westminster Confession of Faith) and sets them against the Scripture itself. Their position is not Reformed in any sense, but is nearly identical with Catholicism in its rejection of the Protestant doctrine of infallible assurance.

More than a century ago, the great Southern Presbyterian theologian, Robert L. Dabney, wrote:

> The Calvinistic world has now generally settled down upon the doctrine of the Westminster Assembly, that assurance of hope is not of the essence of saving faith; so that many believers may be justified though not having the former: and may remain long without it; but yet an infallible assurance, founded on a comparison of their hearts and lives with Scripture, and the teaching and light of the Holy Ghost, through and in the Word, is the privilege, and should be the aim of every true believer.[28]

---

28 Robert L. Dabney, *Lectures in Systematic Theology* (Grand Rapids, Michigan: Zondervan Publishing House, 1972), 702.

The primary ground of assurance, therefore, is the finished work of Christ; His atoning blood and His imputed righteousness. The secondary grounds of assurance are not substitutes for the objective ground. As Beeke notes:

> The activity of the Spirit is essential in every part of assurance. Without the application of the Spirit, the promises of God lead to self-deceit and carnal presumption. Without the illumination of the Spirit, self-examination tends to introspection, bondage, and legalism. The witness of the Spirit, divorced from the promises of God, and from inward evidences, can degenerate into unbiblical mysticism and excessive emotionalism. These great stands cannot be separated from each other.[29]

---

29   Beeke, *Quest for Full Assurance*, 147.

-19-

The Federal Vision and Perseverance

> "All in covenant are given all that is true of Christ. If they persevere in faith to the end, they enjoy these mercies eternally. If they fall away in unbelief, they lose these blessings and receive a greater condemnation than Sodom and Gomorrah. Covenant can be broken by unbelief and rebellion, but until it is, those in covenant with God belong to Him and are His. If they do not persevere, they lose the blessings that were given to them (and all of this works out according to God's eternal decree which He ordained before the foundation of the world)."[1]
>
> STEVE WILKINS, FEDERAL VISION PROPONENT

---

1 Guy Prentiss Waters, *The Federal Vision and Covenant Theology: A Comparative Analysis* (Phillipsburg, New Jersey: P&R Publishing, 2006), 164.

This statement by Federal Vision advocate, Steve Wilkins, denies the certainty of perseverance for all true believers and gives no explanation of whether a person who has true faith can lose spiritual blessings which he received from Christ. In their emphasis on the objectivity of the covenant, Federal Vision advocates deny the inward, subjective aspects of the covenant. Thus, those who are in covenant with Christ are only in covenant with Him concerning the outward, objective aspects of that covenant. Yet, Francis Turretin exposed the fallacy of universal objective grace:

> Since universal objective grace is vain and illusory without subjective grace, we must either say that sufficient strength is restored to each and all, by which they can (if they will) obey God and be received into the covenant (which is nothing else than to sacrifice to the idol of free will and wholly to abolish discriminating grace, against Paul; as if something is or can be in us which is our own [according to Pelagius] and does not proceed from the unmerited grace of God, 1 Cor. 4:7; or that God intends something under an impossible condition which neither man can have himself, nor does God, who alone can, will to bestow upon him).[2]

There is no middle ground or third option between Augustinianism and Pelagianism on this point. Objective grace without subjective grace is illusory. Such a theory of objective grace necessarily must be based on the sufficiency of the natural man to live in covenant with God. Yet, that very idea confuses nature with grace and knowledge with faith.[3] The devastating consequence of the Federal Vision system is that man's free will is exalted above God's sovereign and electing grace. Men are left to persevere by the strength of their will, not by the power of God's redeeming grace which grants true saints certain perseverance. All who are baptized have the same starting point according to them. Some persevere in faith to the end and receive the eternal mercies of God. Others fall away in unbelief and receive a greater condemnation than Sodom or Gomorrah. Thus, according to the system of the Federal Vision, it is the person who is baptized who makes himself or herself to differ from others in contradiction to the apostle's words in 1 Corinthians 4:7. The Federal Vision does not believe in universal objective grace to all people, but, rather, in universal

---

[2] James T. Dennison, ed., George Musgrave Giger, trans., Francis Turretin, *Institutes of Elenctic Theology*, Volume 2 (Phillipsburg, New Jersey: P&R Publishing Company, 1994), 211.

[3] Ibid.

objective grace to all who are within the covenant by virtue of their baptism.

Key Assessment: The Federal Vision denies the certainty of perseverance and disconnects perseverance from the other benefits of Christ while the Scripture and the Westminster Standards teach the certain perseverance of all those who are effectually called.

Scripture Teaching on Perseverance

John 15 is a favorite passage of the Federal Vision proponents which they incorrectly interpret as teaching that a person can fall from grace—from a real relationship with Christ. In his commentary on the Gospel of John, William Hendriksen made the following remarks concerning John 15:

> In no sense whatever do such passages as 15:2 and 15:6 suggest that there is a falling away from grace, as if those who were once actually saved finally perish. This allegory plainly teaches that the branches which are taken away and burned represent people who never once bore fruit, not even when they were "in" Christ. Hence, they were never true believers; and for them the in-the-vine relationship, though close, was merely outward.[4]

John 15 never says that such people had "real, personal, and deep communion" with Christ. They had a formal relationship with Christ only which is not the same as a real relationship with Him or a true marriage to Him. As Hendriksen further comments:

> Speaking in terms of the metaphor, both groups of branches were in the vine. . . That this relationship of having been in the vine (or, dropping the metaphor, in Christ) does not have to refer to the spiritual, saving union with Christ is easy to see. Not all those who are in the covenant are of the covenant. Not all those who were baptized into Moses were saved (1 Cor. 10:1-5).[5]

A fundamental problem of the Federal Vision is the failure to make this distinction between being "in" the covenant, but not "of" the covenant. Leithart makes this mistake when he says:

> These reprobates really were joined to Christ, really were enlightened

---

4 William Hendriksen, *New Testament Commentary: The Gospel of John* (Edinburgh, Scotland and Carlisle, Pennsylvania: The Banner of Truth Trust, 1976), 296.

5 Ibid., 295.

and fed, really shared in the Spirit, and yet did not persevere and lost what they had been given... The New Testament says pretty plainly that they have lost something real, which includes a relationship with the Spirit, union with Christ, and knowledge of the Savior.[6]

The New Testament never says that apostates lose something that is real. The New Testament teaches very plainly that apostates lose their souls because they never truly receive Christ and never have a real relationship with Him. The apostasy side of this issue was explored earlier in Chapter 17, but in this chapter we are interested in the certain perseverance of all true saints. The difference between the saved and the lost is not that the lost merely failed to persevere, but that they never had a real relationship with Christ. Without true saving grace, they were incapable of persevering. As Edward D. Griffin, former pastor of Park Street Church in Boston from 1811 to 1815, said concerning the doctrine of the perseverance of the saints:

> After what has been proved in former lectures in regard to election, the question respecting the perseverance of the saints is reduced to this: *Are any regenerated besides the elect*? For if none but the elect are regenerated, none of the regenerate can finally apostatize.[7]

The Scriptures, likewise, make it clear that perseverance is a grace or benefit of Christ which is always given to true believers. Hebrews 3:14 says: "For we have become partakers of Christ, if we hold fast the beginning of our assurance firm until the end." The verb translated, *we have become partakers*, is the perfect tense which, according to J. Gresham Machen, "denotes the present state resultant upon a past action."[8] All believers partook of Christ in the past and are holding fast in perseverance unto the end. Calvin, in commenting on Romans 11:22, said perseverance is a grace God gives to all the elect and only the elect:

> Paul adds the condition, *if thou continue in his goodness*, because he is not arguing about individuals who are elected, but about the whole body. I grant that as soon as any one abuses the goodness of God, he deserves to be deprived of the grace which is offered to him. It would, however, be improper to say in particular of any of the godly that God

---

6 Peter J. Leithart, *The Baptized Body* (Moscow, Idaho: Canon Press, 2007), 91.

7 Edward D. Griffin, *A Series of Lectures* (Boston: Doctrinal Tract and Book Society, 1855), 263.

8 J. Gresham Machen, *New Testament Greek for Beginners* (Toronto: The Macmillan Company, 1951), 187.

had mercy on him when he chose him, on condition that he should continue in his mercy. The perseverance of faith, which perfects the effect of God's grace in us, flows from election itself.[9]

In Romans 5:2-5, several benefits of Christ are mentioned—faith, grace, perseverance, proven character, hope, and the love of God poured out through the Holy Spirit. Separating perseverance from the other benefits of Christ makes it a work of man and, therefore, opens the door for a Pelagian scheme of salvation.

In his commentary on the Westminster Standards, Francis R. Beattie remarks concerning the perseverance of the saints taught in 1 Peter 1:5 and other passages:

> The term preservation is one which would, in some respects, more accurately express the truth here. Believers persevere because they are preserved; they follow because they are led by divine grace.[10]

Perseverance in the Scripture and the Reformed Confessions is never the result of man's free will or effort. The certainty of perseverance is the result of God's preservation of His people. The Federal Vision turns this matter around and makes perseverance hypothetically possible for all those who are baptized. Such a scheme makes perseverance dependent on man's faithfulness—not God's. The error is in maintaining that some who have received true, saving benefits from Christ can fall away from Him.

Perseverance and the Federal Vision System

When they first began constructing their system, many of the adherents of the Federal Vision taught that even perseverance was among the gifts bestowed on all who are baptized. Steve Wilkins and Peter Leithart are two examples of that position. Their earlier position meant that every baptized person would be saved. Thus, they changed their position to avoid this obvious error. Peter Leithart explains why he made this change:

> I retracted that because there were, as was pointed out by the study committee and others, that there's obvious gifts that the elect receive

---

9   John Calvin, *The Epistles of Paul to the Romans* (Grand Rapids: Wm. B. Eerdmans Publishing Co., 1979), 252-253.

10   Francis R. Beattie, *The Presbyterian Standards: An Exposition of the Westminster Confession of Faith and Catechisms* (Greenville, South Carolina: Southern Presbyterian Press, 1997), 239.

that, from Christ, that gifts that Christ has to offer that don't go to every baptized person. Perseverance was the obvious one.[11]

There certainly are gifts from Christ which do not go to every baptized person. Indeed, the benefits of Christ's redemption are given to the elect alone in their effectual calling. None of the saving benefits of Christ are given to all who are merely baptized with water. As the Westminster Shorter Catechism #32 teaches:

> They that are effectually called do in this life partake of justification, adoption, and sanctification, and the several benefits which in this life do either accompany or flow from them.

Or, as Shorter Catechism #36 says:

> The benefits which in this life do accompany or flow from justification, adoption, and sanctification, are, assurance of God's love, peace of conscience, joy in the Holy Ghost, increase of grace, and perseverance therein to the end.

In contradiction to the Scripture and the Shorter Catechism, the Federal Vision separates perseverance from the other benefits supposedly bestowed through baptismal efficacy. This new position on perseverance allows the Federal Vision adherents to hold to the apostasy of those they assume to be truly united with Christ. Leithart, therefore, gives a typical Federal Vision perspective on perseverance:

> I do believe that some are united to Christ yet do not persevere (John 15). During the time they are branches in the vine, they do receive benefits from Christ through the Spirit and may enjoy real, personal, and deep communion with Jesus for a time.[12]

No matter how often they revise their position to make it seem more consistent, their system still contradicts the Scriptures and the Westminster Standards. Their present position is that there are two groups of people who both enjoy "real, personal, and deep communion with Jesus." Some enjoy those benefits for all eternity, if they persevere. Others enjoy those benefits only "for a time," if they fail to persevere. For the Federal Vision adherents, perseverance does not so much evidence a true union with Christ as that it simply makes that true union last.

---

11 Record of the Case, Standing Judicial Commission of the Presbyterian Church in America, Case 2012-5, RE Gerald Hedman vs. Pacific Northwest Presbytery, 545.

12 Record of the Case, Standing Judicial Commission, 2012-5, 63.

Various Views of Perseverance

The error of the Federal Vision concerning perseverance is similar to Arminianism, Lutheranism, and Catholicism. A. A. Hodge described the Arminian doctrine on perseverance as follows:

> It is an inseparable part of the Arminian system, flowing necessarily from their views of election, of the design and effect of Christ's death, and of sufficient grace and free will, that those who were once justified and regenerated may, by neglecting grace and grieving the Holy Spirit, fall into such sins as are inconsistent with true justifying faith, and continuing and dying in the same, may consequently finally fall into perdition.—"Confession of the Remonstrants," xi.7. The Lutherans and the Arminians agree on this point. They both believe that the "elect" (those whom God has chosen to eternal life because he has certainly foreseen their perseverance in faith and obedience to the end) can not finally apostatize. The true question between them and the Calvinists, therefore, is not whether the "elect", but whether those who once were truly "regenerate and justified" can finally apostatize and perish.[13]

Hodge's assessment of Arminianism and Lutheranism clarifies the issue with the Federal Vision concerning perseverance. The issue is not whether the elect will persevere, but whether a regenerate and justified person can fail to persevere. The Federal Vision says all those who are baptized are "ecclesiastically" regenerated and justified, but only some of them persevere to final justification and salvation.

The Catholic position on this same question is given in the Council of Trent's *Concilii Tridentini*, session 6, chapter 15, which says:

> It is to be maintained that the received grace of justification is lost, not only by infidelity, whereby even faith itself is lost, but also by any other mortal sin whatever, though faith be not lost[14]
>
> If any one saith, that a man once justified can sin no more, nor lose grace, and that therefore he that falls and sins was never truly justified... let him be anathema[15]

Likewise, the Formula of Concord of the Lutherans says:

---

13 A. A. Hodge, *Outlines of Theology* (Grand Rapids, Michigan: Zondervan Publishing House, 1972), 543.

14 Ibid, 546.

15 Ibid.

> That false opinion is to be earnestly confuted and rejected, which certain feign, that faith and realized justification and sanctification itself, can not be lost by any sins or crimes whatsoever.[16]

Key Assessment: The Federal Vision, Arminianism, Catholicism, the Lutheran Formula of Concord, and Pelagianism all deny the certainty of perseverance.

Thus, the crux of the matter is the same one which Hodge elucidated between the Reformed on the one hand and Lutherans, Arminians, and Catholics on the other. The Scripture and the Westminster Standards state very clearly that no one who is truly regenerated or justified can ever lose those saving graces. Arminians, Lutherans, Catholics, and the Federal Vision proponents object to the Reformed position. For instance the summary statement of the Auburn Avenue Presbyterian Church in Monroe, Louisiana, where Steve Wilkins is pastor, says:

> In some sense they were really joined to the elect people, really sanctified by the Holy Spirit, really recipients of new life given by the Holy Spirit. God, however, withholds from them the gift of perseverance, and all is lost. They break the gracious new covenant they entered into at baptism.[17]

The denial of certain perseverance by the Federal Vision adherents, who hold to baptismal efficacy, is not surprising. Thus, J. C. Ryle observed the effect that baptismal efficacy views have on the doctrine of perseverance:

> I believe another most common reason why many do not hold to perseverance, is *an incorrect view of the effect of baptism.* They lay it down, as a cardinal point in their theology, that all who are baptized are born again in baptism, and all receive the grace of the Holy Ghost. Without a single plain text in the Bible to support their opinions, and in the face of the 17th Article[18], which many of them as Churchmen have subscribed, they still tell us that all baptized persons are necessarily "regenerate." Of course such a view of baptism is utterly destructive of the doctrine that true grace can never be overthrown. It is as plain as daylight, that multitudes of baptized persons never show a spark of grace all their lives, and never give the slightest evidence of having

---

16 Ibid.

17 Waters, *Federal Vision and Covenant Theology*, 155.

18 Ryle (1816-1900) was a minister in the Church of England and is referring to the 17th of the 39 Articles of Religion of that denomination.

been born of God. . . . According to the view which I am now referring, "they have all fallen from grace! They all had it! They were made God's children! But they lost their grace! They have all become children of the devil!". . . All I say is, that "if baptismal regeneration" be true, there is an end of final perseverance.[19]

As Ryle stated, it is impossible to hold to both certain perseverance and baptismal efficacy. Wrong views on baptismal efficacy necessarily lead to the denial of certain perseverance. Where the efficacy of baptism is lifted up, the sovereign work of God in salvation is brought down. What is overlooked by the Federal Vision is that salvation is a work of God, from beginning to end, that depends on His grace. True believers may backslide and depart from a life of holiness for a period of time, but can never lose grace or fall away from salvation. Their perseverance is as certain as the promises of God to His elect. As Francis Turretin said concerning perseverance:

> Faith is not true because it perseveres, but it perseveres because it is true. Thus perseverance is not the cause of the verity of faith, but the consequent and the effect—for because it has solidity and a deep root in the heart, on this account it is constant and perpetually endures.[20]

The Federal Vision reverses this order. It insists that faith is not true unless it perseveres, which makes perseverance the verity of faith. In reality, faith perseveres because it is true faith and endures because it has been planted in the believer's heart by God's grace through the work of the Holy Spirit. To reverse this order is to make man, rather than God, responsible for his own perseverance.

Summary
The Federal Vision advocates use language that beguiles many people because it sounds similar to biblical teaching. They make eternal salvation dependent on perseverance and final justification. In their scheme, perseverance becomes a work or a condition of salvation. Faith is proven to be true faith only if it perseveres in their system. This subtle change is a redefinition of perseverance and saving faith in a man-centered direction and is a denial of certain perseverance. Augustinians and Calvinists believe in the certain perseverance of

---

19 John Charles Ryle, *Old Paths: Being Plain Statements on Some of the Weightier Matters of Christianity* (Cambridge and London: James Clarke & Co. LTD., 1972), 501-502.
20 Turretin, *Institutes of Elenctic Theology*, Volume 2, 592.

all true believers. All Pelagians of whatever degree deny certain perseverance and make perseverance dependent on the diligence of the individual. Contrariwise, the Scripture teaches that perseverance is dependent on the grace of God.

Conclusion

Perseverance is a gift of God and a blessing of the covenant of grace. There are benefits of Christ's redemption given to all true believers, and perseverance is one of them. Those benefits form an unbroken chain from election to glorification. The impossibility of a true saint losing his salvation can be approached from another perspective. Herman Bavinck, always insightful, expressed it this way:

> When Scripture expressly states that it is impossible to restore to repentance those who are in view in these texts (Heb. 6:4; 10:26; 2 Peter 2:20; 1 John 5:16), it cannot be denied that the reference is to a sin that carries with it a judgment of hardening and that the reference is to a sin that makes repentance impossible. And of such a sin—also according to the confession of those who hold to the impossibility of a falling away—there is only one, namely, the sin of the blasphemy against the Holy Spirit. Now if this is true, then the doctrine of the falling away of the saints leads to the conclusion that either the sin of blaspheming the Holy Spirit can be committed also, or perhaps only, by those who are born again, or the above mentioned texts lose all their evidential value against the doctrine of the perseverance of the saints.[21]

Perhaps no one has more succinctly stated the issue concerning perseverance than the first Presbyterian missionary to America, Francis Makemie, who wrote:

> We do not maintain a perseverance depending on the will of man but on the gracious covenant, the everlasting purpose of God, the unchangeableness of his love, and efficaciousness of Christ's death.[22]

The great error of the Federal Vision concerning perseverance is that it makes it dependent on the will of man, rather than the unchangeableness of God's covenant of grace.

---

21 John Bolt, ed., John Vriend, trans., Herman Bavinck, *Reformed Dogmatics*, Volume IV, *Holy Spirit, Church, and New Creation* (Grand Rapids, Michigan: Baker Academic, 2008), 268.

22 Littleton Purnell Bower, *The Days of Makemie: or, The Vine Planted. 1680-1708* (Philadelphia: Presbyterian Board of Publication, 1833), 328.

-20-
The Federal Vision and Final Justification

> "Final justification, however, is according to works. This pole of justification takes into account the entirety of our lives—the obedience we've performed, the sins we've committed, the confessions and repentance we've done... God's verdict over us will be in accord with, and therefore in some sense based upon, the life we've lived."[1]
>
> RICH LUSK, FEDERAL VISION PROPONENT

---

[1] Guy Prentiss Waters, *The Federal Vision and Covenant Theology: A Comparative Analysis* (Phillipsburg, New Jersey: P&R Publications, 2006), 90.

There are two primary pillars that support the heretical views of the Federal Vision. The first pillar is an unscriptural doctrine of the covenant and what that means for the baptized children of believers. The second pillar is the heretical doctrine of final justification. These pillars are at the opposite ends of this new—yet old—theological system. There is a sense in which the Federal Vision heresy is essentially an unbiblical doctrine of the covenant. Yet, there is an even greater sense in which the heresy of final justification is the key doctrine in the whole Federal Vision system. All of the Federal Vision's errors concerning the *ordo salutis* coalesce in the heresy of final justification. Those other errors are absolutely necessary to the whole of the system because of this doctrine of final justification.

Errors Involved with Final Justification

For instance, the Federal Vision cannot hold solely and only to the doctrine of unconditional election if a person's justification is not final until the very end of his life, based on the totality of his whole life. Unconditional election makes one's ultimate salvation certain according to God's eternal purpose of grace in Christ before the foundation of the world. Final justification, conversely, makes salvation uncertain until the end of life. Those are two very different positions. Thus, the Federal Vision essentially replaces unconditional election with the doctrine of a conditional, covenantal election in which people can move in and out of an elect standing with Christ.

The Federal Vision cannot logically and consistently hold to a doctrine of supernatural regeneration because of its heresy of final justification. Supernatural regeneration is the implantation of the seed of God in the hearts of God's elect; the seed of eternal life. Eternal life, according to the false theology of the Federal Vision, is indeterminate until the end of life. Thus, the doctrine of final justification, in order to be self-consistent, requires that man's nature cannot be eternally, supernaturally, and permanently renovated before the end of his life.

Union with Christ is restricted to an outward and formal union by the doctrine of final justification for the same reasons that militate against supernatural regeneration. If union with Christ is inward and spiritual, as the Scripture defines it, then the doctrine of final justification is overturned. Thus, the Federal Vision is compelled by the doctrine of final justification to define union with Christ as formal and outward.

The doctrine of the imputation of Christ's righteousness, His active obedience, is in conflict with the doctrine of final justification. Those who hold to final justification teach that one's whole life of righteous deeds will be the basis for his final vindication before God. Such a view leaves no place for the imputation of Christ's perfect righteousness to the believer.

The doctrine of final justification is based on the view that the members of the covenant must live in obedience to God's laws in order to be finally vindicated. Covenant faithfulness is taught as the way to salvation. There are various names given to this theory. Neonomianism is one of them. It means "new law." Salvation is made easier in the New Testament, according to this theory, by the relaxation of the strictness of the Mosaic law. Interestingly, many people in the Federal Vision hold that the Old Testaments laws are still applicable today in exhaustive detail, but their neonomian theories of salvation are in dynamic conflict with theonomy. Is the Mosaic law relaxed or is it still applicable in exhaustive detail? If final justification is correct, then there must be some standard by which covenant members are judged. That standard is God's new law, *neonomianism*, which requires our faithful, sincere efforts to obey Him. Final justification necessitates this doctrine of neonomianism.

If final justification is correct, then no one is really in or out of salvation until the end of life. Final justification, therefore, changes the meaning of apostasy. Apostasy, according to the Federal Vision, is not necessarily permanent unless it is persisted in. Yet, the Scripture says that those who fall away cannot be renewed "again to repentance" (Hebrews 6:6), a passage which is hotly debated by the Federal Vision proponents. The theory of final justification requires that no one's status is permanent until that person's last breath is past.

The Federal Vision is opposed to the subjective experience of the assurance of salvation and ridicules it as introspective and pietistic. In a system which teaches final justification, it follows that no one can really be assured of his salvation until the judgment of God is declared at that last day.

The certainty of persevering grace for all of God's elect is a cornerstone doctrine of the Reformed faith, but it is in conflict with the doctrine of final justification. Perseverance must inevitably be conditional—uncertain, not certain—in such a scheme. Thus, final justification requires that perseverance be qualified with an "if." According to the Federal Vision, if a person perseveres in faithfulness he will be saved. If he fails to persevere, he will be lost. There are no "ifs" in the unconditional election of God's grace.

Assessment of Final Justification

Therefore, more is at stake in this debate with the Federal Vision than mere quibbling over semantics. The Federal Vision denies justification by faith alone in its doctrine of final justification. That denial necessarily involves the Federal Vision system in heretical views concerning all the doctrines of salvation. Augustine saw this issue very clearly in his writings against the Pelagians and he stated:

> For "If righteousness come by nature, then Christ is dead in vain." If, however, Christ did not die in vain, in Him only is the ungodly man justified, and to him, on believing in Him who justifies the ungodly, faith is reckoned for righteousness. . .
>
> When, however, the Pelagians say that the only grace which is not given according to our merits is that whereby his sins are forgiven to man, but that which is given in the end, that is, eternal life, is rendered to our preceding merits: they must not be allowed to go without an answer.[2]

Augustine saw clearly that if the Pelagian theory of a justification based on works at the end of life was true, then it rendered the gospel and the work of Christ meaningless. Likewise, John Owen, in his masterly work on the doctrine of justification by faith, clearly denied that there is any second or subsequent justification to the one justification by faith alone which is once-for-all. Owen acknowledged that there is a manifestation and declaration of our justification at the final judgment but he denied the Roman Catholic doctrine of a double justification:

> Yet, is it not a *second justification*: for it depends wholly on the *visible effects* of that faith whereby we are justified, as the apostle James instructs us; yet is it only one single justification before God, evidenced and declared, unto his glory, the benefit of others, and increase of our own reward. . .
>
> This distinction of *two justifications*, as used and improved by those of the Roman church, leaves us indeed, no justification at all. . .

---

2 Philip Schaff, ed., Peter Holmes and Robert Ernest Wallis, trans., *St. Augustin's Anti-Pelagian Works* (Peabody, Massachusetts: Hendrickson Publishers, Inc., 1999), 122, 450.

> The second branch of the distinction hath much in it like *unto justification by the law*, but nothing of that which is declared in the gospel. So that this distinction, instead of *coining us two justifications*, according to the gospel, hath left us *none at all*.[3]

Despite the claim by N. T. Wright and the Federal Vision proponents that final justification does not affect the Protestant doctrine of justification by faith alone, we must not be beguiled. A second justification at the judgment based on works strips the Scripture of its most important truth. It leaves us with no justification at all.

Defense of the Doctrine of Final Justification

When the Presbyterian Church in America voted in 2007 on the Ad-Interim Committee Report on the New Perspectives on Paul, the Federal Vision, and the Auburn Avenue Theology, the doctrine which was most defended afterwards by Internet bloggers and supporters of the Federal Vision was the theory of final justification. Without that doctrine, their whole system crumbles like a house of cards. A friend of mine told me that he was at a conference where N. T. Wright spoke several years ago. Wright supposedly defended his views with the caveat that if he was wrong on the front end at least he was right in the end. As I have thought about that statement over the years, I am convinced Wright must have been referring to the doctrine of final justification. In his view, such a statement would mean that final justification is an undeniable fact, one that is beyond dispute. In other words, if his doctrine of initial justification is wrong, at least his doctrine of final justification is correct. Quite to the contrary! He is wrong on both counts. His views, and those of the Federal Vision, are outside of Scripture and the historic Christian faith.

Key Assessment: The Federal Vision teaches that final justification is based on works according to the totality of the life lived, a position also held by the Pelagian spectrum of heresies.

That final justification is the view of the proponents of both the Federal Vision and N. T. Wright is easy to prove. One of the leading proponents of the Federal Vision, Rich Lusk, is quoted at the beginning

---

3 William Goold, ed., *The Works of John Owen*, Volume V (London: The Banner of Truth Trust, 1967), 139-141.

of this chapter. N. T. Wright said nearly the same thing in his book *Justification*, as well as in other places:

> It is "justification" in the present, anticipating the verdict of the future. God will declare on the last day that certain people are "in the right," by raising them from the dead, and that verdict has been brought forth into the present.[4]

If justification is according to works, then salvation also is based on works. If salvation is based on works, then it is no longer based on grace. And if it is not based on grace, then the whole message of the gospel is overturned. As Paul wrote, "[I]f righteousness comes through the law, then Christ died needlessly" (Galatians 2:21). The hope of the Federal Vision, according to Lusk's quote above, is that God will vindicate those whose obedience, works, confessions (for sins committed), and repentance meets the requirements of His standards (law) in some sense. In other words, God will vindicate people based on the curve. There is nothing especially enlightening about such a view. It does not take a theological education to construct it. Final justification, in that sense, is the prized theological opinion of every person who has ever lived apart from and been destitute of the saving knowledge of the gospel. All men hope that God will grade them on the curve in comparison to others. They naturally hold that if they sincerely strive to please God, He will be merciful to them. Perhaps the only unique thing about this position of the Federal Vision is that its proponents basically restrict this option to those who are baptized members of the covenant. It is justification (vindication) by works only for those within the covenant community; whereas the natural man believes that each person who has ever lived will be saved by works based on the totality of his whole life. N. T. Wright, who is something of a mentor to the Federal Vision proponents, takes the same tack concerning final justification:

> Justification, at the last, will be on the basis of performance, not possession. . .
>
> Future justification, acquittal at the last great Assize, always takes place on the basis of the totality of the life lived.[5]

---

4 N. T. Wright, *Justification: God's Plan and Paul's Vision* (Downers Grove, Illinois: IVP Academic, 2009), 147.

5 Guy Prentiss Waters, *Justification and the New Perspectives on Paul: A Review and Response* (Phillipsburg, New Jersey: P&R Publishing, 2004), 171.

There are certainly statements from the Federal Vision proponents where they try to soften the blow of such quotes concerning final justification, but those are not to be taken seriously. Either justification by faith alone is once-for-all at the moment of initial faith or it is not. Either final justification is based on the totality of one's life or it is not. In neither case can it be both, no matter how much the Federal Vision proponents equivocate. As Francis L. Patton commented concerning heresies that are based on half-truths in his memorial address for Caspar Wistar Hodge:

> A lie that is all a lie can be met and fought with outright,
> But a lie that is half a truth is a harder matter to fight.[6]

Anyone familiar with the Federal Vision is aware of the constant state of flux in that system. Its advocates make a statement about final justification or some other doctrine, and when they are challenged, they equivocate and redefine their position without really retracting their errors. This has happened so frequently in recent years that it cannot seriously be considered as an honest error. Dissembling and equivocation are essential to the tradecraft of heretics in all ages. John Calvin accused Albertus Pighius of something similar:

> Even readers of a modest intellect will recognize here Pighius's usual system of logic, the first rule of which is: Always split one thing into many, and mix up things which are different into one![7]

Final Justification and Richard Baxter

The Federal Vision finds support for its views on final justification from such men as the Puritan minister of Kidderminster in England, Richard Baxter, who was rightly described by J. I. Packer as a "disaster" of a theologian. Baxter adopted a political method of theology in which God was the governor and the gospel was His legal code which must be obeyed to earn salvation. His theology was natural, not scriptural. This political method led Baxter to adopt a theory of final justification which he described in his own words:

---

6 James M. Garretson, *Pastor-Teachers of Old Princeton: Memorial Addresses for the Faculty of Princeton Theological Seminary 1812-1921* (Edinburgh, Scotland and Carlisle, Pennsylvania: The Banner of Truth Trust, 2012), 466.

7 A. N. S. Lane, ed., G. I. Davies, trans., John Calvin, *The Bondage and Liberation of the Will* (Grand Rapids, Michigan: Baker Books, 1996), 221.

> To conclude, it is most clear in Scripture, that our Justification, at the great Judgment, will be according to our Works, and to what we have done in Flesh, whether good or evil; which can be no otherwise than as it was the Condition of that Justification.[8]

In those words, Baxter lent his support for the doctrine that justification on the day of judgment will be according to works. Baxter's system, like the Federal Vision, allowed room for an initial justification based on faith, but the full or final justification—which he said determines everlasting salvation—was based on works. He was well aware of the consequences of his position and knew that it would cause others to accuse him of "Heresy, Popery, Socinianism! and what not."[9] Baxter's theological method resulted in him defining sin as primarily external which is the error of Popery, Socinianism, and even Pelagianism. On that count, Baxter's fear was prophetic. Proponents of the Federal Vision are guilty of the same externalizing of sin and salvation in their agreement with the doctrine of final justification.

Final Justification, Ritualism, and Rationalism
As we have observed throughout this book, the heresies of the Federal Vision often combine rationalism and ritualism, as well as legalism and liberalism. All of them are opposed to the scriptural doctrines of salvation. Baxter was certainly not the first person to believe in final justification. Similar views were held by the professors at the Huguenot seminary in Saumur, France, particularly by the Scottish theologian, John Cameron. Final justification is a doctrine which is essential to any form of nomism, as Bavinck states, and has been held by numerous heretical groups:

> Under the influence of Socinianism and Remonstrantism, Cartesianism and Amyraldianism, there sprang up the neonomian view of the order of salvation, which made the forgiveness of sins and eternal life dependent on faith and obedience, which, in keeping with the new law of the gospel, had to be accomplished by the human agent.[10]

Before that controversy among the French Protestants, the Council

---

8 Richard Baxter, *An Extract of Richard Baxter's Aphorisms of Justification* (Newcastle upon Tyne, England: John Gooding, 1745), 32.

9 Ibid., 31.

10 John Bolt, ed., John Vriend, trans., Herman Bavinck, *Reformed Dogmatics*, Volume 4: *Holy Spirit, Church and New Creation* (Grand Rapids, Michigan: Baker Academic, 2008), 201.

of Trent had clearly articulated a similar view of final justification in the sixteenth chapter of their sixth session, which says:

> And for this cause, life eternal is to be proposed to those working well *unto the end*, and hoping in God, both as grace mercifully promised to the sons of God through Jesus Christ, and as a reward which is according to the promise of God himself, to be faithfully rendered to their good works and merits.[11]

Calvin repudiated that definition of justification in his antidote to Trent, "On the Sixth Session of the Council of Trent":

> Nay, their definition at length contains nothing else than the trite dogma of the schools: that men are justified partly by the grace of God and partly by their own works; thus only shewing themselves somewhat more modest than Pelagius was.[12]

The Federal Vision on Final Justification

Final justification is a decidedly non-evangelical viewpoint. It is a position held in common by Pelagians, Semi-Pelagians, Arminians, Romanists, Neonomians, and the Federal Vision. As Cornelis Venema says in his work, *The Gospel of Free Acceptance in Christ*, the Roman Catholic Church objected to the doctrine of justification by faith alone because it left no place for "a works based final acquittal before God."[13] The Reformers and the Reformed confessions have unanimously declared that there is a final judgment, but not "a final phase or step in an unfinished process of justification."[14]

As already observed, Richard Baxter and the Neonomians held to a theory of final justification based on one's good works. Likewise, Pelagius taught that justification by faith was only for the present:

> One's initial faith is credited as righteousness to the end that one may be absolved of the past, justified for the present, and readied for the future works of faith.[15]

---

11 Philip Schaff, ed., David S. Schaff, trans., *The Creeds of Christendom: With a History and Critical Notes*, Volume II: *The Greek and Latin Creeds* (Grand Rapids, Michigan: Baker Book House, 1983), 107.

12 John Calvin, *Tracts and Letters*, Volume 3: Tracts, Part 3 (Edinburgh, Scotland and Carlisle, Pennsylvania: The Banner of Truth Trust, 2009), 108.

13 Cornelis P. Venema, *The Gospel of Free Acceptance in Christ* (Edinburgh, Scotland and Carlisle, Pennsylvania: The Banner of Truth Trust, 2006), 259.

14 Ibid., 266.

15 Theodore DeBruyn, trans., *Pelagius' Commentary on St. Paul's Epistle to the Romans* (Oxford,

Pelagius uses the phrase, "at the present," several times in his Romans commentary to limit justification. Justification is not once-for-all, according to Pelagius, but simply "at the present." Pelagius teaches elsewhere that those who are baptized and believe must persevere in order to be saved. If they do so, they will be finally justified as long as "daily good works surpass past misdeeds."[16]

Federal Vision advocate, Peter Leithart, teaches that God justifies a person at baptism; whenever anyone who responds in faith (even temporarily) to his or her baptism; and, whenever a baptized person perseveres unto the end, which is called "final justification." Yet, Leithart stated at his trial that he believed that justification is a once-for-all judicial act. It is very clear that neither of the first two "justifications" can be a once-for-all justification. Thus, "final justification" is the only once-for-all justification possible under his soteriology. Leithart's views are similar to the views of other Federal Vision advocates on final justification.

Key Assessment: The Federal Vision, like Pelagius, teaches that initial faith justifies a person only for the present and there will be a final justification according to the works.

The Federal Vision proponents vainly attempt to support their view of final justification from the thirty-third chapter of the *Westminster Confession of Faith*, particularly the first section of that chapter. That chapter of the *Confession* never defines that judgment as a final justification. Robert Shaw, in his exposition of the Westminster Confession, *The Reformed Faith*, commented on the place of works in the judgment for the righteous:

> It is to be remarked, that the good works of the righteous will be produced in that day, not as the grounds of their acquittal, and of being adjudged to eternal life, but as the evidences of their gracious state, as being interested in the righteousness of Christ.[17]

The denial of the imputation of the righteousness of Christ to believers is part and parcel of the doctrine of final justification. It is the

---

England: Clarendon Press, 1993), 85.

16 Ibid.

17 Robert Shaw, *The Reformed Faith: An Exposition of the Westminster Confession of Faith* (Inverness, Scotland: Christian Focus Publications, 1974), 326.

great dividing line between believers and heretics on this point. Thus, Westminster Confession of Faith 16.6 says:

> Notwithstanding, the persons of believers being accepted through Christ, their good works are also accepted in him, not as though they were in this life wholly unblameable and unreprovable in God's sight; but that he, looking upon them in his Son, is pleased to accept and reward that which is sincere, although accompanied with many weaknesses and imperfections.

The *Confession* also teaches that the good works of believers are only accepted by God because of Christ and that justification precedes sanctification. Pelagius, Rome, and the Federal Vision reverse this order through the doctrine of "final justification." Yet, the issue in the end is not what any creedal statement says, whether the Westminster Confession of Faith or the Council of Trent. Scripture is the great touchstone of truth. In his dispute with the Arian, Maximinus, Augustine wisely limited the debate to the Scriptures:

> I ought neither to adduce the Council of Nice, nor you that of Ariminum[18], as if to prejudge the question. I am not determined by the authority of the latter, nor you by that of the former. Founding on the authority of Scripture not peculiar to either, but the common witness of both, fact contends with fact, plea with plea, reason with reason.[19]

The Federal Vision's Circular Reasoning on Final Justification

In many respects, the Federal Vision proponents engage repeatedly in a kind of twisted circular reasoning. When required to subscribe to the Westminster Confession of Faith as officers in the church, the adherents retort that they find the Scripture to be pushing them in a different direction. When it is demanded of them to prove their views from the Scripture, they claim support for their novel interpretations of Holy Writ from the views of uninspired men. Augustine's determination to limit his debate with Maximinus to the Scriptures only was very wise. Thus, Calvin commented on that matter:

> So much liberty does this holy man concede to himself and others, that he will not allow the Council of Nice to operate as a previous judge,

---

18 The Council of Rimini in 357, also called Ariminum, was held in the Italian city of Rimini for the purpose of resolving the Arian controversy over the divinity of Christ. This council presented a new creed which favored Arianism and was considered a defeat for trinitarianism. Pope Liberius of Rome rejected this creed and favored Nicea.

19 Calvin, *Tracts*, Volume 3, 30.

unless the truth of the case be plainly established from Scripture.[20]

The Scripture proofs against the doctrine of final justification are the same ones examined in the chapter on justification by faith alone. The Federal Vision twists Scripture out of context and finds support for its views by pitting one author of Scripture against another; or, sometimes even pitting an author against himself, as in the case of the Apostle Paul. Paul is clear in Romans and Galatians that justification is through faith alone, apart from works. Yet, the Federal Vision attempts to build a doctrine of final justification on a misinterpretation of Romans 2:13. Thereby, it attempts to make Paul inconsistent with himself in the epistle to the Romans and to destroy the integrity of the Scriptures. It would be far better for proponents of the Federal Vision to remember what Jesus said: "And the Scripture cannot be broken" (John 10:35). That is their first error—they break the unity and integrity of the Scriptures by pitting Scripture against Scripture.

Another fundamental error of the Federal Vision proponents is the failure to interpret the more obscure passages of Scripture in the light of the plain passages of Scripture. Whatever Romans 2:13 or James 2:24 mean, those passages must be understood in consistency with the clear statements of Scripture concerning justification which are found in Romans and Galatians. Without some clear passages of Scripture to prove their doctrine of final justification, then the Federal Vision and others are simply not to be believed. Calvin emphasized the word "plainly" and so should we. Federal Vision teachers attempt to prove their doctrines from obscure, relatively unclear passages of Scripture. For other doctrines, they simply appeal to the views of others, often third-rate theologians, as their authority.

Summary

The doctrine of final justification is, apparently, one of the most prized doctrines for those in the Federal Vision movement. It is a doctrine they hold in common with Pelagians, Neonomians, Catholics, and Socinians. Such a doctrine denies justification by faith alone and the other great truths of the gospel. For that reason, final justification is neither taught in the Scriptures nor in any of the Reformed symbols.

---

20 Ibid.

Conclusion

What is at stake in this controversy with the Federal Vision over the doctrine of final justification? The gospel is at stake. Everything the Bible teaches about salvation through faith in Christ is at stake. It is the reason above all else for this book.

Both the Federal Vision and N. T. Wright are in basic agreement in their denial of the scriptural doctrine of salvation because of their commonly held doctrine of final justification. Whatever differences there are between the Federal Vision and the New Perspectives on Paul, as held by N. T. Wright, those differences are not at the level of soteriology. The Puritan, Robert Traill, summarized the importance of a correct doctrine of justification:

> All the great fundamentals of Christian truth, center in this of justification. The trinity of persons in the God-head; the incarnation of the only begotten of the Father; the satisfaction paid to the law and justice of God, for the sins of the world, by His obedience, and sacrifice of Himself in that flesh He assumed; and the divine authority of the scriptures, which reveal all this, are all straight lines of truth, that center in this doctrine of justification of a sinner by the imputation of and application of that satisfaction.[21]

In the final analysis it does not matter that the Federal Vision proponents profess to believe many truths of the Bible. Their denial of scriptural soteriology will eventually lead to the denial of all the other fundamental doctrines of Christianity as well. All the great truths of Scripture, as Traill eloquently stated, have their center in justification. Justification by faith alone is the article of a standing or falling church. By adhering to final justification (and rejecting justification by faith alone), the Federal Vision teachers have already adopted the religious view of salvation of every natural person in the world. They have sold their birthright for a bowl of stew.

---

21 *The Works of Robert Traill*, Volume I (Edinburgh, Scotland and Carlisle, Pennsylvania: The Banner of Truth Trust, 1975), 289.

-21-
The Federal Vision and Gnosticism

> "Calvin and the Reformed tradition made a huge mistake by substituting metrical psalms for real ones—a gnostic move, since the assumption is that the IDEAS of the text are all that matter, and not the shape thereof."[1]
>
> JAMES JORDAN, FEDERAL VISION PROPONENT

---

[1] Record of the Case, Standing Judicial Commission Case of the Presbyterian Church in America, 2012-5, RE Gerald Hedman vs. Pacific Northwest Presbytery, 316.

In the introduction to *The Federal Vision*, Steve Wilkins makes the following promise:

> By putting forth this collection, we do not intend to make a bad situation worse. We have not (and never will) fling charges of heresy against our brothers who disagree with our position. We refuse to do this because such charges are totally unwarranted.[2]

Yet, the various authors of that symposium make a number of general accusations of heresy against those who differ with the Federal Vision. It is certainly true that there are no charges of heresy against specific individuals, but there are numerous charges of heresy in general. The opponents of the Federal Vision are accused of becoming as Romish as could be in their zeal to avoid Romanism; James Jordan accuses the covenant of works scheme of being "Pelagian in character"[3]; of holding to tradition even more than Catholicism; of being guilty of experientialism; of using the same hermeneutic in interpreting the Scripture as liberals do; of forcing a system of theology on the Scriptures; and, especially, of being Gnostics. This last charge is pervasive in the writings of the proponents of the Federal Vision, as well as those of N. T. Wright, but all these charges are serious and put the lie to Wilkins' quote above. They not only will fling charges of heresy against their opponents; they will do so early and often.

Key Assessment: The Federal Vision accuses most of Christianity, especially Reformed Christianity, of the Gnostic heresy, while warning others not to charge them with any heresies.

The Federal Vision proponents often lecture others not to call them heretics. It would certainly be wrong to fling the charge of heresy against anyone who holds to the orthodoxy of the Scripture, but the Scripture also warns us that there are heretics in the church.

Several of the New Testament epistles were written to combat the various heresies besieging the first-century church, particularly Gnosticism. Philip Schaff, the great church historian, is undoubtedly correct in saying that the letter to the Colossians was written against

---

2 Steve Wilkins & Duane Garner, editors, *The Federal Vision* (Monroe, Louisiana: Athanasius Press, 2004), 13.

3 Ibid., 153.

the Gnostic heresy. According to Polycarp, the Apostle John wrote the fourth Gospel and his first epistle to refute the errors of an early Gnostic heretic named Cerinthus.[4]

What is Gnosticism?

The word Gnostic comes from the Greek word for "knowledge." Gnosticism claimed to impart a higher knowledge or enlightenment that the average Christian did not have. Gnosticism in the era of the apostles, though, was not as fully developed as it would become in the second and third centuries. Schaff describes the Gnostic heresy against which Paul wrote in Colossians:

> The Colossian heresy was an Essenic and ascetic type of Gnosticism; it derived its ritualistic and practical elements from Judaism, its speculative elements from heathenism; it retained circumcision, the observance of the Sabbaths and new moons, and the distinction of meats and drinks; but it mixed with it elements of oriental mysticism and theosophy, the heathen notion of an evil principle, the worship of subordinate spirits, and ascetic struggle for emancipation from the dominion of matter. It taught an antagonism between God and matter and interposed between them a series of angelic mediators as objects of worship. It thus contained the essential features of Gnosticism, but in its incipient and rudimental form, or a Christian Essenism in its transition to Gnosticism.[5]

Most evangelical commentators on Colossians have followed the conclusions of J. B. Lightfoot who defined the Colossian heresy as a type of Gnosticism which was essentially Christian Essenism, as opposed to Christian Pharisaism. The three main sects of the Jews were the Sadducees, the Pharisees, and the Essenes. The Sadducees never attempted to integrate with Christianity, but the Pharisees and the Essenes did. The Pharisees tried to bring into Christianity their legalistic ideas, and Paul's letter to the Galatians, in particular, was written to refute that heresy. The Essenes retained the legalism of the Pharisees, but added asceticism and a mystical speculation. Thus, this Essenic Gnosticism that troubled the Colossian church was ascetic, ritualistic, speculative, and mystical; it taught the evil of matter; and,

---

4 John McClintock and James Strong, *Cyclopedia of Biblical, Theological, and Ecclesiastical Literature*, Volume III (Grand Rapids, Michigan: Baker Book House, 1981), 893.

5 Philip Schaff, *History of the Christian Church*, Volume I, "Apostolic Christianity: A.D. 1-100" (Grand Rapids, Michigan: William B. Eerdmans Publishing Company, 1980), 773.

it worshiped subordinate spirits who were angelic mediators between God and men. As Lightfoot wrote:

> Gnosticism strove to establish, or rather, to preserve, an *intellectual oligarchy* in religion. It had its hidden wisdom, its exclusive mysteries, its privileged class.[6]

There is no doubt that many evangelical voices have called the teachings of the Federal Vision heretical. Some would say that this whole matter of name calling is simply a game of tit for tat, but there is a huge difference. The opponents of the Federal Vision have painstakingly documented how and why that teaching is heretical, but the Federal Vision has countered with charges of heresy against the orthodox Christian faith, especially the charge of Gnosticism, without substantiating those charges. They thus run the risk of falsely and slanderously caricaturing their opponents as heretics.

Augustine and Calvin Accused of Gnosticism

Apparently, the Augustinian doctrine of original sin is one of the reasons for the charge of Gnosticism against Augustinians and Calvinists. For instance, A. M. Fairweather, in his introduction to *Aquinas on Nature and Grace*, distinguished between Aquinas and Augustine as follows:

> His predecessor [Augustine] never seems to have freed himself entirely from the Manichean conviction of cosmic evil. His mystical doctrine of the fall extended the effects of a cosmic evil will to nature itself, so that all nature is corrupt, not only human nature. Reason in man remains, but it is helpless since it cannot operate apart from the will, which has lost freedom through sin. There is consequently a sharp division between the realm of nature and the realm of grace, such as renders it impossible to explain how man can be regenerated through grace without destroying the continuity of his own endeavour.[7]

Fairweather's assessment of Aquinas is exactly opposite of what Francis Schaeffer surmised in *Escape from Reason*. It was Aquinas, not Augustine, who was guilty of establishing a nature/grace dualism

---

6   J. B. Lightfoot, *Saint Paul's Epistles to the Colossians and to Philemon* (Grand Rapids, Michigan: Zondervan Publishing House, 1879 Reprint), 98.

7   A. M. Fairweather, trans. and ed., *Nature and Grace: Selections from the Summa Theologica of Thomas Aquinas* (Philadelphia: The Westminster Press, 1954), 21-22.

that resulted in nature becoming autonomous and, as Schaeffer said, "nature began to 'eat up' grace."[8]

Pelagius said Augustinianism was nothing but the Manichean heresy or Gnosticism, as William Cunningham noted:

> Some modern writers have contended, not only that the fathers of the second and third centuries taught anti-Calvinistic doctrines, but also that the Gnostic heretics, against whom they contended, taught Calvinism. This, however, proceeds upon a misrepresentation of Calvinistic doctrines, as if they really made God the author of sin, and took away from man that freedom of will which is necessary to moral agency.[9]

Yet, Bavinck describes Pelagius' cosmology which explains why he accused Augustine of Gnosticism:

> According to Pelagius, the image of God consisted solely in a free personality, not in positive holiness, immortality, and so on. Adam's trespass, according to him, did not deprive humans of the image of God and in fact had no adverse consequences whatsoever. There is no such thing as original sin. . . Hereditary transmission of sin is a Manichean error; sin is not a state but an act and always bears a personal stamp. . . [B]aptized parents can no longer propagate sin since it is eradicated by baptism. Sin, accordingly, is propagated not by generation but by imitation. . . In voicing these ideas, Pelagius did little more than take over the views that had been promulgated long before by Greek and Roman philosophers and had found acceptance in popular philosophy.[10]

Julian, the disciple of Pelagius, was quoted by Augustine as leveling this charge of Manichaeism (Gnosticism) against the Catholics for their doctrine of original sin:

> Those Manicheans say, with whom now we do not communicate,—that is, the whole of them with whom we differ,—that by the sin of the first man, that is, of Adam, free will perished: and that no one has now the power of living well, but that all are constrained into sin by the necessity of their flesh.[11]

---

8 Francis A. Schaeffer, *Escape From Reason* (London, England and Downers Grove, Illinois: Inter-Varsity Press, 1968), 13.

9 William Cunningham, *Historical Theology: A Review of the Principal Discussions in the Christian Church since the Apostolic Age*, Volume One (London: The Banner of Truth Trust, 1969), 182.

10 John Bolt, ed., John Vriend, trans. Herman Bavinck, *Reformed Dogmatics, Volume 3: Sin and Salvation in Christ* (Grand Rapids: Baker Academic, 2008), 86.

11 Philip Schaff, ed., Peter Holmes and Robert Ernest Wallis, trans., *Saint Augustin's Anti-Pelagian Writings* (Peabody, Massachusetts: Hendrickson Publishers, Inc., 1999), 378.

The next point in the acrostic T-U-L-I-P, unconditional election, has also resulted in that same charge. In the Reformation debate between Albertus Pighius (1490-1542), a zealous Dutch Roman Catholic, and John Calvin, Pighius assailed the doctrine of predestination with charges of heresies. In his work *The Bondage and Liberation of the Will*, Calvin comments on Pighius' accusations:

> [Pighius] mentions that it is derived from the ancient heretics, Priscillian, Mani, Marcion, Cerdo, and even Simon Magus himself, all of whom however, he says, Luther surpassed in impiety. . . The charge is an ancient and well-worn one, not discovered first by Pighius. For so once the Pelagians harassed Augustine, as though he held the same opinions as the Manichees. But truth always has a defence ready against empty, unfounded abuse.[12]

Key Assessment: Pelagius accused Augustine of Gnosticism and various Pelagians have accused other Reformed theologians, including Calvin, of being Gnostics.

Fairweather, Pighius, and others to the contrary, the Reformed and Augustinian doctrine of original sin is nothing like the Manichean/Gnostic heresy. Gnosticism, as this chapter will show, teaches that matter is essentially evil. The Scripture teaches that man's nature is corrupted by the fall, but was formerly upright and holy. In the Manichean theory of creation, Adam and Eve were created by the King of Darkness which made their human body of devilish substance and design.[13] J. B. Lightfoot describes the dilemma which faced the Gnostics in explaining the presence of sin in this world:

> To reconcile the creation of the world and the existence of evil with the conception of God as the absolute Being, was the problem which all Gnostic systems set themselves to solve. . . The Gnostic argument ran as follows: Did God create the world out of nothing, evolve it from Himself? Then, God being perfectly good and creation having resulted from His sole act without any opposing or modifying influence, evil would have been impossible; for otherwise we are driven to the conclusion that God created evil.
>
> The solution being rejected as impossible, the Gnostic was obliged to postulate some antagonistic principle independent of God, by which His creative energy was thwarted and limited. This opposing principle,

---

12 A. N. S. Lane, ed., G. I. Davies, trans., John Calvin, *The Bondage and Liberation of the Will* (Grand Rapids, Michigan: Baker Books, 2002), 42.

13 Hans Jonas, *The Gnostic Religion* (Boston: Beacon Press, 1963), 227.

the kingdom of evil, he conceived to be the world of matter. The precise idea of its mode of operation varies in different Gnostic systems. . . Thus Gnostic speculation on the existence of evil ends in a dualism.[14]

Christian theology is opposed to such dualism, and Calvin's comment on man's fall in Genesis 3 evidences his total rejection of the Manichean/Gnostic cosmology:

> God, therefore, permitted Satan to tempt man, who was conformed to His own image, and not yet implicated in any crime, having, moreover, on this occasion, allowed Satan the use of an animal which otherwise would never have obeyed him; and what else was this, than to arm an enemy for the destruction of man? This seems to have been the ground on which the Manicheans maintained the existence of two principles. Therefore, they have imagined that Satan, not being in subjection to the divine will, and was superior not to man only, but also to God himself. Thus, for the sake of avoiding what they dreaded as an absurdity, they have fallen into execrable prodigies of error; such as, that there are two Gods, and not one sole Creator of the world, and that the first God has been overcome by his antagonist.[15]

Thus, the primary reason for the charge of Gnosticism against Calvinists is the rejection of either original sin or God's sovereign grace in salvation by the accusers. Both Pelagius and Pighius denied those scriptural truths. The Manicheans taught that the substance or essence of man was evil which is not the same thing as the doctrine of original sin. Calvin clarifies the issue for us:

> Those who say that the [human] nature must be healed differ greatly from the Manichees, because it could not be healed if the evil were eternal and unchangeable, as in Mani's dreams. Those who say that evil is accidental to our nature are greatly opposed to the Manichees, who assign it to its substance. Those who teach that [human] choice is free only to do evil, but at the same time acknowledge that it originated from that which is not evil, are not at all close to the Manichees, but powerfully refute their error.[16]

From these quotes, it can clearly be seen that Augustinianism/Calvinism has nothing in common with the dualistic view of creation

---

14 Lightfoot, *Colossians and Philemon*, 77-78.

15 John King, trans. and ed., John Calvin, *Genesis* (Edinburgh, Scotland and Carlisle, Pennsylvania: The Banner of Truth Trust, 1975), 143, 144.

16 Lane, ed., Calvin, *Bondage and Liberation of the Will*, 48.

and the entrance of sin into the world held by the Manichees and the Gnostics. It is simply a scurrilous lie to paint Augustine, Calvin, and the Protestant Reformers as adherents to Gnosticism.

The Federal Vision's Charge that Protestants are Gnostics

One of the interesting things about proponents of both the New Perspectives of Paul and the Federal Vision is their repeated accusations that Protestant Christians today are guilty of the heresy of Gnosticism. In that aspect, they are following Pelagius, Julian, Pighius, and others who have protested against Augustinianism/Calvinism with the same charge. For instance, N. T. Wright quotes favorably from a book by Philip J. Lee, *Against the Protestant Gnostics*, that American Protestant Christianity is rife with Gnosticism. Wright's assessment of Lee's thesis is as follows:

> His thesis, which has received enthusiastic reviews from theologians and cultural critics alike, is that a kind of Gnosticism has been deeply entrenched in North American Protestant Christianity, and that it has generated all kinds of ills not only in the church but in the wider society. His book... is a polemic whose time has, I believe, more than fully come.
>
> Lee categorizes the typical American religion as elitist: it favors the self-knowing individual over the believing community. It has regularly opted for what he calls "selective syncretism" over against the particularity of actual religious traditions. It is both escapist, withdrawing from the world of politics and society, and narcissistic, seeking its identity and fulfillment. In its rejection of the goodness of creation, it has invited Americans to think of the natural world simply as a place to exploit, opening up the imagination to embrace ecological carelessness and wanton violence—which as Lee points out in the preface to the paperback edition, has been an increasingly disturbing feature of American public life.[17]

Lee says that Gnosticism in America goes all the way back to the Calvinistic Founding Fathers of America—an opinion which even Wright admits goes too far. Lee's assertion of what constitutes Gnosticism in American Protestantism is hard to justify according to what that heresy actually taught. The essence of his accusation seems to be that American Protestants are escapists who fail to see the goodness of creation and who view the creation as inherently evil. Gnosticism

---

17 N. T. Wright, *Judas and the Gospel of Jesus: Have We Missed the Truth about Christianity?* (Grand Rapids, Michigan: Baker Books, 2006), 125-126.

certainly taught the evil of matter, but that is not the position of Protestantism as we have shown above.

An example of the autonomy of nature which Schaeffer said resulted from Aquinas' theology can be found in Doug Wilson's response to B. B. Warfield's statement, that "any view which says God uses any means to accomplish His purposes in salvation is a corrupted or impure salvation,"[18] by accusing him of Gnosticism:

> What Warfield thought of as "pure supernaturalism" is actually closer to a refried Gnosticism, an invisible conduit from God to man, with no contact made with contaminating earthly, incarnational influences.[19]

Wilson is keen on putting words in other people's mouths and marshaling his forces against straw men. His objection to Warfield's quote above is driven by his own emphasis on the "objectivity of the covenant" in which the external elements of the sacraments become the conduits for salvation. Thus, salvation in Wilson's view is through the means of the external sacraments.

Wilson, of course, is not the only Federal Vision proponent to charge his opponents with being Gnostics. Another one who does so is Peter Leithart who, in *Against Christianity*, made this provocative statement which has more heat than light, and is unsubstantiated by facts:

> The Bible never mentions Christianity. It does not preach Christianity, nor does it encourage us to preach Christianity. Paul did not preach Christianity, nor did any of the other apostles. During centuries when the Church was strong and vibrant, she did not preach Christianity either. Christianity, like Judaism and "Yahwism", is an invention of biblical scholars, theologians, and politicians, and one of its chief effects is to keep Christians and the Church in their proper marginal place. The Bible speaks of Christians and of the Church, but Christianity is gnostic, and the Church firmly rejected gnosticism from her earliest days.[20]

The same people—Wright, Wilson, Wilkins, Leithart and others—lecture others not to refer to them as heretics, but they have been call-

---

18 Guy Prentiss Waters, *The Federal Vision and Covenant Theology* (Phillipsburg, New Jersey: P&R Publishing, 2006), 198.

19 Ibid.

20 Peter J. Leithart, *Against Christianity* (Moscow, Idaho: Canon Press, 2003). Accessed at: http://www.goodreads.com/author/quotes/68223.Peter_J_Leithart on October 22, 2014.

ing evangelical and Reformed Christians heretics since at least 2004. They accuse them of being Gnostics. There is nothing new about this charge.

Ebionism and Gnosticism

Heresy appeared in two leading forms during the first centuries of Christianity, and these two forms were polar opposites. One form was Ebionism and the other was Gnosticism. Ebionism was an effort to Christianize Judaism. Gnosticism was an effort to Christianize heathenism. Philip Schaff describes the difference between them:

> Ebionism is a particularistic contraction of the Christian religion; Gnosticism, a vague expansion of it. The one is a gross realism and literalism; the other a fantastic idealism and spiritualism. In the former the spirit is bound in outward forms; in the latter it revels in licentious freedom. Ebionism makes salvation depend on observance of the law; Gnosticism, on speculative knowledge. Under the influence of Judaistic legalism, Christianity must stiffen and petrify; under the influence of Gnostic speculation, it must dissolve into empty notions and fancies.[21]

Making a chart of Schaff's quote will help us to see the differences between these two heresies.

EBIONISM	GNOSTICISM
Jewish Contraction of Christianity	Heathenistic Expansion of Christianity
Grossly Realistic and Literal	Idealistic and Spiritual
Outward Forms	Licentious Freedom
Observance of the Law	Speculative Knowledge
Christianity Stiffens and Petrifies	Empty Notions and Fancies

From this chart, it is easy to see that the Federal Vision is similar, in many ways, to the ancient heresy of Ebionism. It is a Judaizing of Christianity; as was Ebionism. It places great emphasis on the literal. For instance, its advocates interpret every mention of baptism in the New Testament as a reference to water. Like Pelagius, they emphasize the objective, external, and mediate aspects of the sacraments while denying the subjective, internal, and immediate aspects of them. Out-

---

21 Philip Schaff, *History of the Christian Church,* Volume II, "Ante-Nicene Christianity: A.D. 100-325" (Grand Rapids, Michigan: William B. Eerdmans Publishing Company, 1980), 429-430.

ward forms are important in their scheme. Participation in the rite of baptism and the Lord's Supper, membership in the visible church, and other things give an outward, formal tint to their religion. Observance of the law, particularly with many of them adhering to theonomy, is another characteristic of the Federal Vision. Covenant faithfulness is another name for legalism or law-keeping. In all these ways, the Federal Vision is similar to Ebionism. Therefore, they view those who disagree with them as being opposed to their legalism—as being licentious, speculative, falsely spiritual, fanciful, and antinomian. The true Christian position is neither of these polar opposite heresies; both Gnosticism and Ebionism are wrong.

Yet, there were ways in which these polar opposite heresies, Ebionism and Gnosticism, were combined. One of those was the Judaizing Gnosticism of Cerinthus who was opposed by the Beloved Disciple, John. It is this writer's opinion, after careful reflection, that the Federal Vision is guilty of a Judaizing Gnosticism. No matter how their system is analyzed by others, the proponents of the Federal Vision dismiss such assessments as not really understanding them. How can the Federal Vision be a theology which appeals to the masses if it is so difficult to understand that even theologians are incapable of so doing? Of course, it cannot, but the objection they make to assessments of their views reveals their latent Gnosticism. Their system is misunderstood even by theologians, they say. You have to be inside the Federal Vision movement before you can really understand it.

Summary

N. T. Wright, Doug Wilson, Steve Wilkins, and Peter Leithart, among others in the Federal Vision or New Perspectives movements, frequently accuse Protestant and Reformed Christians of being Gnostic in their views. This chapter references several of those accusations. Pelagius accused Augustine of Gnosticism. Julian accused Catholicism of being Gnostic. Calvin was accused of the same thing. There are a few illegitimate reasons for such accusations. First, legalists always accuse their opponents of being antinomian which was one of the errors of Gnosticism. Therefore, the charge of Gnosticism naturally follows. Second, the charge of Gnosticism is often made by legalists and Pelagians against those who hold to the innate sinfulness of mankind and to the divine sovereignty. The Federal Vision clearly has problems with unconditional election, as Chapter 11 of this book documented. All of their other positions are pushing them in the direction of also denying the innate sinfulness of mankind at some point. Accusing evangelical Christians of being Gnostic will only speed up that process.

Conclusion

The history of doctrine shows that when an ancient heresy is revived it usually begins by people adopting the conclusions of that heresy and working their way back to the first principles. Whereas Pelagius started with the principle of the innocence of infants and developed his whole theology around it, those who rediscover his system will usually start at the opposite end. The Federal Vision movement has not yet denied the innate sinfulness of mankind—not yet, but they will do so, or their children will. Yet, it is a mistake to reduce Pelagianism to only an heretical view of man. Pelagianism is a full-orbed system, as A. A. Hodge stated, that includes wrong views of man, Christ, salvation, the atonement, the Law, the Gospel, the covenants, the Spirit, the sacraments, regeneration, free grace, election, perseverance, and all the doctrines of salvation. A person can be Pelagian in his or her theology on most of the above doctrines without having already adopted all the view of Pelagianism.

That false doctrine of anthropology will probably enter their theology through their decision to cast their opponents as Gnostics. History shows that flinging the charge of Gnosticism against one's opponents without justification is usually an indication that the doctrine of sin is being denied. That was the case with Pelagius, Julian, and Pighius, among many others, and it will probably also prove to be the case with the Federal Vision proponents. In fact, there are already disturbing trends that indicate the scriptural doctrine of total depravity will be the next domino to fall. One of those trends is the development of the doctrine of infant faith which is moving forward at breakneck speed among them. Another trend is their denial of the necessity of supernatural regeneration. What Bavinck wrote concerning Old Testament scholarship will prove prophetic for the Federal Vision also:

> In Old Testament biblical criticism today, accordingly, all the opinions have returned that in the past were advocated by the Gnostics, Anabap-

tists, Socinians, and Rationalists concerning the Old Testament.[22]

N. T. Wright and the Federal Vision proponents are redefining the sinfulness of man (or lack thereof) by their constant attacks against Protestant Christianity as being Gnostic. There might be some doubt in the minds of some people concerning the Federal Vision at the moment, but in another generation or two it will all be clear. It will then be obvious that this movement is Pelagianism revived.

---

22 Bavinck, *Reformed Dogmatics*, Volume 3, 212.

-22-

The Federal Vision: Another Gospel

"I am convinced that what the Federal Vision offers is not a renewal or improvement of the historic Reformed faith but a wholesale replacement of it with a curious hybrid affecting soteriology, sacramentology, and ecclesiology, closely similar to and heavily influenced by the New Perspectives on Paul associated with James D. G. Dunn, E. P. Sanders, and N. T. Wright."[1]

CALVIN BEISNER IN THE FOREWORD TO GUY PRENTISS WATERS' BOOK, "THE FEDERAL VISION AND COVENANT THEOLOGY: A COMPARATIVE ANALYSIS"

---

1 E. Calvin Beisner in Guy Prentiss Waters, *The Federal Vision and Covenant Theology: A Comparative Analysis* (Phillipsburg, New Jersey: P&R Publishing, 2006), viii.

George Gillespie, one of the Scottish commissioners to the Westminster Assembly in 1643, once defined heresy with these words:

> Heresy is a gross and dangerous error, voluntarily held and factiously maintained by some person or persons within the visible church, in opposition to some chief or substantial truth or truths grounded upon and drawn from the holy Scripture by necessary consequences.[2]

In writing this book, the title, *The Federal Vision: None Dare Call it Heresy*, was considered for two reasons. First, there is a strange reluctance in Reformed denominations to exercise discipline on the proponents of the Federal Vision or the New Perspectives on Paul. Perhaps the courts of Reformed denominations think they are being more loving by accommodating these false views, but the Scripture counsels otherwise. Second, both the proponents of the Federal Vision and their defenders lecture others not to accuse them of heresy. Yet, there is nothing that the Scripture warns against more frequently than false doctrine or heresy.

False Prophets

In Matthew 7:15, Christ says, "Beware of the false prophets, who come to you in sheep's clothing, but inwardly are ravenous wolves." A wolf in sheep's clothing is pretending to be something it is not. In Jesus' parable of the Good Shepherd, the wolf "comes only to steal and kill and destroy."[3] Dr. D. Martyn Lloyd-Jones, in his *Studies in the Sermon on Mount*, makes the following comment on such false prophets:

> You notice the very terms in which He puts it, this picture of the sheep's clothing. He suggests that the real difficulty about this kind of false prophet is that at first you never imagine that he is such. The whole thing is extremely subtle, so much so that God's people can be misled by it. . . They look like the right people; they have sheep's clothing on, no one suspects anything false. Now the Bible, in the Old and Testament and in the New, always brings out that characteristic of the false prophet. It is his subtlety that really constitutes the danger.[4]

---

2 George Gillespie, *The Works of George Gillespie*, Volume 2 (Edmonton, Alberta, Canada: Still Water Revival Books, 1991), 49.

3 John 10:10.

4 D. Martyn Lloyd-Jones, *Studies in the Sermon on the Mount*, Two volumes in one, Volume II (Grand Rapids, Michigan: William B. Eerdmans Publishing Company, 1972), 243.

Moses warned the Israelites not to be deceived by false prophets (Deuteronomy 18:20-22). The Old Testament prophets themselves often warned against false prophets who proclaim, "Peace, peace, but there is no peace" (Jeremiah 8:11). In the New Testament, every author warns against heresy or false doctrine. Paul counsels Christians to watch "those who cause dissensions and hindrances contrary to the teaching which you have learned, and turn away from them" who "by their smooth and flattering speech. . . deceive the hearts of the unsuspecting" (Romans 16:17, 18; cf. also 1 Corinthians 16:13; 2 Corinthians 11:3,4; Galatians 1:6-8; Ephesians 4:14; Philippians 3:2, 18; Colossians 2:6-8; and 2 Thessalonians 2:2, 3). James counsels Christians to try to win back those who stray from the truth (James 5:19, 20). Peter prophesies of the rise of false teachers who will "introduce destructive heresies" (2 Peter 2:1-3) and "distort. . . the Scriptures, to their own destruction" (2 Peter 3:16-18). John advises his readers to "test the spirits to see whether they are from God" (1 John 4:1) and that "anyone who goes too far and does not abide in the teaching of Christ, does not have God" (2 John 9). Jude, after encouraging believers to "contend earnestly for the faith which was once for all handed down to the saints" (Jude 3), describes the heretics as "certain persons who have crept in unnoticed. . . who turn the grace of our God into licentiousness" (Jude 4), who "revile the things which they do not understand" (Jude 10), and "who are hidden reefs in your love feasts" (Jude 12). Christ, in His letters to the seven churches, commended the church at Ephesus because they "put to the test those who call themselves apostles, and they are not, and you found them to be false" (Revelation 2:2), but rebuked the churches at Pergamum and Thyatira because they endured false teaching (Revelation 2:14, 15, 20).

The Heresy of Pelagianism
In chapter after chapter, this book has documented that the Federal Vision is guilty of heresy, particularly Semi-Pelagianism and Pelagianism. The similarities between the Federal Vision / New Perspectives on Paul and such heresies are remarkable and striking. The Federal Vision and the New Perspectives on Paul agree with the Pelagian spectrum of heresies in the following areas:

- in either denying supernatural regeneration by the Spirit is necessary or making it a non-essential doctrine;
- in defining grace in an overly objective and external sense;
- in denying the necessity of the subjective, internal grace of the Holy Spirit;
- in denying the distinction between the law and the promise; or, the distinction between the covenant of works and the covenant of grace;
- in making infant baptism the paradigm for all baptism, contrary to Scripture;
- in asserting that the benefits and graces of Christ are bestowed through the act of water baptism;
- in teaching a form of baptismal regeneration;
- in denying or downplaying the distinction between common and special grace;
- in denying that the grace that bestows the benefits of Christ's redemption is always efficacious;
- in teaching a covenant election of all the baptized that is conditional;
- in denying that justification is by faith alone and is once-for-all;
- in denying that the perfect righteousness of Christ is imputed to all His people;
- in teaching that salvation is by covenant faithfulness or the keeping of the law;
- in denying the certainty of perseverance;
- in teaching that justification is not final until the judgment when it will be based on one's faithful good works.
- in accusing its opponents of Gnosticism and antinomianism.

There is only one soteriological doctrine in which the Federal Vision or the New Perspectives on Paul does not yet *overtly* agree with Pelagianism. That is the Pelagian doctrine of the native innocence of all humans from birth. Yet, that doctrine is essential to all their other views on soteriology. Eventually the Federal Vision and New Perspectives on Paul will adopt that view also—probably sooner than later.

Thus, the Federal Vision proponents are in the unusual position of trying to hold to two different and contradictory systems of theology in a very tenuous relationship. Their membership and ordination in Reformed denominations require them to affirm the Reformed faith, but their views on the Federal Vision are contrary to that profession. Christ said no man can serve two masters. What B. B. Warfield once said about Lewis Sperry Chafer can be said about them:

> Mr. Chafer is in the unfortunate and, one would think, very uncomfortable condition of having two inconsistent systems of religion struggling together in his mind.[5]

Only One Gospel

In the scholarly debates with and analyses of the Federal Vision and the New Perspectives of Paul, the essential issue can easily be missed. That issue is that there is only one gospel. There cannot be two very different messages of the gospel. There is only one way for a sinner to gain reconciliation and justification with God. The Apostle Paul made that point very clear in Galatians:

> I am amazed that you are so quickly deserting Him who called you by the grace of Christ, for a different gospel; which is really not another; only there are some who are disturbing you and want to distort the gospel of Christ. But even if we, or an angel from heaven, should preach to you a gospel contrary to what we have preached to you, he is to be accursed! As we have said before, so I say again now, if any man is preaching to you a gospel contrary to what we have preached to you, he is to be accursed! (Galatians 1:6-9).

B. B. Warfield, in *The Plan of Salvation*, succinctly stated the difference between true and false doctrines concerning the gospel:

> There are fundamentally only two doctrines of salvation: that salvation is from God, and that salvation is from ourselves. The former is the doctrine of common Christianity; the latter is the doctrine of universal heathenism.[6]

Later in that same chapter, Warfield identified Pelagianism as the doctrine of heathenism which teaches that salvation is from man's efforts or works. Thus, the conflict is between salvation by free grace alone and salvation by works; between the gospel of God's free grace in Christ and the doctrines of heathenism. Whereas A. A. Hodge saw

---

5 Waters, *Federal Vision and Covenant Theology*, 300.

6 B. B. Warfield, *The Plan of Salvation* (Grand Rapids, Michigan: Wm. B. Eerdmans Publishing Co., 1970), 33.

only two complete, self-consistent systems of theology (Augustinianism completed in Calvinism or Pelagianism completed in Socinianism), Warfield identifies the latter system of works salvation with heathenism. Both those great theologians are correct. Between these two positions, there is no stable, middle ground.

Every theological system, ancient or modern, can be grouped broadly under one or the other of these two complete, self-consistent systems. Arminianism and Semi-Pelagianism are simply incomplete and unstable systems arising from Pelagianism. At various times, those systems of compromise approximate closer to either Calvinism or Pelagianism. Defining precisely the inconsistent systems of Christian theology, such as Semi-Pelagianism, is difficult, as William Cunningham acknowledged in the first volume of *Historical Theology*:

> Semi-pelagianism—which may be regarded as describing, in general, views that make some approach to Pelagianism, but do not go quite so far—is of a much more vague and indefinite character.[7]

Are the Federal Vision and the New Perspectives on Paul Heresies?

The two best books on the New Perspectives on Paul are Cornelis P. Venema's *The Gospel of Free Acceptance in Christ* and Waters' *Justification and the New Perspectives on Paul*. Both books refer to the theology of the New Perspectives on Paul (NPP) as being essentially Semi-Pelagian. For instance, Waters comments:

> NPP teaching undercuts Paul's repeated affirmation that the doctrine of justification by faith is one of "grace" (Rom. 4:4-5; 11:6) and that it precludes "boasting" (Eph. 2:9). If, as we have seen, Paul counterposes works and grace (Roman. 11:6; 4:4-6), and pairs works and boasting (Eph. 2:9), then the scheme of the NPP (which make faith in justification effectively faithfulness) are defective. In other words, the apostle and the NPP define grace in entirely different ways. For justification to be of grace to Paul, it must not embrace human activity (even the activity of the renewed) in any way. For the NPP, justification may still be gracious although it takes into consideration the labors of a believer assisted by grace. We might anachronistically speak of Paul as an Augustinian and his NPP interpreters as semi-Pelagians. However we define this difference, there is a theological divide between Paul and the proponents of the NPP.[8]

---

7 William Cunningham, *Historical Theology*, Volume I, (London: The Banner of Truth Trust, 1969), 323.

8 Guy Prentiss Waters, *Justification and the New Perspectives on Paul* (Phillipsburg, New Jersey:

In Chapter 16, we quoted from Venema's book, *The Gospel of Free Acceptance in Christ*, where he defined covenantal nomism as similar to Semi-Pelagianism.[9] Nomism is what Pelagius taught according to Augustine and is identified by Herman Bavinck and others as a form of Pelagianism. For instance, David J. Engelsma, in *Federal Vision: Heresy at the Root*, wrote that the Federal Vision is a form of Pelagianism:

> In addition, the theology of the federal vision openly teaches the semi-Pelagian, Roman Catholic doctrine of justification by faith and works. The federal vision is a form of Arminianism and Pelagian doctrine, the origin of which is hell.[10]

When the Synod of Dort repudiated the theology of the Remonstrants, which is known popularly as Arminianism, they compared it to Pelagianism:

> For they have too low an opinion of the death of Christ, do not at all acknowledge the foremost fruit or benefit which it brings forth, and summon back from hell the Pelagian error.[11]

The Puritans, according to J. I. Packer, likewise saw the fraternal relationship between Pelagianism and Counter-Reformation Romanism:

> The Puritans saw that trio of theological relatives, Pelagianism, Arminianism, and Counter-reformation Romanism, as the bastard offspring of natural religion fertilized by the gospel.[12]

The Reformers Accused the Papacy of Pelagianism

The Catholic Church at the time of the Reformation acknowledged the native depravity of humanity in some sense and taught that grace was necessary as an aid to salvation. Yet, the following quotes from the Reformers prove conclusively that they saw many of the errors of

---

P&R Publishing, 2004), 174.

9 Cornelis P. Venema, *The Gospel of Free Acceptance in Christ* (Edinburgh, Scotland and Carlisle, Pennsylvania: Banner of Truth Trust, 2006), 300.

10 David J. Engelsma, *Federal Vision: Heresy at the Root* (Jenison, Michigan: Reformed Free Publishing Association, 2012), 178.

11 Canons of Dort, Rejection of Errors, Second Head, Paragraph 3. Accessed at: http://carm.org/canons-of-dort on October 22, 2014.

12 J. I. Packer, *A Quest for Godliness; The Puritan Vision of the Christian Life* (Wheaton, Illinois: Crossway Books, 1990), 151.

the Papacy during the Medieval Ages and the Reformation as being Pelagian in root.

Almost two hundred years before the Reformation, Thomas Bradwardine, chaplain to the King of England, Edward III, wrote against the abuses perpetuated by the sale of indulgences:

> The number of those who strive with Pelagius against thy free grace cannot be counted. They pretend not to receive grace freely, but to buy it.[13]

Bradwardine goes beyond merely condemning the selling of indulgences as an abuse, and asserts that the entire practice was an attempt to buy God's grace. Philip Schaff tells us what these Medieval indulgences were:

> The ultimate and, as it proved, a most vicious form of priestly absolution was the indulgence. An indulgence is a remission of the guilt and punishment by a mitigation or a complete setting aside of the works of satisfaction which would otherwise be required... Towards the close of this period this substitution usually took the form of a money payment. For a lump sum absolution for the worst offences might be secured.[14]

Indulgences were sold by the church for almost any offence and usually consisted of a piece of paper which declared the guilt and punishment for the sin was remitted. Indulgences were also secured through crusades or pilgrimages to certain churches. Indulgences were a lesser form of works salvation than works of penance. Pelagianism provided the theological basis for the selling of indulgences which led to Martin Luther nailing his ninety-five theses to the door of the Wittenberg Church on October 31, 1517. The greatest historian of the Reformation, J. H. Merle d'Aubigne, said that the "ninety-five propositions that Luther put forth in the Church [were] against the Pelagian rationalism of the scholastic theology."[15] d'Aubigne also put his finger on the fundamental issue between the Reformers and the Papists:

---

13 J. H. Merle d'Aubigne, *The Reformation in England*, Volume One (London: The Banner of Truth Trust, 1971), 76.

14 Philip Schaff, *History of the Christian Church*, Volume V, The Middle Ages (Grand Rapids, Michigan: Wm. B. Eerdmans Publishing Company, 1981), 737.

15 J. H. Merle d'Aubigne, *History of the Reformation of the Sixteenth Century*, Volume I (Grand Rapids, Michigan: Baker Book House, 1976), 82.

The Papists with Pelagius asserting man's freedom would keep him in slavery, the Reformers showing him his fetters and how they may be struck off, were the true advocates of liberty, the questions were between a liberty proceeding from man's nature and a liberty that cometh from God.[16]

d'Aubigne's assessment of the theological situation at the time of the Reformation is further supported by direct quotes from the Reformers themselves. In the third chapter of the second book of the *Institutes of the Christian Religion*, John Calvin said:

> Now let us hear Augustine speaking in his own words, lest the Pelagians of our own age, that is the Sophists of the Sorbonne[17], according to their custom, charge that all antiquity is against us.[18]

Concerning the Roman Catholic Church doctrines on God's grace and man's good works, from the time of the Schoolmen forward, Calvin said:

> These schools have gone continually from bad to worse until, in headlong ruin, they have plunged into a sort of Pelagianism.[19]

Martin Luther, in his *Bondage of the Will*, which was known as the "Manifesto of the Reformation," accuses Erasmus and the Roman Catholic Church of being even lower than the Pelagians in their selling of indulgences:

> This hypocrisy of theirs results in their valuing the grace of God at a much cheaper rate than the Pelagians. The latter assert that it is not by a feeble something within us that we obtain grace, but by efforts and works that are complete, entire, perfect, many and mighty; but our friends here tell us that it is something very small, almost nothing, that we merit grace.[20]

---

16 Lewis Cheeseman, *Differences Between Old and New School Presbyterians* (Rochester, New York: Erastus Darrow, 1848), 10. Quoted from the introduction by John C. Lord.

17 This phrase, "Sophists of the Sorbonne," refers to the faculty of the University of Paris, a medieval Roman Catholic university. Calvin, as a Frenchman, was very familiar with this institution and singles them out as Pelagians. Calvin believed that what was true of the "Sophists of the Sorbonne" was also true about the Roman Catholic Church as a whole.

18 John T. McNeill, ed., Ford Lewis Battles, trans., *Calvin: Institutes of the Christian Religion*, Volume One (Philadelphia: The Westminster Press, 1967), 307.

19 Ibid., 745.

20 Martin Luther, *Bondage of the Will* (Old Tappan, New Jersey: Fleming H. Revell Company, 1957), 293-294.

Philip Melancthon, the intellectual leader of the Lutheran branch of the Reformation, likewise accused the Papists of being Pelagians:

> Although the papists speak of original sin, they are fundamentally Pelagian, for they say that inborn doubt and evil tendency are not sins, but things indifferent, like eating and drinking. . .
>
> They further say that a man can, with natural strength, entirely fulfill God's law, that man can merit forgiveness of sins through good works, that man thus becomes upright before God, and that God is pleased on account of the external good works. . .
>
> From the time of Cain human reason in certain people has thus rationalized this matter. So the Pharisees taught, and until the end of the world such pharisaic, Pelagian errors will be voiced by many people. The true Church, knowing divine judgment against sin, must combat this error, and must preach the voice of the gospel of the Son of God, as John says, "Behold, the Lamb of God, who takes away the sin of the world" [1:29]! He who imagines, as do the Pharisees, Pelagians, and papists, that our works merit forgiveness of sins robs the Lord Christ of his glory.[21]

William Tyndale, called the Apostle of England for his work in translating the New Testament and the Pentateuch into vernacular English, accused the priests of the Roman Catholic Church of being Pelagians in his exposition of Matthew 6:22, 23:

> Faith of works[22] is that belief of the Turks and Jews, which driveth them ever away from Christ. Faith of works hath been that light of darkness in which a great part of us Christen have walked ever since Pelagius and Faustus, well about twelve hundred years, and ever more and more too, this four or five hundred year; and in which the priests also have walked a long season: the Lord bring them out again.
>
> Finally: how dark is the darkness, when a Pharisee and a very Pelagian standeth up, and preacheth against the Pharisees and Pelagians, and is allowed of all the audience! And, in conclusion, when the world, ever since it began, hath and doth of natural blindness believe in their own works: then, if scripture be perverted to confirm that error, how sure are their hearts hardened, and how deep is that darkness.[23]

---

21 Clyde L. Manschreck, trans. and ed., *Melancthon on Christian Doctrine* (New York: Oxford University Press, 1965), 79.

22 By this phrase, "faith of works," Tyndale means faith in works or trusting in works for salvation.

23 Henry Walter, ed., *Works of William Tyndale*, Volume 2 (Edinburgh, Scotland and Carlisle, Pennsylvania: The Banner of Truth Trust, 2010), 104. This work is a reprint from the Parker Society which was first published in 1849.

The Federal Vision: Another Gospel

Tyndale was referring to the practice of the Papists to deny that they were Pelagians in their doctrine. The Papists were well aware that Pelagianism had been condemned by the Council of Ephesus in A.D. 431, but they did not want to come down on the side of Augustinianism either. When the Council of Trent was called by Rome in 1546, the Council members attempted to frame their general statements in such ways that both Protestants and Catholics would be pleased. Yet, Trent is a deceptive creed which led William Cunningham to declare that "on many points the decisions of the Council of Trent are expressed with deliberate and intentional ambiguity."[24] The Council of Trent was a ruse in an effort to draw back the Protestants to Rome. Thus, Cunningham concluded:

> There is certainly not so much Pelagianism[25] in the decrees and canons of the Council of Trent as appears in the writings of the earlier Romish opponents of Luther, though there is enough to entitle us to charge the Church of Rome with perverting the gospel of the grace of God, and subverting the scriptural method of salvation.[26]

Nicholas Ridley, Bishop of London, was a martyr for the faith during the Marian Persecutions and was burned at the stake in Oxford England in October 16, 1555, along with Thomas Cranmer and Hugh Latimer. Ridley wrote to John Bradford, prebendary of St. Paul's Church in London, in the middle of April, 1555. At that date, Ridley was imprisoned at the Bocardo Prison in Oxford and Bradley was a prisoner in the London Tower. Ridley accused the Papacy of being guilty of the heresy of Pelagianism:

> Whereas you write of the outrageous rule, that Satan our ghostly enemy beareth abroad in the world—whereby he stirreth and raiseth so pestilent and heinous heresies—as some deny the blessed Trinity, some the Divinity of our Savior Christ, some the divinity of the Holy Ghost, some the baptism of infants, some original sin, and to be infected with the error of the Pelagians, and to re-baptize those that have been baptized with Christ's baptism already—alas! Sir, this doth declare that this time and these days to be wicked indeed.[27]

---

24 Cunningham, *Historical Theology*, Volume I, 493.

25 A. A. Hodge referenced Cunningham's chapter, "Council of Trent" in the first volume of *Historical Theology* to prove that the Council of Trent was Semipelagian, not Pelagian. Yet, Cunningham never used the phrase "semipelagianism" in this chapter.

26 Cunningham, *Historical Theology*, Volume I, 494.

27 Aubrey Townsend, ed., *The Writings of John Bradford*, Volume 2 (Edinburgh, Scotland and

Bradford had written to Cranmer, Ridley and Latimer on January 18, 1555, shortly after his imprisonment, concerning a man named Harry Hart and some others who had separated from the Reformed churches in England and "held the opinions of the Anabaptists and Pelagians."[28] These men particularly denied the grace of God in election. Bradford said:

> In free-will they are plain papists, yea Pelagians.[29]

Concerning Pelagianism in the Church of Rome, Cunningham wrote two centuries ago:

> The apostate Church of Rome has preserved throughout an orthodox profession on the subject of the Trinity; but though precluded by her avowed principles from professing Pelagian doctrines, which have been frequently anathematized by popes and councils, she has always, in her practical teaching, exhibited a large amount of Pelagian error, and may be said to have become formally liable to the charge of teaching Pelagianism, in consequence of the general adoption by the church of the famous Bull Unigenitus, against the Jansenists, published in the early part of the last century.[30]

It is clear, therefore, that the Protestant Reformers believed the specific heresy they were combating at the time of the Reformation was Pelagianism. There has never been a distinct body of Christians or any particular denomination which has formally adopted Pelagianism as its confession of faith. While few people have fully agreed with Pelagius in denying original sin, the errors of Pelagianism on other important doctrines have been asserted by many people in various denominations, including some people even in the Reformed and Presbyterian branches of the church.

Carlisle, Pennsylvania: The Banner of Truth Trust, 1979), 213. This work also is a reprint from the Parker Society of 1849 and 1853.

28 Waters, *Justification and the New Perspectives*, 171.

29 Ibid.

30 Cunningham, *Historical Theology*, Volume 1, 322. The Jansenists were a party in the Roman Catholic Church led by Cornelius Jansen. They emphasized predestination, denied free will and maintained human nature is incapable of doing what is good. Pope Clement XI anathematized the doctrines of the Jansenists as heresy on September 8, 1713.

Summary

That the Federal Vision system is heresy can scarcely be denied by any Reformed theologian. Every Reformed scholar who has written on the subject has accused the system of at least the heresy of Semi-Pelagianism. It is probably better to simply state concerning the Federal Vision what William Cunningham said about Rome at the time of the Reformation, that is, that the system exhibits a large amount of Pelagian error.

Conclusion

The charge of Semi- Pelagianism or Pelagianism against the Federal Vision and the New Perspectives on Paul seems unfounded to many people. The Reformed faith is the opposite of Pelagianism. Thus, it is unimaginable to some that ministers who subscribe to a Reformed confession could imbibe Pelagianism in any form. Yet, such a scenario is more realistic than seems at first glance. Pelagianism has been a problem in Reformed churches on many occasions. The Reformed faith is a very cerebral system, and the intellectual stimulation of it is attractive to many people. Therein is the danger. The objective truths of the gospel can become intellectually intoxicating while the subjective necessity of regeneration and the indwelling of the Holy Spirit are denied or ignored. Pelagianism is the inevitable result either way. Some become Pelagians in practice while others are Pelagians by conviction. People who initially espouse Reformed doctrine can easily slide into the error of Pelagianism through the denial of subjective grace and the neglect of heart religion.

Dr. G. Aiken Taylor, former editor of *The Presbyterian Journal* and former moderator of the Presbyterian Church in America, now deceased, once wrote about theonomy and theonomists that tying them to a position was tantamount to trying to pick up quicksilver with your fingers. The same thing could be written about the advocates of the Federal Vision. The problem is that they use theological terms and nomenclature in ways different from the accepted meaning of the words. That is their problem, not ours. When the theological nomenclature of the proponents of the Federal Vision is the same as the theological nomenclature of the heretics of the past, then we must recognize the essential agreement of the Federal Vision with those heresies.

On July 17, 2014, *The Aquila Report* reprinted online the response of Clarence McCartney to the well-known sermon of Harry Emerson

Fosdick, "Shall the Fundamentalists Win?", which was preached at the First Presbyterian Church of New York City on May 21, 1922.

McCartney responded six weeks later with a message which asked the question, "Shall Unbelief Win?" In that message, he wrote a poem which poignantly framed the issue in that great battle between fundamentalism and modernism:

> To sin by silence when we should protest
> Makes cowards out of men. The human race
> Has climbed on protest. Had no voice been raised
> Against injustice, ignorance and lust,
> The Inquisition yet would serve the law,
> And guillotines decide our least disputes.
> The few who dare must speak, and speak again,
> To right the wrongs of many.[31]

Despite all the arguments against the Federal Vision and the irrefutable proofs that the Federal Vision is a revival of the Pelagian spectrum of heresies, there are still many churchmen in all the Reformed denominations who are unwilling to discipline those who imbibe these heresies. No doubt they are persuaded by the claim of the Federal Vision proponents themselves that they hold to Reformed theology. Their adherence to Reformed theology, whether sincere or merely with their lips, is not the reason to be lax in disciplining them. Rather, their adherence to the teaching of the Federal Vision, which has been demonstrated to be a heresy, is the reason such discipline is needed. The Federal Vision is not a benign addition to Reformed theology on minor matters. It is a complete denial and replacement of the scriptural doctrine of salvation. Like all heresies, it will rule over those who adhere to it.

In this great contest with the Federal Vision, the question we must ask today is this: Shall legalism win? Shall works salvation win? Shall the gospel be perverted in our day by our guilty silence while martyred saints stand ready to testify against us in the Great Day? The few who dare must speak out against this heresy, and they must speak again to right the wrongs of many. There is only one gospel, as the apostle wrote, and the Federal Vision is not it. But the free grace of God in Christ Jesus is.

---

31 Clarence McCartney, "Shall Unbelief Win?", in *The Aquila Report*, July 17, 2014. Accessed at http://theaquilareport.com/?s=%22Shall+Unbelief+Win%3F%22 on July 20, 2014.

Appendix A

Chart Showing the Various Theological Positions of Pelagianism, Semi-Pelagianism, and Calvinism

As the following chart shows, Pelagianism and Semi-Pelagianism differ with each other at several points, but also agree with each other on other points. The Federal Vision is a system that generally takes the Pelagian position in those places where Pelagianism and Semi-Pelagianism differ. While many of those who hold to the Federal Vision system claim also to be Calvinistic or Reformed, that system is inconsistent at every point with Reformed theology. It is illogical and inconsistent to believe that justification is by faith alone, once-for-all, but also not final until the judgment day. It is illogical to hold that election is both unconditional and conditional. It is illogical to hold that new life in the Spirit is different from the new birth or regeneration. There are many other inconsistencies involved in trying to meld the Federal Vision together with Reformed theology. They are two different systems.

THEOLOGICAL ISSUE	PELAGIANISM	SEMI-PELAGIANISM	CALVINISM OR REFORMED
Original Sin	Man is born in a state of innocence, but still commits sin	Man is sick but not spiritually dead	Man is spiritually dead by nature
Free will	Man has the same free will that Adam had	Man has free will despite his sinful condition	The natural man has lost ability to choose spiritual good; Christians have free will imperfectly
Unconditional Election	No; election is conditional and based on God's foresight	No; election is conditional and based on God's foresight	Yes; election is unconditional
Effectual Calling	No	No	Yes
Regeneration	No, it is unnecessary	Yes, but it can be lost	Yes
Justification by Faith Alone, once-for-all	No	No	Yes
Imputation of Christ's Active Obedience	No	No	Yes
Imputation of Christ's Passive Obedience	Yes, for past sins	Yes, for past sins	Yes, for all sins: past, present, and future
Baptismal Efficacy	Objectively efficacious for all but often is temporary	Subjectively efficacious for all but often is temporary	Efficacious only for the elect in God's timing

Appendix A

THEOLOGICAL ISSUE	PELAGIANISM	SEMI-PELAGIANISM	CALVINISM OR REFORMED
Union with Christ	External, objective union that can be lost	Internal, subjective union that can be lost	Vital, spiritual union that cannot be lost
The relationship of Justification and sanctification	Sanctification and justification are interwoven	Sanctification or infused grace is the basis for justification	Justification is a once-for-all act of God's free grace; sanctification is an ongoing work of God's free grace in the believer
Indwelling of Holy Spirit	No, internal, subjective grace is not needed	Yes, the subjective grace of the Spirit is needed but can be lost	Yes, the indwelling of the Spirit is needed and is permanent for the elect
Saving Faith and Good Works	Faith plus good works saves us	Faith plus good works saves us	Faith alone saves, but true faith is always evidenced by good works
Assurance of Salvation	No	No	Yes
Certain Perseverance	No	No	Yes
Apostasy of real Christians	Yes	Yes	No
Final Justification	Yes, based on totality of whole life	Yes, based on totality of whole life	No, the final judgment is not a final justification

389

Appendix B

Definition of Pelagianism

Pelagianism is often reduced to a single doctrine concerning anthropology or the doctrine of sin. It is a mistake to view Pelagianism in this way. Pelagianism is a complete system, but there are three interconnected doctrines that are closely related: the doctrines of sin, freedom of the will, and grace. John McClintock and James Strong, in *Cyclopedia of Biblical, Theological, and Ecclesiastical Literature* give a fuller, more accurate definition as follows:

"Though the Pelagian builds the chief doctrines of his system on the doctrine of the original perfection of human nature, yet, in a just development of Pelagianism, which stands in antagonism to the whole doctrines of anthropology, we regard the freedom of the will as forming the fundamental conception or principle on which the whole depends. We begin, therefore, our representation of Pelagianism with the doctrine of the freedom of the will, because the doctrine of sin is conditioned upon it, and the doctrine of grace depends on both."

John McClintock and James Strong, *Cyclopedia of Biblical, Theological, and Ecclesiastical Literature*, Volume VII (Grand Rapids, Michigan: Baker Book House, 1981), 873.

Select Bibliography

A Joint Federal Vision Profession. Accessed at: http://www.federal-vision.com/resources/joint_FV_Statement.pdf on October 20, 2015.

A' Brakel, Wilhelmus. *The Christian's Reasonable Service*, Volume 1. Translated by Bartel Elshout. Ligonier, Pennsylvania: Soli Deo Gloria Publications, 1992.

Alsted, Johann Heinrich. *Theologica didacta, exhibens locos communes theologica methodo scholastica*. Hanover, Germany: C. Eifrid, 1618.

Ante-Nicene Fathers, Latin Christianity: Its Founder, Tertullian, Volume 3. Edited by Alexander Roberts and James Donaldson. Peabody, Massachusetts: Hendrickson Publishers, 1999.

Aquinas, Thomas. *Summa Contra Gentiles*. Translated by Charles J. O'Neill. Garden City, NY: Image Books, 1957.

Augustin: Anti-Pelagian Writings, Nicene and Post-Nicene Fathers, First Series, Volume 5. Edited by Philip Schaff. Peabody, Massachusetts: Hendrickson Publishers, 1999.

Augustine. *Confessions*. Translated and Introduced by R. S. Pine-Coffin. London, England: Penguin Books, 1961.

Aurelius, Marcus. *Meditations*. Translated by Martin Hammond. New York, New York: Penguin Group (USA), 2006.

Bahnsen, Greg L. *Theonomy in Christian Ethics*. Nutley, New Jersey: The Craig Press, 1977.

Baird, Samuel J. *A History of the New School*. Philadelphia: Claxton, Remsen, and Haffelfinger, 1868.

Bannerman, James. *The Church of Christ: A treatise on the nature, powers, ordinances, discipline, and government of the Christian Church*, Volume 2. Edinburgh, Scotland and Carlisle, Pennsylvania: The Banner of Truth Trust, 1974.

Bannerman, James. *The Doctrine of Justification: An Outline of its History in the Church and of its Exposition from Scripture*. London: The Banner of Truth Trust, 1961.

Barker, William S. *Puritan Profiles: 54 Influential Puritans at the Time When the Westminster Confession of Faith was Written*. Fearn, Scotland: Christian Focus Publications, 1996.

Bavinck, Herman. *Our Reasonable Faith: A Survey of Christian Doctrine*. Grand Rapids, Michigan: Wm. B. Eerdmans Publishing Company, 1956.

Bavinck, Herman. *Reformed Dogmatics*, 4 Volumes. Edited by John Bolt. Translated by John Vriend. Grand Rapids, Michigan: Baker Academic, 2003-2008.

Baxter, Richard. *An Extract of Richard Baxter's Aphorisms on Justification*. New Castle upon Tyne, England: John Gooding, 1745.

Beattie, Francis R. *The Presbyterian Standards: An Exposition of the Westminster Confession of Faith and Catechisms*. Greenville, South Carolina: Southern Presbyterian Press, 1997.

Beeke, Joel R. *The Quest for Full Assurance: The Legacy of Calvin and His Successors*. Edinburgh, Scotland and Carlisle, Pennsylvania: The Banner of Truth Trust, 1999.

Bellarmine, Robert. *Spiritual Writings*. Edited and translated by John Patrick Donnelly and Ronald J. Treske. Malwah, New Jersey: Paulist Press, 1989.

Berkhof, Louis. *The History of Christian Doctrines*. Edinburgh, Scotland and Carlisle, Pennsylvania: The Banner of Truth Trust, 1975.

Bonar, Andrew A. *Memoir and Remains of R. M. McCheyne*. London: The Banner of Truth Trust, 1966.

Bower, Littleton Purnell. *The Days of Makemie: or, The Vine Planted. 1680-1708*. Philadelphia: Presbyterian Board of Publications, 1833.

Brown, John. *Hebrews*. London, England and Carlisle, Pennsylvania: The Banner of Truth Trust, 1972.

Buchanan, James. *The Doctrine of Justification: An Outline of Its History in the Church and of its Exposition from Scripture*. London: The Banner of Truth Trust, 1961

Burges, Cornelius. *Baptismal Regeneration of Elect Infants by the Church of England, According to the Scriptures, the Primitive Church, the Present Reformed Churches, and Many Particular Divines Apart*. Oxford, England: I. Litchfield for Henry Curteyn, 1629.

Calvin: Institutes of the Christian Religion, Volume Two. Edited by John T. McNeill. Translated by Ford Lewis Battles. Philadelphia: Westminster Press, 1960

Calvin, John. *A Commentary on Jeremiah*, Volumes One and Four. Edinburgh, Scotland and Carlisle, Pennsylvania: The Banner of Truth Trust, 1989.

Calvin, John. *Genesis*. Edited and Translated by John King. Edinburgh, Scotland and Carlisle, Pennsylvania: The Banner of Truth Trust, 1975.

Calvin, John. *Sermons on the Epistle to the Ephesians*. Edinburgh, Scotland and Carlisle, Pennsylvania: The Banner of Truth Trust. 1973.

Calvin, John. *Sermons on Galatians*. Translated by Kathy Childress. Edinburgh, Scotland and Carlisle, Pennsylvania: The Banner of Truth Trust, 1997.

Calvin, John. *The Bondage and Liberation of the Will*. Edited by A. N. S. Lane. Translated by G. I. Davies. Grand Rapids, Michigan: Baker Books, 1996.

Calvin's Commentaries: A Harmony of the Gospels, Volume II. Edited by David W. Torrance and Thomas F. Torrance. Translated by T. H. L. Parker. Grand Rapids, Michigan: Wm. B. Eerdmans Publishing Company, 1979.

Calvin's Commentaries: The Acts of the Apostles, 1-13. Edited by David W. Torrance and Thomas F. Torrance. Translated by John W. Fraser and W. J. G. McDonald. Grand Rapids, Michigan: Wm. B. Eerdmans Publishing Company, 1979.

Calvin's Commentaries: The Epistles of Paul to the Galatians, Ephesians, Philippians and Colossians. Edited by David W. Torrance and Thomas F. Torrance. Translated by T. H. L. Parker. Grand Rapids, Michigan: Wm. B. Eerdmans Publishing Company, 1972.

Calvin's Commentaries: The Gospel According to St. John. Edited by David W. Torrance and Thomas F. Torrance. Translated by T. H. L. Parker. Grand Rapids, Michigan: Wm. B. Eerdmans Publishing Company, 1959.

Calvin's Commentaries: The Epistles to the Romans and the Thessalonians. Edited by David W. Torrance and Thomas F. Torrance. Translated by Ross MacKenzie. Grand Rapids, Michigan: Wm. B. Eerdmans Publishing Company, 1979.

Catechism of the Catholic Church. New York, New York: Doubleday, 1992.

Cheeseman, Lewis. *Differences Between

Select Bibliography

Old and New School Presbyterians. Rochester, New York: Erastus Darrow, 1848.

Cunningham, William. *Historical Theology*, 2 Volumes. London: The Banner of Truth Trust, 1969.

Cunningham, William. *The Reformers and the Theology of the Reformation*. London: The Banner of Truth Trust, 1967.

Dabney, Robert L. *Discussions: Evangelical and Theological*, Volume 1. London: The Banner of Truth Trust, 1967.

Daillie, John. *An Exposition of Philippians*. MacDill AFB, Florida: Tyndale Bible Society, n.d.

d'Aubigne, J. H. Merle. *History of the Reformation of the Sixteenth Century*, Volume I. Grand Rapids, Michigan: Baker Book House, 1976.

d'Aubigne, J. H. Merle. *The Reformation in England*, Volume One. London: The Banner of Truth Trust, 1971.

Davenant, John. *An Exposition to the Epistle of St. Paul to the Colossians*. Lynchburg, Virginia: James Family Christian Publishers, 1979.

Dickson, David. *A Commentary on the Psalms*. Edinburgh, Scotland and Carlisle, Pennsylvania: The Banner of Truth Trust, 1995.

"Dialogue with Trypho the Jew." In *A Treasury of Early Christianity*. Edited by Anne Fremantle. New York: Viking Press, 1953.

Engelsma, David. *Federal Vision: Heresy at the Root*. Jenison, Michigan: Reformed Free Publishing Association, 2012.

Evans, Robert F. *Pelagius: Inquiries and Reappraisals*. London: Adam & Charles Black, 1968.

Evans, William. *Imputation and Impartation: Union with Christ in American Reformed Theology*. Eugene, Oregon: Wipf and Stock Publishers, 2009.

Faber, George Stanley. *The Primitive Doctrine of Justification Investigated*. London: R. B. Seeley and W. Burnside, 1837.

Ferguson, Sinclair. *In Christ Alone*. Orlando, Florida: Reformation Trust, 2008.

Flavel, John. *The Union of the Believer with Christ a Principal Part of Effectual Application*. In *The Method of Grace in the Gospel redemption*. In *The Works of John Flavel*, Volume II. London: The Banner of Truth Trust, 1969.

Garretson, James M. *Pastor-Teachers of Old Princeton*. Edinburgh, Scotland and Carlisle, Pennsylvania: The Banner of Truth Trust, 2012.

Gillespie, George. *Aaron's Rod Blossoming*. Harrisonburg, Virginia: Sprinkle Publications, 1985.

Gillespie, George. *The Works of George Gillespie*, Volume 2. Edmonton, Alberta, Canada: Still Water Revival Books, 1991.

Goode, William. *The Doctrine of the Church of England as to the Effects of Baptism in the Case of Infants*. London: J. Hatchard and Son, 1850.

Griffin, Edward D. *A Series of Lectures*. Boston: Doctrinal Tract and Book Society, 1855.

Haldane, Robert. *An Exposition of the Epistle to the Romans*. MacDill AFB, Florida: MacDonald Publishing Company, n.d.

Hall, Peter. *The Harmony of the Protestant Confessions: Exhibiting the Faith* of the Churches of Christ, Reformed After the Pure and Holy Doctrine of the Gospel. Edmonton, Alberta, Canada: Still Water Revival Books, 1992.

Hendriksen, William. *Exposition of Galatians*. Grand Rapids, Michigan: Baker Book House, 1974.

Hendriksen, William. *The Gospel of John*. Edinburgh, Scotland and Carlisle, Pennsyalvania: The Banner of Truth Trust, 1976.

Hislop, Alexander. *The Two Babylons*. Neptune, New Jersey: Loizeaux Brothers, Inc., 1959.

Hodge, A. A. *Outlines of Theology*. Grand Rapids, Michigan: Zondervan Publishing House, 1972.

Hodge, A. A. *The Confession of Faith*. London: The Banner of Truth Trust, 1961.

Hodge, Charles. *An Exposition of the First Epistle to the Corinthians*. Grand Rapids, Michigan: Wm. B. Eerdmans Publishing Company, 1969.

Hodge, Charles. *An Exposition of the Second Epistle to the Corinthians*. Grand Rapids, Michigan: Wm. B. Eerdmans Publishing Company, 1970.

Hodge, Charles. *Commentary on the Epistle to the Ephesians*. Old Tappan, New Jersey: Fleming H. Revell Company, n.d.

Hodge, Charles. *Systematic Theology*, 3 Volumes. Grand Rapids, Michigan: Wm. B. Eerdmans Publishing Co., 1970.

Hughes, Philip Edgcumbe. *Paul's Second Epistle to the Corinthians*. Grand Rapids, Michigan: Wm. B. Eerdmans Publishing Company, 1971.

Irenaeus. *Against the Heresies*. Edited by John Keble. Oxford, London, and Cambridge: James Parker and Co., 1872.

John Calvin: Tracts and Letters, Volume 1: Tracts, Part 1. Edited and Translated by Henry Beveridge. Edinburgh, Scotland and Carlisle, Pennsylvania: The Banner of Truth Trust, 2009.

John Calvin: Tracts and Letters, Volume 2: Tracts, Part 2. Edited and Translated by Henry Beveridge. Edinburgh, Scotland and Carlisle, Pennsylvania: The Banner of Truth Trust, 2009.

John Calvin: Tracts and Letters, Volume 3: Tracts, Part 3. Edited and Translated by Henry Beveridge. Edinburgh, Scotland and Carlisle, Pennsylvania: The Banner of Truth Trust, 2009.

Jonas, Hans. *The Gnostic Religion*. Boston: Beacon Press, 1963.

Justified in Christ: God's Plan for us in Justification. Edited by K. Scott Oliphant. Fearn, Scotland: Christian Focus Publications, 2007.

Kelly, Douglas F. *Systematic Theology: Grounded in Scripture and Understood in Light of the Church*, Volume Two. Fearn, Ross-Shire, Scotland: Christian Focus Publications, 2014.

Kevan, Ernest F. *The Grace of Law: A Study of Puritan Theology*. Grand Rapids, Michigan: Baker Book House, 1976.

Kirk, James R. Daniel. "The Sufficiency of the Cross." In *Scottish Bulletin of Evangelical Theology*, 2006.

Lane, Anthony N. S. *Bernard of Clairvaux: Theologian of the Cross*. Collegeville, Minnesota: Liturgical Press, 2013.

Lane, A. N. S. "Calvin's Doctrine of

Assurance Revisited." In *Tributes to John Calvin: A Celebration of his Quincentenary*. Edited by David W. Hall. Phillipsburg, New Jersey: P & R Publications, 2010.

Leithart, Peter. *Against Christianity*. Moscow, Idaho: Canon Press, 2003.

Leithart, Peter. *The Priesthood of the Plebs: The Baptismal Transformation of Antique Order*. Eugene, Orgeon: Wipf and Stock Publishers, 2003.

Leithart, Peter. *The Baptized Body*. Moscow, Idaho: Canon Press, 2007.

Lightfoot, J. B. *Saint Paul's Epistles to the Colossians and to Philemon*. Grand Rapids, Michigan: Zondervan Publishing House, Reprint of 1879 edition.

Lightfoot, J. B. "The Epistle Of Barnabas." In *The Apostolic Fathers*. Edited by J. R. Harmer. Grand Rapids, Michigan. Baker Book House, 1973.

Litton, Edward Arthur. *Introduction to Dogmatic Theology*. Edited by Philip E. Hughes. London, England: James Clarke & Co. Ltd, 1960.

Lloyd, Jones, D. Martyn. *Romans: An Exposition of Chapter 8:5-17, The Sons of God*. Grand Rapids, Michigan: Zondervan Publishing House, 1975.

Lloyd- Jones, D. Martyn. *Studies in the Sermon on the Mount*. Two Volumes in One, Volume II. Grand Rapids, Michigan: William B. Eerdmans Publishing Company, 1972.

Lusk, Rich. *Paedofaith: A Primer on the Mystery of Infant Salvation and a Handbook for Covenant Parents*. Monroe, Louisiana: Athanasius Press, 2005.

Luther, Martin. *Bondage of the Will*. Old Tappan, New Jersey: Fleming H. Revell Company, 1957.

Machen, J. Gresham. *Christianity and Liberalism*. Grand Rapids, Michigan/Cambridge, U.K.: William B. Eerdmans Publishing Company, 2009.

Machen, J. Gresham. *New Testament Greek for Beginners*. Toronto: The MacMillan Company, 1951.

Macleod, John. *Scottish Theology: In Relation to Church History Since the Reformation*. Edinburgh, Scotland and Carlisle, Pennsylvania, 1974.

Matthew Henry's Commentary on the Whole Bible, Volume III. Old Tappan, New Jersey: Fleming H. Revell Company, n. d.

McClintock, John and Strong, James. *Cyclopedia of Biblical, Theological, and Ecclesiastical Literature*, Volumes II and III. Grand Rapids, Michigan: Baker Book House, 1981.

Melancthon on Christian Doctrine. Edited and translated by Clyde L. Manschreck. New York: Oxford University Press, 1965.

Miller, Samuel. *Infant Baptism Scriptural and Reasonable: and Baptism by Sprinkling or Affusion the Most edifying Mode*. Philadelphia: Presbyterian Board of Publication, 1835.

Milman, Henry Hart. *The History of Christianity, From the Birth of Christ to the Abolition of Paganism in the Roman Empire*, Volume I. London: John Murray, 1867.

Mitchell, Alexander F. *The Westminster Assembly: Its History and Standards*. Philadelphia: Presbyterian Board of Publications, 1897.

Moore, Thomas V. *A Commentary on*

Zechariah. London: The Banner of Truth Trust, 1968.

Muller, Richard A. *Calvin on the Reformed Tradition: On the Work of Christ and the Order of Salvation*. Grand Rapids, Michigan: Baker Academic, 2012.

Mullins, E. Y. *The Axioms of Religion*. Macon, Georgia: Mercer University Press, 2010.

Murray, John. *Redemption Accomplished and Applied*. Grand Rapids, Michigan: Wm. B. Eerdmans Publishing Company, 1970.

Murray, John. *The Epistle to the Romans*, Volume I, two volumes in one. Grand Rapids, Michigan: Wm. B. Eerdmans Publishing Company, 1968.

Nature and Grace: Selections from the Summa Theologica of Thomas Aquinas. Edited and translated by A. M. Fairweather. Philadelphia: The Westminster Press, 1954.

Nicene and Post-Nicene Fathers, Volume V. Edited by Philip Schaff. Grand Rapids, Michigan: Wm. B. Eerdmans Publishing Co., 1971.

Owen, John. *An Exposition of the Epistle to the Hebrews*, Volume IV. Edited by W. H. Goold. Grand Rapids, Michigan: Baker Book House, 1980.

Packer, J. I. *A Quest for Godliness: The Puritan Vision of the Christian Life*. Wheaton, Illinois: Crossway Books, 1990.

Pelagius' Commentary on St. Paul's Epistle to the Romans. Translated by Theodore DeBruyn. Oxford, England: Clarendon Press, 1993.

Phillips, Richard D. *Zechariah*. Phillipsburg, New Jersey: P & R Publishing, 2007.

Record of the Case, Standing Judicial Commission of the Presbyterian Church in America, Case 2012-5, RE Gerald Hedman vs. Pacific Northwest Presbytery.

Rees, B. R. *The Letters of Pelagius and His Followers*. Rochester, New York: Boydell Press, 1991.

Ryle, John Charles. *Knots Untied: Being Plain Statements on Disputed Points in religion from the Standpoint of and Evangelical Churchman*. Edited by G. E. Duffield. Cambridge, England: James Clarke & Co. LTD., 1977.

Ryle, John Charles. *Old Paths: Being Plain Statements of Some Weightier Matters of Christianity*. Cambridge & London: James Clarke & Co. LTD., 1972.

Saint Augustin's Anti-Pelagian Writings. Edited by Philip Schaff. Translated by Peter Holmes and Robert Ernest Wallis. Peabody, Massachusetts: Hendrickson Publishers, Inc., 1999

Sanders, E. P. *Paul and Palestinian Judaism: A Comparison of Patterns of Religion*. Philadelphia: Fortress Press, 1977.

Sandlin, Andrew. "Covenant Redemptive History." In *A Faith That Is Never Alone: A Response to Westminster Seminary California*. Edited by Andrew Sandlin. LaGrange: Kerygma Press, 2007.

Schaff, Philip. *The Harmony of the Reformed Confessions: As Related to the Present State of Evangelical Theology*. New York: Dodd, mead, and Company, 1877.

Schaff, Philip. *History of the Christian Church*, Volumes III and V. Grand Rapids, Michigan: Wm. B. Eerdmans Publishing Company, 1981.

Scott, Thomas. *The Articles of the Synod of Dort*. Harrisonburg, Virginia: Sprinkle

Publications, 1983.

"Select Lectures in Systematic Theology." In *Collected Writings of John Murray*, Volume Two. Edinburgh, Scotland and Carlisle, Pennsylvania: The Banner of Truth Trust, 2009.

Select Sermons of George Whitefield. London: The Banner of Truth Trust, 1964.

Selected Shorter Writings of Benjamin B. Warfield, Volume 1. Edited by John E. Meeter. Nutley, New Jersey: Presbyterian and Reformed Publishing Company, 1970.

Shaw, Robert. *The Reformed Faith: An Exposition of the Westminster Standards*. Inverness, Scotland: Christian Focus Publications, 1974.

Shepherd, Norman. *The Call of Grace: How the Covenant Illuminates Salvation and Evangelism*. Phillipsburg, New Jersey: P & R Publishing, 2000.

Shedd, William G. T. *A History of Christian Doctrine*, Volume II. Edinburgh, Scotland: T. & T. Clark, 1877.

Shedd, William G. T. *Theological Essays*. Minneapolis, Minnesota: Klock & Klock Christian Publishers, Inc., 1981.

Smeaton, George. *The Doctrine of the Holy Spirit*. Edinburgh, Scotland and Carlisle, Pennsylvania: The Banner of Truth Trust, 1974.

Smeaton, George. *The Apostle's Doctrine of the Atonement*. Grand Rapids, Michigan: Zondervand Publishing House, 1957.

Smith, Ralph. *Eternal Covenant: How the Trinity Reshapes Covenant Theology*. Moscow, Idaho: Canon Press, 2003.

St. Thomas Aquinas. *Summa Theologica*, Volume II. Translated by the Fathers of the English Dominican Province. New York, Boston, Cincinnati, Chicago, San Francisco: Benziger Brothers, Inc., 1947.

St. Augustine's City of God. Translated by J. W. C. Wand. London: Oxford University Press, 1963.

Strickler, G. B. *Sermons*. New York: Fleming H. Revell Company, 1910.

Sulpitius Severus, Vincent of Lerins, John Cassian. *Nicene and Post-Nicene Fathers*, Second Series, Volume 11. Peabody, Massachusetts: Hendrickson Publishers, Inc., 2004.

The Auburn Avenue Theology, Pros and Cons: Debating the Federal Vision. Edited by E. Calvin Beisner. Fort Lauderdale, Florida: Knox Theological Seminary, 2004.

The Collected Writings of James Henley Thornwell, Volumes 1 and 2. Edinburgh, Scotland and Carlisle, Pennsylvania: The Banner of Truth Trust, 1974.

The Creeds of Christendom: With a History and Critical Notes, 3 Volumes. Edited by Philip Schaff. Grand Rapids, Michigan: Baker Book House, 1983.

The Early Christian Fathers: A Selection from the Writings of the Fathers from St. Cyril of Jerusalem to St. Leo the Great. Edited and translated by Henry Bettenson. London, New York, Toronto: Oxford University Press, 1974.

The Federal Vision. Edited by Steve Wilkins and Duane Garner. Monroe, Louisiana: Athanasius Press, 2004.

The Golden Treasury of Puritan Quotations. Compiler I. D. E. Thomas. Chicago: Moody Press, 1975.

The Select Works of Robert Rollock. Edited by William M, Gunn. Edinburgh,

Scotland: The Woodrow Society, 1844.

The Works of John Owen, Volumes V and X. Edited by William H. Goold. London: The Banner of Truth Trust, 1967.

The Works of Robert Traill, Volume I. Edinburgh, Scotland and Carlisle, Pennsylvania: The Banner of Truth Trust, 1975.

The Writings of John Bradford, Volume 2. Edited by Aubrey Townsend. Edinburgh, Scotland and Carlisle, Pennsylvania, 1979.

Turretin, Francis. *Institutes of Elenctic Theology*, 3 Volumes. Edited by James T. Dennison, Jr. Translated by George Musgrave Giger. Phillipsburg, New Jersey: P & R Publishing, 1992-1997.

Vaughn, C. R. *The Gifts of the Holy Spirit: To Believers and Unbelievers*. Edinburgh, Scotland and Carlisle, Pennsylvania: The Banner of Truth Trust, 1975.

Venema, Cornelis. *The Gospel of Free Acceptance*. Edinburgh, Scotland and Carlisle, Pennsylvania: The Banner of Truth Trust, 2006.

Vos, Geerhardus. *Biblical Theology: Old and New Testaments*. Edinburgh, Scotland and Carlisle, Pennsylvania: The Banner of Truth Trust, 1975.

Walker, James. *Theology and the Theologians of Scotland*. Edinburgh, Scotland: Knox Press, 1982.

Warfield, B. B. "Introductory Essay on Augustin and the Pelagian Controversy." In Saint Augustin. *Anti-Pelagian Writings*, Volume V of *A Select Library of the Nicene and Post-Nicene Fathers of the Christian Church*. Grand Rapids, Michigan: Wm. B. Eerdmans Publishing Company, 1978.

Warfield, B. B. *The Plan of Salvation*. Grand Rapids, Michigan: Wm. B. Eerdmans Publishing Company, 1970.

Waters, Guy Prentiss. *The Federal Vision and Covenant Theology: A Comparative Analysis*. Phillipsburg, New Jersey: P & R Publishing, 2006.

Waters, Guy Prentiss. *Justification and the New Perspectives on Paul: A Review and Response*. Phillipsburg, New Jersey: P & R Publishing, 2004.

Watson, Thomas. *A Body of Divinity*. London: The Banner of Truth Trust, 1970.

Wiggers, G. F. *An Historical Presentation of Augustinism and Pelagianism from the Original Sources*. Andover, Connecticut: Gould, Newman & Saxton, 1840.

Wilson, Douglas. "Can a Nature/Grace Dualism Be Born Again?" *Credenda Agenda*, Volume 19, Series 3, Special Edition, 2007.

Wilson, Douglas. "Credos: On Baptism." *Credenda Agenda*, Volume 15, Series 5.

Wilson, Douglas. *Reformed is Not Enough: Recovering the Objectivity of the Covenant*. Moscow, Idaho: Canon Press, 2002.

Wilson, Geoffrey B. *Ephesians: A Digest of Reformed Comment*. Edinburgh, Scotland and Carlisle, Pennsylvania: The Banner of Truth Trust, 1978.

Wilson, Geoffrey B. *Romans: A Digest of Reformed Comment*. Edinburgh, Scotland and Carlisle, Pennsylvania: The Banner of Truth Trust, 1977.

Wood, James. *Old and New Theology*. Philadelphia: Presbyterian Board of Publications, 1845.

Works of William Tyndale, Volume 2. Edited by Henry Walter. Edinburgh,

Scotland and Carlisle, Pennsylvania: The Banner of Truth Trust, 2010.

Wright, N. T. *Judas and the Gospel of Jesus: Have We Missed the Truth about Christianity?* Grand Rapids, Michigan: Baker Books, 2006.

Wright, N. T. *Justification: God's Plan and Paul's Vision.* Downers Grove, Illinois: IVP Academic, 2009.

Wright, N. T. *Surprised by Hope: Rethinking Heaven, the Resurrection, and the Mission of the Church.* New York: HarperCollins Publishers, 2008.

Writings and Disputations of Thomas Cranmer. Edited by John Edmund Cox. Cambridge, England: The University Press, 1844.

Index of Names

A
Abelard, Peter 57
a' Brakel, Wilhelmus 86, 87, 91, 393
Alexander, Archibald 24, 26, 27, 284
Alexander, James Waddell 60
Alsted, Johann Heinrich 246, 393
Ambrose 152, 153, 154, 260
Amyraut, Moses 235
Aquinas, Thomas 135, 136, 137, 138, 139, 140, 141, 142, 146, 154, 155, 156, 165, 228, 259, 316, 328, 329, 362, 367, 393, 398, 399
Arius 235
Arminius, Jacobus 21, 34, 73, 82, 235
Athanasius 103, 201, 213, 217, 239, 245, 247, 259, 316, 360,
Atkinson, James 156, 157
Augustine, Bishop of Hippo 23, 42, 52, 56, 57, 62, 64, 67, 68, 69, 70, 73, 74, 82, 83, 96, 105, 139, 140, 150, 151, 153, 154, 155, 156, 178, 227, 228, 257, 259, 260, 262, 292, 293, 294, 295, 299, 301, 315, 348, 355, 362, 363, 364, 366, 369, 379, 381, 393, 399
Aurelius, Marcus 72, 260, 393

B
Bahnsen, Greg 28, 183, 184, 185, 186, 187, 188, 189, 191, 193, 194, 195, 196, 197, 198, 393
Bannerman, James 106, 107, 108, 121, 260, 393
Barach, John 28, 42, 125, 185, 213, 215, 216, 217, 221, 236, 319, 320, 330
Barker, William 63, 64, 160, 161, 277, 393
Barnes, Albert 21, 26, 34, 51, 53, 235, 277, 283, 284, 287
Barth, Karl 235
Basil the Great 259, 262
Bavinck, Herman 63, 66, 75, 91, 95, 100, 101, 106, 107, 108, 110, 111, 142, 165, 168, 169, 217, 225, 226, 242, 289, 300, 301, 302, 309, 310, 344, 352, 363, 370, 371, 379, 393
Baxter, Richard 20, 21, 34, 94, 95, 208, 277, 281, 282, 351, 352, 353, 393
Beattie, Francis R. 339, 393
Beeke, Joel 332, 334, 393
Bellarmine, Robert 328, 393
Berkhof, Louis 77, 81, 109, 393
Bernard of Clairvaux 57, 58, 74, 261, 262, 272, 273, 396
Berthoud, Jean-Marc 96, 97
Booth, Randy 42, 185
Bradford, John 383, 384, 400
Bradwardine, Thomas 380
Brown, John 98, 99, 306, 394
Bucer, Martin 159, 161
Buchanan, James 31, 32, 68, 268, 276, 287, 394

Index of Names

Bullinger, Heinrich 83, 161, 280
Burgess, Cornelius 161, 162
Byrne, Brendan 251, 253

C

Calvin, John 43, 44, 63, 68, 69, 70, 76, 82, 84, 85, 100, 128, 129, 132, 136, 137, 147, 153, 161, 172, 189, 190, 195, 196, 197, 203, 204, 205, 206, 223, 224, 246, 254, 255, 261, 262, 263, 274, 275, 283, 284, 292, 299, 302, 309, 311, 313, 322, 323, 324, 325, 326, 332, 338, 339, 351, 353, 355, 356, 359, 362, 364, 365, 366, 369, 381, 393, 394, 396, 397, 398
Cameron, John 75, 352
Chrysostom, John 76, 152, 153, 154, 260
Cicero, Tullius 72, 73, 74, 140
Clark, R. Scott 20, 21, 22, 26, 39, 185, 186
Clement of Alexandria 258, 384
Colquhoun, John 91
Cox, Samuel H. 54, 55, 147, 401
Cranmer, Thomas 147, 383, 384, 401
Cruso, Thomas 305
Cunningham, William 36, 50, 51, 74, 110, 158, 159, 161, 162, 163, 227, 241, 242, 256, 257, 297, 363, 378, 383, 384, 385, 395
Cyprian, Bishop of Carthage 151, 154
Cyril of Alexandria 91
Cyril of Jerusalem 153, 399

D

Dabney, Robert L. 123, 333, 395
Daillie, John 298, 395
d'Aubigne, J. H. Merle 380, 381, 395
Davenant, John 151, 163, 395
Dickson, David 221, 286, 395
Dunn, James D. G. 249, 250, 373

E

Edersheim, Alfred 215
Engelsma, David J. 20, 82, 379, 395
Episcopius, Simon 73

F

Fairweather, A. M. 362, 364, 398
Featley, Daniel 161
Fesko, John V. 20
Finney, Charles G. 20, 21, 26, 34, 53, 55, 284, 285, 286, 287
Flavel, John 242, 243, 395
Fosdick, Harry Emerson 386

403

G

Gallant, Tim 42, 185
Garver, Joel 28, 31
Gataker, Thomas 276, 278, 279
Gillespie, George 160, 161, 162, 163, 374, 395
Girardeau, John L. 214
Godfrey, Robert 32
Goode, William 158, 159, 395
Gregory, Bishop of Nyssa 153
Griffin, Edward D. 338, 395

H

Haldane, Robert 88, 173, 219, 248, 395
Hedman, Gerald 19, 46, 92, 103, 104, 115, 125, 149, 176, 201, 214, 232, 245, 270, 340, 359, 398
Hendriksen, William 32, 238, 239, 291, 337, 396
Henry, Matthew 128, 314
Hodge, Archibald Alexander, (A. A.) 24, 91, 116, 117, 118, 146, 159, 160, 162, 163, 220, 221, 236, 237, 240, 249, 286, 301, 341, 351, 370, 378, 383, 396
Hodge, Charles 42, 51, 52, 53, 54, 55, 59, 60, 106, 108, 133, 157, 204, 218, 219, 249, 251, 254, 274, 321, 322, 323, 342, 396
Horne 28, 31, 38, 42, 120, 122
Hughes, Philip E. 53, 274, 396, 397

I

Ignatius 257
Illyricus, Matthias Placius 51, 52
Innocent IV, Pope 154, 155
Irenaeus 83, 258, 396

J

Jerome 71, 91, 151, 153, 154, 211, 260
Jordan, James 28, 41, 42, 43, 47, 57, 59, 62, 185, 359, 360
Jue, Jeffrey K. 278
Julian 67, 363, 366, 369, 370
Junckheim, Johann Z. 49
Justin Martyr 82, 257, 258

K

Kelly, Douglas F. 96, 132, 396
Kevan, Ernest F. 89, 90, 396
Kline, Meredith 32
Knight III, George 32

L

Lane, Anthony N. S. 12, 13, 58, 70, 273, 299, 325, 351, 364, 365, 394, 396
Latimer, Hugh 383, 384

Index of Names

Lee, Philip J. 366
Leithart, Peter 19, 27, 32, 42, 46, 47, 61, 62, 63, 64, 66, 85, 92, 94, 103, 104, 106, 112, 113, 115, 116, 125, 126, 127, 134, 135, 137, 139, 140, 141, 145, 147, 149, 150, 160, 167, 168, 176, 177, 178, 179, 180, 185, 201, 203, 208, 209, 210, 215, 232, 236, 245, 246, 247, 252, 253, 255, 264, 270, 271, 282, 283, 284, 285, 286, 299, 300, 304, 307, 319, 337, 338, 339, 340, 354, 367, 369, 397
Lenski, R. C. H. 255, 256
Letham, Robert 161
Lightfoot, J. B. 82, 128, 258, 361, 362, 364, 365, 397
Litton, Edward A. 53, 397
Lloyd-Jones, D. Martyn 32, 174, 175, 220, 321, 322, 328, 374
Lombard, Peter 136
Lusk, Rich 28, 41, 42, 49, 50, 59, 62, 79, 81, 87, 98, 103, 107, 159, 161, 185, 186, 198, 213, 218, 221, 222, 223, 226, 231, 232, 235, 245, 247, 255, 267, 268, 312, 313, 314, 315, 345, 349, 350, 397
Luther, Martin 20, 51, 69, 91, 156, 157, 211, 246, 292, 364, 380, 381, 383, 397

M

Machen, J. Gresham 15, 32, 33, 36, 214, 226, 282, 338, 397
MacKnight, James 216, 217
MacLeod, John 94, 282
Makemie, Francis 344, 394
Martin, Albert N. 32
Martyr, Peter 159
McCartney, Clarence 385, 386
McCheyne, Robert Murray 326, 327, 394
Melancthon, Phiip 382, 397
Meyers, Jeff 42
Miller, Samuel 144, 145, 146, 150, 157, 235, 397
Milman, Henry Hart 71, 130, 131, 132, 397
Mitchell, Alexander F. 84, 397
Moore, Thomas V. 275, 397
Muller, Richard A. 332, 398
Mullins, E. Y. 130, 132, 398
Murray, John 90, 91, 92, 131, 148, 169, 171, 172, 175, 176, 177, 250, 253, 271, 397, 398, 399

N

Nicole, Roger 32

O

Origen 260
Otis, John 20
Owen, John 72, 73, 74, 98, 225, 232, 237, 238, 285, 286, 348, 349, 398, 400

P

Packer, J. I. 94, 282, 351, 379, 398

405

Pajon, Claude 48, 49, 75
Patton, Francis L. 351
Pelagius 21, 34, 38, 50, 56, 57, 63, 64, 65, 66, 67, 69, 71, 75, 76, 77, 93, 94, 99, 100, 104, 105, 113, 135, 136, 137, 138, 139, 141, 146, 154, 156, 170, 171, 178, 197, 221, 222, 225, 229, 235, 251, 252, 257, 260, 264, 271, 272, 279, 285, 287, 293, 294, 295, 298, 299, 300, 336, 353, 354, 355, 363, 364, 365, 366, 368, 369, 370, 379, 380, 381, 382, 384, 395, 398, 405
Phillips, Richard 275, 276, 398
Philpotts, Henry 158
Pighius, Albert 76, 299, 351, 364, 365, 366, 370
Polycarp 257, 361

R
Reid, W. Stanford 32
Reymond, Robert 32
Ridley, Nicholas 383, 384
Robertson, O. Palmer 32
Rollock, Robert 84, 307, 399
Rushdoony, R. J. 191
Ryle, J. C. 35, 36, 37, 45, 107, 108, 151, 158, 163, 164, 224, 234, 342, 343, 398

S
Sadolet, James 262, 263, 264
Sanders, E. P. 290, 291, 292, 296, 373, 398
Sandlin, Andrew 86, 185, 398
Schaeffer, Francis 140, 141, 304, 362, 363, 367
Schaff, Philip 51, 52, 56, 57, 59, 62, 63, 65, 67, 69, 72, 75, 93, 96, 151, 152, 155, 177, 197, 198, 202, 206, 207, 211, 272, 279, 280, 293, 295, 296, 299, 301, 312, 348, 353, 360, 361, 363, 368, 380, 393, 398, 399
Schlissel, Steve 28, 79, 81, 87, 185, 245, 247, 253, 255, 330
Schubert, Ernst 49
Scott, Thomas 235, 398
Scotus, Duns 154, 156, 228
Shaw, Robert 163, 354, 399
Shedd, William G. T. 212, 250, 269, 399
Shepherd, Norman 28, 29, 32, 143, 150, 238, 253, 255, 285, 399
Smeaton, George 49, 76, 270, 273, 329, 399
Smith, Morton H. 13, 15, 16, 32, 105,
Smith, Peter 278
Smith, Ralph 28, 42, 82, 90, 105, 399
Socinus, Faustus 50, 285, 286, 287
Sproul, R. C. 9, 32
Strickler, Givens B. 310, 311, 399

T
Taylor, G. Aiken 385
Tertullian 87, 131, 132, 393

Theodoret 151, 153, 154
Thornwell, James Henley 23, 38, 88, 91, 92, 97, 98, 216, 218, 399
Traill, Robert 357, 400
Trapp, John 304
Turretin, Francis 68, 71, 73, 75, 76, 77, 87, 91, 126, 146, 147, 190, 191, 229, 316, 317, 318, 336, 343, 400
Twisse, William 279
Tyndale, William 382, 383, 395

V
Vaughan, C. R. 44, 45, 50
Venema, Cornelis 20, 23, 189, 290, 292, 353, 379, 400
Vines, Richard 276, 278, 279
Vos, Geerhardus 23, 24, 25, 83, 91, 129, 130, 132, 400

W
Walker, James 36, 74, 400
Warfield, Benjamin Breckinridge 55, 62, 69, 71, 75, 91, 119, 122, 367, 377, 378, 399, 400
Waters, Guy Prentiss 19, 20, 22, 26, 31, 41, 43, 49, 58, 61, 79, 85, 90, 98, 120, 125, 126, 143, 149, 192, 213, 216, 223, 231, 236, 280, 307, 312, 315, 317, 319, 326, 330, 331, 332, 335, 342, 345, 350, 367, 373, 377, 378, 384, 400
Watson, Thomas 269, 400
Whately, Richard 223
Whitefield, George 88, 399
Wiggers, G. F. 104, 105, 400
Wilkins, Steve 19, 27, 28, 32, 42, 61, 62, 143, 145, 149, 150, 185, 201, 203, 217, 221, 222, 223, 231, 232, 239, 245, 247, 264, 306, 307, 316, 317, 326, 327, 330, 331, 335, 336, 339, 342, 360, 367, 369, 399, 406
Wilson, Douglas 28, 42, 47, 48, 59, 80, 115, 117, 118, 145, 317, 331, 367, 369, 400
Witsius, Herman 91
Wright, N. T. 22, 29, 32, 33, 82, 148, 149, 150, 163, 187, 189, 253, 255, 264, 277, 291, 292, 296, 349, 350, 357, 360, 366, 367, 369, 371, 373, 401

Z
Zwingli, Ulrich 83

www.ingramcontent.com/pod-product-compliance
Lightning Source LLC
Chambersburg PA
CBHW052008070526
44584CB00016B/1663